The United Nations and nucle

ial
The United Nations and nuclear orders

Edited by Jane Boulden, Ramesh Thakur, and
Thomas G. Weiss

United Nations University Press
TOKYO · NEW YORK · PARIS

© United Nations University, 2009

The views expressed in this publication are those of the authors and do not necessarily reflect the views of the United Nations University.

United Nations University Press
United Nations University, 53-70, Jingumae 5-chome,
Shibuya-ku, Tokyo 150-8925, Japan
Tel: +81-3-5467-1212   Fax: +81-3-3406-7345
E-mail: sales@hq.unu.edu   general enquiries: press@hq.unu.edu
http://www.unu.edu

United Nations University Office at the United Nations, New York
2 United Nations Plaza, Room DC2-2062, New York, NY 10017, USA
Tel: +1-212-963-6387   Fax: +1-212-371-9454
E-mail: unuona@ony.unu.edu

United Nations University Press is the publishing division of the United Nations University.

Cover design by Joyce C. Weston

Printed in United States of America

ISBN 978-92-808-1167-4

Library of Congress Cataloging-in-Publication Data

The United Nations and nuclear orders / edited by Jane Boulden, Ramesh Thakur and Thomas G. Weiss.
    p. cm.
 Includes bibliographical references and index.
 ISBN 978-9280811674 (pbk.)
 1. Nuclear nonproliferation. 2. United Nations. I. Boulden, Jane, 1962–
II. Thakur, Ramesh Chandra, 1948– III. Weiss, Thomas George.
JZ5675.U53   2009
341.7′34—dc22   2009006980

Contents

Tables	vii
Contributors	viii
Foreword by *Jayantha Dhanapala*	xiii
Acknowledgements	xvi
Abbreviations	xviii
1 The United Nations and nuclear orders: Context, foundations, actors, tools, and future prospects Jane Boulden, Ramesh Thakur, and Thomas G. Weiss	1
Part I: Actors	29
2 The Security Council and nuclear disarmament Ernie Regehr	31
3 General Assembly majorities on the preferred nuclear order M. J. Peterson	52
4 The Secretary-General and the Secretariat Randy Rydell	73

Part II: Actual and potential tools 109

5 United Nations sanctions and nuclear weapons 111
   George A. Lopez and David Cortright

6 The use of force 132
   Ian Johnstone

7 Verification and compliance 151
   Harald Müller

8 Codification and legal issues....................................... 170
   Lori Fisler Damrosch

Part III: Looming threats, new challenges 189

9 Technology proliferation, globalization, and the role of the
   United Nations 191
   Brian Finlay and Rita Grossman-Vermaas

10 Dealing with extra-NPT actors and non-state actors 210
   Waheguru Pal Singh Sidhu

11 The international nuclear trade: Harnessing peaceful use
   while preventing proliferation 230
   Nicole C. Evans

12 Nuclear proliferation and regional security orders: Comparing
   North Korea and Iran 248
   Amitav Acharya

13 NPT regime change: Has the good become the enemy of the
   best? 273
   Ramesh Thakur

Index 298

Tables

12.1	Theories of regional security orders	253
12.2	North Korea and Iran	258
13.1	Number of nuclear warheads in the inventory of the five NPT nuclear weapons states, 1945–2005	288
13.2	Public opinion on nuclear weapons	292

Contributors

Amitav Acharya is Professor of Global Governance in the Department of Politics at the University of Bristol, UK, and Director of its Centre for Governance and International Affairs. His books include *Constructing a Security Community in Southeast Asia* (2001); *Crafting Cooperation: Regional International Institutions in Comparative Perspective* (2007); and *Whose Ideas Matter: Agency and Power in Asian Regionalism* (2009). His recent journal articles have appeared in *International Organization*, *International Security*, and *World Politics*.

Jane Boulden holds a Canada Research Chair in International Relations and Security Studies at the Royal Military College of Canada. She is also the Associate Chair of War Studies and is a Senior Research Associate at the Centre for International Studies at the University of Oxford, UK. She has written widely on the United Nations and on arms control and disarmament, and has been a consultant to governments on those issues. From August 2000 until December 2003 she was a MacArthur Research Fellow at the Centre for International Studies, University of Oxford. Her recent books as author or editor include *Terrorism and the UN: Before and After September 11* (2004), co-edited with Thomas G. Weiss; *Dealing with Conflict in Africa: The United Nations and Regional Organizations* (2003); and *Peace Enforcement* (2001).

David Cortright is Research Fellow at the Joan B. Kroc Institute for International Peace Studies at the University of Notre Dame, USA, and president of the Fourth Freedom Forum. He has served as consultant or adviser to agencies of the United Nations, international think tanks, and the foreign ministries of Canada, Japan, and several European countries. He has written widely on nuclear disarmament, multilateral counter-terrorism, and the use of incentives and sanctions as tools of international peacemaking. He is the author or editor of 15 books, including, most recently, *Peace: A History of Movements and Ideas* (2008); *Uniting Against Terror: Cooperative Nonmilitary Responses to the Global Terrorist Threat* (2007), co-edited with George A. Lopez; and *Gandhi and Beyond: Nonviolence in an Age of Terrorism* (2006).

Lori Fisler Damrosch is the Henry L. Moses Professor of Law and International Organization at Columbia University, USA, where she has taught since 1984. She was an attorney with the US Department of State (1977–1981) and practiced law in New York (1981–1984). In 1995–96 she was a fellow at the United States Institute of Peace in Washington, DC. Her books include *The International Court of Justice at a Crossroads* (1987); *Enforcing Restraint: Collective Intervention in Internal Conflicts* (1993); *Beyond Confrontation: International Law for the Post-Cold War Era* (1995); and *International Law: Cases and Materials* (2001). She has been co-editor in chief of the *American Journal of International Law* since 2003.

Nicole Evans is the Deputy Director (Senior Program Manager) for Nuclear and Radiological Security in the Global Partnership Program at Canada's Department of Foreign Affairs and International Trade (DFAIT). In this capacity, she manages Canada's efforts to secure nuclear and radiological materials internationally in order to help prevent terrorist acquisition and use. While at DFAIT, she was also a Sessional Lecturer in Political Science at Carleton University in Ottawa. Prior to joining DFAIT in 2005, she was the Retained Lecturer in International Relations at Wadham College, University of Oxford, UK, specializing in Soviet and Russian strategic nuclear policies. She has published on missile defense and nuclear strategy.

Brian Finlay is a Senior Associate at the Henry L. Stimson Center, USA, where he co-directs the Cooperative Nonproliferation Program. Prior to joining the Center, he served as Director of the Threat Reduction Campaign, a Senior Researcher at the Brookings Institution, and a Program Officer at the Century Foundation. Before emigrating from Canada, he was a Project Manager for the Laboratory Center for Disease Control in Ottawa. He has also served as a consultant to the Canadian Department of Foreign Affairs. He sits on the board of directors of Information Management and Mine Action Programs (iMMAP), a pioneering organization leading the way forward in the effective use of information management practices in the service of humanitarian relief and development.

Rita Grossman-Vermaas is an analyst at the US Department of the Treasury, focusing on financial networks that facilitate the spread of weapons of mass destruction and related technologies. From 2006 to 2008, she was a Research Associate with the Cooperative Nonproliferation Program at the Henry L. Stimson Center, USA, where she worked on issues of weapons proliferation, the nexus between proliferation and development, and scientist redirection in the former Soviet Union. She spent four years in Ottawa, Canada, working on WMD verification and compliance issues with the Canadian Department of Foreign Affairs and International Trade, as well as with the Canadian Centre for Treaty Compliance, Norman Paterson School of International Affairs. She began her career in the field as a researcher at the Center for Biosecurity at the University of Pittsburgh Medical Center, USA.

Ian Johnstone is an Associate Professor of International Law at the Fletcher School of Law and Diplomacy, Tufts University, USA. From 1991 to 2000, he held various positions in the United Nations Secretariat, including five years in the Executive Office of the Secretary-General, as well as the Department of Peacekeeping Operations and the Office of the Legal Counsel. From 2005 to 2007, he served as Editor and Lead Scholar of the *Annual Review of Global Peace Operations*. In addition to the 2006 and 2007 volumes of the *Annual Review*, his recent publications include: *The United States and Contemporary Peace Operations: A Double-Edged Sword?* (2008); "Legislation and Adjudication in the UN Security Council: Bringing Down the Deliberative Deficit," *American Journal of International Law* (2008); "Law-making through the Operational Activities of International Organizations," *George Washington International Law Review* (2008); "The Secretary-General as Norm Entrepreneur," in *Secretary or General? The Role of the UN Secretary-General in World Politics* (2007).

George A. Lopez holds the Rev. Theodore M. Hesburgh, C.S.C. Chair in Peace Studies at the Joan B. Kroc Institute for International Peace Studies at the University of Notre Dame, USA. His research interests focus primarily on the problems of state violence and coercion, especially economic sanctions, gross violations of human rights, and ethics and the use of force. Working with David Cortright since 1992, he has written more than 25 articles and book chapters, as well as five books, on economic sanctions, including *The Sanctions Decade: Assessing UN Strategies in the 1990s*, which was named a Choice Outstanding Academic Title in 2000; *Towards Smart Sanctions: Targeting Economic Statecraft* (2002), co-edited with Cortright; and *Sanctions and the Search for Security* (2002), co-authored with Cortright. Their co-edited *Uniting Against Terror* (2007) details their more recent work in sanctions applications and counter-terrorism.

Harald Müller is Director of the Peace Research Institute Frankfurt, Germany, and Professor of International Relations at Frankfurt University. He was a member of the Advisory Council on Disarmament

Matters of the UN Secretary-General (1999–2005), which he chaired in 2004. He was also a member of the German delegation to the NPT Review Conferences in 1995, 2000, and 2005. He was a member of the International Atomic Energy Agency Expert Group on Multilateral Nuclear Arrangements (2004–2005) and is the author of many books and articles on arms control, non-proliferation, and disarmament. His most recent book in English, edited with Matthew Evangelista and Niklas Schörnig, is *Democracy and Security: Preferences, Norms and Policy-making* (2008). His most recent article in English is "The Future of Nuclear Weapons in an Interdependent World," *The Washington Quarterly* (2008).

M. J. Peterson is a Professor of Political Science at the University of Massachusetts Amherst, USA, and has held visiting appointments at the University of Maryland College Park, the University of California Berkeley, and the University of Chicago. Her research focuses on multilateral cooperation, intergovernmental and transnational organizations, and international law. She is the author of *The General Assembly in World Politics* (1986), *The UN General Assembly* (2005), and other books on the development of regimes for outer space, the Antarctic Treaty system, and recognition of governments. Her articles have appeared in the *American Political Science Review*, *International Organization*, *Millennium*, *World Politics*, the *American Journal of International Law*, and other journals.

Ernie Regehr is co-founder of and now Senior Policy Advisor to Project Ploughshares, a Canadian non-governmental organization (NGO). He is a Fellow at the Centre for International Governance Innovation, Ontario, Canada, and is Adjunct Associate Professor in Peace and Conflict Studies at Conrad Grebel University College, Waterloo, Canada. He has served as NGO representative and expert adviser on various Government of Canada delegations to multilateral disarmament forums, including Review Conferences of the Nuclear Non-Proliferation Treaty. His publications on peace and security issues include books, monographs, journal articles, policy papers, parliamentary briefs, and op-eds, and he appears regularly before Parliamentary Committees. He is an officer of the Order of Canada.

Randy Rydell is Senior Political Affairs Officer in the Office of the High Representative for Disarmament Affairs at the United Nations. He was Senior Counsellor and Report Director of the international Weapons of Mass Destruction Commission under Hans Blix (2005–2006). Before working at the United Nations, he served as a nuclear non-proliferation adviser to US Senator John Glenn, as a member of the professional staff of the Senate Committee on Governmental Affairs (1987–1998). He has also worked as an international political analyst at the Lawrence Livermore National Laboratory, USA (1980–1986).

CONTRIBUTORS

Waheguru Pal Singh Sidhu is Director of the New Issues in Security Course at the Geneva Centre for Security Policy. He has written extensively on regionalism and the United Nations as well as on disarmament, arms control, and non-proliferation in leading international journals, including *Arms Control Today, Asian Survey, Disarmament Forum, International Peacekeeping, Politique Etrangère*, and *Bulletin of the Atomic Scientists*. He is also co-editor of *The Iraq Crisis and World Order: Structural, Institutional and Normative Challenges* (2006); and *Arms Control After Iraq: Normative and Operational Challenges* (2006).

Ramesh Thakur is Foundation Director of the Balsillie School of International Affairs and Distinguished Fellow of the Centre for International Governance Innovation in Waterloo, Canada. He was Senior Vice Rector of the United Nations University and Assistant Secretary-General from 1998 to 2007. He was a Professor of International Relations at the University of Otago in New Zealand and Professor and Head of the Peace Research Centre at the Australian National University, during which time he was also a consultant/adviser to the Australian and New Zealand governments on arms control, disarmament, and international security issues. The author or editor of over 30 books and 300 articles and book chapters, he also writes regularly for quality national and international newspapers around the world. His two most recent books are *The United Nations, Peace and Security: From Collective Security to the Responsibility to Protect* (2006) and *War in Our Time: Reflections on Iraq, Terrorism and Weapons of Mass Destruction* (2007).

Thomas G. Weiss is Presidential Professor of Political Science at the City University of New York Graduate Center and Director of the Ralph Bunche Institute for International Studies, where he is co-director of the United Nations Intellectual History Project. He is President of the International Studies Association (2009–2010) and Chair of the Academic Council on the UN System (2006–2009). Previously, he was editor of *Global Governance*, Research Director of the International Commission on Intervention and State Sovereignty, Research Professor at Brown University's Watson Institute for International Studies, Executive Director of the Academic Council on the UN System and of the International Peace Academy, a member of the UN Secretariat, and a consultant to several public and private agencies. He has written or edited some 35 books and 150 articles and book chapters about multilateral approaches to international peace and security, humanitarian action, and sustainable development. His most recent book is *What's Wrong with the United Nations and How to Fix It* (2009).

Foreword

Jayantha Dhanapala

The centrality of nuclear weapons in Cold War international relations is returning, almost two decades after that phase of global politics ended. Four factors may be identified as leading to this situation.

The first is the new global issue of international terrorism (as distinct from national terrorist movements) that emerged on 11 September 2001, which has raised the real threat of nuclear terrorism. Actual evidence of terrorist groups such as al-Qaeda seeking to acquire nuclear materials together with the startling revelations of Dr A. Q. Khan's network of clandestine operations to market nuclear technology and nuclear materials gives this threat credence.

The second factor is a "nuclear renaissance," or a heightened interest in the use of nuclear energy. This reflects, in part, the incontrovertible scientific evidence of climate change resulting from the indiscriminate use of fossil fuels, as embodied in the reports of the Intergovernmental Panel on Climate Change. Although peaceful use of nuclear energy is an "inalienable right" under Article IV of the Nuclear Non-Proliferation Treaty (NPT), alarm bells are ringing about the absence of a credible firewall between peaceful and non-peaceful uses of nuclear energy. A plethora of proposals are being put forward on internationalizing the fuel cycle so as to discourage national uranium enrichment facilities or plutonium reprocessing.

Proven instances of nuclear weapons proliferation among NPT parties constitute the third factor, beginning with Iraq's clandestine program of weapons of mass destruction, which the International Atomic Energy

Agency and the UN Special Commission on Iraq destroyed after the first Gulf war. This was followed by pull-backs by the Democratic People's Republic of Korea and Libya. Suspicions linger over the nuclear program being developed by Iran. Outside the NPT, India and Pakistan have developed nuclear weapons capability and it is credibly assumed that Israel has had nuclear weapons for some time.

The fourth factor is that the nuclear doctrines of some nuclear weapons states have now adopted the actual and pre-emptive use of nuclear weapons even against non-nuclear weapons states and not just their political use as a weapon of deterrent value. This change occurred during the George W. Bush administration and has been followed by the development of nuclear weapons designed for actual use on the battlefield. Today, in the absence of transparent declarations by nuclear weapons states, it is estimated that more than 25,000 nuclear weapons exist in the world, with 10,183 of them deployed warheads ready to be launched. With the Comprehensive Nuclear-Test-Ban Treaty not in force, only a brittle voluntary moratorium prevents further testing and refinement of nuclear weapon technologies.

All of the above point to a highly dangerous situation, which the 2006 report of the Weapons of Mass Destruction Commission encapsulated in the following terms: "So long as any state has such weapons – especially nuclear arms – others will want them. So long as any such weapons remain in any state's arsenal, there is a high risk that they will one day be used, by design or accident. Any such use would be catastrophic."[1] To cope with this threat to international peace and security and the very survival of humanity we have to look to cooperative multilateral action as the only effective and durable way out of this crisis. At the center of multilateral activity is the United Nations, with its unparalleled universality of membership and its legitimacy.

This volume seeks to evaluate the role that the United Nations has played in the past in attenuating the risks of nuclear weapons possession and proliferation, in creating a negotiating and norm-building machinery, in verifying treaties that have been negotiated, and in preventing nuclear war. Jane Boulden, Ramesh Thakur, and Tom Weiss have assembled a brilliant team. They collectively provide the backdrop to an analysis of what the United Nations can do in the current situation and the future. It is an analysis by widely respected scholars from an impressive variety of disciplines.

I am sure all students of the United Nations will welcome this invaluable addition to the growing literature on the world organization. And the disarmament community will be encouraged by the fact that the United Nations has the potential to play a significant role in the vital issue of nuclear disarmament and nuclear proliferation.

Note

1. Hans Blix et al., *Weapons of Terror: Freeing the World of Nuclear, Biological and Chemical Arms* (Stockholm: Weapons of Mass Destruction Commission, 2006): 17.

Acknowledgements

This book had its origins in the aftermath of the Iraq war and in the midst of mounting concerns about nuclear weapons in North Korea, along with the nature of Iran's nuclear research program. The project that resulted in this book grew from the long-standing friendship and professional collaboration by the editors. Building on the work done by Boulden and Weiss on terrorism and the United Nations,[1] by Thakur and Weiss on global governance,[2] and by Thakur and colleagues on Iraq (in which Boulden, Weiss and some of the other participants in this project were also involved),[3] we sought to explore the role being played by the United Nations in response to various nuclear weapons-related developments.

The editors are extremely grateful to the authors of the chapters included in this volume. They rose to the challenge and provided us with a set of provocative, informative, and analytically challenging chapters. All of the contributors benefitted from the comments of the participants at the second authors' workshop: Hossam Eldeen Aly, Ummu Salma Bava, Kennette Benedict, Denise Heinz, James O. C. Jonah, Gabriele Kraatz-Wadsack, Georges Landau, Peter Lieberman, Zia Mian, Rolf Mützenich, Dingli Shen, and Nina Tannenwald.

The project was generously funded by the Friedrich-Ebert-Stiftung and the United Nations University, as well as by the Academic Council of the United Nations System and the Ralph Bunche Institute for International Studies at The Graduate Center of the City University of New York (CUNY).

Special mention must be made of Volker Lehmann and Jürgen Stetten of Friedrich-Ebert-Stiftung New York. Not only did they believe in the project from the beginning, but their presence and engagement during all of its phases at both substantive and administrative levels ensured that the final product is as strong as it is; and they published an abbreviated version of our opening and concluding chapters in order to get the conclusions quickly into the hands of officials, especially in New York.[4]

As always, the Ralph Bunche Institute for International Studies provided a supportive and congenial location for the workshops and acted as the project's central locus point. None of this would have been possible without the assistance of the professional staff there. In particular, the editors owe an expression of thanks to Michael Busch, an advanced graduate student in political science at The CUNY Graduate Center. He acted as a steady hand throughout the project's duration. His attention to detail, his research support, and his overall willingness to help were greatly appreciated; neither this book nor the gatherings that led to it would have been as solid without the efforts from this promising young professional.

As ever, we welcome comments from our readers.

J.B., R.T., and T.G.W.
New York
October 2008

Notes

1. Jane Boulden and Thomas G. Weiss, eds, *Terrorism and the UN: Before and After September 11* (Bloomington: Indiana University Press, 2004).
2. Thomas G. Weiss and Ramesh Thakur, *The UN and Global Governance: An Unfinished Journey* (Bloomington: Indiana University Press, forthcoming).
3. Ramesh Thakur and Waheguru Pal Singh Sidhu, eds, *The Iraq Crisis and World Order: Structural, Institutional and Normative Challenges* (Tokyo: United Nations University Press, 2006); Waheguru Pal Singh Sidhu and Ramesh Thakur, *Arms Control After Iraq* (Tokyo: United Nations University Press, 2006).
4. Ramesh Thakur, Jane Boulden, and Thomas G. Weiss, *Can the NPT Regime Be Fixed, or Should It Be Abandoned?* Dialogue on Globalization Occasional Paper Series, No. 40 (New York: Friedrich-Ebert-Stiftung, 2008).

Abbreviations

ABACC	Brazilian-Argentine Agency for Accounting and Control of Nuclear Materials [Agência Brasileiro-Argentina de Contabilidade e Controle de Materiais Nucleares]
ARF	ASEAN Regional Forum
ASEAN	Association of Southeast Asian Nations
CD	Conference on Disarmament
CTBT	Comprehensive Nuclear-Test-Ban Treaty
DDA	Department of Disarmament Affairs
DPA	Department of Political Affairs
DPRK	Democratic People's Republic of Korea
DPSCA	Department of Political and Security Council Affairs
EU	European Union
EU-3	France, Germany and the United Kingdom
FMCT	Fissile Material Cut-off Treaty
G-8	Group of Eight
G-77	Group of 77
GCC	Gulf Cooperation Council
HEU	highly enriched uranium
HLP	High-level Panel on Threats, Challenges and Change
IAEA	International Atomic Energy Agency
ICJ	International Court of Justice
IHL	international humanitarian law
ILC	International Law Commission
LTBT	Limited Test Ban Treaty
N-5	five NPT-licit nuclear states
NAM	Non-aligned Movement

NATO	North Atlantic Treaty Organization
NGO	non-governmental organization
NNWS	non-nuclear-weapon state(s)
NPT	Treaty on the Non-Proliferation of Nuclear Weapons
NSG	Nuclear Suppliers Group
NSS	National Security Strategy
NWFZ	nuclear-weapon-free zone
NWS	nuclear weapons state(s)
ODA	Office for Disarmament Affairs
OMV	Ongoing Monitoring and Verification
OPCW	Organisation for the Prohibition of Chemical Weapons
OSCE	Organization for Security and Co-operation in Europe
P-5	five permanent members of the Security Council
PSI	Proliferation Security Initiative
SALT-I	Strategic Arms Limitation Talks Treaty I
SSOD	Special Session on Disarmament
START	Strategic Arms Reduction Treaty
UFP	Uniting for Peace
UK	United Kingdom
UN	United Nations
UNMOVIC	United Nations Monitoring, Verification and Inspection Commission
UNSCOM	United Nations Special Commission on Iraq
US	United States
WHO	World Health Organization
WMD	weapon(s) of mass destruction

1

The United Nations and nuclear orders: Context, foundations, actors, tools, and future prospects

Jane Boulden, Ramesh Thakur, and Thomas G. Weiss

Since the end of the Cold War, the status of nuclear weapons has been in constant flux, an extension of a longer pattern of changes relating to the existence of such arms in world politics. This collection of essays sheds light on the subject of the past, present, and future roles of the United Nations and the nuclear challenges that confront the planet as well as the world body. To that end, our chapter acts as both introduction and conclusion. We begin by outlining the context framing the book, then offer a brief discussion of the provisions of the UN Charter that are central to the problématique. Next, mirroring the book's structure, we briefly examine the actors, tools, and issues that form the backbone of our study. A final section looks at future threats looming on the horizon. In addition to establishing the rationale and the framework for analysis, we conclude by drawing together key themes and ideas that emerge from other chapters in order to highlight the resulting conclusions and questions about the role of the United Nations and where the world organization might, and should, be headed.

The context

On what basis do we argue that the status of nuclear weapons is so constantly variable? A few examples help to provide the context for this generalization. Three former Soviet republics became nuclear weapons

---

The United Nations and nuclear orders, Boulden, Thakur and Weiss (eds), United Nations University Press, 2009, ISBN 978-92-808-1167-4

states (NWS) on achieving independence and then relinquished that status. South Africa announced its renunciation of a nuclear weapons program that few knew existed. India and Pakistan arrived and consolidated themselves as NWS a decade ago. Libya pursued nuclear weapons programs only to pull back from the brink. Its reversal and re-entry into the international community contributed to the revelation that a Pakistani government official, Abdul Qadeer Khan, had been selling nuclear weapons information and technology to a variety of clients over a considerable period of time. North Korea has pursued a policy of nuclear brinkmanship, including testing, for a decade or two, while Iran continues to test the limits of its credibility and the world's patience by arguing that it is pursuing peaceful uses of potentially fissile materials.

Moreover, in 1995 the Nuclear Non-Proliferation Treaty (NPT) was made permanent, although the five-year Review Conference in 2005 ended without an agreed document. Nor has the world been any more successful in the pursuit of a non-discriminatory, multilateral, and verifiable convention banning the production of fissile material for weapons purposes, which would greatly strengthen the non-proliferation regime. On top of these developments, the United States removed one of the cornerstones supporting the bilateral nuclear arms control edifice by withdrawing from the Anti-Ballistic Missile treaty.

Meanwhile, globalization has been gathering momentum, fueled by the accelerating technological capabilities of states and instantaneous communication. On the supply side, a major proliferation challenge is the globalization of the arms industry, the flooding of the global arms market, and a resultant loosening of supplier constraints. These changes have increased the number of states that may potentially have the capability to develop a nuclear weapons program should they choose to pursue one. Leaving aside weapons aspirations, the number of states that might be able or may choose to pursue peaceful nuclear energy programs is now considerably larger than it has ever been. Along with the increased pressure for cleaner and less expensive energy sources, the combined effects of these trends undoubtedly will increase the level of trade in nuclear material and equipment as well as the number of nuclear-capable powers generally.

A further factor compounding the complexity of the situation is the rise of terrorism and the associated fear that a terrorist group might succeed in obtaining some form of nuclear material. Many see the advent of al-Qaeda, especially since the attacks of 11 September 2001, as an indication of a particularly lethal new form of terrorism. In addition to their willingness to commit suicide as part of an attack, the newest generation of terrorists seek not just to make a political statement through violent acts, but to do so while maximizing the level of destruction and instability involved. For them, therefore, access to nuclear materials of any kind, but especially weapons-grade, is assumed to be an important goal. The combined effects of these developments led to an arms control regime under deep stress. The global consensus underpinning the normative architecture of arms control is itself being strained. The 2004 UN Secretary-General's High-level Panel on Threats, Challenges and Change (HLP) warned bluntly: "We are approaching a point at which the erosion of the non-proliferation regime could become irreversible and result in a cascade of proliferation."[1]

Examining the UN role in this context reveals a paradox. On the one hand, the unique legitimacy of the organization, deriving from its universal membership, makes it the normative center of gravity either for re-affirming the existing consensus or for refashioning a new one. On the other hand, the world organization's balance sheet is unimpressive in this regard. Symptomatic of this, in September 2005, over 150 heads of state gathered to consider the proposals of the Secretary-General's HLP on the occasion of the United Nations' sixtieth anniversary. Billed as the "World Summit" – the largest gathering ever of heads of state and government – the meeting sought to establish a new path for the world organization. The final outcome document addressed issues ranging from terrorism to human rights to UN reform, but made no mention of arms control and disarmament, a gap that Secretary-General Kofi Annan called a "disgrace."[2] Nor is the idea that the United Nations has a role to play a natural one. There is little tradition of the United Nations as a key player on nuclear weapons issues. The Charter was developed before the potential of atomic weapons was understood or demonstrated, and thus it has no provisions directly geared to dealing with them. Early UN-based efforts to develop and negotiate controls on atomic materials and weapons were almost instantly stymied by the politics of the Cold War. This early failure was symptomatic of the long struggle to come between East and West. The decades-long superpower stalemate that would infect the newly formed world organization was accompanied by the attendant argument that nuclear-weapons-based strategic deterrence was a key pillar supporting the "long peace" until 1989.[3] A number of arms control and disarmament agreements and actions, resulting from negotiations conducted outside the United Nations, both resulted from, and also in turn contributed to, the ending of the Cold War. One of the best examples is the Intermediate Range Nuclear Forces agreement between Moscow and Washington.

On the other side of the equation, however, the United Nations – whose foremost purpose is the maintenance of international peace and security – has played a significant and varied role in this area from its inception. Of course, it has not been the central forum for decisions relating to nuclear weapons. Nonetheless, the Security Council has been a setting for discussions about crises over nuclear weapons (e.g. in Cuba and Iraq), the source of decisions relating to how states respond to other potential nuclear states (e.g. the Israeli bombing of the Osirak reactor), and a standard-setter for member states seeking nuclear weapons and materiel (e.g. Security Council resolution 1540). Perhaps even more pertinently, the strong, if unsuccessful, efforts made in early 2003 to secure a second Council resolution explicitly authorizing war in Iraq demonstrated just how powerful the United Nations' legitimizing role remains.[4] Then, as the war was waged anyway, the desperate but unrewarded search for non-existent weapons of mass destruction (WMD) proved conclusively the success of UN inspections in disarming Saddam Hussein of all such weapons.

Critics and proponents alike often overlook the fact that the General Assembly's very first resolution on 24 January 1946 established a commission to deal with "the problems raised by the discovery of atomic energy." From the 1950s and into the 1960s, the Assembly was the forum for a series of proposals on general and complete disarmament. Since then, the Assembly has passed scores of resolutions on nuclear weapons and has held three special sessions on disarmament. In 1996, in an Advisory Opinion requested by the General Assembly, the International Court of Justice (ICJ) gave its views on the legality of nuclear weapons. At the center of, and in many ways the most consistent actor in, the UN family is the International Atomic Energy Agency (IAEA), formed in 1957. The IAEA's role has evolved and expanded in response to the changing environment and its requirements. Its mandate involves monitoring, verifying, and reporting on nuclear programs in a large number of states, making it the central UN actor in an increasingly complex and politicized environment, as experience with Iraq, North Korea, and Iran has demonstrated.

This brief survey suggests that, although the United Nations may not be the central forum for negotiations and discussions concerning nuclear weapons, and it may not be living up to its full potential, it would be wrong to count the United Nations out of the nuclear weapons picture. Two critical questions remain: Is the United Nations a credible or desirable actor in this realm? And, if so, to what end? These queries provide the analytical framework of this book.

There is little in the way of sustained or focused research on the United Nations' role in this area, which further complicates the reality that numerous previous predictions about nuclear weapons and nuclear power have been so wrong – aptly called "the sky-is-still-falling profession."[5] To the extent such work exists, it relates to specific cases or to specific tools. Research on the Council or the Assembly, for example, might include reference to their role on nuclear weapons as one of a number of issues with which they deal, but certainly not as a central factor. There is a wealth of work on the United Nations' role and experience with Iraq, but it focuses primarily on questions specific to that experience.[6] Similarly, work on the NPT or other arms control efforts might mention the UN role, but the focus is the arms control efforts in question, not the United Nations. In addition to the fact that little exists on the subject, an added push comes from the fact that the United Nations is considerably changed from its Cold War days. The world organization, especially in the form of the Security Council, has demonstrated a greater willingness to use the international peace and security tools at its disposal to deal with situations in new and creative ways. Much of the literature dealing with that shift, however, is focused on issues such as the use of force, terrorism, and an ever-broadening definition of threats to international peace and security – ranging from human rights and humanitarian disasters to HIV/AIDS.

There is, therefore, a gap to be filled in taking on this kind of study, which is why we assembled a richly diverse team of analysts to help us illuminate this issue. The assumptions that form the foundation of analyses in this volume are:

- There is an increased desire on the part of key actors and of member states generally that the United Nations, and in particular the Council, play a greater role in dealing with nuclear issues.
- There are Charter grounds for such a role as well as some past experience, including the concrete case of Iraq, to build upon.
- The current political, legal, normative, and military contexts, however, are considerably different from those in which many of the previous UN goals were established and experiences accumulated. Indeed, many precepts once taken as givens are now openly questioned.
- Many of the questions relating to how, when, and in what context the United Nations plays a role in, or might make a contribution to, the nuclear issue require far greater research and reflection.

In hoping to evaluate the past and look toward the future, we asked contributors to keep in mind common considerations. Thus, the analytical framework here was focused on finding better answers than previous ones to three interrelated questions:

- What is the nature of the current environment in which the United Nations is operating on these issues?
- Who and what are the actors and tools the United Nations has available to it with respect to questions about nuclear weapons?
- What do the answers to those two questions tell us about whether and how the organization could, or should, play a role in these issues, as well as the kind of role that it might assume?

The foundation: The UN Charter

The framers of the UN Charter began their task with a shared sense of two key objectives: the desire to prevent a third world war and the need to avoid the pitfalls of the League of Nations. The result was a determination that the new organization would have an effective system of enforcement with military teeth to ensure compliance with its decisions. To that end, the Charter framers had already agreed that states would be required to provide military forces to the organization for the purposes of undertaking enforcement operations, and that the great powers would shoulder the brunt of this burden. They also agreed that the organization should play a role in establishing a system for the regulation of armaments, although the need for regulation had to be balanced against the need for states to maintain a level of armaments sufficient to allow them to fulfill their duty to provide troops for the implementation of the planned collective security system. Another critical lesson learned from the interwar experience was that the allies had not rearmed sufficiently strongly and sufficiently in advance of Nazi aggression. This too dampened interest in general and complete disarmament.

Although the Charter's framers saw the control of national armaments as fundamentally tied to the envisaged system of mandatory enforcement, they judged it sufficiently important to keep it separate from the broader Article 24 Council responsibilities for maintaining international peace and security. Thus, Article 26 requires the Council to establish a plan for regulating arms as a special and specific function, in addition to its primary responsibility for the maintenance of international peace and security:

> In order to promote the establishment and maintenance of international peace and security with the least diversion for armaments of the world's human and economic resources, the Security Council shall be responsible for formulating, with the assistance of the Military Staff Committee referred to in Article 47, plans to be submitted to the Members of the United Nations for the establishment of a system for the regulation of armaments.

Consideration of arms regulation and disarmament was also established as a specific function for the General Assembly. Article 11(1) states that:

> The General Assembly may consider the general principles of cooperation in the maintenance of international peace and security, including the principles governing disarmament and the regulation of armaments, and may make recommendations with regard to such principles to the Members or to the Security Council or to both.

The explosion of atomic weapons at Hiroshima and Nagasaki and the onset of the Cold War not long thereafter fundamentally altered the environment in which the United Nations found itself operating. Both the ideas that member states would provide troops for the enforcement of Council decisions and that the Council would develop a system for regulating armaments fell by the wayside. As has been the case in other issue areas, however, the absence of a willingness to use the Charter machinery as originally designed has not stopped the various actors within the system from playing a role, developing proposals, or designing new mechanisms for addressing the issue.

UN arms control and disarmament machinery

The machinery and the program of action for disarmament were established at the first UN Special Session on Disarmament (SSOD-I) in 1978.[7] The final document established the Conference on Disarmament (CD) as the "single multilateral disarmament negotiating forum." Its origins lie in the Ten-Nation Committee on Disarmament of 1959 (five members each from the North Atlantic Treaty Organization and the Warsaw Pact). Just as the Security Council's and the Economic and Social Council's numbers were increased to reflect the changing UN membership after decolonization, so too the CD was expanded to include eight neutral and non-aligned countries and then further enlarged to its present strength of 65. The CD is not a true UN body and it has its own rules and procedures, but the links are intimate: its budget is included in the UN budget, its meetings are serviced by the UN Secretariat, its Secretary-General is the Director-General of the United Nations Office at Geneva, and its Deputy Secretary-General is the head of the Geneva Branch of the UN Office for Disarmament Affairs. Moreover, it submits its annual report to the Assembly.

The consensus rule for making any decisions in the CD, originally designed to help states find agreement, is now providing a convenient cover for countries that want to block progress. Since the completion of the Comprehensive Nuclear-Test-Ban Treaty (CTBT) in 1996, the CD has been unable to begin negotiations on banning fissile materials or any other issue. Apart from a few weeks in August 1998, the CD has been unable to agree even on a program of work. This dreadful state of affairs has been due to a few countries (sometimes only one or two) thwarting the majority. In the process, the CD is bringing the whole of the multilateral disarmament process into disrepute.

Another body, the First Committee of the General Assembly, is charged with considering disarmament and international security. Its resolutions cover the gamut of disarmament and security issues: landmines, small arms, terrorism, biological weapons, information technology, and nuclear weapons. Many resolutions are mere repeats of previous years' resolutions, but new ones are introduced every year and serve as a litmus test of progress or lack thereof, and as weathervanes of current international thinking on disarmament and international security. Voting is by a simple majority. Resolutions may be adopted by acclamation, without objection or without a vote, or the vote may be recorded or taken by roll-call. After the Committee has completed its consideration of items and submitted draft resolutions, all issues are voted on through resolutions passed in plenary meetings of the Assembly, usually towards the end of the regular session each December.

The UN Disarmament Commission is one body where all member states can come together to examine the framework for disarmament and set a discussion agenda. It is a deliberative body mandated to make recommendations in the field of disarmament and to follow up the decisions and recommendations of SSOD-I. Unlike the First Committee, the Commission does not pass resolutions. Instead, it focuses on a limited number of agenda items each session to allow for in-depth discussion. However, its work too has become moribund owing to the politicization of all its discussions amidst the prevailing distrust and suspicions of one another's motives, intentions, and agendas by the various groups of member states.

Several international bodies are linked to the UN framework as part of the implementation mechanism for disarmament – for example, the IAEA in Vienna and the Organisation for the Prohibition of Chemical Weapons (OPCW) at The Hague.[8] In addition, there are the mechanisms established with specific mandates associated with Council decisions in the aftermath of the UN-authorized action in response to Iraq's invasion of Kuwait. In 1999, the Council created the UN Monitoring, Verification and Inspection Commission (UNMOVIC) to replace the UN Special Commission (UNSCOM). The Council mandated UNMOVIC with verifying the disarmament of the weapons of mass destruction in Iraq under Security Council resolutions 687, 1284, and 1441. Previously, UNSCOM had succeeded in determining the extent of the Iraqi WMD program and in disarming Iraq without the cooperation of the Iraqi government. It also oversaw the destruction of missiles and Iraq's chemical warfare agent arsenal. But an attack on Iraq by the United States with cruise missiles and damning revelations about the use of UNSCOM by US intelligence brought about its downfall. UNMOVIC was established with a clean slate, but it was not until the 2002 showdown with Washington and the threat of massive military action by the United States that Iraq allowed Executive Chairman Hans Blix and the UNMOVIC inspectors into the country to carry out its mandate.[9]

The international inspection record in Iraq prior to 2003 has important implications for the United Nations and future efforts to foster disarmament. UNSCOM did a very good job. Despite all the cat-and-mouse games, obfuscation, subversion, and evasion by Iraq, UNSCOM succeeded in mapping large parts of Iraq's WMD programs between 1991 and 1998.[10] UN sanctions and national export controls worked better than expected. The painstaking analysis of all the UNSCOM data that UNMOVIC carried out in the period 1999–2002 paid off. However, UNMOVIC found little new evidence of weapons of mass destruction in the few months of in-country inspections that it carried out because it had very little useful and original intelligence information and only partial cooperation from the Iraqi government. However, the post-invasion Iraq Survey Team was not able to achieve more, even without those constraints.

The actors

The political science literature informs us of the fallacy of the rational actor model of state decision-making. This is even truer of the United Nations. It is not a unitary actor. There is no such thing as *the* United Nations. Instead, there are several United Nations, each with its own balance of composition and political interests. We recall Inis Claude's classic twofold distinction between the world organization as an intergovernmental arena and as a secretariat,[11] and the more recent distinction of a "Third United Nations" consisting of certain non-governmental organizations (NGOs), external experts, scholars, consultants, and committed citizens who work closely with the United Nations' intergovernmental machinery and secretariats.[12] The psychology and logic of these networks and groups are distinct yet relatively unknown, another topic for future research.[13]

Our discussion of the nuclear challenges involves mainly the First United Nations, an arena where states make decisions, with due consideration of the Second United Nations. The Charter establishes a rough division of labor between the two principal organs associated with the United Nations' core functions relating to international peace and security (the Council and the Assembly) and the third principal organ (the Secretariat, headed by the Secretary-General). Each has distinct advantages and disadvantages in its respective roles, as well as in the issues that arise in areas where those roles cross paths. We discuss them in this chapter in reverse order.

The Secretariat and the Secretary-General

Of the three actors discussed here, the Secretary-General and the Secretariat are the least obvious choices as key actors for the nuclear weapons agenda. Yet, as Randy Rydell establishes in Chapter 4, there is ample ground for the Secretary-General to play an important role. He is the chief administrative officer of the organization and as such able to restructure the Secretariat; and the unit dealing with disarmament has been a particular target with successor secretaries-general. In addition, however, the Secretary-General is the chief symbol of the international interest, advocate of law and rights, general manager of the global agenda, and a focal point in setting the direction of world affairs.

The status, authority, and powers of the Secretary-General are derived chiefly from the Charter, but his success depends also invariably on the skills and personality of the incumbent and on relations among the major powers of the world. The political role of the Secretary-General in turn is a function of the interplay between Charter functions and powers, personal attributes, and the political equations among the member states. Charter Article 99 authorizes the Secretary-General to bring to the attention of the Council "any matter which in his opinion may threaten the maintenance of international peace and security." This article and other Charter provisions can be interpreted expansively by an incumbent Secretary-General under the doctrine of implied powers. The single most important political role of the Secretary-General is to provide leadership – that elusive ability to make others connect emotionally and intellectually to a larger cause that transcends their immediate, perceived self-interests.

Because the Security Council and the General Assembly are often split, the Secretary-General can sometimes maneuver to advance his own priorities by indicating possible points of agreement. He has the right to be present and take part in the debates in the political organs, and often does. He provides the logistical and intellectual basis for many Council and Assembly resolutions and may urge particular courses of action. He is expected to implement the most controversial of decisions with the most scrupulous impartiality, exercising political judgment while avoiding the twin temptations of inflating or deflating the role of the office. He is also at the nerve center of a sensitive communications network. He can, and generally does, speak directly to governments, civil society representatives, and business leaders. He is asked to submit reports and analyses on a vast range of topics. As well as using the budget as a vehicle for inserting his priorities into the organization's work agenda, he submits an annual report on the work of the organization that gives him a guaranteed instrument for outlining his vision for the

United Nations. All these avenues allow the Secretary-General to shape the institutional context and normative milieu within which he must wield influence.

The General Assembly

The most significant advantage of the Assembly is its universality. Every member state has a voice and a vote, which lends considerable legitimacy to Assembly efforts. That universality is also a disadvantage. With 192 members (not to mention many observers), the Assembly is unwieldy. Its sheer size makes it an unlikely source for efficient or effective negotiation, and consensus almost guarantees sinking to the lowest common denominator. In addition, as M. J. Peterson argues in Chapter 3, the nature of the debate in the Assembly has shifted from one characterized by discussion and consensus-seeking to one where divisions are articulated and reinforced. In spite of the discord and stalemate that have characterized the debate in recent years, the Assembly has been the source or motivator for some important developments in the efforts to control nuclear weapons.

The Assembly was the first UN actor to move on the issue of nuclear weapons and, as mentioned, devoted its very first resolution to creating the UN Atomic Energy Commission. The Assembly was the forum in which the major proposals for controlling atomic material and weapons were put forward and debated during the early years of the atomic age and the US monopoly. Perhaps the most ambitious instance came in 1946. Financier Bernard Baruch devised a plan to place the entire nuclear fuel cycle under the control of the United Nations while the United States still possessed the monopoly on atomic weapons. Many believed that it signaled an American willingness eventually to disarm its nuclear weapons. The Soviet Union refused to sign the proposed agreement.[14] The Assembly also provided the stage for President Dwight Eisenhower's historic "Atoms for Peace" address to the United Nations in 1953. Eisenhower used the speech to highlight the dual nature of atomic energy: catastrophically dangerous in the form of weapons, potentially productive as a peaceful power source. "Atoms for Peace" provided the blueprint for the creation of an international agency charged with managing the world's stockpiles of fissionable materials, consistent with the United Nations' mission of maintaining international peace and security. Four years later, Eisenhower's call was realized with the establishment of the IAEA.

Since then, the Assembly has continued to consider the question of nuclear weapons in various ways, mainly through resolutions and three special sessions on disarmament. The Assembly has played an important role in setting standards for the development of nuclear-weapon-free zones, and in advocating greater progress on key issues such as the CTBT. Nevertheless, this level of activity obscures the erratic and limited nature of the progress that this represents. A fourth special session on disarmament was approved in 1995, for example, but 13 years, many debates, and two open-ended working groups later, there is still no agreement on establishing its objectives.

As the only authentic and truly representative body of the international community of states, the General Assembly functions as the normative center of gravity and can set and articulate standards of conduct and norms of appropriate behavior. Judgment about the Assembly's record should be balanced against its overall functions. Its resolutions are non-binding and represent recommendations only. Nonetheless, the Assembly's inability or unwillingness to harness the power inherent in the universality of its membership towards basic common goals may have left open an opportunity for the Security Council to play a greater role on this front than in the past. This could be one of the reasons we now see a shift in the balance of activity towards the Council.

The Security Council

For a body able to establish binding requirements and the ability to enforce them, we must look to the Security Council. Although international agreements and treaty negotiations are conducted in other forums, Ernie Regehr recalls in Chapter 2 that violations and transgressions can be brought to the Council. Its activity on issues relating to nuclear weapons was quite sparse during the Cold War. Perhaps the most notable action was resolution 487, passed unanimously by the Council in 1981, soundly condemning the Israeli attack on an Iraqi nuclear research facility located in Osirak.[15]

A decade later, with the Cold War clearly over, the Council entered more fully into the nuclear weapons realm. Beginning with resolution 687, which ended the Gulf war in 1991, it initiated a long, complicated effort to deal with Iraq's chemical, biological, and nuclear weapons programs. Those efforts have been joined by Council action in response to the arrival of other actual or potential nuclear weapons states. So, it has taken action of varied intensity and impact in response to developments in India, Pakistan, Iran, and North Korea, as Amitav Acharya details in Chapter 12 on cases in Asia.

At the level of process, Council activity on nuclear weapons can be divided into two streams: reactive case-oriented action and proactive thematic efforts. The development of a thematic or issue-oriented approach is a general trend in Council work, seen most clearly in its response to terrorism. The thematic efforts on nuclear weapons occur in the 2004 resolution 1540, in which the Council built on concerns about terrorism and established a set of minimum standards for member state action on nuclear, chemical, and biological weapons. Echoing the novel approach in resolution 1373 on terrorism, in 1540 the Council directed, rather than merely recommended, states to take measures at the national level in order to ensure the security of any material, equipment, or weaponry relating to nuclear, chemical, or biological weapons.

The overall record of Council case-oriented action on nuclear weapons is mixed. Although the possibility that Libya was pursuing a nuclear weapons program was never dealt with head-on, there is little doubt about the impact of the sanctions that the Council imposed in response to Libya's unwillingness to hand over suspects in the Lockerbie bombing. This stance contributed to Libya's eventual decision to re-enter the international community of states as a full-fledged member in good standing. Doing so meant coming clean on its nuclear program, and then forfeiting it. Similarly, there are positive signs with respect to North Korea's nuclear weapons program. But here again, it seems likely that it is pressure in the form of Council-imposed sanctions in conjunction with separate regionally based negotiations on the status of the program that has contributed to steps in the right direction. In other words, the Council has been a key player in some of these situations, but certainly not the only one.

On India and Pakistan, the Council's approach has little to commend it.[16] It suffered from a triple handicap. First, neither India nor Pakistan had signed the NPT. Any attempt to penalize them for violating a treaty that they had explicitly rejected would constitute so revolutionary a departure from the widely accepted norms of sovereign statehood that it would run tremors of apprehension up the spines of most states. Second, and very much by contrast, the continued possession and deployment of nuclear weapons by the NPT-licit five nuclear weapons states (the N-5) are considered by many to violate their NPT Article 6 disarmament obligations, which all five have voluntarily signed. They thus had little moral authority to lecture and censure India and Pakistan. And third, it is difficult to apply moral and economic coercion on two states while ignoring Israel as the singular exemption with respect to de facto NWS status, as opposed to nuclear testing.

In 1998, Security Council resolution 1172 condemned the weapons tests by India and Pakistan and called on both to cease their weapons programs and to join the NPT. That initial effort was undermined, if not completely abandoned, by the lack of any follow-up. Moreover, a de facto acceptance of both states' nuclear weapons status has been in evidence through the policies of all of the permanent members, especially the United States. No better example can be found than the agreement reached between the United States and India in March 2006. The deal grants India US nuclear power assistance and expertise in exchange for New Delhi's acceptance of international monitoring of its civilian nuclear power program. At the same time, however, India's military nuclear programs remain unmolested. The Council's actions have similarly worked against it with respect to Iraq. Although the Council did not approve the use of force against Iraq in 2003, the fact that the United States and the United Kingdom violated the provisions of the Charter under the guise of responding to Iraqi violations of Council resolutions relating to WMD had an enormous impact on the perception of the Council's authority. All in all, the many instances of double standards frustrate most member states and undermine the Council's claim to be a legitimate actor.

Compared with the Assembly, however, we see much in the Council's actions to demonstrate an evolution and responsiveness to the changing nature of the international environment and new threats. The Council's overall approach might be characterized as one focused on denial, prevention, and pressure rather than direct action. The Council has done this by making use of the tools available to it through the Charter, sometimes very creatively.

Tools

Of all the UN tools available, sanctions represent one that has considerable potential for adaptation. Indeed, to the extent that we might identify success stories in UN efforts to deal with nuclear weapons, David Cortright and George Lopez argue in Chapter 5 that sanctions have been the explanation. Yet barriers remain that prevent any blanket endorsement of sanctions as the tool of choice in dealing with all aspects of the nuclear challenge. The ongoing expansion of technological capabilities, and the extent to which states might vary in their susceptibility to sanctions as a tool, stand out as key obstacles that need to be addressed – not to mention the negative humanitarian consequences of sanctions.[17] What is clear is that, in order to work, sanctions must be consistently applied, be coupled with inducements, and involve other forms of engagement. Using sanctions effectively also draws in a variety of other actors. Increasingly, for example, sanctions are targeted at the financial assets of states and individuals, drawing in financial institutions as key players in this equation. And sometimes they are used in situations where the lead political role is being taken by states outside of the UN umbrella, such as the Six-Party Talks on North Korea.

Inside the First United Nations, the use of force as a response to nuclear weapons situations is the most contentious and most problematic tool for individual states and groups of states. The use or misuse of the threat and use of force has the potential to undermine the organization as a whole as it goes to the very heart of the United Nations' collective security bargain. The Charter provides that force may be used only in self-defense or in pursuit of the collective interest contingent upon Council authorization. Therefore, it is difficult to underestimate the impact of the unauthorized war launched against Iraq in 2003. Despite the fact that it was waged under the banner of Iraq's non-compliance with UN provisions calling for the elimination of its weapons of mass destruction,[18] this act confirmed for some the perception that the United Nations remains an organization based on a double standard. In the eyes of the most severe critics, the Iraq war confirmed that permanent members, in this case the United States and the United Kingdom, can violate the terms of the Charter with impunity.

Recent experience, and not just in Iraq, raises broad questions about the use of force in response to nuclear weapons. Ian Johnstone takes on these issues in Chapter 6, focusing in particular on questions relating to self-defense and the grounds for preventive and pre-emptive use of force. In many ways this is the source of the most profound potential dilemmas for the United Nations, especially in the years to come. At what point is it appropriate to authorize the use of force when considering nuclear weapons? On what basis should the Council make decisions about nuclear weapons? Where does its information come from, and what kinds of judgments are Council members able to make based on that information? As noted by the Secretary-General's HLP, "The maintenance of world peace and security depends importantly on there being a common global understanding, and acceptance, of when the application of force is both legal and legitimate."[19] In his chapter, Johnstone forges into this debate by suggesting a list of factors the Council might take into account when considering its reaction to situations involving nuclear weapons or nuclear weapons proliferation.

Questions about information lead us to the issues surrounding the United Nations' role in verification and compliance. As with Council activity generally, we can identify two streams here: case-based approaches and those that are preventive and issue oriented. This is a potential growth area for the world organization. In order to ensure Iraqi compliance with its resolutions, the Council established UNSCOM and UNMOVIC. As Harald Müller argues in Chapter 7, the IAEA is the central and critical body, the only existing organization with an institutional foundation and experience in this field that are sufficiently robust to take on these tasks. It has the added benefit of being outside of the politicking of the United Nations, but with a large enough membership, through its board of governors and its international staff, to offer a high degree of legitimacy in its efforts. That legitimacy will begin to erode commensurately with efforts to politicize its technical tasks and challenges.

Of course, no discussion of tools to meet the nuclear challenge is complete without a consideration of international law. As mentioned above, Security Council resolution 1540 mandated, rather than recommended, that states secure any weapons-related nuclear material. This is a critical international legal development. This resolution crossed a conceptual and legal Rubicon of sorts in directing sovereign states to enact non-proliferation legislation. The Council called WMD proliferation a threat to international peace and security, and expressed concern over the threat of WMD terrorism and of illicit trafficking in WMD material, weapons, and delivery systems. Resolution 1540 called on all states to enact and enforce laws to prohibit non-state actors to develop, acquire, transfer, or use WMD; to take and enforce effective domestic control, physical protection, accounting, and border control measures to prevent proliferation; and to set up a committee of the whole to oversee implementation of the resolution.

Its very existence may provide a foundation for broader (rather than case-specific) non-proliferation action. The unprecedented intrusion into national law-making authority can be read as the toughened new determination by the international community of states to take effective action. But it certainly was not without controversy. A former member of the Joint UN/Organisation of African Unity Group of Experts on the Denuclearization of Africa noted that "by arrogating to itself wider powers of legislation," the Council was departing from its Charter-based mandate, and that excessive recourse to Chapter VII could signal a preference for coercion over cooperation.[20] Many NGOs too criticized the resolution's silence on the role of disarmament in promoting non-proliferation, as well as the Council's effort to transform itself into a world legislature.[21]

There is some important historical background in the linkage between the Security Council and international legal limits on nuclear weapons. In 1968, Council resolution 255 backed the NPT by committing the Council, "above all its nuclear-weapon state permanent members," to take action in any instance of aggression involving nuclear weapons against a non-nuclear-weapon state. The NPT requires that any state withdrawing from the NPT provide notice to the Council outlining the "extraordinary" events that prompt this decision. In addition, the IAEA Statute requires that the Council be notified if any issues falling within its competence or non-compliance arise. Lori Fisler Damrosch examines several legal issues around the NPT in Chapter 8. In addition to the longstanding debate about the precise nature of the Article VI requirements placed on the nuclear weapons states, these issues range from questions about the exact scope of the obligations to cooperate in pursuing civilian nuclear use, to issues associated with the provision for member state withdrawal from the Treaty, and the legal standing of NPT Review Conference decisions. The extent and number of the legal debates surrounding the Treaty reflect the changing landscape of nuclear weapons states, and the state of flux of the proliferation regime more broadly.

As indicated in several of the book's chapters, in 1996, the International Court of Justice, another principal organ, set forth a legal opinion that impinges upon our treatment of nuclear weapons. Charter Article 96 authorizes the Assembly or the Council to seek Advisory Opinions of the ICJ "on any legal question." Advisory Opinions, although not binding, are considered to be authoritative interpretations of the law at the time that the opinions are delivered. The World Health Organization in 1993 and the Assembly in 1994 asked the World Court to render Advisory Opinions on the legality of the use or threat of nuclear weapons.

Delivering its opinion on 8 July 1996, the Court found that there is neither a specific authorization (unanimously) nor a comprehensive and universal prohibition (11–3) of the threat or use of nuclear weapons in customary or conventional international law. On the central question before it, it was split 7–7. The ICJ President, Judge Mohammad Bedjaoui of Algeria, cast the deciding vote in favor of the opinion that the threat or use of nuclear weapons would generally be contrary to the rules of international law, and in particular humanitarian law. However, the Court could not conclude definitively whether the threat or use of nuclear weapons would be lawful or unlawful in an extreme circumstance of self-defense in which the very survival of a state was at stake. As Damrosch points out in Chapter 8, the outcome of the decision raises as many questions as it answers. Although the ICJ opinion affirmed that any threat or use of force involving nuclear weapons must comply with the provisions of the Charter, the fact that the justices left open the possibility of nuclear weapons use in self-defense prompted some analysts to worry that the ICJ had in effect undermined arguments for complete disarmament. Others, however, concluded that the ICJ opinion gave new impetus to efforts to pursue disarmament.

Changing environment

At the outset of this chapter we indicated that the changing nature of the international environment, with respect to both nuclear weapons and the United Nations itself, was a key factor in prompting this study. The idea that this is a time of new threats and challenges has been implicit in this discussion and explicit in everything from the innovations that we have witnessed in Security Council action, to the adaptation and evolution of the tools the United Nations has available, to the lack of action in forums such as the General Assembly and the NPT Review.

As Brian Finlay and Rita Grossman-Vermaas argue in Chapter 9, there is a level of unpredictability in the current changes associated with globalization and shifting power hierarchies that accentuates the nature of the current and especially future challenges. One of the main changes in the environment in which the United Nations operates is the advent of a variety of new actors, including many different types of non-state actor. Resolution 1540 anticipates the continued development with specific reference to and concern for non-state terrorists. But as W. P. S. Sidhu asserts in Chapter 10, we need to expand the non-state envelope to include a whole range of entities. He paints a spectrum of non-state actors ranging from terrorists and economically motivated individuals and groups at the threat end to private and public economic actors (e.g. banks and industry) to NGOs and other civil society actors at the responsive end of the continuum. For the United Nations as a state-based organization, therefore, the challenge includes non-state actors not just as a threat to international peace and security but also as potential partners or potential sources of additional tools in responding to those threats.

Other types of non-state actor, namely many members of global civil society, have brought to bear more beneficent influences. Although NGOs typically have the least influence on matters of high politics – and what could be higher than nuclear weapons? – they have been important players at a number of stages in a number of negotiating contexts, as several chapters hint. This must be balanced against the fact that there are a number of state-based actors and mechanisms that have taken on a nuclear weapons role outside the United Nations – for example, the Proliferation Security Initiative and the Group of 8 – consolidating and reaffirming the initial disconnect between concrete action and the United Nations established at its origins.

This is an area of potentially significant growth and strength for the United Nations. There is a large pool of non-state actors that could be drawn into support of UN goals on nuclear weapons if the United Nations so chooses. This could be done directly by actively working to engage key actors through information-sharing mechanisms. Elsewhere – for instance, especially in the realm of the environment and global climate change – groups of experts have played an essential role in moving a threat to the forefront of intergovernmental attention. Although we do not have an answer at this juncture, we should certainly ask ourselves to what extent the burgeoning epistemic community of nuclear disarmament specialists can be mobilized. At a time when former US secretaries of defense and state are writing op-eds in the *Wall Street Journal* that call for disarmament,[22] there should be creative ways to build on resolution 1540 and counter-terrorism efforts to pull these actors into the equation through state action and legislation. Indeed, no less than two-thirds of all living secretaries of state support this general orientation. This "remarkable bipartisan consensus," note Ivo Daalder and Jan Lodal, provides a framework "to make the elimination of all nuclear weapons the organizing principle of US nuclear policy" during the new administration of the forty-fourth president of the United States, Barack Obama.[23]

Another set of challenges and potential threats rests in the international nuclear trade. As Nicole Evans makes clear in Chapter 11, the nuclear trade should have two overarching objectives: to harness nuclear technology for the benefit of all people, on the one hand, and to stem the tide of nuclear proliferation, on the other. Two main dangers threaten these goals, however. In the first place, illicit networks have emerged to deal in the illegal trade of nuclear technology. This threat highlights a second problem, namely the possibility of unauthorized access to weapons-grade nuclear material and highly radioactive substances. Compounding these concerns is the so-called "nuclear renaissance." Whether real or perceived, this renaissance presents further challenges, whether in the form of nuclear weapons theft or the increasing odds that states will divert their nuclear materials to the enhancement of military capability. Evans argues that only a triumvirate of cooperation between the United Nations, member states, and industry can formulate solutions to combat these various threats and dilemmas.

The dovetailing of responsibilities between the United Nations and regional organizations is another variable of a viable future international approach to controlling and regulating nuclear weapons. As Amitav Acharya indicates in Chapter 12, regional organizations often have room for maneuver and can act where the United Nations has great difficulty or actually cannot. His examination of the Iran and North Korea cases emphasizes the importance of the regional dimension in working towards addressing the potential and actual nuclear developments in those states. However, his analysis also reveals the extent to which no two regions can be considered alike. The nature and extent of a regional role will, therefore, vary depending on the circumstances. In the North Korean situation, for example, the Six-Party Talks played an important role in developing an agreed path out of the crisis. In Iran's case, however, the absence of a strong regional entity able to play a role and the differing regional dynamics of the Middle East make the situation there quite different. Nonetheless, Acharya argues that the United Nations should make a far greater effort to draw on regional entities in its nuclear weapons initiatives. As we go to press, the election of Barack Obama to the

US presidency on 4 November 2008 perhaps opens the door for renewed talks with the remaining two members of the "axis of evil" immediately following the January inauguration. Indeed, both Tehran and Pyongyang made public overtures for possible talks with Washington in the future.

Concluding thoughts

The Manhattan project was well under way while Charter negotiations were ongoing. However, knowledge of the program and its potential was very tightly held and played no role in the public discussions in 1945. How different would the Charter be if the framers had known of what was to come?[24] Arguably, if inadvertently, by establishing very broad provisions for regulation and avoiding more specific guidance on the question of arms regulation,[25] the framers of the Charter created a system sufficiently flexible to withstand the advent of fundamentally different and devastatingly more destructive weapon systems.

At the same time, it is not too much of a stretch to argue that the advent of nuclear weapons altered the political and military landscape in fundamental ways. Nuclear weapons surely played a role in consolidating, fueling, and stabilizing the Cold War.[26] The depth and scope of the superpower antagonism virtually paralyzed the United Nations, and certainly contributed to disempowering the enforcement apparatus established in Chapter VII of the Charter and considered so vital to the success of the collective security system. As a result, the world organization suffered a profound loss of legitimacy and confidence in the early years that affected every aspect of its work. The repercussions still reverberate today.

The challenges posed by nuclear weapons extend across the United Nations' international peace and security mandate. Although the Charter has the benefit of inherent flexibility in the general nature of its terms, that malleability has never been used to establish effective controls on nuclear weapons or to make the world body a leader in decision-making about them. The disconnect established at the very origins of the United Nations, between the goals and structure of the collective security framework and the fundamental change in the nature of military power in the international system, established a pattern that has yet to be broken. The United Nations still follows the first footsteps that the infant organization took at its birth – one or two behind the military and political dynamics set in motion by the advent of the nuclear age.

There is an alternative interpretation of that last image. It is possible to argue that the United Nations began and continues to be a few steps behind in dealing with the implications of the nuclear age precisely because this suits the interests of the five permanent members of the Security Council (the P-5). For many, there is no coincidence that the P-5 eventually all became nuclear weapons states, and that they then locked in their status through the NPT. For those who see the situation in this way, the challenge is not in how or whether to make the United Nations more effective in dealing with nuclear weapons. The challenge lies in the very nature of the power structure of the Council and the way in which it undermines the principle of universality that is, in every other way, the foundation stone of the world organization. Viewing the issue from this vantage point affirms the importance of the United Nations in the nuclear weapons equation but not necessarily in a positive way. As editors we chose to frame the debate in the context of the idea of "nuclear orders" in recognition of the fact that the structure of the current environment with respect to both nuclear weapons states and the United Nations is not value neutral and also is not fixed.

This alternative perspective also drives home the point that legitimacy is not divisible. The roles and responsibilities of the P-5 and the N-5 are linked, as is the legitimacy of the orders that they uphold. Further pressure on that power structure comes in the form of the two fully declared nuclear powers that exist outside both the N-5 and the P-5: India and Pakistan. In setting the context at the beginning of this chapter we spoke of the situation as in constant flux. Of all the factors outlined, the existence and de facto acceptance of India and Pakistan as nuclear powers touch on every possible fault-line associated with the United Nations and the various nuclear weapons control regimes. This factor reveals the fundamental disjuncture between the formal structures under discussion here and the shifting nature of the balance of power occurring outside those structures.

This returns us to our initial questions – can or should the world organization play a role here, and if so to what end? The United Nations has played three linked but analytically distinct roles as a funnel, forum, and font for norms:[27]

- A funnel for processing ideas into norms and policies and for transmitting information from national sources to the international community of states[28]
- A forum for discussion and negotiation of common international positions, policies, conventions, and regimes
- A font of international legitimacy for the authoritative promulgation of international norms, appeals for adherence to global norms and regimes, and coercive measures to enforce compliance with them

From one point of view, it could be argued that the United Nations has not been the chief architect of nuclear arms control and disarmament.

The bilateral treaties signed by Moscow and Washington during the Cold War on intermediate range and strategic forces were all negotiated and implemented outside UN auspices.

At one level, this is of course true. At another level, the literal truth masks a deeper underlying reality. The ideas behind many of the existing regimes were often first funneled through the UN system. Thus the idea for a total cessation of nuclear testing was proposed by India at the General Assembly in December 1954, although not put to a vote.[29] In January 1957, the United States submitted a five-point plan to the General Assembly proposing an end to the production and testing of nuclear weapons. Throughout the 1980s and the mid-1990s, pressure for a comprehensive test ban was funneled through the General Assembly. Similarly, the idea of negotiating a South Pacific nuclear-weapon-free zone (NWFZ) was submitted to the Assembly for endorsement in 1975 under the joint sponsorship of Fiji, New Zealand, and Papua New Guinea; and the 1985 South Pacific Nuclear Free Zone Treaty links the regional verification system for the South Pacific to the global IAEA inspections regime within the UN system.[30] Indeed, the closest approximation to a widely acceptable definition of nuclear-weapon-free zones was contained in criteria identified in 1975 by a group of experts commissioned by the Assembly.[31] The origins of the NPT are also within the United Nations. Early proposals to curb proliferation, for example, were submitted to the Disarmament Commission, the Disarmament Committee, and the General Assembly in the late 1950s and early 1960s. These were the foundation for the negotiations that led to agreement on the NPT.

The United Nations has thus historically been the funnel for processing arms control and disarmament proposals and this role continues today. Two recent initiatives to generate ideas are worth keeping in mind. In 2008, a follow-up commission to the earlier Canberra Commission and Tokyo Forum was announced with the joint sponsorship of Australia and Japan, co-chaired by former foreign ministers Gareth Evans and Yoriko Kawaguchi. The International Commission on Nuclear Nonproliferation and Disarmament aims to strengthen the NPT, which is up for review in 2010, but it will also focus explicitly on nuclear disarmament as well as non-proliferation.[32] The New Agenda Coalition, building on the Eight-Nation (Brazil, Egypt, Ireland, Mexico, New Zealand, Slovenia, South Africa, and Sweden) Initiative of June 1998 (following the nuclear tests by India and Pakistan in May), has used the United Nations essentially as the funnel through which to advance the twin agenda of non-proliferation and disarmament. The basic policy positions are agreed to among coalition countries directly, and then taken to the international community of states through UN structures. As with many other examples in the past, the final treaty may well be negotiated in forums outside the United Nations. Nevertheless, this reality should not take away due credit from the world organization for its invaluable funnel role.

The Assembly, with universal membership, houses the divided fragments of humanity and, when united, speaks with the collective voice of the international community of states. This is what makes it the arena where contested norms can be debated and reconciled, the unique *forum of choice* for articulating global values and norms. It is to the Assembly that civil society actors look and member states go when they wish to proclaim and reaffirm arms control and disarmament norms. This is the chief explanation for so many declarations and resolutions first being adopted by the world organization before producing conventions and treaties – norms followed by laws – in UN as well as non-UN forums.

There is no substitute for the United Nations as a *font* of international authority and legitimacy. This was reflected in the manner in which the campaign to ban landmines was careful to keep in touch with the UN system. The four countries most active in the Ottawa process – Austria, Belgium, Canada, and Norway – are members of the CD. The October 1996 Ottawa conference developed a resolution that was adopted by the General Assembly in December by a vote of 156–0 (with 10 abstentions). In the final conference a year later, negotiators were careful not to quarantine themselves from the world organization, but to integrate their process with the UN system with regard to review, reporting, and depositary functions. Treaties, even if negotiated outside UN forums, are often submitted to UN machinery for formal endorsement, which has no bearing on the legal standing of the treaty but does substantially enhance its moral weight. This has been true, for example, of the various regional NWFZs. India's protestations notwithstanding, probably the clearest example of the United Nations as a font of authority for global arms control treaties came with the CTBT in 1996. When India vetoed the final product in the CD in Geneva, Australia initiated to use a constitutional maneuver to move the text from the CD in Geneva to the Assembly in New York.[33] On 10 September 1996, the Assembly approved the text of the CTBT by a vote of 158–3. Only Bhutan and Libya supported India in rejecting it.

Calling on the moral authority of the United Nations to ensure compliance with global norms is especially relevant when behavior considered to be normatively unacceptable is not in fact proscribed by any treaty to which a state may be party. Such was the case with India and Pakistan's successive nuclear tests in May 1998. At the same time, the United Nations' ineffective response to the India and Pakistan tests shows that the world organization's moral authority is not a very effective substitute for legally binding treaty obligations.

As for compliance, the core of the international law enforcement system with respect to non-proliferation and disarmament, as with everything else, is the Security Council. Faced with a challenge to the norms and laws governing the acquisition, production, transfer, and use of arms, the P-5 may have to resort to measures of coercion ranging from diplomatic and economic to military action. With the Assembly having little substantial power and the Council often deadlocked, the weight of UN decision-making frequently falls on the Secretary-General. He may be ignored, but he is not easily de-legitimized. However, on the issue of armaments and weapons platforms involving national security, the Secretary-General is not in the best position to issue judgments and edicts against member states, unless perhaps they have violated specific and binding obligations.

The chapters in this book confirm one of the starting assumptions of this study – namely, that this particular point in the evolution of the United Nations comes at a critical moment of transition in the current nuclear weapons regime. In providing a forum of universal membership, the United Nations can overcome what Ramesh Thakur in Chapter 13 calls the "NPT anomalies" – the fact that three of the world's nuclear weapons states are not signatories to the NPT. There is thus an opportunity for the United Nations to play a role in trying to establish a new and desperately needed path forward for the non-proliferation regime, by pulling the actors and tools of the regime together. The division of labor among the three principal international peace and security organs established under the Charter provides cross-cutting mandates that leave the door wide open for action on nuclear weapons using a variety of tools and drawing in any number of outside actors. The chapters of this volume outline the key issues and challenges that need to be addressed and offer a number of different ideas of how to do so.

There are significant obstacles to overcome, to be sure. As the chapters also indicate, nuclear weapons expose the numerous pitfalls in the UN structure and the propensity for discord and dissonance in difficult times. These tendencies are not exclusive to nuclear weapons but apply to UN action across virtually every issue area. But none of the obstacles discussed here is, as yet, insurmountable. At the outset, we sought to determine if the United Nations does and should have a role to play on nuclear weapons, and, if so, what kinds of challenges and issues the current environment poses.

The question we did not ask is *whether* the United Nations will play that role, whatever it might be. As always, progress will ultimately depend on member states wanting to make the system work, not just for their own purposes but for those of the collectivity. Here a particular burden falls most crucially on the permanent members of the Council. The

Charter grants and enshrines for them a leadership role – it is up to them to take it.

Notes

1. *A More Secure World: Our Shared Responsibility. Report of the High-Level Panel on Threats, Challenges and Change* (New York: United Nations, 2004), UN document A/59/565, 2 December 2004, para. 111.
2. Kofi Annan, press conference at United Nations Headquarters, 13 September 2005, available at ⟨http://www.un.org/News/Press/docs/2005/sgsm10089.doc.htm⟩ (accessed 30 October 2008).
3. John Lewis Gaddis, *The Long Peace: Inquiries into the History of the Cold War* (Oxford: Oxford University Press, 1989).
4. For the charge of irrelevance, see for example Richard Perle, "Thank God for the Death of the UN," *The Guardian*, 13 March 2003. For a response, see Ramesh Thakur and Andrew Mack, "More Relevant Than Ever," *Japan Times*, 23 March 2003.
5. William M. Arkin, "The Sky-Is-Still-Falling Profession," *Bulletin of the Atomic Scientists* 50, no. 2 (1994): 64. For a useful review of the literature, see William C. Potter and Gaukhar Mukhatzhanova, "Divining Nuclear Intentions: A Review Essay," *International Security* 33, no. 1 (2008): 139–169.
6. See, for example, W. P. S. Sidhu and Ramesh Thakur, eds, *Arms Control After Iraq: Normative and Operational Challenges* (Tokyo: United Nations University Press, 2006).
7. This sub-section draws on Patricia Lewis and Ramesh Thakur, "Arms Control, Disarmament and the United Nations," *Disarmament Forum* 1, no. 1 (2004): 17–28.
8. See Ramesh Thakur and Ere Haru, eds, *The Chemical Weapons Convention: Implementation, Challenges and Opportunities* (Tokyo: United Nations University Press, 2006).
9. Hans Blix, *Disarming Iraq* (New York: Pantheon, 2004) and *Why Nuclear Disarmament Matters* (Cambridge, MA: MIT Press, 2008).
10. See Jean E. Krasno and James S. Sutterlin, *The United Nations and Iraq: Defanging the Viper* (Westport, CT: Praeger, 2003).
11. Inis L. Claude, Jr, *Swords into Plowshares: The Problems and Prospects of International Organization* (New York: Random House, 1956) and "Peace and Security: Prospective Roles for the Two United Nations," *Global Governance* 2, no. 3 (1996): 289–298.
12. Thomas G. Weiss, Tatiana Carayannis, and Richard Jolly, "The 'Third' United Nations," *Global Governance* 15, no. 1 (2009): 123–142. This is also a major theme in Richard Jolly, Louis Emmerij, and Thomas G. Weiss, *UN Ideas Changing History* (Bloomington: Indiana University Press, 2009).
13. See Jacques E. C. Hymans, *The Psychology of Nuclear Proliferation: Identity, Emotions, and Foreign Policy* (New York: Cambridge University Press, 2006); and Etel Solingen, *Nuclear Logics: Alternative Paths in East Asia and the Middle East* (Princeton, NJ: Princeton University Press, 2007).
14. For a rich account of the Baruch plan, see Evan Luard, *A History of the United Nations, Volume I: The Years of Western Domination, 1945–1955* (New York: Palgrave Macmillan, 1982).
15. The Council took the opportunity to note that Iraq was a member of the NPT and to call on Israel to put its nuclear facilities under IAEA safeguards.
16. See Ramesh Thakur, "The South Asian Nuclear Challenge," in *Alternative Nuclear Futures: The Role of Nuclear Weapons in the Post-Cold War World*, ed. John Baylis and Robert O'Neill (Oxford: Oxford University Press, 2000), 101–124.

17. Thomas G. Weiss, David Cortright, George A. Lopez, and Larry Minear, eds, *Political Gain and Civilian Pain: Humanitarian Impact of Economic Sanctions* (Lanham, MD: Rowman & Littlefield, 1997).
18. See Ramesh Thakur and W. P. S. Sidhu, eds, *The Iraq Crisis and World Order: Structural, Institutional and Normative Challenges* (Tokyo: United Nations University Press, 2006).
19. *A More Secure World*, para. 184.
20. Abdalnahmood Abdalhaleem Mohammad, "Security Council and Non-Proliferation," *Hindu* (Chennai), 28 May 2004.
21. Jim Wurst, "NGOs Criticize Non-proliferation Draft for Ignoring Disarmament," *U.N. Wire*, 1 April 2004; ⟨http://www.unwire.org/⟩ (accessed 30 October 2008).
22. George P. Shultz, William J. Perry, Henry A. Kissinger, and Sam Nunn, "A World Free of Nuclear Weapons," *Wall Street Journal*, 4 January 2007; and George P. Shultz, William J. Perry, Henry A. Kissinger, and Sam Nunn, "Toward a Nuclear-Free World," *Wall Street Journal*, 15 January 2008.
23. Ivo Daalder and Jan Lodal, "The Logic of Zero," *Foreign Affairs* 87, no. 6 (2008): 81.
24. In 1945 the US Secretary of War, Henry Stimson, was one of the few to articulate this possibility. In a note to US President Truman he stated: "To approach any world peace organization of any pattern ... without an appreciation by the leaders of our country of the power of this new weapon, would seem to be unrealistic. No system of control heretofore considered would be adequate to control this menace. Both inside any particular country and between the nations of the world, the control of this weapon will undoubtedly be a matter of the greatest difficulty and would involve such thorough-going rights of inspection and internal controls as we have never heretofore contemplated." Henry L. Stimson and McGeorge Bundy, *On Active Service in Peace and War* (New York: Hippocrene Books, 1947), 636.
25. More detailed provisions were discussed, including specific guidance on the principles that should guide the nature of the goals. See Ruth B. Russell, *A History of the United Nations Charter: The Role of the United States, 1940–1945* (Washington, DC: Brookings Institution, 1958).
26. See Kenneth N. Waltz, *The Spread of Nuclear Weapons: More May Be Better*, Adelphi Paper No. 171 (London: International Institute for Strategic Studies, 1981); Waltz, "Nuclear Myths and Political Realities," *American Political Science Review* 84, no. 3 (1990): 731–745; John Mearsheimer, "Back to the Future: Instability in Europe after the Cold War," *International Security* 15, no. 1 (1990): 5–56; Bruce D. Berkowitz, "Proliferation, Deterrence, and the Likelihood of Nuclear War," *Journal of Conflict Resolution* 29, no. 1 (1985): 112–136; John Lewis Gaddis, *The Cold War* (London: Allen Lane, 2005).
27. This conceptual terminology comes from Margaret Joan Anstee, a former Under-Secretary-General of the United Nations, who proposed the categorization in the context of the UN Intellectual History Project. See Thomas G. Weiss, Tatiana Carayannis, Louis Emmerij, and Richard Jolly, *UN Voices: The Challenge of Development and Social Justice* (Bloomington: Indiana University Press, 2005), chapter 10; Lewis and Thakur, "Arms Control, Disarmament and the United Nations."
28. For example, the United Nations publishes a disarmament yearbook. See *The United Nations Disarmament Yearbook Volume 31: 2006* (New York: UN Department for Disarmament Affairs, 2007); available online at ⟨http://disarmament.un.org/e-yearbook.html⟩ (accessed 30 October 2008).
29. Savita Pande, *India and the Nuclear Test Ban* (New Delhi: Institute for Defence Studies and Analyses, 1996), 25.
30. See Ramesh Thakur, "The Treaty of Rarotonga: The South Pacific Nuclear-Free Zone," in *Nuclear-Free Zones*, ed. David Pitt and Gordon Thompson (London: Croom Helm, 1987), 23–45.

31. *Comprehensive Study of the Question of Nuclear-Weapon-Free Zones in All of Its Aspects* (New York: United Nations, Special Report of the Conference of the Committee on Disarmament, 1976), UN document A/10027/Add.1.
32. For additional information, see ⟨http://www.icnnd.org/⟩ (accessed 30 October 2008).
33. See Ramesh Thakur, "Get On with the Test Ban Treaty and Warn India," *International Herald Tribune*, 22 August 1996, and "Get Test Ban Treaty Operational and Let India Join Later," *International Herald Tribune*, 9 September 1996.

Part I
Actors

2

The Security Council and nuclear disarmament

Ernie Regehr

It was never part of a formal plan that the five permanent members of the United Nations Security Council (the P-5) should also be the five nuclear weapons states (NWS), later to be recognized and accepted as such under the Treaty on the Non-Proliferation of Nuclear Weapons (NPT). By now, however, these two distinct attributes have been so fully fused in the multilateral consciousness that it seems as if nature intended it this way. Indeed, permanent membership in the Council could only have added to the drive by the United Kingdom, France, and China to follow the United States and the then Soviet Union to acquire credible nuclear arsenals. Possession of nuclear weapons was seen as a desirable if not essential accoutrement of the global gravitas attaching to any states assuming the mantle of ultimate custodians of international peace and security. And though this commingling of the P-5 with the nuclear five (N-5) now seems normal, it is an arrangement that has bedeviled the Council's performance in one key part of its assigned job of keeping the peace and enforcing global norms.

The focus of this chapter is the Security Council's attention to vertical non-proliferation, that is, nuclear disarmament, rather than horizontal non-proliferation. It begins by laying out the framework provided by the UN Charter before discussing the multilaterally defined disarmament agenda – the principles, objectives, and practical steps toward disarmament – that the P-5/N-5 have fully endorsed in forums or contexts outside the Council. The chapter then discusses the importance of disarmament efforts to curb horizontal proliferation. Next, two specific Council

---

The United Nations and nuclear orders, Boulden, Thakur and Weiss (eds),
United Nations University Press, 2009, ISBN 978-92-808-1167-4

engagements – on negative security assurances and the response to Indian and Pakistani nuclear weapons developments – are addressed. They provide valuable insights into considering ongoing impediments to the P-5/N-5 giving attention to the imperative of nuclear disarmament within the practical and more demanding business of the Security Council. The chapter concludes by exploring what the Council might realistically do to advance the agreed nuclear disarmament agenda.

The Charter framework

Nuclear disarmament is not directly mandated by the UN Charter, but Article 26 does assign to the Security Council the task of establishing "a system for the regulation of armaments." Furthermore, on 31 January 1992, during its early post–Cold War period of activism and innovation, the Council declared the proliferation of nuclear weapons, along with chemical and biological weapons, to be a threat to international peace and security.[1] The statement reinforced the logic that nuclear arms control and disarmament should be essential components of the Council's pursuit of its Article 24 responsibility for the maintenance of international peace and security. At the same time, the fact that the P-5 are also the N-5, at least since 1971 when mainland China assumed the Chinese seat, explains another inescapable fact – that nuclear disarmament has never found its way directly onto the Council agenda. Now, in the seventh decade of the organization's life and the Council's work, the P-5 continue to give every indication that they also regard themselves as a permanent N-5. Indeed, the Stockholm International Peace Research Institute, the pre-eminent tracker of global nuclear arsenals and NWS policies, is led to say in the measured tone of its *Yearbook 2008* that "all of the five legally recognized nuclear weapon states ... appear determined to remain nuclear powers for the foreseeable future and are in the midst or on the verge of modernizing their nuclear forces."[2]

Modernization of nuclear forces among the P-5/N-5 does not necessarily mean expanding arsenals. The number of deployed nuclear warheads worldwide is in decline, but the warheads, the delivery hardware, and the strategies to employ them are continuously being revised, rebuilt, and updated, despite legal obligations under the NPT to eliminate arsenals altogether, and despite the judgments of the P-5/N-5 themselves that those weapons represent a threat to international peace and security.

Article 11 explicitly mandates the General Assembly to "consider the general principles governing disarmament and the regulation of armaments," and over the past six-plus decades, beginning with its very first resolution, the Assembly has pursued its disarmament mandate with considerable vigor (discussed elsewhere in this volume). Neither dominated nor constrained by the nuclear retentionist interests of the P-5/N-5, the Assembly – now through the First Committee – has focused broadly on norm-building[3] and the development of a global consensus in support of particular disarmament measures. The Geneva-based Conference on Disarmament is the United Nations' disarmament negotiating forum and, notwithstanding its current stalemate and failure to negotiate anything in well over a decade, has historically made contributions to particular treaties – the Comprehensive Nuclear-Test-Ban Treaty (CTBT) most recently – and sought to accommodate and create consensus among nuclear have and have-not communities. The more marginal Disarmament Commission meets as a deliberative body when the Assembly is not in session in the interests of exploring a more limited range of issues in greater depth.

The Security Council is charged in Article 47(1) with establishing a Military Staff Committee to advise and assist it on all military issues, including "the regulation of armaments, and possible disarmament." It has never functioned as designed, but nuclear issues should still come before the Council by virtue of its mandate to maintain international peace and security. It does receive referrals from the International Atomic Energy Agency (IAEA), the NPT, and potentially nuclear-weapon-free zone (NWFZ) treaties. In particular, Article III.B.4 of the IAEA Statute sets out the Agency's general obligation to report to the Council, "as the organ bearing the main responsibility for the maintenance of international peace and security." Article XII.C requires the Agency's board of governors to report instances of non-compliance to all members of the IAEA board, the Council, and the Assembly. According to Article X of the NPT, any state party to the NPT has the right to withdraw from the Treaty in the event of developments that "have jeopardized the supreme interest of its country," but notice of withdrawal must be given three months in advance to all other states parties and to the Security Council.

Of course, the Council has a responsibility to address threats to international peace and security wherever they occur and does not have to wait for referrals from other multilateral bodies or from individual states. Nevertheless, these all have the right and opportunities to bring such threats to the attention of the Council.

In the Security Council, with its unambiguous obligation to advance the regulation of arms, the NWS or P-5/N-5 states have been in full control since 1971, and in the two decades following the entry into force of the NPT in 1970 they treated the world to an extraordinary (that is to say, profligate) episode of the vertical proliferation of nuclear weapons. At its peak, the nuclear arms race accumulated more than 70,000 nuclear warheads linked to a dazzling array of delivery vehicles and security doctrines. This race was a largely bilateral US–Soviet affair, but all of the P-5/N-5 were participants. Therefore, for the international community to now look to the Council to take a greater role in advancing nuclear disarmament might charitably be thought of as the rough equivalent of an assembly of hens handpicking a small group of leading foxes to take over all henhouse security responsibilities. At the same time, of course, given that the P-5/N-5 foxes must ultimately lead and implement the global nuclear disarmament effort, it makes even less sense to sideline their central forum from the process.

During the Cold War the Security Council was sidelined, not by the rest of the international community, but by the shared interests and strategic competition among the P-5/N-5. The politics of nuclear disarmament, arms control, and non-proliferation were submerged by the bilateral dynamics of the two primary nuclear powers, guaranteeing that nuclear arms control and disarmament would never find a way onto the Council agenda. Aside from resolutions on Iraq, in the first six decades of its work the Council managed to pass only six substantive resolutions linked to nuclear weapons (two on negative security assurances, and one each on Israel, North Korea, India/Pakistan, and non-state actors).[4] Recently, the Council has also taken on the issue of Iran as a result of an IAEA referral.

The agreed nuclear disarmament agenda

The Security Council's inaction on nuclear disarmament obscures the extent to which, beyond the Council table, the P-5/N-5 states have signed on to a well-defined nuclear disarmament agenda. The end of the Cold War opened the door to the slow and painstaking construction, through the consensus decision-making processes of the NPT review process in particular, of a plan for global nuclear disarmament. The NPT is, of course, the primary international agreement imposing a legally binding obligation to disarm,[5] and NPT states parties have collectively been identifying a set of principles and steps, notably at the 1995 and 2000 Review Conferences, that the NWS are to follow in progressive fulfillment of that obligation. The legal meaning of Review Conference decisions or agreements is discussed by Lori Damrosch in Chapter 8 in this volume, but it is important to note that the tradition of decision by consensus at the Review Conferences – though not a specific requirement of the Treaty – suggests that these unanimous agreements on substantive questions linked to the implementation of the Treaty can be taken as authoritative. Damrosch points out that, according to the law of treaties, the collective agreements among states parties to a treaty must inform interpretations of what measures or actions represent appropriate implementation of the treaty. In the NPT review process, those agreements received the explicit approval or endorsement of all P-5/N-5 states, and together the Review Conference agreements of 1995 and 2000, linked to Article VI, must be understood as setting out specific priority issues or actions that states are to follow to fulfill the requirements of the Treaty.

These statements were hotly debated at each Review Conference. Each word was in effect negotiated between the NWS and the non-nuclear-weapon states (NNWS) in the Treaty, and each word was unanimously approved. The 2000 agreement was reached six months before George W. Bush was first elected president of the United States. Although his administration specifically and repeatedly distanced itself from these agreements, fighting against any reference to them in the agendas of subsequent review process meetings, there is no retreating from the fact that the states parties to the Treaty have provided a clear interpretation of the steps required to move toward implementation of Article VI. Nor can it be denied that the government of the United States, along with the other P-5/N-5 states, formally agreed to that interpretation.

The 1995 Decision on "Principles and Objectives for Nuclear Non-Proliferation and Disarmament" said that "effective implementation of article VI" would require the negotiation of a CTBT and, pending its entry into force, the exercise of "utmost restraint" by the NWS.[6] The P-5/N-5 have to date honored that commitment. The CTBT was negotiated and signed by all the P-5/N-5 and each has committed to a moratorium on testing (ratification and entry-into-force of the CTBT is another matter). The decision also called for immediate negotiations to ban the production of fissile material for weapons purposes – a commitment that remains unfulfilled, although the P-5/N-5 declared a moratorium on such production.[7] The P-5/N-5 also agreed through the 1995 decision (paragraph 4(c)) to "the determined pursuit by the nuclear-weapon States of systematic and progressive efforts to reduce nuclear weapons globally, with the ultimate goal of eliminating those weapons."

In 2000, the P-5/N-5 were even more explicitly abolitionist when they joined all other states parties to the NPT in "an unequivocal undertaking by the nuclear-weapon States to accomplish the total elimination of their nuclear arsenals leading to nuclear disarmament, to which all States parties are committed under article VI." The 2000 agreement identified a set of "practical steps for the systematic and progressive efforts to implement article VI of the Treaty," which include:[8]

- The early entry into force of a Comprehensive Nuclear-Test-Ban Treaty
- A moratorium on testing in the meantime
- The verifiable fissile material production ban already called for in 1995

- Formation of a subsidiary body on nuclear disarmament within the Conference on Disarmament
- Adherence to the principle of irreversibility in nuclear disarmament;
- Unilateral initiatives to reduce arsenals
- Increased transparency by the nuclear weapon states
- Further reductions in non-strategic nuclear weapons
- Reductions in the operational status of weapons systems
- "[A] diminishing role for nuclear weapons in security policies to minimize the risk that these weapons will ever be used and to facilitate the process of their total elimination"
- Placing of fissile material no longer required for military purposes under IAEA inspections to keep them permanently out of military programs
- "[R]egular reports" by all states parties on the implementation of Article VI in the context of the Advisory Opinion of the International Court of Justice (ICJ)
- "[T]he further development of the verification capabilities that will be required to provide assurance of compliance with nuclear disarmament agreements for the achievement and maintenance of a nuclear-weapon-free world"

Obviously this list does not exhaust the actions required to reach full nuclear disarmament, but it does represent the considered judgment of the parties to the Treaty on the priority actions that are required. These steps have been collectively defined through formal and participatory processes and have earned virtually universal support and, more to the point, the support of the P-5/N-5 states. This agreed agenda is the product of post–Cold War cooperation and in a real sense vindicates the optimism present at the Security Council's 1992 heads of government meeting. The presidential statement approved at the meeting welcomed the "favourable international circumstances under which the Security Council has begun to fulfil more effectively its primary responsibility for the maintenance of international peace and security" and expressed their agreement that "the world now has the best chance of achieving international peace and security since the foundation of the United Nations."[9]

The inescapable vertical–horizontal connection

Actual implementation of the agreed disarmament agenda has certainly not matched the optimism of 1992 or the enthusiasm with which the final document of the 2000 Review Conference was greeted. The point in elaborating specific disarmament steps toward the full implementation of the

NPT was to try to match the concrete obligations of NNWS to meet the requirements of Articles II and III with the concrete obligations of NWS to meet the requirements of Article VI and, in the process, to acknowledge the inescapable links between vertical and horizontal nonproliferation.

The P-5/N-5 have in fact cautiously but unmistakably recognized that link. To begin with, the 1992 Security Council summit declared that "the proliferation of *all* weapons of mass destruction constitutes a threat to international peace and security" (emphasis added). In 1992, as well as with resolution 1172 (6 June 1998), in response to the 1998 nuclear tests by India and Pakistan, and resolution 1540 (2004), the P-5/N-5 and the Council were acknowledging the need for disarmament and reductions to their own arsenals in the context of addressing horizontal proliferation questions. In the 1992 presidential statement and in resolution 1540 the P-5/N-5 joined the other members of the Council to reaffirm "the need for all Member States to fulfil their obligations in relation to arms control and disarmament," and to encourage "all Member States to implement fully the disarmament treaties and agreements to which they are party."[10] On 5 June 1998, the P-5/N-5 issued a joint communiqué in which they said: "They remain determined to fulfil their commitments relating to nuclear disarmament under article VI of the Treaty on the Non-Proliferation of Nuclear Weapons."[11] Resolution 1172 then welcomed that commitment.[12] The 1992 Security Council presidential statement was slightly more pointed on the subject of disarmament agreements with its call to "emphasize the importance of the early ratification and implementation by the States concerned of all international and regional arms control arrangements, especially the START [Strategic Arms Reduction] and CFE [Conventional Forces in Europe] Treaties."[13]

Resolution 1540 refers to the need to "prevent proliferation *in all its aspects*," implying both vertical and horizontal proliferation, and affirms the Council's "support for the multilateral treaties whose aim is to *eliminate* or prevent the proliferation of nuclear, chemical or biological weapons and the importance for all States parties to these treaties to implement them fully in order to promote international stability" (emphasis added). These are all preambular references; in other words, they set the context for the more specific aim of 1540, namely to require states to "adopt and enforce appropriate laws which prohibit any non-State actor to manufacture, acquire, possess, develop, transport, transfer or use nuclear, chemical or biological weapons and their means of delivery" (operative paragraph 2). But the operative section of 1540 also includes state disarmament obligations inasmuch as operative paragraph 8 calls upon all states to "promote the universal adoption and *full implementation*, and, where necessary, strengthening of multilateral treaties to which they are parties, whose aim is to prevent the proliferation of nuclear, biological or chemical weapons" (emphasis added).

In other words, resolution 1540 is appropriately understood as targeting both the vertical and the horizontal proliferation of nuclear weapons.[14] The effort to prevent the spread of weapons of mass destruction (WMD) to non-state actors cannot finally be separated from the effort to control and eliminate state arsenals of WMD.

The centrality of this link has recently been emphasized by some key and decidedly mainstream figures within NWS states. In January 2007 and again in January 2008, Henry Kissinger, George Shultz, William Perry, and Sam Nunn used the op-ed page of the *Wall Street Journal* to issue a clear call to address nuclear dangers, to take "a series of steps that will pull us back from the nuclear precipice," and to rekindle "the vision of moving toward zero" nuclear weapons.[15] Without that vision and some practical steps in that direction, they argue, "we will not find the essential cooperation required to stop our downward spiral" toward accelerated horizontal proliferation, including the threat that nuclear weapons will come into the hands of non-state actors. Indeed, they say, articulation of the goal of elimination "is the only way to build the kind of international trust and broad cooperation that will be required to effectively address today's threats."

That the NPT's Article VI embodies the requirement to eliminate the nuclear weapons of the P-5/N-5 signatories to the Treaty was of course confirmed in the ICJ's 1996 unanimous opinion that the Treaty obligates NWS to enter into and conclude disarmament negotiations: "There exists an obligation to pursue in good faith *and bring to a conclusion* negotiations leading to nuclear disarmament in all its aspects under strict and effective international control" (emphasis added).[16] The Court's approach and decision are explored in detail elsewhere in this volume. Of course, the vertical–horizontal connection is now a common theme within the NPT review process, emphasized by a host of arms control advocates and experts. The primary idea is that the credibility with which the Security Council pursues its horizontal non-proliferation responsibilities cannot be separated from the diligence with which the P-5/N-5 carry out their own nuclear disarmament (vertical non-proliferation) responsibilities – the P-5/N-5 failure in the latter explaining the Council's failure in the former.

The challenge of the outliers

The context of the Security Council's decisive action in response to the May 1998 nuclear tests by India and Pakistan is that Council demands tend to be ignored "if the intended recipient does not regard the pronouncement as authoritative or legitimate."[17] Resolution 1172 "demands that India and Pakistan refrain from further nuclear tests" and then calls on them to, among other things, adhere to the provisions of the CTBT, "stop their nuclear weapons development programs," cease production of fissile materials for nuclear weapons, and cease development of ballistic missiles capable of delivering nuclear warheads. But resolution 1172 is above all a potent example of the impotence of Council action when its P-5/N-5 members fail to adhere consistently to non-proliferation laws or principles.[18] The point is not the absence of relevant law. Although India and Pakistan did not violate the NPT (because they were not and are not signatories to the Treaty), Patricia Lewis and Ramesh Thakur point out that the two were in violation of a global norm against the spread of nuclear weapons beyond the NPT's N-5. But the more consequential issue, they say, is the fact that "the Security Council was in a peculiarly difficult position, for the simple reason that the P-5 are caught in a particularly vicious conflict of interest with regard to nuclear non-proliferation."[19] They point out that the condemnation of the 1998 Indian and Pakistani tests – "when not one of the over 2,000 previous tests [by the P-5/N-5] had ever been so condemned by the Council – inflamed opinion in the subcontinent." So the Council's presidential statement of 14 May 1998, strongly deploring India's tests, was rejected by the Indian government as "completely unacceptable."[20] In fact, after the initial statements of outrage, the P-5/N-5 paid no further attention to these particular instances of proliferation, despite their earlier assertion that all instances of proliferation are a threat to international peace and security.

The Council is now left with having one of its rare resolutions on nuclear disarmament rendered irrelevant and ineffective – overtaken, subsequently, by the decision by the Nuclear Suppliers Group (NSG) to exempt India from the central non-proliferation guideline: the prohibition on civilian nuclear cooperation with states whose nuclear facilities are not under full-scope safeguards of the IAEA. Experts at the Carnegie Endowment have proposed that resolution 1172 be replaced with a new resolution that would apply to the three non-NPT states,[21] all of which also have nuclear weapons. The point would be to once again appeal to universalism over exceptionalism. The suggestion is for a new resolution to formally welcome explicit commitments by the three states to forgo nuclear explosive tests, to implement and enforce comprehensive national laws barring sensitive exports, to adopt state-of-the art technologies and practices to secure all nuclear materials, to participate constructively in Conference on Disarmament negotiations to ban production of fissile material for nuclear weapons or other nuclear explosive purposes, to refrain from increasing the declared and undeclared role of nuclear weapons in their national security policies, and to commit to the peaceful resolution of conflicts.[22]

The list of commitments links in part to key elements of the disarmament agenda to which the NPT signatories have committed. The proponents of such an action judge that it would at least minimally advance non-proliferation objectives, whereas resolution 1172 has no chance of being heeded. But it has also become clear that, in the absence of discernible action on these same demands by the P-5/N-5 themselves, such a new resolution would suffer the same fate as 1172.

In the run-up to the NSG exemption, India agreed to "assume the same responsibilities ... as other leading countries with advanced nuclear technology" (a euphemism for nuclear weapons states),[23] which presumably is its way of saying that it will do what the P-5/N-5 do, not what they say.[24] Even so, India's promise to assume the same responsibilities as the P-5/N-5 is a political commitment although, just as the P-5/N-5 have resisted transforming their NPT-related disarmament declarations into legally binding obligations, India rejected all efforts to make the NSG waiver formally conditional on fulfilling its promises.

Consistent and accountable non-proliferation, horizontal and vertical, depends on agreed universal standards, not unilateral political declarations. The P-5/N-5, and now India as well, have shown themselves willing to make individual declarations of intent but, by keeping the disarmament agenda far away from the collective action and mutual commitments of the Council, the P-5/N-5 remain true to their respective national interests in acknowledging their disarmament obligations in general while ensuring that none of them becomes a time-bound legal obligation. It should be axiomatic that the Council, having recognized that all nuclear proliferation is a threat to international peace and security, has a clear obligation to demand concrete and accountable action to address the apprehended threat of nuclear proliferation.

Negative security assurances

Negative security assurances have twice made it onto the Security Council agenda. Both instances illustrate the skill of the P-5/N-5 in keeping concrete commitments at bay and accountability off the table and in ensuring that collective Council action on disarmament questions does not impinge on their respective national prerogatives. In 1968 it was clear that the NPT, by virtue of which all states other than the P-5/N-5 were to forgo the acquisition of nuclear weapons, would not be adopted unless the NNWS received some assurance that the NWS would not use or threaten to use their nuclear weapons against them. Egypt's permanent representative to the United Nations recalled in 1996 that the NNWS were not simply looking for individual declarations from each of the P-5/N-5 states; rather they wanted the collective assurance of the international community "and to have assurances that if they were threatened or attacked by nuclear weapons, the Security Council would react."[25] To that end, the pursuit of security assurances was also linked to the emergence of NWFZs – both measures being efforts to limit the geographical scope of the political pressures and influence that nuclear weapons exert.

The P-5/N-5 refused to allow text on security assurances into the NPT itself; instead, the Council undertook to set out these assurances in a separate resolution (Security Council resolution 255, 19 June 1968). In fact, the resolution did not offer any security assurances; it simply said that, in the event of an attack or threat of it, the P-5/N-5 were obligated to act in accordance with the Charter: "The Security Council ... recognizes that aggression with nuclear weapons or the threat of such aggression against a non-nuclear-weapon State would create a situation in which the Security Council, and above all its nuclear-weapon State permanent members, would have to act immediately in accordance with their obligations under the United Nations Charter." The resolution also welcomed "the intention expressed by certain States that they will provide or support immediate assistance, in accordance with the Charter, to any non-nuclear-weapon State Party to the Treaty on the Non-Proliferation of Nuclear Weapons that is a victim of an act or an object of a threat of aggression in which nuclear weapons are used."[26]

Thus, the P-5/N-5 offered after-the-fact fidelity to the Charter and assistance to the victims of attack, but no assurance that there would be no nuclear attack or, more saliently, no threat of attack against NNWS signatories to the NPT. Furthermore, France, then not a party to the NPT, abstained, and the Chinese vote was cast by Taiwan, which at that time occupied China's chair on the Council.

It took another 27 years for the Council to make another attempt to meet the ongoing request of NNWS. In this case, the resolution (Security Council resolution 984, 11 April 1995) once again recognized the requirements of the Charter to bring security crises to the Security Council and "takes note with appreciation of the statements made by each of the nuclear-weapon States ..., in which they give security assurances against the use of nuclear weapons to non-nuclear-weapon States that are Parties to the Treaty on the Non-Proliferation of Nuclear Weapons."[27] The individual statements by France, Russia, the United Kingdom, and the United States all reaffirm that they "will not use nuclear weapons against non-nuclear-weapon States parties to the [NPT], except in the case of an invasion or any other attack on [the NWS], its territory, its armed forces or other troops, its allies, or on a State towards which it has a security commitment, carried out or sustained by such a non-nuclear-weapon State in association or alliance with a nuclear-weapon state."[28] The Chinese statement (S/1995/265, 11 April 1995) excludes the exception added by the other four states and declares that "China undertakes not to use or threaten to use nuclear weapons against any non-nuclear-weapon States or nuclear-weapon-free zones at any time or under any circumstances." China's statement also includes a pledge not to be the first to use nuclear weapons. The Council itself does not undertake any action, demand any firm commitment, or impose any obligation on the P-5/N-5. Resolution 984 reflects the fundamental aversion of the P-5/N-5 to collective commitments that make them accountable to others. Their interests are better served by a general collective statement that avoids commitment but references individual national statements that offer political commitments through unilateral declarations without incurring particular legal obligations.

The international community has called for these unilaterally declared commitments to become mutual and to be girded by a legally binding international instrument to convert national political commitments into legal obligations under international law, but such an agreement is not forthcoming. Indeed, since making these 1995 statements, France, Russia, and the United States have each cast doubt on them by saying they would not rule out the use of nuclear weapons, including pre-emptive use, against states that threatened them with chemical weapons or major conventional attack.[29]

Does the Security Council have a future as a disarmament body?

The global consensus on nuclear weapons and disarmament is unambiguous. NNWS within the NPT are legally bound to remain so and to arrange for ongoing safeguards to continuously verify their non-nuclear-weapon status. NWS within the NPT are legally bound to (eventually) disarm and in effect become non-nuclear-weapon states. The outlier states – those still outside the NPT, whether or not they now have nuclear weapons (and they all currently do) – are also instructed by Security Council (in resolution 1172, for example) and General Assembly actions to become non-nuclear-weapon states within the non-proliferation regime.

Undermining these widely agreed norms and objectives is certainly not in the interests of the P-5/N-5. In the long run, if any one of these three objectives is hopelessly compromised, all risk being abandoned. In the first half-century of the nuclear age the primary mechanism for preventing the horizontal spread of nuclear weapons was tight controls over knowledge, technology, and materials. It was largely successful. But in the second half-century of the nuclear age, that approach will largely fail. Nuclear knowledge, technology, and materials can no longer be confined to the few. The peaceful uses of nuclear knowledge and materials are encouraged and any state with institutions of advanced education and emerging research and industrial capabilities will essentially have the technical option of pursuing a nuclear weapons capability. The only way to keep such non-nuclear-weapon states from exercising a weapons option will be to persuade them that their own long-term security, not to mention the common good, is best served by forgoing nuclear weapons. Coming to such a judgment depends on a variety of factors, including the presence of widely respected global norms and laws, as well as confidence that other states will honor all three norms in the long-term future – and that finally all states will join the view, supported by a global convention, that their interests are best served by verifiably forgoing nuclear weapons.

Can the international community look to the Security Council to build support for these norms? The short answer would seem to be "no." As Tsutomu Kono put it, "in the absence of agreement among [the] five veto-holding countries, the United Nations does not work properly."[30] And there is no denying that on the matter of vertical non-proliferation there is little agreement among the veto powers.

Currently the challenge of persuading the Council's P-5 to honor the NPT-mandated disarmament imperative and to become actively engaged in promoting nuclear disarmament – especially to persuade NNWS that Article VI obligations will be treated as seriously as the NNWS are expected to treat Article I and III obligations – is the challenge of persuading the P-5/N-5 to act collectively in pursuit of a common objective that they have not truly embraced. Nuclear disarmament has become a larger part of their rhetorical postures, but it is not owned as a pillar of strengthened peace and security.

Richard Butler, the former chair of the UN Special Commission responsible for disarming Iraq after the 1991 Gulf war, states unambiguously that it is the Council's responsibility to enforce compliance with treaties on the non-proliferation of weapons of mass destruction: "The Security Council is the custodian of nonproliferation. It has the task of providing confidence to the international community that the tapestry of treaties designed to ensure that weapons of mass destruction do not spread is enforced and kept whole. There is simply no other body that can do this job, and this is widely understood."[31] But the obstacles and objections to the Council as the institution guiding vertical non-proliferation or disarmament remain daunting.

The P-5/N-5 states have made important strides toward cooperation in pushing horizontal non-proliferation objectives, gradually coming together in particular on Iran, North Korea, and the threat of the acquisition of WMD by non-state actors. But they still seem to regard their primary shared interest in vertical non-proliferation and implementation of Article VI of the NPT to be in stalling. The United States and Russia do share some disarmament interests inasmuch as both seek significant and further reductions in their respective nuclear arsenals, but neither has yet displayed a compelling desire to embrace a global interest that would lead them to accept collective limits on national prerogatives and embrace institutionalized accountability to the international community. John Burroughs of the Lawyers' Committee on Nuclear Policy thus cautions against putting much hope in or emphasis on the Council as the body to shape the non-proliferation agenda. "Especially absent reform of the Security Council to make it more representative and accountable, the emphasis going forward should be on making the existing treaty regimes – including review processes, implementing agencies, and governance mechanisms – more effective, and on negotiating new multilateral treaties as needed."[32]

Resolution 1540, a most ambitious piece of global non-proliferation legislation, is credible to the extent that it actually reflects a broad global consensus that non-state access to nuclear materials or even weapons is a grave risk, whose prevention is a matter of high urgency. Notwithstanding its lack of political legitimacy as a law-making body relevant to nuclear weapons, the Security Council can legislate successfully when it has the clear support of a broad global consensus and when its mandated actions have a strong buy-in from all regions.

The Security Council cannot credibly make the disarmament rules, even though nuclear disarmament enjoys overwhelming global support among populations and governments, because the P-5/N-5 – the five that would be the core rule-makers – are not prepared themselves to be legally bound by such rules.[33] Disarmament legislation, therefore, must remain the province of more representative and inclusive mechanisms, notably the Conference on Disarmament in direct treaty negotiations, treaty review processes, and ultimately the General Assembly. These time-consuming and difficult processes are still the best way to ensure that the norms, commitments, and institutions that result will reflect the collective will and will be honored by the states involved.

The Council is broadly mandated to perform simultaneously legislative, executive, judicial, and policing functions but, given the overweening influence of the veto-wielding P-5/N-5, the Weapons of Mass Destruction Commission was led to ask, rather modestly: "Is the Council sufficiently representative of the world to carry such responsibility?"[34] The Commission then asks, among other things, whether new practices need to be developed to provide for better consultation with other members of the United Nations.

The current urgent need to foster transparency may provide the primary potential for new Council practices in support of nuclear disarmament efforts. The P-5/N-5 have obviously not all embraced the principle of openness when it comes to their weapons programs and intentions for disarmament, but they have made some important advances. Once again, it is through the NPT process, notably the reporting provision, that the P-5/N-5 have been drawn into some concessions to transparency. The 1995 agreement to extend indefinitely the NPT rested fundamentally on the principle of "permanence with accountability." Accountability was to be strengthened through refinements to the review process, and at the 2000 Review Conference a new reporting requirement was added. Step 12 of the final document's "practical steps" to implement the Treaty's disarmament provisions called for "regular reports, within the framework of the strengthened review process for the Non-Proliferation Treaty, by all States parties on the implementation of article VI and paragraph 4 (c) of the 1995 Decision on 'Principles and Objectives for Nuclear Non-Proliferation and Disarmament', and recalling the advisory opinion of the International Court of Justice of 8 July 1996."[35]

The reporting requirement, agreed to by the P-5/N-5, is thus framed by the objectives of three internationally agreed nuclear disarmament decisions:

- "Cessation of the nuclear arms race" (Article VI of the NPT)[36]
- Reduction of nuclear weapons globally, "with the ultimate goal of eliminating those weapons" (paragraph 4(c) of the 1995 Decision on "Principles and Objectives for Nuclear Non-Proliferation and Disarmament")[37]
- The "obligation to achieve a precise result – nuclear disarmament in all its aspects" (the Advisory Opinion of the International Court of Justice of 8 July 1996)[38]

The P-5/N-5 states have certainly resisted the idea that they are actually obliged to report, and China and Russia are the only ones to have submitted formal reports (in 2005). The other P-5/N-5 states have not submitted reports that they specifically identify as being in response to the 2000 agreement on reporting, but, at the same time, all five regularly report to NPT review process meetings (including annual preparatory committees) by informally distributing national statements, working papers, fact sheets, and other background material. It must be said that such reporting, although it varies considerably, has increased in detail and scope since 2000.

The principle of mutual accountability has been a long time developing within the NPT. The degree to which the reporting obligation is honored by the P-5/N-5 will reflect the degree to which the P-5/N-5 regard themselves as accountable to other states parties to the Treaty. Non-nuclear-weapon states parties to the Treaty see reporting as a formal expression of accountability to other states parties. They expect it to become much more detailed and systematic and to mature into an effective tool with which states parties can assess each other's compliance with Treaty obligations. Accountability is the fundamental purpose or objective of reporting, and reporting even at current minimal levels has begun to help states to better understand the approaches and activities of other states parties and to generate a general attitude that each owes the others an accounting of what they are doing to implement and strengthen the disarmament and non-proliferation regime.

The NPT has no permanent secretariat, so there is in effect no body to receive reports. States parties to the Treaty are really the recipients, and the only formal opportunities for them to act on the received reports are at the Review Conferences every five years. Thus, in addition to reporting to the NPT Review Conferences, the annual reports of states parties could go directly to the Council, with the Secretary-General tasked to compile and assess them and then report annually to the Council on the state of progress toward meeting the international community's agreed nuclear disarmament objectives. In October 2008, the Secretary-General encouraged the nuclear weapons states to provide the Secretariat with expanded information on "the size of their arsenals, stocks of fissile material and specific disarmament achievements."[39]

Until resolution 1540, the Security Council had never requested or received reports on nuclear weapons and disarmament to serve as the basis for an assessment of progress in pursuit of the objectives set by Articles 11 and 26 (it has, of course, received reports on specific horizontal non-proliferation situations on its agenda, such as that in Iraq).[40] Council resolution 487 (19 June 1981), in response to Israel's attack on Iraq's nuclear research reactor, called on Israel to place its nuclear facilities under safeguards and asked the Secretary-General to inform the Council of implementation of the resolution, but it was not followed up. Nor has the Council called for any updates on progress in meeting "the need for all Member States to fulfil their obligations in relation to arms control and disarmament," as its 1992 summit statement put it. As the Egyptian diplomat Nabil Elaraby noted in 1996, given that the Council summit in 1992 concluded that "the proliferation of all weapons of mass destruction constitutes a threat to international peace and security," it would be reasonable to "expect the Council to look at that statement, adopted at the highest possible level, and to see if it should do something about it."[41] Lucy Webster, former political affairs officer with the UN Office of Disarmament, has proposed the appointment by the Secretary-General of a special rapporteur to investigate and submit regular reports to the Council on nuclear weapons proliferation.[42] Other analysts have proposed that the Council elaborate benchmarks to help it to determine, according to objective criteria, "whether to designate a situation one of nuclear proliferation, and therefore a threat to the peace, triggering chapter VII."[43] Pierre Goldschmidt, the former deputy director general of the IAEA, calls for horizontal non-proliferation enforcement mechanisms that are objective and consistently applied:

> *The most effective, unbiased, and feasible way to establish a legal basis for the necessary verification measures in circumstances of non-compliance is for the United Nations Security Council (UNSC) to adopt (under Chapter VII of the UN Charter) a **generic** (i.e. not state specific) and legally binding resolution stating that if a state is reported by the IAEA to be in non-compliance, a standard set of actions would result.*[44]

The question is whether it is possible to establish a similar mechanism and objective benchmarks to assess compliance and define non-compliance regarding Article VI. Peter van Ham and Olivia Bosch point out that resolution 1540 "provides a framework within which nations can question one another about activities that suggest illicit trafficking or other proscribed activity."[45] The Council could set up a similar mechanism to facilitate the same kind of questioning and accountability for getting first-hand accounts of Article VI compliance efforts. The priority disarmament agenda articulated in the NPT review process essentially defines the key benchmarks for progress and there is no doubt that, in the context of the NPT review process, the P-5/N-5 already have an obligation to outline steps taken toward compliance.

There remains the obvious but critical question of political will. It is true that consensus against horizontal proliferation is well advanced within the P-5/N-5. But there should be no doubt that any moves toward tougher and more coercive approaches to horizontal non-proliferation compliance will be increasingly challenged by NNWS members if compliance with Article VI obligations continues to be kept away from multilateral scrutiny. The Council should pass a resolution to formalize the understanding that *all* nuclear proliferation is a threat to international peace and security, and within that to set the framework for regular reports, deliberations on the implications of those reports, and efforts to agree on follow-on undertakings to meet agreed benchmarks. Transparency is not compliance, but it is a large step toward accountability, which in turn encourages compliance. In the absence of effective legislative, judicial, or enforcement action on disarmament, a Security Council commitment to promoting and formalizing transparency and accountability could still encourage discernible progress toward the "unequivocal undertaking" in 2000 "to accomplish the total elimination of nuclear weapons," as promised in Article VI of the NPT.

Notes

1. "Note by the President of the Security Council," UN document S/23500, 31 January 1992, 4.
2. Shannon N. Kile, Vitaly Fedchenko, and Hans M. Kristensen, "World Nuclear Forces, 2008," in *SIPRI Yearbook 2008: Armaments, Disarmament and International Security* (New York: Oxford University Press, 2008), 366.
3. "If the UNSC is the geopolitical centre of gravity," notes Ramesh Thakur, "the GA, with universal membership, is the normative centre of gravity." Ramesh Thakur, *The United Nations, Peace and Security* (Cambridge: Cambridge University Press, 2006), 162.
4. Tsutomu Kono, "The Security Council's Role in Addressing WMD Issues: Assessment and Outlook," in *Arms Control After Iraq: Normative and Operational Challenges*, ed. Waheguru Pal Singh Sidhu and Ramesh Thakur (Tokyo: United Nations University Press, 2006), 83.
5. Other elements of existing international and humanitarian law involve legally binding principles related to proportionality, the obligation that military action distinguish between combatants and noncombatants, and so on, that challenge the legitimacy of nuclear arsenals and nuclear use planning.
6. *1995 Review and Extension Conference of the Parties to the Treaty on the Non-Proliferation of Nuclear Weapons: Final Document*, Part I, Annex, Decision 2, "Principles and Objectives for Nuclear Non-Proliferation and Disarmament," NPT/CONF.1995/32 (Part I), New York, 1 June 1995.
7. "In the 1990s, the United States, Russia, France and the United Kingdom officially ended their production of plutonium and HEU for weapons and China communicated unofficially that it had joined the moratorium." *Global Fissile Material Report, 2007*, Second report of the International Panel on Fissile Materials, Princeton University Program on Science and Global Security, 4; available at ⟨http://www.fissilematerials.org/ipfm/site_down/gfmr07.pdf⟩ (accessed 15 January 2009).
8. *2000 Review Conference of the Parties to the Treaty on the Non-Proliferation of Nuclear Weapons: Final Document*, Volume I, Part I, "Review of the operation of the Treaty, taking into account the decisions and the resolution adopted by the 1995 Review and Extension Conference: Improving the effectiveness of the strengthened review process for the Treaty," NPT/CONF.2000/28, New York, 2000; available at ⟨http://daccessdds.un.org/doc/UNDOC/GEN/N00/453/64/PDF/N0045364.pdf?OpenElement⟩ (accessed 3 November 2008).

9. "Note by the President of the Security Council," 2 and 5.
10. Resolution 1540 (2004), UN document S/RES/1540 (2004), 28 April 2004.
11. "Joint communiqué adopted during the meeting of the Ministers for Foreign Affairs of China, France, the Russian Federation, the United Kingdom of Great Britain and Northern Ireland and the United States of America at Geneva on 4 June 1998," UN document S/1998/473, 5 June 1998, p. 3.
12. Resolution 1172 (1998), UN document S/RES/1172 (1998), 6 June 1998.
13. "Note by the President of the Security Council," 4.
14. This is the central point argued by Alyn Ware in "International Ju-Jitsu: Using United Nations Security Council Resolution 1540 to Advance Nuclear Disarmament," July 2004, International Association of Lawyers Against Nuclear Arms, Wellington, New Zealand, available at ⟨http://www.wagingpeace.org/articles/2004/07/00_ware_ju-jitsu.htm⟩ (accessed 3 November 2008).
15. Both statements are available at ⟨http://www.2020visioncampaign.org/pages/113/Kissinger_Shultz_Perry__Nunn_call_for_A_World_Free_of_Nuclear_Weapons⟩ (accessed 3 November 2008).
16. The complete text of the International Court of Justice Advisory Opinion on Nuclear Weapons (*Advisory Opinion on the Legality of the Threat or Use of Nuclear Weapons*, International Court of Justice, 8 July 1996) is available at the website of the Lawyers' Committee on Nuclear Policy Inc., ⟨http://www.un.org/law/icjsum/9623.htm⟩ (accessed 3 November 2008).
17. Steven R. Ratner, "The Security Council and International Law," in *The UN Security Council: From the Cold War to the 21st Century*, ed. David M. Malone (Boulder, CO: Lynne Rienner, 2005), 604 and 603.
18. John Burroughs, "The Role of the UN Security Council," in *Nuclear Disorder or Cooperative Security? U.S. Weapons of Terror, the Global Proliferation Crisis, and Paths to Peace*, ed. Michael Spies and John Burroughs (New York: Lawyers' Committee on Nuclear Policy, 2007); available at ⟨http://wmdreport.org/ndcs/online/⟩ (accessed 3 November 2008).
19. Patricia Lewis and Ramesh Thakur, "Arms Control, Disarmament and the United Nations," *Disarmament Forum* 1, no. 1 (2004): 22.
20. Ibid.
21. This group does not include North Korea. It has formally withdrawn from the NPT, but at the time of its withdrawal it was in serious non-compliance, and there is a broad understanding that it cannot be absolved of the obligations of the Treaty as long as it retains nuclear materials and technologies acquired in violation of the Treaty while it was a member.
22. George Perkovich, Jessica T. Mathews, Joseph Cirincione, Rose Gottemoeller, and Jon B. Wolfsthal, *Universal Compliance: A Strategy for Nuclear Security* (Washington, DC: Carnegie Endowment for International Peace, March 2005), 47; available at ⟨http://www.carnegieendowment.org/files/UC2.FINAL3.pdf⟩ (accessed 3 November 2008).
23. "Joint Statement Between President George W. Bush and Prime Minister Manmohan Singh," White House, July 18, 2005; available at ⟨http://www.whitehouse.gov/news/releases/2005/07/20050718-6.html⟩ (accessed 3 November 2008).
24. In statements in 2005, when the agreement was first announced, and in 2008 when the waiver decision was before the NSG, India made nearly a dozen significant disarmament and non-proliferation commitments. In the statements, India (1) agrees to separate civilian and military nuclear facilities and programs and to "place voluntarily its civilian nuclear facilities under IAEA safeguards"; (2) promises to sign and adhere to an Additional Protocol with respect to civilian nuclear facilities; (3) promises to work with the United States and others for the conclusion of a multilateral Fissile Material Cut-off

Treaty that is "universal, non-discriminatory and verifiable"; (4) agrees to a policy of "refraining from the transfer of enrichment and reprocessing technologies to states that do not have them and supporting international efforts to limit their spread"; (5) declares its interest in participating as a supplier nation in the establishment of international fuel banks; (6) declares that it maintains comprehensive export controls; (7) promises the harmonization of its export controls with the Missile Technology Control Regime and the Nuclear Suppliers Group; (8) remains committed to "a voluntary, unilateral moratorium on nuclear testing"; (9) supports the elimination of nuclear weapons and the negotiation of a convention toward that end; (10) agrees "to assume the same responsibilities ... as other leading countries with advanced nuclear technology"; and (11) affirms a policy of no-first-use of nuclear weapons. See, for example, "Statement by External Affairs Minister of India Shri Pranab Mukherjee on the Civil Nuclear Initiative," 5 September 2008; available at ⟨http://meaindia.nic.in/pressbriefing/2008/09/05pb01.htm⟩ (accessed 3 November 2008).
25. Nabil Elaraby, "The Security Council and Nuclear Weapons," presentation to the NGO Working Group on the Security Council, Global Policy Forum, 28 May 1996; available at ⟨http://www.globalpolicy.org/security/docs/elaraby.htm⟩ (accessed 3 November 2008).
26. Security Council resolution 255 on "Questions Relating to Measures to Safeguard Non-Nuclear-Weapon States Parties to the Treaty on the Non-Proliferation of Nuclear Weapons," UN document S/RES/255 (1968), adopted 19 June 1968; available at ⟨http://daccessdds.un.org/doc/RESOLUTION/GEN/NR0/248/36/IMG/NR024836.pdf?OpenElement⟩ (accessed 3 November 2008).
27. Security Council resolution 984 on "Security Assurances," UN document S/RES/984 (1995), adopted 11 April 1995.
28. The four statements are included in UN documents S/1995/261, S/1995/262, S/1995/263, and S/1995/264, 6 April 1995.
29. The Weapons of Mass Destruction Commission, *Weapons of Terror: Freeing the World of Nuclear, Biological and Chemical Arms* (Stockholm: The Weapons of Mass Destruction Commission, 2006); available at ⟨http://www.wmdcommission.org/⟩ (accessed 3 November 2008).
30. Kono, "The Security Council's Role in Addressing WMD Issues," 98.
31. Richard Butler, "Bewitched, Bothered, and Bewildered: Repairing the Security Council," *Foreign Affairs*, 78, no. 5 (1999): 11.
32. Burroughs, "The Role of the UN Security Council," 42.
33. On the matter of controlling proliferation-sensitive fuel cycle technologies, the consensus problem is reversed. The P-5/N-5 share an interest in severely limiting the spread of those technologies, and it is a concern that is shared by many other states as well, but there is also a significant group of states that do not favor replicating the NPT's have/have not divide in fuel cycle technologies that are verifiably used for peaceful purposes.
34. Weapons of Mass Destruction Commission, *Weapons of Terror*, 182.
35. *2000 Review Conference of the Parties to the Treaty on the Non-Proliferation of Nuclear Weapons: Final Document*, 15.
36. Non-Proliferation Treaty, Article VI: "Each of the Parties to the Treaty undertakes to pursue negotiations in good faith on effective measures relating to cessation of the nuclear arms race at an early date and to nuclear disarmament, and on a Treaty on general and complete disarmament under strict and effective international control."
37. *1995 Review and Extension Conference of the Parties to the Treaty on the Non-Proliferation of Nuclear Weapons*, Decision 2, para. 4(c): "The determined pursuit by the nuclear-weapon States of systematic and progressive efforts to reduce nuclear weapons globally, with the ultimate goal of eliminating those weapons, and by all States of general and complete disarmament under strict and effective international control."

38. Relevant excerpts from the Advisory Opinion of the International Court of Justice of 8 July 1996 on Nuclear Weapons (available at ⟨http://www.un.org/law/icjsum/9623.htm⟩) include paragraph 99: "The legal import of that (Article VI) obligation goes beyond that of a mere obligation of conduct [of negotiations in good faith]; the obligation involved here is an obligation to achieve a precise result – nuclear disarmament in all its aspects – by adopting a particular course of conduct, namely the pursuit of negotiations in good faith"; and paragraph 100: "This twofold obligation to pursue and to conclude negotiations formally concerns the [then] 18 States parties to the Treaty on the Non-Proliferation of Nuclear Weapons, or, in other words, the vast majority of the international community."
39. Early on, after the formation of the Atomic Energy Commission in 1946, the Council received reports from the Commission but simply passed them along to the General Assembly. For more, see Kono, "The Security Council's Role in Addressing WMD Issues," 83.
40. Quoted in UN Secretary-General Ban Ki-moon's address to the EastWest Institute (EWI), New York, 24 October 2008.
41. Elaraby, "The Security Council and Nuclear Weapons."
42. Lucy Webster, "The Security Council and Nuclear Weapons," speech to the NGO Working Group on the Security Council, Global Policy Forum, 28 May 1996; available at ⟨http://www.globalpolicy.org/security/pubs/webster.htm⟩ (accessed 3 November 2008).
43. Jack I. Garvey, "A New Architecture for the Non-Proliferation of Nuclear Weapons," *Journal of Conflict and Security Law*, 12, no. 3 (2007): 339–357.
44. Pierre Goldschmidt, "Priority Steps to Strengthen the Nonproliferation Regime," *Policy Outlook*, February 2007, Carnegie Endowment for International Peace, 3, emphasis in the original; available at ⟨http://www.carnegieendowment.org/files/goldschmidt_priority_steps_final.pdf⟩ (accessed 3 November 2008).
45. Peter van Ham and Olivia Bosch, "Global Non-Proliferation and Counter-Terrorism: The Role of Resolution 1540 and Its Implications," in *Global Non-Proliferation and Counter-Terrorism: The Role of Resolution 1540 and Its Implications*, ed. Peter van Ham and Olivia Bosch (Washington, DC: Brookings Institution Press, Chatham House and Clingendael Institute, 2007), 19–20.

3

General Assembly majorities on the preferred nuclear order

M. J. Peterson

Efforts to abolish or to limit the number and type of nuclear weapons are one element of a broader program of activities intended, in the words of the preamble of the UN Charter, "to save succeeding generations from the scourge of war" by establishing an international order in which armed conflict is removed from member states' repertoire of choices. The Charter incorporates three methods of working toward this goal: peaceful settlement of disputes, collective security, and disarmament. As Inis Claude pointed out in 1956, each works in a different way: "Whereas pacific settlement of disputes proposes to leave states with nothing to fight about, and collective security proposes to confront aggressors with too much to fight against, disarmament proposes to deprive nations of anything to fight with."[1] Denial of means alone cannot end international hostilities because even complete elimination of modern weapons systems and military organizations would not prevent a populous state from overwhelming a significantly less populous one; other state agencies can supply the needed coordination of effort against another state and a wide array of everyday objects can be used to kill or intimidate people.

The Charter acknowledges this in establishing the triad of peaceful settlement, collective security, and disarmament and also suggests a division of labor between the General Assembly as a forum for deliberative and normative efforts to reduce both the will and the means to fight and the Security Council as manager of the collective security system. Yet each of the two organs has sought a role in all three areas, with the balance depending on the extent to which the five veto-wielding permanent

---

The United Nations and nuclear orders, Boulden, Thakur and Weiss (eds), United Nations University Press, 2009, ISBN 978-92-808-1167-4

members of the Council or a coalition of any two-thirds of the members of the Assembly – the number needed to adopt resolutions on "important" questions under Assembly voting rules – succeed in pursuing a unified program.

With this tension in mind, this chapter focuses on the role of General Assembly majorities in tackling the problem of nuclear weapons. It begins by highlighting the Assembly's approach to nuclear issues and the working methods it has adopted as both "forum" and "arena" for international politics. Next, the chapter establishes a context for understanding the considerable variation between Assembly resolutions through time on nuclear weapons issues. This is followed by a detailed examination of the resolutions themselves from the United Nations' founding to the present day. Finally, the chapter concludes with a look at the limits and potential of the Assembly on nuclear issues, arguing that its greatest utility lies in setting agendas, defining important issues, designing policies, and fostering norm development.

The Assembly's approach and working methods

The particular dread inspired by nuclear weapons, whether in the possession of states or of non-state entities, led to considerable overlap of effort in the United Nations' first decade and in recent years. In 1947–1952, bodies reporting to the Security Council took the lead, with the Commission on Atomic Energy addressing both civilian and weapons uses in its discussions of "international control of atomic energy," and the parallel Commission on Conventional Arms addressing limitation of conventional arms. When the UN membership acknowledged the failure of efforts to secure Soviet–American consensus on atomic issues, the two commissions were merged into a single Disarmament Commission reporting to the Assembly. In the next half-century, the Council addressed nuclear issues only when they provoked disputes among particular states or when the International Atomic Energy Agency (IAEA) reported concerns over compliance with Safeguards Agreements. In adopting its resolution 1540 (28 April 2004), the Council returned to general nuclear weapons issues by launching its own effort to prevent further diffusion to states or non-state entities of all weapons of mass destruction and of missiles capable of delivering them. This created a divergence of approach between the two bodies as the Council picked up only the non-proliferation aspect of the broader nuclear order, including the elimination of nuclear weapons and the right of access to civilian nuclear technologies supported by the Assembly majority.

Successive Assembly majorities have taken a remarkably consistent approach to the problem of nuclear weapons. Starting with resolution 1/1 of 24 January 1946, they have defined the goal as "elimination from national armaments of atomic weapons and all other weapons adaptable to mass destruction."[2] The predominance in the Assembly of comparatively small states unable to match global or regional powers in military effort has also translated into a strong preference for assuring elimination through multilateral agreements containing effective "international" (jointly organized and implemented) verification measures and/or controls. While acknowledging and encouraging unilateral, bilateral, small group, and regional approaches, Assembly majorities have consistently affirmed the centrality of globally agreed measures.

Assembly majorities have also acknowledged that the Assembly itself cannot serve as the primary negotiating forum on arms issues or as the leader of compliance promotion or enforcement. Faced with the need to address an agenda of more than 200 items in its approximately 14 weeks of regular session a year, it does not have the time for detailed negotiation. Nor is it small enough or possessed of resources for handling compliance problems effectively. Thus it leaves detailed negotiation to subsidiary bodies, primarily the all-inclusive Disarmament Committee, serving as an exploratory forum for airing broad ideas, and the now 65-member Conference on Disarmament, which it designated as the United Nations' "single multilateral disarmament negotiating forum" in 1978.[3] Similarly, it leaves compliance promotion and enforcement efforts to the Security Council, the IAEA, and bodies established by particular treaties.

Yet Assembly majorities often seek to steer negotiations by adopting resolutions instructing the Committee or the Conference to accord priority to particular items, to consider particular proposals, or to report to the Assembly on some matter by a particular deadline. Similarly, they often use the Secretary-General or the Secretariat in attempts to break stalemates by commissioning studies or requesting a canvassing of member state views on some question.

A majority's ability to steer rests on effective use of the Assembly's unique legitimacy in a world order based on the notion of the sovereign equality of states. It is the only UN principal organ open to all member states and giving each an equal vote. All the smaller member states, not just those belonging to the Non-aligned Movement (NAM) or located in the "global South," prize these features of the Assembly and dislike efforts to eclipse it by resort to limited-membership UN bodies or non-UN forums. However, using the Assembly effectively requires paying constant attention to the two major limits on its influence. First, its formal authority vis-à-vis member states is confined to the adoption of recommendations. Assembly majorities work hard to create and maintain the impression that they express "the will of the international community" to which all states should defer. However, states are legally free to ignore Assembly resolutions and will ignore any resolution they find distasteful unless the political cost of doing so is particularly high. Most of the time the cost is low; the Assembly's resolutions are not well publicized, domestic opinion usually backs the government (particularly when a resolution can be presented as the product of a hostile majority), and a reasonably clever government can usually develop an explanation of how the terms of a particular resolution fail to adequately address the situation that domestic audiences, and at least some other governments, will accept. Second, the United Nations lacks the taxing, administering, and enforcing capacities needed to promote compliance or punish non-compliance. This means Assembly majorities must pay attention to the divergence between control of votes within the Assembly and its capability to influence other states outside it. These limitations mean the Assembly can provide UN member states with an issue definition, a preferred solution to some problem, and a preferred path to that solution, but its impact on a reluctant member state is best described in the traditional English saying that "you can lead a horse to water but you can't make it drink," unless powerful states are prepared to provide the needed backup.

Understanding the Assembly's efforts and impact is complicated by its dual function as both "forum" for broad-minded deliberation meant to produce agreement on addressing a common problem, and "arena" in which pairs or groups of member states pursue their conflicts in front of, and with the hope of eliciting support from, other states. Governments pursue state interests in both the forum and the arena; but there are important differences in the sorts of interests pursued and the intensity of advantage-seeking. In deliberation, member governments are trying to develop shared normative statements, policy guidelines, and implementation plans that promote broad national interests over the medium to long term. In pursuit of conflict, they are seeking immediate advantage over one or more particular competitors or enemies. Governments and their delegates in the Assembly are acutely aware – even if the public is not – about which resolutions originate in the forum and which in the arena. The weight they attach to any particular resolution as a statement of general norms or policy guidelines is influenced by that origin.

The political context of Assembly resolutions on nuclear weapons issues

Assembly statements on nuclear weapons questions occur in resolutions expressing broad goals, setting work programs for the UN disarmament bodies, or addressing some particular issue regarding nuclear weapons or uses of atomic energy.[4] The ensemble of adopted statements combine periodic reassertion of the primary goal of eliminating nuclear weapons with endorsement of a changing set of immediate measures that the majority of the day regards as likely to contribute to attaining the primary goal. The content of these immediate measures has varied considerably over the years for three reasons.

First, from resolution 1/1 onward, the effort to eliminate nuclear weapons has been paired with an assurance that states are free to pursue all peaceful uses of radioactive materials. Many of these "peaceful" or "civilian" uses employ relatively weak radioactive isotopes of elements not suited to weapons applications. However, the uranium and plutonium fuels used in electricity-generating reactors can be made into weapons material, and the potential for diverting fuels to bomb-making has inspired a long search for effective means of keeping the two activities separate.

Second, states accumulate weapons because of mutual distrust. Even groups of states that completely trust one another accumulate weapons to guard against others that they distrust. Thus, the UK, French, and US governments have never regarded each other's nuclear arsenals as a threat; however, the Russian and Chinese governments regard all Western arsenals as well as each other's as threats. The Indian government had China's arsenal and conventional threat in mind when it began its nuclear weapons program in the 1960s, but Pakistan has always regarded Indian nuclear weapons as more dangerous to itself than Chinese ones. Willingness to forgo a weapon rests either on low levels of mistrust or on a military consensus across countries that a particular weapon is either too heinous or too cost ineffective to be used in warfare. Norm entrepreneurs seek to establish inhibitions against the possession and use of nuclear weapons strong enough to prevail even among the very distrustful,[5] but governments appear more attuned to the Russian maxim "trust but verify." The general human tendency to seek assurance that no one is preparing to take unfair advantage of cooperative action is heightened among governments because of their institutional role as protector of the nation. Thus governments regard eliminating any type of weapon, including nuclear ones, as requiring levels of mutual trust sufficient to support the operation of verification systems robust enough to compensate for variation in levels of trust.

Third, efforts to attain the shared goal of eliminating nuclear weapons occur in a political context characterized by varying degrees of turbulence resulting from the simultaneous pursuit of deliberation and political conflict in the Assembly. Similar statements about the ultimate goal appear both in resolutions reflecting wide agreement on some points and in resolutions reflecting one group of states' success at securing Assembly endorsement of its partisan positions. Conflict-related invocation does not discredit the goal, but it does cause governments regarding themselves as the target of partisan efforts to suspect that the actions, or sequences of actions, suggested by the resulting resolutions will weaken them relative to their competitors or enemies.

The Assembly's resolutions on nuclear weapons

Between 1946 and 1953 the Assembly followed the contentions over US proposals for international control of atomic energy occurring inside and outside the UN Commission on Atomic Energy, and held debates of its own on nuclear issues. Yet it adopted very few resolutions. As the Cold War deepened, the prime contenders used a variety of forums, most often their own Foreign Ministers' Conferences, to air positions and appeal to global opinion. A 1953 Soviet effort to enlist Assembly support for its version of how to end the Cold War was rejected by the US-led majority then controlling the Assembly.[6] This reinforced Soviet perceptions of the Assembly as an unpromising forum for pursuing nuclear weapons initiatives.

The easing of tensions after Stalin's death in 1953 and the first steps towards an organization of the NAM affected politics in the Assembly in several ways. Most noticeably, they were traceable in discussions on civilian uses of nuclear technology, slowing the nuclear arms race, and preventing the acquisition of nuclear weapons by additional states. The IAEA, initially seen as a provider of technical assistance for civilian programs, came to be viewed as a mechanism for separating the civilian and weapons uses of nuclear materials through "safeguards" against the diversion of reactor fuel to weapons programs. Competitive testing of increasingly large bombs inspired widespread public dread as awareness of attendant radiation hazards spread. Tentative discussions of nonproliferation also began. The European neutrals were already urging "international" approaches to verification, but these got swamped by continuing Soviet–US contention over on-site inspections.

The advent of intercontinental missiles in the early 1960s decreased the time needed to get weapons to overseas targets but did not affect the strategic balance between the blocs in Europe. This balance rested on a tradeoff between US possession of a larger nuclear arsenal and Soviet possession of a clear superiority in conventional arms. US deflection of a Soviet effort to alter the nuclear situation in the 1962 Cuban missile crisis triggered new nuclear efforts on both sides as the Soviets sought nuclear parity and the Americans sought to avert this because of continuing Soviet conventional advantages. By the end of the decade, each superpower possessed a nuclear arsenal large enough to provide second-strike capability and together they created the "nuclear balance of terror."

Simultaneously, the superpowers shifted diplomatic efforts from the broad general disarmament approach endorsed unanimously in Assembly resolution 14/1378 to more limited arms control measures, to the dismay of those preferring either the elimination of nuclear weapons or multilateral processes, or both.[7] Much superpower effort now went into bilateral agreements on arms limitation and the avoidance of accidental war. When stability of rules required other states' participation, the superpowers' bilateral approach merged with the multilateral preferences of the now third-world-dominated Assembly majority, leading to the 1963 Limited Test Ban Treaty (LTBT) and the 1968 Treaty on the Non-Proliferation of Nuclear Weapons (NPT). The United Kingdom (1952), France (1960) and China (1964) had all tested nuclear weapons and publicly stated their possession of nuclear arsenals, and there was considerable concern that possession would spread unless actively discouraged.

The LTBT addresses states with nuclear weapons, recording their agreement to ban tests on land, in the atmosphere, and in outer space and to test only in underground facilities. The NPT is a much more complex arrangement among a wider group of states. It contains a three-part bargain between parties possessing nuclear weapons by 1 January 1967 (nuclear weapons states or NWS)[8] and parties not possessing nuclear weapons (non-nuclear-weapon states or NNWS): (a) the NWS would refrain from using nuclear weapons against any NNWS, (b) both NWS and NNWS would cooperate in ensuring non-proliferation of nuclear weapons, and (c) the NWS would pursue nuclear disarmament. Yet even with this undertaking, expressed in the Article VI provision that "[e]ach of the Parties to the Treaty undertakes to pursue negotiations in good faith on effective measures relating to cessation of the nuclear arms race at an early date and to nuclear disarmament, and on a treaty on general and complete disarmament under strict and effective international control," the NPT was criticized then and later for creating an obviously two-tier system. Even so, 43 states became parties in 1968–1970; today all but three of the United Nations' 192 members – India, Israel, and Pakistan – are parties. Calls for NWS to abide by Article VI became stronger when China and France joined the NPT in August 1992, finally bringing all five Council permanent member states with "NWS" status into the bargain.

The close relation of bilateral and multilateral processes was indicated by the fact that the LTBT and the NPT were negotiated by the Eighteen-Nation Disarmament Committee established by the superpowers. This Committee was composed of six Western, six Soviet bloc, and six neutral states, it operated by consensus, and it was only nominally associated with the United Nations. The Assembly was thus trying to influence proceedings at arm's length. This did not inhibit the newly forming majority of non-aligned and European neutral states, which affirmed preferences for a comprehensive over a limited test ban, for avoiding the development of "new types" of nuclear weapons, and for an early start to discussions on a treaty or other modes of assurance against the use of nuclear weapons. For the moment, the superpowers kept to issues where public pressure for agreement was high and verification from a distance sufficiently reliable. The LTBT and NPT did not get tangled up in the ongoing superpower stalemate over on-site inspection of nuclear weapons facilities because of improved seismic detectors capable of distinguishing nuclear explosions from earthquakes.

Between 1960 and 1977 the Assembly adopted no more than eight resolutions a year on nuclear weapons questions, with another two or three on civilian uses of atomic technology and the IAEA's activities. These included expressions of interest in using nuclear explosions for civilian purposes (such as canal-building),[9] a line of debate that gave India the ability to claim its 1974 nuclear test involved a "peaceful nuclear device" rather than a weapon. The non-aligned and neutral majority continued to press further than either Cold War bloc was willing to go in advocating early conclusion of a comprehensive test ban, stronger assurances on non-use of nuclear weapons than contained in the NPT, and a moratorium on the development of "new types" of nuclear weapons. It also mandated Secretariat assistance for a conference of NNWS to parallel and put additional pressure on the negotiations in the Eighteen-Nation Disarmament Committee.[10]

Increasing third world assertiveness on a wide range of international issues in the early 1970s was reflected in Assembly resolutions on nuclear questions. Resolution 26/2828A (16 December 1971), drafted by the more assertive members of the NAM and adopted over Chinese opposition and superpower bloc abstention, deplored "the fact that the General Assembly has not yet succeeded in its aim of achieving a comprehensive test ban, despite eighteen successive resolutions on the subject," and urged the NWS "to bring to a halt all nuclear weapons tests at the earliest possible date and, in any case, not later than 5 August 1973."[11] Resolution 30/3478 (11 December 1975) marked the first step in bringing nuclear negotiations within the United Nations by calling on the five nuclear weapons possessors to meet in a conference with 25–30 non-possessors, to be selected by the president of the Assembly after consultations with the regional groups, and to start negotiations on a comprehensive test ban "not later than 30 March 1976." Also that year, resolution 30/3472B (11 December 1975) took discussion of nuclear-weapon-free zones to a new level by offering a definition and telling weapons possessors that they should make binding legal commitments to respect such zones and refrain from "contributing in any way" to any acts in the zone that violate the nuclear-weapons-free status.

Superpower attention focused on the bilateral relationship after 1968, and continued negotiations led in the early 1970s to several agreements, most notably the first Strategic Arms Limitation Talks Agreement (SALT-I) and the Treaty on the Limitation of Anti-Ballistic Missile Systems (ABM Treaty). These were carefully limited to what each side could verify with its own "national technical means of verification" – seismic detectors, radar, photo or signals-intercepting reconnaissance satellites – and capped, but did not reduce, nuclear arsenals. While welcoming the agreements, Assembly majorities continued to emphasize the goal of eliminating nuclear weapons and in the meantime urged the adoption of a moratorium on testing and the development of "new types" of nuclear weapons, as well as a ban on any use, or at least first use, of nuclear weapons. Most of these resolutions elicited grudging acceptance or abstentions from the rival blocs; calls for ceasing all tests elicited Chinese opposition because China's arsenal was far less developed than others'.

The highlight of the Assembly's more general disarmament debate in the 1970s was the First Special Session on Disarmament in 1978. Its resolutions specified broad statements of objectives, separated discussions of disarmament from discussions of other political issues by putting the former in the First Committee and the latter in the Special Political Committee, and adopted a reorganization of UN disarmament bodies that tied them more clearly to the Assembly.[12]

Starting in 1979 as the Cold War re-intensified, Assembly debates took on a very different tone as the Soviet Union enjoyed considerable success in mobilizing the Assembly majority against the harder line of US policy, particularly by the Reagan administration in 1981–1985. The number of resolutions on nuclear weapons (excluding nuclear-weapon-free zones) rose from approximately 7 a year in 1975 to approximately 15 a year in 1979 and reached a high of 24 in 1983. The number of separate topics also increased as the Soviets introduced drafts on preventing nuclear war, the non-stationing of nuclear weapons on the territory of NNWS, the climate impact of nuclear war, banning neutron bombs, and adopting a nuclear freeze. The Soviets were also able to get their drafts of a comprehensive test ban treaty and a treaty banning use of nuclear weapons annexed to resolutions 37/85 (9 December 1982) and 38/73G (15 December 1983) referred to the Conference on Disarmament as "a basis" for negotiating. The Assembly usually avoids such detailed guidance, and the votes, 115–5–25 with all four other weapons possessors in opposition on 37/85 and 104–17–6 with only China supporting 38/73G, suggested that the drafts were unlikely to advance negotiations.[13]

Soviet eagerness to use the Assembly for mobilization was most apparent in proposals that the United Nations support active public information campaigns and encourage the collection of citizen signatures on petitions demanding the elimination of nuclear weapons for presentation to the Assembly's Second Special Session on Disarmament in 1982. Both harkened back to the Soviet sponsorship of "spontaneous" public campaigns in the mid-1950s and, like those earlier campaigns, corresponded to a spike in public fear of nuclear war. Though perceived by Western policy-makers as cynical attempts to manipulate and intensify public disapproval of Reagan administration policies while clamping down on criticism at home, Western governments agreed to revised resolutions that channeled projected UN activities in less partisan directions.

The NAM had re-intensified Assembly criticism of nuclear war doctrines in 1978 by adopting the first in a string of resolutions[14] reviving the assertion first made in resolution 16/1653 of 1961 that "[a]ny State using nuclear and thermo-nuclear weapons is to be considered as violating the Charter of the United Nations, as acting contrary to the laws of humanity and as committing a crime against mankind and civilization."[15] Yet the strongest statements in this sequence of resolutions were suggested by the Soviets. Resolution 36/100 (9 December 1981), titled "Declaration on the Prevention of Nuclear Catastrophe," included operative paragraphs expressing the views that:

1. "States and statesmen" using nuclear weapons first commit "the gravest crime against humanity"
2. There will never be "any justification or pardon" for leaders who are the first to use nuclear weapons
3. Doctrines that allow for first use and actions pushing the world towards catastrophe "are incompatible with human moral standards and the lofty ideals of the United Nations"
4. Leaders of nuclear weapons states have a "supreme duty and direct obligation" to eliminate the risk of outbreak of nuclear conflict, and should exert "joint efforts, through negotiations conducted in good faith and on the basis of equality," to stop and reverse the nuclear arms race with the eventual goal of eliminating nuclear weapons
5. "Nuclear energy should be used exclusively for peaceful purposes and only for the benefit of mankind"

Resolution 38/75 (15 December 1983) had the majority stating that it:

1. *Resolutely, unconditionally, and for all times condemns* nuclear war as being contrary to human conscience and reason, as the most monstrous crime against peoples and as a violation of the foremost human right – the right to life
2. *Condemns* the formulation, propounding, dissemination and propaganda of political and military doctrines and concepts intended to provide "legitimacy" for the first use of nuclear weapons and in general to justify the "admissibility" of unleashing nuclear war

The partisan circumstances of the adoption of these resolutions meant that their political weight did not match the strength of their language. Resolution 36/100 was adopted by a vote of 82 to 19 with 41 abstentions and 38/75 by a vote of 95 to 19 with 30 abstentions. China announced its non-participation in both votes.[16] European neutrals and some third world states figured among the abstainers because they were aware of the impact of continuing Soviet superiority in conventional weapons on the bipolar competition. China dissociated itself from the whole debate by non-participation to maintain its distance from both superpowers, a notable departure from its usual support for positions also adopted by a majority of the non-aligned. Later evidence of low impact was supplied when the International Court of Justice (ICJ) did not take up these themes in its Advisory Opinion on nuclear weapons.[17]

Yet the NAM needed no outside encouragement to link the existence of nuclear weapons with international instability. The final communiqué of the Seventh Non-Aligned Summit (New Delhi, 1983) noted that the renewed arms race and continued reliance on doctrines of nuclear deterrence "had heightened the risk of the outbreak of nuclear war and led to greater insecurity and instability in international relations,"[18] and that of the Eighth Summit (Harare, 1986) further asserted that "the idea that world peace can be maintained through nuclear deterrence, a doctrine that lies at the root of the continuing escalation in the quantity and quality of nuclear weapons, is the most dangerous myth in existence."[19] The non-aligned continued to press for negotiations on the whole range of pre-existing nuclear issues, and in particular for holding another UN conference on peaceful uses of nuclear energy so that civilian uses would not be sacrificed to proliferation concerns. They also needed no Soviet prompting to issue annual Assembly condemnations of the South African and Israeli nuclear programs.[20]

Though the level of contention declined with the end of the Cold War, the arena fights of the early 1980s cast a continuing shadow over later debates for two reasons. First, they hardened the attitudes of many US officials and commentators who returned to responsible government positions or greater public prominence when George W. Bush became president in January 2001. Like their conservative supporters in Congress and among the public, they are strongly skeptical of general arms control – as distinct from efforts to keep weapons of mass destruction out of the hands of "mad" or "rogue" governments that are typically unreceptive to Assembly recommendations on nuclear questions.

Second, majorities were slow to adjust Assembly routine to the changed conditions. The number of separate resolutions on specifically nuclear weapons questions (again excluding those on nuclear-weapon-free zones) dropped from the 1983 high of 24 to about 15 in 1987–1989, hit a low of 7 in 1997, and returned to between 14 and 15 in the mid-2000s. Use of neutron bombs, nuclear freezes, and the climate effects of nuclear war as distinct agenda items streamlined debate after 1990. Yet the "threat of proliferation in the Middle East," the 1996 ICJ Advisory Opinion on the use of nuclear weapons, and reducing nuclear dangers re-expanded debate after 1995. The Assembly also continued its habit, first apparent in the early 1960s in relation to issues of the test ban and assurances of non-use against NNWS, of handling disagreements about priorities or issue definitions by adopting multiple resolutions on a single topic. Multiple resolutions were particularly prevalent on three issues in the 1990s. One stream of resolutions on a comprehensive test ban treaty (CTBT) suggested amending the LTBT, while another suggested negotiating in the Conference on Disarmament or some other forum. One stream of resolutions on providing assurance that NWS would not use nuclear weapons against NNWS urged negotiation of a single multilateral treaty, while a second endorsed unilateral pledges by the NWS. The annual output of resolutions on the elimination of nuclear weapons featured at least three resolutions offering various suggestions about negotiation.

Stalemate on nuclear weapons issues was mirrored in persisting disagreement on convening a world disarmament conference or holding a fourth Special Session on Disarmament. The conference was proposed by the Soviet Union in the early 1980s and still figures in Assembly debates. Proponents' hopes of holding a fourth Special Session in 1997[21] faded when the qualification was added that the objectives and agenda should be agreed before a date was set.[22]

The 1995 and 2000 reviews of the NPT, which ended with agreed statements on how to proceed on nuclear weapons issues, and the 2000 Millennium Declaration suggested grounds for optimism that nuclear weapons, like anti-personnel landmines, chemical weapons, and biological and toxin weapons, were about to be banned. The NWS were widely believed to have undertaken to reduce their nuclear arsenals and were prepared to begin discussions aimed at complete elimination of nuclear weapons.[23] The Millennium Declaration recorded that the heads of state and government participating in the Millennium Summit "will spare no effort to free our peoples from the scourge of war, whether within or between States, which has claimed more than 5 million lives in the past decade," and "will also seek to eliminate the dangers posed by weapons of mass destruction." However, the following paragraph of the declaration suggested that there was no agreement on how to reach this goal; the leaders resolved to "strive for the elimination of weapons of mass destruction, particularly nuclear weapons, and to keep all options open for achieving this aim, including the possibility of convening an international conference to identify ways of eliminating nuclear dangers."[24]

That optimism soon receded. In late 2004 the UN Secretary-General's High-level Panel on Threats, Challenges and Change (HLP) saw no progress and observed that the five permanent Security Council member states had "all but renounced" their earlier commitments during the 2004 session of the preparatory committee for the 2005 NPT Review. It urged the five to honor their NPT commitments, to "reaffirm" assurances they would not use nuclear weapons against NNWS, and in the meantime to work to reduce the risk of nuclear war.[25] The HLP also took the view, increasingly shared among experts, that addressing nuclear weapons issues requires paying attention to both the "supply" (availability of weapons-usable materials) and the "demand" (motivations for acquiring nuclear weapons) dimensions of the problem.[26]

The vociferous unilateralism of the United States under George W. Bush and its isolated stances on certain issues, particularly the CTBT and controls on fissile materials, encourage a view of the United States as the main obstacle to progress. The change of administration after the election of Barack Obama certainly weakens neoconservative influence and reduces obstacles. As long as there are no reliable defenses against them, nuclear weapons are very attractive to states that feel threatened by larger conventionally armed enemies, whether great powers, regional rivals, or coalitions of regional neighbors.[27] Though chemical and biological weapons also have a deterrent effect and cost less to develop, some experts believe that the greater possibilities of post-attack damage mitigation make them less attractive deterrents than nuclear weapons,[28] a supposition receiving some support in the greater progress on agreements to ban them.

A close look at Assembly debates and votes suggests that the current nuclear weapons stalemate pleases a number of governments. The Chinese and Russian governments have contributed to stalemate by insisting on a linkage between discussions of nuclear weapons and weapons in outer space that they know the United States will reject. There is currently no way to formulate a resolution addressing nuclear-weapons-related issues in the Middle East that will elicit "yes" votes from all states in the region. None of the competing resolutions on reducing nuclear arsenals or eliminating nuclear weapons gains support from all five NWS. India, Pakistan, and Israel vote against or abstain on resolutions addressing proliferation in the Middle East or nuclear-weapon-free zones in South Asia, and adamantly reject majority calls to adhere to the NPT as a NNWS. Neither the Assembly as a whole nor the smaller coalitions pressing most urgently for movement toward elimination – the Group of 21 non-aligned states, the New Agenda Coalition (Brazil, Egypt, Ireland, Mexico, New Zealand, South Africa, and Sweden), and the Norway Group (Norway, Australia, Chile, Indonesia, Romania, South Africa, and the United Kingdom) – have been able to unite on a common approach.

Though the so-called "four statesmen" – Henry Kissinger, George P. Schultz, William J. Perry, and Sam Nunn – have called for nuclear disarmament,[29] which affected the dynamics of US domestic debates and was noticed in other parts of the world, the Assembly's 2007 debates proceeded in similar fashion. The only resolutions on a nuclear weapons issue that won consensus addressed preventing terrorist acquisition of fissile and radioactive materials.[30] The continuing impasse on how to eliminate nuclear weapons was reflected in the adoption of six resolutions on the topic by votes ranging from 170-3-9 for resolution 62/37 affirming the goal with no detail ("Renewed determination towards the total elimination of nuclear weapons"), to 127-27-27 for resolution 62/39 on "Follow-up to the advisory opinion of the International Court of Justice on the *Legality of the Threat or Use of Nuclear Weapons*," to 109-55-15 for resolution 62/24 urging implementation of all the measures outlined in the Final Documents of the 1995 and 2000 NTP Review Conferences.[31]

The depth of the continuing stalemate was further revealed in the travails of the 2008 session of the Conference on Disarmament. The co-presidents' draft work plan featuring the appointment of "Co-ordinators" to lead discussions on seven issues included the qualification that it was offered "without prescribing or precluding any outcome(s) for the substantive discussions" on nuclear disarmament and the prevention of nuclear war, the prevention of an arms race in outer space, or assuring NNWS against threats or use of nuclear weapons. Further, it was not meant to "prejudice any past, present or future position, proposal or priority of any delegations, nor any commitment undertaken in any other multilateral fora related to disarmament."[32]

What the General Assembly can and cannot do

Some observers have wondered about the efficacy of the Assembly's tendency to pile up multiple resolutions on nuclear weapons issues. In 1983, when the Assembly was fully mobilized as an arena for Cold War contentions and North-South disagreement on other issues was very strong, the president of the 38th session, Jorge Enrique Illueca of Panama, asked delegates: "does it really help the cause of disarmament and do we obtain the desired results by the adoption at this session of 63 resolutions on the subject? True, it is a complex issue, but I have the feeling that many of those resolutions are so complicated as to be incomprehensible to anyone other than the group of experts that drafted them."[33] In 2004, the HLP warned that the Assembly's "norm-making capacity is often squandered on debates about minutiae or thematic topics outpaced by real-world events" and, after commenting on the unwieldy and static disarmament agenda, concluded that member governments need to "put behind them the approach which they have applied hitherto."[34]

The clutter persists because some actors regard it as useful. Assembly insiders, government experts, and the Secretariat regard particular countries' shifts among the yes/no/abstain possibilities on different resolutions in any one year or on resolutions with the same title (whether with identical or modified text) in successive years as providing information about individual governments' positions. However, that is probably not the real reason for multiple resolutions because discussions in the Disarmament Commission and the Committee on Disarmament, and the more formalized debates in the Assembly's First Committee, provide far more detail about positions. The real attraction of resolutions is that votes provide summary counts of how many states adopt what broad attitude. The summary counts provide more vivid evidence than excerpts from debates for anyone seeking to further some position or policy by demonstrating to national legislatures or the general public that opponents are isolated. Thus advocates of eliminating nuclear weapons would like to use Assembly votes to create an impression that states possessing or seeking nuclear weapons are a small group clinging to outmoded ideas. That tactic would work if all resolutions on nuclear weapons issues attracted some 170 "yes" votes, only 3–5 "no" votes, and 10 or fewer abstentions. However, as long as some resolutions attract 47–55 "no" votes, it is difficult to suggest isolation without being so selective in presentation that the argument becomes self-discrediting.

The overlapping provisions and varying votes on Assembly resolutions also contribute little to the efforts of disarmament advocacy groups seeking to mobilize citizen pressure on national governments.[35] These efforts have increased in recent years, but currently have nowhere near the impact of the antinuclear movement of the 1950s or the freeze movement of the early 1980s. The annual Assembly endorsement of multiple competing notions of how to get to elimination merely invites confusion, and the varying votes weaken the resolutions' usefulness as evidence of the "international opinion" that many non-governmental groups invoke when lobbying national governments.

Outlining a useful role for the Assembly on nuclear issues can profitably begin by considering how nuclear issues would be handled if it did not exist. There would be other forums – the Security Council, NPT Review Conferences, the IAEA Assembly – but none of them would have the same combination of nearly universal membership, annual sessions, and broad political mandate that characterizes the General Assembly. Expressions of support for the elimination of nuclear weapons would be fragmented across many forums, most likely attracting even less media and public attention than Assembly proceedings. Nor would there be a place of last resort permitting revival of negotiations producing near-consensus in a more specialized forum. This happened in 1996 when India sought to delay adoption of the draft CTBT to force repair of what it regarded as serious weaknesses, but Australia acted for the overwhelming majority of states supporting the draft despite those imperfections in bringing it to the Assembly and securing resolution 50/250 recommending it to UN member states for their adherence.[36]

The Assembly's size, length of sessions, and Charter mandates mean that its potential for affecting outcomes is greatest in agenda-setting, issue or problem definition, policy design, and norm development. Its potential is smallest in policy implementation and enforcement, and is relevant to compliance promotion only if the governments whose compliance is desired will be swayed by statements of opinion. There is no shortage of thinking on the matter, including the recent review of the whole nuclear order by the IAEA's Commission of Eminent Persons,[37] but the Assembly can reach its full potential for influencing developments only if the overwhelming majority of its members, including all states capable of accomplishing or forestalling the desired outcome, speak in unison.

Some proponents of stronger Assembly action on nuclear issues have suggested invoking the "Uniting for Peace" (UFP) procedure or the Assembly's control over the UN budget to push back against what they regard as efforts by the permanent members of the Council to marginalize the Assembly on nuclear issues. Even under the UFP procedure, the Assembly's resolutions are recommendations; implementation follows only if the majority supporting the resolution has the capacity to implement it. Unless it can come up with a program that all nuclear weapons possessors and considerers will abide by, an Assembly majority invoking UFP would only give a more public demonstration of the Assembly's limitations.[38] Leaving aside the complication stemming from the agreement since the early 1980s that budget and assessment decisions will be adopted by consensus,[39] the ability of the Assembly to affect outcomes through the budget appears rather limited. It can increase the budgets of the various UN public information campaigns and regional centers for disarmament, though in periods when the major payers insist on a no-growth budget this has to come from other areas. None of the UN programs relating to nuclear issues seems to be a useful target for emulating national legislatures' habit of expressing disapproval by denying funds to particular programs.

The Assembly acts less as the original source than as an amplifier of ideas for agenda items, issue or problem definitions, policy designs, or international norms. It amplifies by accelerating the diffusion of ideas in two ways. First, Assembly consideration permits the introduction of a new idea simultaneously to a large number of governments and to the public in many states. Second, Assembly debate puts new ideas through a multi-perspective deliberative process. When the members can get beyond least-common-denominator sentiments or employing language so vague that governments are free to interpret resolutions in different or even directly opposite ways, the Assembly can still provide the global endorsement or condemnation that Inis Claude long-ago identified as one of the primary functions of the United Nations.[40]

It is not quite correct to say, as has Seymour Maxwell Finger, that the piling up of resolutions leads states to take their serious talks elsewhere.[41] While the Assembly is capable of repairing omissions in, or modifying particular parts of, agreements developed in other UN bodies,[42] or of rescuing agreements from last-minute derailment, it cannot undertake detailed negotiations of particular agreements. Efforts to "micro-manage" negotiations proceeding in other forums by endorsing particular drafts indicate stalemate rather than progress since any draft eliciting consensus in the Assembly would have enjoyed enough support in the negotiating body to be used without Assembly prompting.

Some efforts to micro-manage may be a weak-state response to the "go-it-alone" power[43] enjoyed by strong states able to create the outcomes they desire outside the Assembly. Resentment of foot-dragging by the five NWS is deep; India's and Pakistan's publicly affirmed nuclear weapons possession, Israel's unaffirmed but generally presumed possession, and other states' apparent desire to possess also inspire concern. Although efforts to eliminate nuclear weapons remain stalled, support for limiting the spread of fissile materials convertible into weapons and of missiles capable of delivering nuclear weapons over long distances is broad, and is registered in other states' willingness to join the Western-led Nuclear Suppliers Group, the Proliferation Security Initiative, and the Missile Technology Control Regime, despite their origins outside the United Nations.

The politics of disarmament is always fraught because any agreement either solidifies or modifies the existing balance of capabilities among states. Agreements to eliminate a particular weapon are no exception to that rule, though they can draw on the underlying dynamics of weapons choices summarized by Thomas Schelling in 1975. He noted that those preferences are usually arrayed in the order (1) only we have, (2) both we and our rivals have, (3) no one has, and (4) only our rivals have. A stable agreement to eliminate any particular weapon requires shifting the order of preferences.[44] One way involves moving "no one has" into the first slot out of normative or pragmatic considerations. Another, which can develop as long as "only we have" appears unattainable, involves "no one has" coming to rank ahead of "both we and our rivals have." Since the stability of the re-ranking of the middle terms depends on a continued perception that "only we have" is unattainable, it is easy to see why disarmament advocates stress the building up of normative inhibitions against possession and use. Yet normative inhibitions can erode as well, so focusing only on norm development (and implicitly relying on "no one has" ranking first) does not resolve the problem. Since nuclear weapons cannot be "un-invented," elimination intensifies the normal concerns about verification because small numbers of nuclear weapons can make a very big difference in a largely non-nuclear world.

Conclusion

There is a wealth of ideas about how to end the nuclear weapons impasse, particularly the anxiety arising from the continued existence of imperfect verification and imperfect trust. Perfection of either would eliminate the anxiety, but perfect verification is not possible and imperfect trust appears likely to persist except among members of the most strongly established "security communities."[45] Yet Assembly discussions of other arms control and disarmament issues have suggested several useful approaches to the problem of reducing anxiety: confidence-building, timely detection, transparency, and irreversibility. Confidence-building covers a wide array of measures meant to lower distrust among states, particularly those likely to continue or to develop significant political rivalries. Timely detection emphasizes the need for continued improvement of verification technologies and learning from recent inspection controversies. Transparency emphasizes dealing with distrust through public disclosure of basic information about military arsenals and budgets. Irreversibility encourages the development of normative and technical barriers to re-acquiring nuclear weapons, such as the efforts in the IAEA and elsewhere to break the link between nuclear fuel and weapons material or the environmentalist argument that putting more effort into the development of other energy sources would be as effective in reducing greenhouse gas emissions and less dangerous overall than increasing reliance on nuclear power generation.

The Assembly's resolutions have been important in keeping elimination on the nuclear agenda but are not currently contributing to progress toward that goal because the annual pile of overlapping statements winning widely varying support reveals so much disagreement. Beyond that, the domestic politics of states is more important to nuclear disarmament than intergovernmental pressures. The likelihood of significant movement toward elimination in the near future will depend on who comes to power in several major countries where elections will occur in 2008 and

2009.[46] Further, the record of past nuclear agreements – particularly the LTBT, the NPT, and the nuclear freeze – suggests that parallel pressures from both intergovernmental and civil society sources have more impact on nuclear arms control or disarmament than intergovernmental pressures alone.

Majorities can position the Assembly to exert more influence if they acknowledge that wielding the body's potential as a global legitimator at present requires doing something they have not done – avoid adopting resolutions about nuclear issues that cannot attract consensus. This does not require complete silence; it means adopting a single resolution reaffirming the goal of elimination without getting tangled in details. Once the details creep in, consensus evaporates and, with it, most of the Assembly's potential to contribute to the interconnected vision of peaceful use and nuclear disarmament envisioned since 1946.

Notes

1. Inis L. Claude, Jr, *Swords into Plowshares* (New York: Random House, 1956), 296.
2. References to Assembly resolutions have been standardized to the current format of session number/resolution number even for resolutions adopted before that system came into effect in 1976. In the older system, resolutions were numbered consecutively and the session number then given in roman numerals enclosed in parentheses; in the current system, resolution numbers are reset to 1 at the start of each session. Texts of and votes on resolutions appear in the annual *Yearbook of the United Nations* and texts at ⟨http://www.un.org/documents/resga.htm⟩ (accessed 5 November 2008).
3. *Final Document of the Tenth Special Session of the General Assembly*, annexed to General Assembly resolution S-10/2, 30 June 1978.
4. Both civilian uses and weapons were "atomic" in the 1940s and 1950s; weapons became "nuclear" in the 1960s, whereas civilian uses remained "atomic."
5. For an analysis see Nina Tannenwald, *The Nuclear Taboo: The United States and the Non-Use of Nuclear Weapons since 1945* (Cambridge: Cambridge University Press, 2007).
6. *Yearbook of the United Nations, 1953* (New York: United Nations, 1954), 272–276.
7. Lawrence Freedman, *The Evolution of Nuclear Strategy* (London: Palgrave Macmillan, 2003), chapter 13, discusses the formulation of, diffusion of, and reaction to this approach between the mid 1950s and 1960s.
8. NPT, Article IX(3) definition of "nuclear-weapon state." Text of the Treaty on the Non-Proliferation of Nuclear Weapons available at ⟨http://disarmament.un.org/wmd/npt/npt%20authenticated%20text-English.pdf⟩ (accessed 5 November 2008).
9. General Assembly resolutions 23/2456C, 20 December 1968, 24/2605B, 16 December 1969, 26/2829, 16 December 1969, and 30/3484, 12 December 1975.
10. General Assembly resolutions 21/2153B, 17 November 1966, and 22/2346B, 19 December 1967.
11. General Assembly resolution 26/2828A, 4th preambular paragraph and operative paragraph 2, 16 December 1971.
12. See the *Final Declaration of the First Special Session on Disarmament* annexed to General Assembly resolution S-10/2, 30 June 1978.

13. *Yearbook of the United Nations, 1982* (New York: United Nations, 1983), 81–83 and *Yearbook of the United Nations, 1983* (New York: United Nations, 1984), 34–36.
14. First in General Assembly resolution 33/71B, 14 December 1978.
15. General Assembly resolution 16/1653, operative para. 1d, 24 November 1961.
16. *Yearbook of the United Nations, 1981* (New York: United Nations, 1982), 44, and *Yearbook of the United Nations, 1983* (New York: United Nations, 1984), 29.
17. "Legality of the Threat or Use of Nuclear Weapons," Advisory Opinion of 8 July 1996, General List No. 95. *International Legal Materials* 35: 809. Also available at ⟨http://www.icj-cij.org/docket/index.php?p1=3&p2=4&k=e1&p3=4&case=95⟩ (accessed 5 November 2008).
18. 1983 Non-Aligned Summit declaration, reproduced in UN Doc. A/38/132-S/15675, 30 March 1983 and Corr.1&2.
19. 1986 Non-Aligned Summit declaration, reproduced in UN Doc. A/41/697-S/18392, 14 October 1986.
20. The different titles, "South Africa's nuclear capabilities" and "Israeli nuclear armament," reflected the majority's understanding of expert opinion about their nuclear programs.
21. Indicated in General Assembly resolution 49/75[I], 15 December 1994.
22. By resolution 51/45[C], 10 December 1996.
23. Compilers of the *Yearbook of the United Nations, 2000* (New York: United Nations, 2001) described the Final Document of the 2000 NPT review as including "the unequivocal commitment by nuclear-weapon States, for the first time, to totally eliminate their nuclear arsenals," 487.
24. United Nations Millennium Declaration, Section II, paras 8 and 9, *Yearbook of the United Nations, 2000*, 50–51.
25. Secretary-General's High-level Panel on Threats, Challenges and Change, *A More Secure World: Our Shared Responsibility* (New York: United Nations, 2004), paras 120–121. Accessible on the United Nations' website at ⟨http://www.un.org/secureworld/⟩ (accessed 5 November 2008).
26. High-level Panel, *A More Secure World*, paras 127–138 and 122–124. In this discussion the Panel expanded its suggestions for nuclear weapons possessors beyond the NPT five by referring to "the United States, Russia, other nuclear weapons states, and states not party to the NPT."
27. For instance, Robert J. Powell, "Nuclear Deterrence Theory, Nuclear Proliferation, and National Missile Defense," *International Security* 27, no. 4 (Spring 2003): 86–118.
28. See, for example, Andy Butfoy, *Disarming Proposals: Controlling Nuclear, Biological, and Chemical Weapons* (Sydney: University of New South Wales Press, 2005), 54.
29. George P. Schultz, William J. Perry, Henry A. Kissinger, and Sam Nunn, "A World Free of Nuclear Weapons," *Wall Street Journal*, 4 January 2007, and "Toward a Nuclear-free World," *Wall Street Journal*, 15 January 2008.
30. General Assembly resolutions 62/33, 5 December 2007, and 62/46, 5 December 2007. Votes in Official Records of 61st Plenary Meeting, UN Doc. A/62/PV.61 (5 December 2007), 18 and 23; available at ⟨http://daccessdds.un.org/doc/UNDOC/GEN/N07/626/70/PDF/N0762670.pdf?OpenElement⟩ (accessed 5 November 2008).
31. Votes on General Assembly resolutions 62/24, 62/25, 62/37, 62/39, 62/42, and 62/51 in UN Doc. A/62/PV.61, 10–27.
32. Proposed programme of work, document CD/1840 of 13 March 2008; available at ⟨http://daccessdds.un.org/doc/UNDOC/GEN/G08/604/95/PDF/G0860495.pdf?OpenElement⟩ (accessed 5 November 2008).
33. Closing remarks of the President, General Assembly, 38th session, 104th plenary meeting, 20 December 1983, UN Doc. A/38/PV.104 (provisional text), 52–53.

34. High-level Panel, *A More Secure World*, para. 241.
35. Many of the groups are local or regional; those with the widest transnational reach include the Reaching Critical Will project of the Women's International League for Peace and Freedom, International Physicians for the Prevention of Nuclear War, and the Campaign for Nuclear Disarmament. The major transnational environmental groups also support the elimination of nuclear weapons.
36. Circumstances summarized in *Yearbook of the United Nations, 1996* (New York: United Nations, 1997), 451–454, with India's objections noted more fully in "Impasse at Geneva," *Bulletin of the Atomic Scientists* 52, no. 5 (1996): 9.
37. Commission of Eminent Persons, *Reinforcing the Global Nuclear Order for Peace and Prosperity: The Role of the IAEA to 2020 and Beyond*, IAEA Doc. GOV/2008/22-GC(52)/Inf/4, May 2008; available at ⟨http://www.iaea.org/NewsCenter/News/2008/2020report.html⟩ (accessed 5 November 2008).
38. A caution also sounded by Jean Krasno and Mitushi Das, "The Uniting for Peace Resolution and Other Ways of Circumventing the Authority of the Security Council," in *The UN Security Council and the Politics of International Legitimacy*, ed. Bruce Cronin and Ian Hurd (London: Routledge, 2006), 191, during a survey more enthusiastic about its use.
39. M. J. Peterson, *The UN General Assembly* (London: Routledge, 2005), 98.
40. Inis L. Claude, Jr, "Collective Legitimation as a Political Function of the United Nations," in *The Changing United Nations* (New York: Random House, 1967), 73–126.
41. Seymour Maxwell Finger, "Foreword," in *Decision-making Strategies for International Organizations*, Frederick K. Lister (Denver, CO: Graduate School of International Studies, University of Denver, 1984), 3–4.
42. As when members of the First Committee persuaded US and Soviet delegates that they needed to revise the definition of adequate compensation and include provision for a review conference in the Convention on International Liability for Damage Caused by Space Objects in 1970–1971. M. J. Peterson, *International Regimes for the Final Frontier* (Albany, NY: State University of New York Press, 2005), 116–117.
43. Lloyd Gruber, *Ruling the World: Power Politics and the Rise of Supranational Institutions* (Princeton, NJ: Princeton University Press, 2000).
44. Thomas Schelling, "A Framework for the Evaluation of Arms Control Proposals," *Daedelus* No. 104 (Summer 1975): 187–200.
45. The best current treatment of the concept and its implications is Emanuel Adler and Michael J. Barnett, *Security Communities* (New York: Cambridge University Press, 1998).
46. Joseph Cirincione, "Arms Control's New Moment," *Bulletin of the Atomic Scientists* 63, no. 4 (2007): 21.

4
The Secretary-General and the Secretariat

Randy Rydell

Inis Claude once wrote that the Secretariat is "the most valuable product to date of the historical process of international organization."[1] At the United Nations, Claude added, the Secretary-General has the role of "international statesman" or, as Trygve Lie once put it, "the spokesman for the world interest."[2]

Claude identified three basic problems facing any such Secretariat. It must perform its mandates in an objective and cost-effective manner, maintain its international status, and, if possible, demonstrate some political leadership. For Dag Hammarskjöld, the fundamental choice facing the UN organization was whether it should function as "static conference machinery" or serve as a "dynamic instrument" to achieve specific political objectives.[3]

All of these observations very much apply to the work of the United Nations and its secretaries-general in dealing with nuclear weapons challenges. Although member states make the most fundamental decisions, the Secretary-General and Secretariat have all made their own unique contributions in addressing such challenges. These contributions merit close attention by all who are concerned about the process of international organization, in particular as it applies to multilateral efforts to address challenges relating to nuclear weapons, the most dangerous of all weapons of mass destruction (WMD).

Since there is little scholarly literature on the role of the Secretary-General and Secretariat in this field, this chapter seeks to fill that gap. In light of growing concerns in the world over the magnitude of the threats

---

The United Nations and nuclear orders, Boulden, Thakur and Weiss (eds), United Nations University Press, 2009, ISBN 978-92-808-1167-4

posed by such weapons, this chapter will address four questions: What have the eight secretaries-general and Secretariat sought to achieve in this field? How has this work changed? Why? And to what effect? It begins by briefly outlining the origin and evolution of the disarmament mandate of the Secretariat and the Secretary-General, followed by a look at the UN machinery designed to fulfill this charge. Next, the chapter turns its attention to various structural changes within the Secretariat for addressing nuclear weapons issues that reflect the different priorities of successive secretaries-general. Following this examination of the Secretariat's institutional change, the chapter focuses on some specific approaches to disarmament offered by each of the secretaries-general. Finally, the chapter closes with some preliminary conclusions and offers a look ahead at three possible futures for the Secretariat in the field of disarmament.

Origin and evolution of the disarmament mandate

The mandates of the Secretary-General and the Secretariat derive first of all from the UN Charter. The Charter was adopted just weeks before the world's first nuclear test. Not surprisingly, the Charter does not contain the term "nuclear weapon" nor does it assign any specific mandate to the Secretary-General or the Secretariat for either "disarmament" or the "regulation of armaments" – both goals that are found in the Charter but that specifically apply to other UN organs.[4]

The five articles of Chapter XV relate to the work of the Secretariat. Under Article 97, the Secretary-General serves as the "chief administrative officer" of the UN organization. Article 98 acknowledges the need for a more flexible mandate by providing that he or she "shall perform such other functions" as the other UN organs may entrust to that office. Article 99 also authorizes the Secretary-General "to bring to the attention of the Security Council any matter which in his opinion may threaten the maintenance of international peace and security." Article 100 establishes the institutional independence of the Secretary-General and Secretariat and obliges each member state to respect their "exclusively international character." Article 101 pertains to the recruitment of staff, including the criteria of "efficiency, competence, and integrity" and geographic diversity.

Although the Charter does not define the terms "disarmament" and "regulation of armaments," their meanings have evolved through practice and customary use in the UN system. Disarmament refers to the elimination of an agreed class of weapon – a goal that the United Nations has specifically applied to all WMD – while "regulation of armaments" has evolved to encompass limits on the production, trade, or use of other types of weaponry.

Virtually throughout its existence, the United Nations has sought to eliminate nuclear weapons, not just to regulate them. The very first resolution adopted by the General Assembly on 24 January 1946 established a commission to "deal with the problems raised by the discovery of atomic energy and related matters," which would be accountable to the Security Council. The resolution identified the goal of eliminating all "weapons adaptable to mass destruction," a term covering nuclear, biological, and chemical weapons. The Council later adopted resolution 18 (13 February 1947), which established a UN Commission for Conventional Armaments, with a regulatory focus.

After neither commission, working in the early years of the Cold War, was able to arrive at a consensus, the General Assembly combined them (by adopting resolution 502(VI) on 11 January 1952) into the UN Disarmament Commission, also under the Security Council. This Commission had the mandate to prepare a draft treaty to eliminate WMD, to regulate and reduce other armaments, and to ensure the peaceful use of atomic energy. Following extensive but unsuccessful diplomatic efforts throughout the 1950s to achieve these goals – both within the Commission and separately among the great powers – the Assembly adopted a Soviet proposal (in resolution 1378, 20 November 1959) to combine the WMD disarmament and conventional arms regulation goals into a joint term – "general and complete disarmament under effective international control" – which has remained ever since the ultimate goal of the United Nations in this field.

The UN disarmament machinery and its mandates

The institutional structures of the United Nations have varied widely over the years. The current arrangement was largely a product of the General Assembly's first Special Session on Disarmament (SSOD-I) in 1978. Its final document (in General Assembly resolution S-10/2, 30 June 1978, referenced below by paragraph number) set forth a declaration of principles, a "programme of action," and a description of the relevant institutional machinery. Although the "ultimate objective" was "general and complete disarmament under effective international control" (para. 19), the document identified nuclear weapons as the first priority in disarmament negotiations (para. 45).

A key paragraph declared that the United Nations has "a central role and primary responsibility in the sphere of disarmament" and that it "should play a more active role in this field" (para. 114). The final document reasoned that, since "little progress has been made since the end of the Second World War," especially in nuclear disarmament, the solution lay in the following:

> In addition to the need to exercise political will, the international machinery should be utilized more effectively and also improved to enable implementation of the Programme of Action and help the United Nations to fulfil its role in the field of disarmament.... There is ... an urgent need that existing disarmament machinery be revitalized and forums appropriately constituted for disarmament deliberations and negotiations with a better representative character. (para. 113)

The new disarmament machinery would have its own division of labor, with the UN Disarmament Commission performing a purely deliberative role, the First Committee being responsible for preparing resolutions for adoption by the General Assembly, and the Committee (later Conference) on Disarmament serving as the world's "single multilateral disarmament negotiating forum" (para. 120).

Although the final document never referred explicitly to the "Secretariat" per se, it did identify many roles for the Secretary-General and the Centre for Disarmament. It stated that the Secretary-General "shall furnish such experts, staff and services as are necessary for the effective accomplishment of the Commission's functions" (para. 118d). It requested the Secretary-General "to appoint the Secretary of the Committee [on Disarmament], who shall also act as his personal representative, to assist the Committee and its Chairman in organizing the business and timetables of the Committee" (para. 120c). It also requested the Secretary-General "to set up an advisory board of eminent persons" to advise that office on UN studies on disarmament and arms regulation (para. 124).[5]

The Programme of Action also addressed the role of the Secretary-General in generating studies and reports and in preparing guidelines for the United Nations' program of fellowships on disarmament, which was created to train government officials, especially from developing countries. The final document stressed the roles of the Centre for Disarmament in gathering information and performing research and in coordinating with other offices in the UN system, as well as with intergovernmental and non-governmental organizations (NGOs).

Also considered at SSOD-I was a French proposal to establish an international institute for research on disarmament, which later evolved into the autonomous UN Institute for Disarmament Research based in Geneva.

The Secretariat has acquired many additional mandates pursuant to General Assembly resolutions and requests by states parties to multilateral disarmament and arms control treaties. Each year, the Secretary-General presents numerous reports to the Assembly on various disarmament issues, including reports of groups of governmental experts, statistical information, and, most commonly, reports conveying the views of member states, as requested by the General Assembly. In recent years, the Secretariat has launched a program on disarmament and non-proliferation education, which addresses a wide variety of issues relating to nuclear weapons (disarmament, non-proliferation, and counter-terrorism). It has for over three decades served as the de facto secretariat for the states parties to the Treaty on the Non-Proliferation of Nuclear Weapons (NPT) and has for over a decade promoted the entry into force of the Comprehensive Nuclear-Test-Ban Treaty (CTBT).

In summary, the Secretariat handles all *administrative* issues relating to disarmament in the UN organization. It serves an *advisory* function – primarily through the provision of information and advice to the Secretary-General and by assisting missions of the member states. It undertakes *research* and performs substantive analyses of policy issues, publishes reports and papers, and monitors worldwide developments. It also performs *advocacy* and *educational* functions.

Organizational change within the Secretariat

Just as the United Nations' mandates have varied over the years, so too have the structures of the Secretariat for addressing nuclear weapons issues. As the "chief administrative officer" of the United Nations under the Charter, the Secretary-General has some flexibility in organizing the Secretariat and, in fact, the organization of the Secretariat in disarmament often has reflected the personal priorities of the Secretary-General. Yet other organizational changes have been affected by the general climate of international relations outside the United Nations, including the status of relations between the great powers, especially the United States and the Russian Federation, which have the largest nuclear arsenals. There have also been organizational changes owing more to purely internal administrative factors. In short, organizational change in the United Nations is multi-causal – and determining the source of a specific institutional change often involves some educated guesses, because the full circumstances behind such changes are not always well documented.

The pattern of organizational change in the Secretariat in the field of disarmament does not fully conform to either of Hammarskjöld's classic models of "static conference machinery" or "dynamic instrument" of political initiative. One could say it has even merged these categories, reflecting at times a kind of "dynamic conference machinery" or a "static instrument." Beyond question, both the structures and the mandates have undergone some significant changes over the years and will likely continue to do so.

The Secretariat has undergone at least nine reorganizations in disarmament, under each Secretary-General with the exception of Hammarskjöld.

The first office in the Secretariat to handle nuclear weapons issues was the Atomic Energy Commission, located in the Department for Security Council Affairs, which was established in 1946. This group became the Disarmament Affairs Group in 1952 after the Commission was abolished, and remained in the newly named Department of Political and Security Council Affairs (DPSCA). The group's small staff of about 10 was organized into an Atomic Energy Section and a Conventional Arms Office.

Though this section was eliminated in 1964, the Disarmament Affairs Group remained responsible for handling nuclear weapons issues. This group became the Disarmament Affairs Division in 1966, though its staff remained quite small. From 1946 to 1976, the disarmament office had a staff of between 10 and 15 people, typically about one-third of whom were clerical.

In his report to the General Assembly on the work of the organization in 1975, Secretary-General Kurt Waldheim stressed the importance that the UN organization attaches to progress in disarmament:

> The long-term reason for the necessity of disarmament ... is that without it our Organization will not be able effectively to play its primary role – a role which in the present circumstances is vital to the survival of organized life on our planet.[6]

In that report, Waldheim concluded "the role which the United Nations is playing in disarmament is far from adequate" and called upon the Assembly to "consider a basic review of the role of the United Nations in disarmament."[7] On 12 December 1975, the General Assembly established an Ad Hoc Committee on the Review of the Role of the United Nations in the Field of Disarmament, with a focus on organizational issues, improvements in "the collection, compilation and dissemination of information," and assistance to states in ensuring the effective functioning of relevant multilateral agreements.[8] In June 1976, Waldheim issued a report elaborating on the need for reform, stressing the United Nations' need to improve its collection and use of information.[9]

The report of the Ad Hoc Committee, chaired by Inga Thorsson of Sweden, identified many proposed reforms, including several applying to the Secretariat.[10] It urged states participating in disarmament negotiations to "give serious consideration" to seeking assistance from the United Nations. It urged the General Assembly to call upon the

Secretary-General to undertake "in-depth studies of the arms race, disarmament and related matters," with the assistance of governmental experts and other sources. It called for the publication of a "United Nations Disarmament Yearbook" and a "disarmament periodical" reporting "current facts and developments" in the field, as well as "annotated bibliographies" and brief summaries of relevant books and articles.[11]

The report also recommended transforming the Disarmament Affairs Division into a "Centre" for Disarmament, endowed with these new or strengthened mandates. On 14 December 1976, the General Assembly adopted Sweden's resolution 31/90, which endorsed these proposals. For the first time, the Secretariat's top official handling disarmament held the rank of Assistant Secretary-General.[12]

The process of organizational reform continued over the years to follow, further raising the profile and status of disarmament in the Secretariat. As noted earlier, the SSOD-I assigned in 1978 a wide variety of responsibilities to the Centre, especially in terms of the public advocacy of disarmament. In 1979, the General Assembly adopted another Swedish resolution, this time requesting the Secretary-General to carry out a "comprehensive study assessing current institutional requirements and future estimated needs in the United Nations management of disarmament affairs."[13] The preamble provided the rationale for the new resolution, noting "the growing disarmament agenda," the "complexity of the issues involved," and the greater participation of states, which was creating "increasing demands" on the United Nations "for purposes such as the promotion, substantive preparation, implementation and control of the process of disarmament."

The study was prepared with the assistance of a group of experts chaired by Argentine Ambassador Carlos Ortiz de Rozas (who presided over SSOD-I).[14] Among other proposals, it supported a stronger role for the Assistant Secretary-General in coordinating disarmament activities in the UN system. It called upon the Secretary-General to consider "possibilities to strengthen" the Centre by giving it additional staff ("within the existing over-all resources" of the United Nations). It also cautiously proposed a possible UN role in verifying disarmament agreements. The group discussed restructuring proposals – including the options of creating a Department for Disarmament Affairs or a World Disarmament Agency – but "did not take a position of its own" on these proposals.[15] The study cautioned, "whatever the adequacy of the means provided by the United Nations in the service of the task of disarmament, it was ultimately the will of States to make the best use of them and their political readiness to negotiate which would determine how much progress was made in that regard."[16]

In 1982, the year Javier Pérez de Cuéllar became Secretary-General, the General Assembly made a new effort to advance organizational reforms in disarmament and raise its priority. The first event was the convening of the second General Assembly Special Session on Disarmament (SSOD-II), which was held from 7 June to 10 July. The session opened with several speeches about the dismal global situation for disarmament following SSOD-I, with many references to the nuclear arms race, rising military expenditures, and the failure to achieve much progress on the goals of the earlier special session.

Although the session did not achieve its primary purpose – to elaborate a Comprehensive Programme of Disarmament for implementing the recommendations of SSOD-I – it did launch a World Disarmament Campaign to "inform, to educate and to generate public understanding and support" for the goals agreed at SSOD-I.[17] The session's concluding document requested the Secretary-General "to make every effort" to promote these goals, but it provided no funds and instead urged the Secretary-General "to explore the possibilities of redeploying existing resources."[18]

With respect to the Secretariat, the annex of the concluding document contained several relevant – though not agreed upon – paragraphs that Working Group I had proposed for inclusion in the draft Comprehensive Programme of Disarmament. These included proposals for: a "Department for Disarmament Affairs"; an "international disarmament organization" under UN auspices with responsibilities that include verification of arms control and disarmament agreements; and a "United Nations Disarmament Agency."

On 13 December 1982, the General Assembly adopted resolution 37/99[K], which requested the Secretary-General to transform the Centre for Disarmament into a Department for Disarmament Affairs that would be "appropriately strengthened with the existing overall resources of the United Nations" and headed by an Under-Secretary-General.[19] This was the highest level that disarmament had ever been handled at within the Secretariat. The resolution was introduced by Norway on behalf of 42 delegations and was adopted without a vote, with the Soviet Union cautioning "against losing sight of the fact that the real reasons for the lack of progress in disarmament lay not in the organization of the work of the United Nations bodies, but in the willingness of certain major States to stop the arms race."[20] The Department of Disarmament Affairs (DDA) was officially established on 1 January 1983.[21]

The *Secretary-General's Bulletin* of 1 June 1983 spelled out the specific functions and structure of the new department.[22] Its functions were to assist and advise the Secretary-General on disarmament issues; provide administrative and substantive services to the various parts of the UN disarmament machinery and to facilitate coordination of activities therein; maintain liaison with other international organizations; coordinate the World Disarmament Campaign; administer the United Nations' program of fellowships on disarmament; and carry out any other tasks that might be assigned by the Secretary-General. Structurally, the department had an office of the Under-Secretary-General – with formal management, policy advice, coordinating, liaison, and analytic responsibilities – as well as three branches: the committee and conference services branch; the information and studies branch; and the Geneva branch.

This structure would soon expand, especially to focus on regional issues. In 1984, the General Assembly asked the Secretary-General to assist member states in the various regions to participate in the World Disarmament Campaign (resolution 39/63[J], 12 December 1984). A year later, the Assembly established the UN Regional Centre for Peace and Disarmament in Africa (resolution 40/151[G], 16 December 1985), and in 1986 it created the UN Regional Centre for Peace, Disarmament and Development in Latin America, later expanded to include the Caribbean.[23] The following year, the General Assembly established the UN Regional Centre for Peace and Disarmament in Asia, later expanded to include the Pacific.[24]

All these resolutions provided, however, that their funds would have to come from "existing resources" and "voluntary contributions." In practical terms, this required the DDA and the Centres to devote considerable effort to fund-raising activities. Although none of these resolutions specifically put these Centres in the DDA, they provided the Secretary-General flexibility to do so and this is where they were placed.

By 1988, the DDA had four branches – the committee and conference services branch; the publications and World Disarmament Campaign branch; the monitoring, analysis and studies branch; and the Geneva branch, in addition to the three regional Centres.[25] It was still, however, the smallest department in the Secretariat.

Coinciding with these developments were growing concerns of member states about the growth and effectiveness of the UN bureaucracy in general. In 1986, a High-Level Group of Intergovernmental Experts issued a report that included recommendations for a "substantial reduction in the number of staff members" as well as for the merger of "departments, offices and other units" when consolidation would improve the efficiency of the organization.[26]

There was little apparent desire among member states, however, to reduce or eliminate the DDA on grounds of inefficiency or over-growth. In June 1990, the Disarmament Commission completed a review of the role of the United Nations in disarmament and concluded that the Secretary-General "should be assisted by an adequately staffed and funded" DDA.[27] The report said that the DDA's resources should be "commensurate with" its mandated tasks "in so far as" UN budget restraints would permit. It also called for the coordinating role of the DDA vis-à-vis other UN activities and relevant specialized agencies to "be strengthened."

By 1991, the DDA had 30 staff members at the professional level or higher and an annual regular budget of just over US$5 million.[28] It continued to acquire new missions and mandates, without additional funding. Following the war in 1991 to expel Iraq from Kuwait, the Security Council established the United Nations Special Commission (UNSCOM) on Iraq, pursuant to resolution 687.[29] This resolution required the Secretary-General to develop and submit to the Council a plan to accomplish several tasks, including: the creation of the Special Commission to carry out on-site inspection of prohibited weapon capabilities in Iraq; the development of measures by which Iraq would turn over to the Commission prohibited items "for destruction, removal or rendering harmless"; and assistance and cooperation between the Commission and the International Atomic Energy Agency (IAEA) in accomplishing the nuclear disarmament of Iraq.[30]

The Secretariat played a significant role in the planning and setting up of UNSCOM, and although UNSCOM and its successor, the United Nations Monitoring, Verification and Inspection Commission (UNMOVIC), were almost entirely staffed by personnel recruited from outside the Secretariat, the Secretariat did provide the commissions with several professional and general service staff members to assist their work.[31] A member of the Secretariat also served as a member of UNMOVIC's College of Commissioners, which was appointed by the Secretary-General after consultations with the Security Council.[32] Both commissions were funded by Iraq, not the regular UN budget.

The arrival of Boutros Boutros-Ghali as Secretary-General in January 1992 began a period of decline for disarmament in the Secretariat. His new spokesman announced on 7 February that the new Secretary-General would soon be implementing a major organizational reform of the Secretariat, one that would abolish several high-level posts and eliminate several departments, including the DDA, whose staff and mandates would merge into a new Department of Political Affairs (DPA).[33] The spokesman said the intent was to "streamline" the Secretariat and make it "more efficient and more economical." Yet on the cost issue, he also said "I don't know about savings," adding that the purpose of the reform was not to save money but to "improve the bureaucracy."[34]

The announcement came on 21 February, when Boutros-Ghali issued a *Note* expressing his intention "to consolidate and streamline" the United Nations in an effort that would include moving the DDA into the new DPA.[35] He pointed to the summit meeting of the Security Council on

31 January 1992, where the members at the level of heads of state and government issued a presidential statement stressing the importance of enhancing the United Nations' capacity for preventive diplomacy, peacemaking, and peacekeeping. Implicitly, the *Note* viewed the function of disarmament as belonging in a department with a mandate in such fields as conflict resolution and the peaceful settlement of disputes. The first phase of the reform would be effective from 1 March 1992.[36] On 2 March, the General Assembly adopted a resolution approving the Secretary-General's proposal, which it called "a vital part of the reform and revitalization of the United Nations."[37]

NGOs appeared to be somewhat surprised by the reform, but initially at least did not vigorously oppose it. In May, the newspaper *Disarmament Times* – issued by the NGO Committee on Disarmament, Peace, and Security – published an interview with former veteran Soviet diplomat Vladimir Petrovsky, the DPA's new Under-Secretary-General with the dossier for disarmament. He said the new disarmament office occupied a "prominent place" in the DPA and that it "has become a part of the political work of the UN Secretariat," adding that the reform "helps to make the work of the Office much more action-oriented and synchronized with the activities of the UN in other areas, especially preventive diplomacy and peacemaking."[38]

In June 1992, Boutros-Ghali issued a report requested in January just after he assumed his position by the Security Council – *An Agenda for Peace* – which focused at length on preventive diplomacy, peacemaking, and peacekeeping, but which made only a brief passing reference to disarmament.[39] In July, the Secretary-General issued his programme budget for the biennium 1992–1993, which indicated a budget reduction of over US$600,000 for disarmament and a reduction of two high-level posts in this area.[40]

Disarmament Times later asked Petrovsky to comment on the treatment of disarmament in *An Agenda for Peace*. His response was that disarmament was outside the mandate of the report, and that it was an issue that "should be treated as a kind of associated measure with preventive diplomacy, peace-making, and peace-keeping."[41] The newspaper also noted that the Secretary-General's 1992 report on the work of the organization, departing from tradition, failed to make any reference to disarmament.[42]

In October 1992, Boutros-Ghali issued *New Dimensions of Arms Regulation and Disarmament in the Post-Cold War Era*, which addressed disarmament issues.[43] The report's preface called disarmament "an inherent part of preventive diplomacy, peacemaking, peace-keeping and peace-building." It added that the end of strategic bipolarity "has not diminished the need for disarmament; if anything, it has increased it."

At the General Assembly First Committee's special meeting on the Secretary-General's new report on 11 November, Under-Secretary-General Petrovsky stated that, to achieve "genuine disarmament," it must be integrated into the "broader structure of an international system of peace and security, along with economic and social concerns."[44] He admitted "quite frankly" that "we do not have any ready-made recipes for the reorganization of the multilateral machinery for disarmament" and that our "only strong intention ... is to strengthen the Office for Disarmament Affairs [ODA] ... as a focal point of the Secretariat in this field."

On 9 December, the General Assembly decided to convene a special meeting of the First Committee from 8 to 12 March 1993 to reassess the multilateral arms control and disarmament machinery.[45] The Secretary-General addressed the First Committee at its meeting on 9 March 1993 and drew upon the themes of his *New Dimensions* report, stressing that the "Secretariat's capabilities are being strengthened," adding that he was also "considering a proposal to relocate units of the Office of Disarmament Affairs to Geneva."[46] On 8 April, the Assembly adopted a resolution urging the Secretary-General "to take concrete steps to strengthen the Office for Disarmament Affairs in order to ensure that it has the necessary means to carry out its mandated tasks."[47] During the debate, the NGO Committee on Disarmament, Peace, and Security sent a letter to the Secretary-General opposing any move of the ODA to Geneva, calling for greater NGO participation in the UN disarmament machinery, and supporting "an over all strengthening of the UN Secretariat resources devoted to disarmament."[48] Many member states also opposed this restructuring.

On 20 September 1993, the Secretary-General informed the General Assembly that the ODA would remain in New York and the office would be renamed the Centre for Disarmament Affairs and headed by a director at an upgraded D-2 level.[49] He also indicated that he would be adding to his budget proposal for the biennium 1994–1995 additions to cover two new posts in the conventional arms area and one additional general service staff for the new Centre.

The Secretary-General issued a formal amendment to the United Nations' *Organization Manual* on 15 February 1996 to describe the new Centre's functions and structure.[50] In this scheme, "the Centre, reporting directly to the Under-Secretary-General for Political Affairs, is responsible for the provision of advice to the Secretary-General" on disarmament issues. The Centre's key functions largely reflected those of the department that preceded it.

Less than a year later, in January 1997, Kofi Annan became Secretary-General and soon indicated his intention to reorganize the Secretariat once again in the field of disarmament. His initial proposal appeared in a lengthy report – *Renewing the United Nations* – which identified broader reforms in the organization of the Secretariat.[51] He indicated his intention to create a "Department for Disarmament and Arms Regulation, headed by an under-secretary-general." He reasoned that disarmament "is a central issue on the global agenda" and that, in the post–Cold War era, the United Nations "has taken centre stage in the worldwide effort to limit both weapons and conflict." He underlined some new or growing threats, including the proliferation of "nuclear weapons technology and material" and the interest of "criminal syndicates and various terrorist groups" in acquiring weapons of mass destruction. On 11 September, he submitted a budget report on his reforms, which included the creation of a new disarmament department with 41 employees and a proposed 1998–1999 biennium budget of just over US$12 million, an increase over the US$10.8 million spent in the 1996–1997 biennium.[52]

Later that month, the NGO Committee on Disarmament, Peace, and Security – then representing some 250 NGOs worldwide – circulated its own resolution, which welcomed the creation of the new department and strongly urged all member states to support it.[53] The US ambassador to the United Nations at the time, Bill Richardson, had circulated a memo on 25 August stating the following about re-establishing the DDA: "While our opposition to this step was conveyed to the secretary-general, we recognize the decision was within his prerogatives and will work with him to ensure the Department will function effectively and efficiently."[54]

In October, Annan issued an "addendum" to *Renewing the United Nations*, focusing specifically on disarmament.[55] He said that nuclear disarmament must "be pursued more vigorously" and that WMD issues "continue to be of primary importance." In November, the General Assembly adopted a resolution that welcomed and commended the Secretary-General's reform initiative (resolution 52/12, 12 November 1997).

At a press briefing on 14 January 1998, the Secretary-General announced the appointment of Jayantha Dhanapala, the Sri Lankan diplomat who had served as president of the 1995 NPT Review and Extension Conference, as the new Under-Secretary-General for Disarmament Affairs. In May, Annan issued the formal description of the functions and structure of the DDA, having dropped "and Arms Regulation" from its original title.[56] The new Department would have 17 enumerated functions, which resembled many of those performed by the previous Department and Centre. The functions included promoting "the goal of nuclear disarmament with a view to progressive reductions in nuclear weapons and their complete elimination at the earliest possible date." In addition to the office of the Under-Secretary-General, there were to be five branches: weapons of mass destruction; conventional arms; monitoring, database, and information; regional disarmament; and the Conference on Disarmament (the Geneva branch) – plus the three regional Centres. Annan informed the General Assembly in 1998 that "my vision of the Organization places disarmament near the centre of its mission of peace and development."[57] He later added that "Disarmament is a critical element of the United Nations strategy for peace and security."[58]

In March 1999, the Secretariat's Office of Internal Oversight Services issued the results of an "in-depth evaluation" of the United Nations' disarmament program.[59] It found that, although delegations were "generally satisfied" with the DDA's support to multilateral bodies, the Department had various "shortcomings" that were "partly, but not entirely" due to a 22 percent decrease in regular budget funds since 1992 (when the DDA was moved into the DPA) and a significant drop in extra-budgetary funds (from US$6.3 million in 1990–1991 to US$1.4 million in 1996–1997).[60]

The Secretary-General issued a new *Bulletin* describing the functions and structure of the ODA in 2004, with the structure of the Department remaining unchanged from the last *Bulletin* issued in 1998.[61] Its norm-creation function in disarmament was somewhat expanded to cover "promoting, strengthening and consolidating such norms and agreements in all the fields of disarmament." Its role vis-à-vis nuclear weapons moved slightly from a specific function concerning the promotion of nuclear disarmament (1998) to promoting multilateral disarmament efforts and the non-proliferation of all WMD and "in particular nuclear weapons." A new function was added: promoting gender-related policies – a role stemming from the Department's "gender mainstreaming action plan" launched by Dhanapala in 2003.

The office of the Under-Secretary-General, instead of "preparing reports and notes," would henceforth provide "authoritative analysis and assessment" of disarmament issues. The WMD branch was also given the responsibility to handle the issue of WMD delivery systems.[62]

The DDA worked hard to promote the negotiation of a nuclear-weapon-free zone in Central Asia, the first such zone entirely north of the equator. In 2002, Dhanapala visited all five states – meeting with all five foreign ministers and three presidents – to promote such a zone. The DDA's Asia Pacific Regional Centre worked for many years to promote the negotiation of a treaty. In their press release issued upon signing the treaty in September 2006, the Central Asian states thanked the United Nations, "which has directly participated, for the first time ever, in drawing up and agreeing on a draft treaty on a nuclear-weapon-free zone."[63]

The DDA's mandates and responsibilities in the field of nuclear non-proliferation have long been focused on its role as the de facto secretariat of the NPT. The DDA's role expanded after the Security Council's adoption of resolution 1540 on 28 April 2004, which required all states to prohibit the proliferation or terrorist acquisition of any weapons of mass destruction.[64] Yet the DDA has had essentially no direct involvement in handling either the Iranian or North Korean nuclear issues in the last several years – these issues have been handled by small groups of states working outside the United Nations, with the exception of the Security Council in terms of its role in adopting sanctions resolutions.

Although Ban Ki-moon rarely spoke on nuclear disarmament before becoming Secretary-General in 2007, he came to office with more personal experience in dealing with nuclear weapons issues than any of his predecessors. He had participated in the Six-Party Talks over North Korea's nuclear weapons program, and had served in 1999 as Chairman of the Preparatory Commission for the CTBT Organization. He had also been vice chair of the South-North Joint Nuclear Control Commission following the Joint Declaration of the Denuclearization of the Korean Peninsula in 1992.

In an interview shortly before being elected Secretary-General, he said his "highest priority" would be reforms of the United Nations, adding that "I will try to change the whole mind-set of the United Nations secretariat."[65] Citing UN sources, Reuters reported that one reform under consideration would be to "combine the existing disarmament and political affairs departments and put them under one undersecretary-general who would also be responsible for leading anti-terrorism programs."[66]

On 16 January 2007, the first press reports appeared that the Secretary-General intended to "downgrade" disarmament in the Secretariat by moving it back into the DPA.[67] Representatives of several NGOs – including the Lawyers' Committee on Nuclear Policy, the International Peace Bureau, and Reaching Critical Will – immediately criticized the proposal.[68]

These criticisms were joined by concerns from the UN diplomatic community.[69] Noting that an American was likely to be the new head of the DPA, one ambassador from the 166-member Non-aligned Movement (NAM) said: "Having an American as head is like putting the fox in charge of the chicken coop." An Asian diplomat called the move "a retrograde step," regardless of who would head the DPA, adding that "We will only be repeating the blunder that Boutros Ghali made and which Kofi rectified." He also said that "[b]urying disarmament in the department of political affairs will kill it, and especially so under a US national as its head."

A proposal was reported on 18 January to keep the DDA intact but place it under the leadership of an Assistant Secretary-General, a rank lower than Under-Secretary-General.[70] The report noted that the proposal was "not likely to fly" given the NAM's preference for leaving the DDA "virtually untouched."

The concerns or outright opposition voiced by the NGOs, the NAM, the 130-member Group of 77 (G-77), and several other delegations (including Austria, Denmark, Japan, New Zealand, Norway, and Sweden) indicated that the proposal was clearly in trouble. As early as 19 January, the Associated Press reported that the Secretary-General had "dropped" the proposal to merge the two departments "because of opposition from a powerful bloc of developing countries."[71]

The report described a meeting between Vijay Nambiar, the Secretary-General's Chef de Cabinet, and the NAM's "troika" (Malaysia, Cuba, and Egypt – NAM's past, current, and future chairs, respectively), at which Nambiar proposed that the DDA would keep its structure but become part of the office of the Secretary-General and be headed by an Assistant Secretary-General "who would be the special representative" for disarmament. Ambassador Maged Abdelaziz of Egypt later warned that the merger would result in "overpoliticization ... particularly if somebody from a nuclear weapons state will occupy the Department of Political Affairs"; he added that the move would "affect the balance between nuclear disarmament and non-proliferation."[72] A representative of Zimbabwe later questioned the motivation for the proposal: "was it a problem of structure which prevented us from making progress on disarmament or was it a more substantive problem?"[73]

On 23 January, *Terra Viva* reported that the Secretary-General was making the reform proposal because he wanted to keep disarmament "closer to him."[74] The article quoted one NAM ambassador as saying the various non-papers were "still vague on details and on reporting lines"; he asked, "why not keep things as they are?" Meanwhile, the article reported that several NGOs "have launched a campaign" against dismantling the DDA.

Other concerns were registered from an unexpected quarter: US Congressmen Ed Markey and Christopher Shays, co-chairs of the Bipartisan Task Force on Nonproliferation in the US House of Representatives, sent the Secretary-General a letter voicing their concerns about reports that the DDA would be "downgraded."[75] In a statement reminiscent of Hammarskjöld's "dynamic instrument" metaphor, they called the DDA "a crucial tool to help the world eliminate weapons of mass destruction and halt illegal arms trafficking."

On 26 January, Reuters reported that it had acquired a UN memo indicating that the DDA would be reorganized into an Office (which the article claimed "carries less weight") that would be headed by a "high representative" reporting directly to the Secretary-General.[76] Included in the rationale for the change was the need for "a greater role and personal involvement" of the Secretary-General in handling disarmament issues.

Reuters reported on 29 January that another motive for the change was that it would enable the Secretary-General "not to increase the number of undersecretaries-general."[77] The report also noted continuing concerns within the NAM, including South Africa's UN Ambassador Dumisani Kumalo and Pakistani Ambassador Munir Akram, the chair of the G-77. One European diplomat later warned that the proposal faced a "death of 1,000 meetings."[78] At a closed-door meeting of the G-77 on 30 January, several states reportedly voiced their concerns over the proposal, including the lack of consultation.[79] The report quoted one South Asian ambassador as saying, "The secretary-general is not the King, and the Secretariat is not the King's court."

The Secretary-General addressed the General Assembly on 5 February and explained his proposal. He highlighted "the need to revitalize the disarmament agenda, through a more focused effort."[80] This requires "sustained and determined leadership at the highest level" and the new Office would therefore have a "direct line to me, thus ensuring access and more frequent interaction." He said that disarmament was "an integral part of the policy decision-making process at the highest level." The Office would be headed "by an SRSG [Special Representative of the Secretary-General] or High Representative" to "maximize the flexibility, agility, and proximity to the Secretary-General" and to permit "a strengthened advocacy role." The Office would keep the DDA's mandates.

There were in this period some reports that the United States was behind the disarmament reform initiative. Inter Press claimed that the United States provided the "strongest support" for the proposal.[81] The Associated Press had earlier cited "U.N. diplomats" as claiming that "Washington has been lobbying for disarmament to be added to the job [at the DPA]."[82] These reports, however, did not provide any evidence to document such claims.

On 6 February, UN spokesperson Michele Montas told reporters that the Secretary-General "had adjusted his proposals in accordance with their concerns" and that "he does not want to downgrade disarmament."[83] The next day, 12 NGOs addressed a joint letter to all 192 permanent missions to the United Nations in support of keeping an independent department with its own mandate and Under-Secretary-General.[84]

On 15 February, the Secretary-General sent a letter to the president of the General Assembly containing a detailed description of the roles and structure of the new Office for Disarmament Affairs, which indicated that there would no downgrading of either.[85] The main change would be in the greater role and personal involvement of the Secretary-General in revitalizing the international disarmament and non-proliferation agenda. In his address the next day to the General Assembly, he stated that, "having heard strong views from member states," he was "ready to propose that the high representative would be appointed at the rank of under-secretary-general."[86]

The reform effort came to closure on 15 March, when the General Assembly formally endorsed the Secretary-General's plan to establish the Office for Disarmament Affairs, headed by a High Representative with the rank of Under-Secretary-General, and maintaining the Office's "budgetary autonomy" and existing structures and functions (resolution 61/257, 15 March 2007). On 2 July, the Secretary-General announced the appointment of Sergio de Queiroz Duarte, a widely respected Brazilian diplomat and former president of the 2005 NPT Review Conference, as the High Representative for Disarmament Affairs.[87]

Some specific approaches to disarmament offered by the secretaries-general

The discussion thus far has focused on organizational mandates and structures. Yet there has also been some considerable variation in specific approaches offered by the secretaries-general to address nuclear challenges.

Trygve Lie

Negotiation on this problem [nuclear disarmament] should not be deferred until the other great political problems are solved, but should go hand-in-hand with any effort to reach political settlements.

Trygve Lie, "Twenty-Year Programme for Achieving Peace through the United Nations" (1950)

On 6 June 1950, days before the start of the Korean war, Lie sent a memorandum to all UN member states containing his "Twenty-Year Programme for Achieving Peace through the United Nations."[88] In this document, he suggested that the Security Council could "instruct" the Secretary-General to "call a conference of scientists," which would serve as a "reservoir of ideas" on the control of WMD and the promotion of peaceful uses of atomic energy. He called for an "interim agreement" to halt "an unlimited atomic arms race."

Dag Hammarskjöld

Now there is, of course, a kind of shuttle traffic between the improvement in the international atmosphere and disarmament. On the one hand ... disarmament is not likely to come about in an efficient, effective way short of a further improvement in the international situation. On the other hand, I do not think any single policy move will contribute more to an improvement in the international atmosphere than an agreement on even the most modest step in the direction of disarmament.
Dag Hammarskjöld, Press Conference, Prague, 7 July 1956

Hammarskjöld had a distinctly analytical approach to disarmament – he understood the value of breaking the disarmament challenge down into its components and making progress by working with these parts:

> [B]y isolating certain non-political, scientific elements from the politically controversial elements in the total problem of disarmament, the area of conflict has been somewhat reduced ... [I]t may be worth considering whether those elements of the problem lending themselves to objective study by experts in science and technology, in military experience, and in law might not be singled out for separate treatment.[89]

He referred to disarmament as a "hardy perennial" at the United Nations, stressing its importance but recognizing that it would take time to achieve.[90]

During his tenure, he called upon the Security Council to request the Secretary-General to prepare a "technical and scientific study of an international control system for the suspension of nuclear tests."[91] A conference of experts did in fact occur in July–August 1958 on this issue, and resulted in a consensus that it was indeed possible to verify a test ban. Hammarskjöld suggested that the Council might sponsor the idea of "a summit meeting on disarmament," a proposal not implemented.[92]

He viewed disarmament not as an issue exclusively for the attention of the great powers, but, as Brian Urquhart once put it, as a "central preoccupation of the UN."[93] Speaking to both UK Houses of Parliament in 1958, Hammarskjöld said: "It is obvious that controlled disarmament will be possible only through the United Nations, because any disarmament system has to be adopted and administered by a world organization whose members include practically all nations of the world."[94] He was critical of the establishment in 1959 of the Ten-Nation Committee on Disarmament, which was outside the United Nations, and his criticisms led to a four-power communiqué stressing that the Committee "in no way diminishes or encroaches upon the UN responsibilities in this field."[95] During the negotiations in 1955 to establish the IAEA, he sought to ensure that the new agency would be closely linked to the United Nations.[96]

He was the only Secretary-General not to reorganize the Secretariat in the field of disarmament. In his words, "[o]rganizational arrangements ... do not change realities ... Essential difficulties encountered within the UN are based on realities and not on the specific constitution of the Organization."[97]

Ironically, three days after his death, the United States and the Soviet Union issued a joint statement of agreed principles on general and complete disarmament.[98]

U Thant

It is not by force of nature but by his own will that man finds himself engaged in a race between building a better world and destroying an imperfect one.
U Thant, *Report of the Secretary-General on the Work of the Organization* (1965)

Like his predecessor, U Thant did not believe that nuclear disarmament was the business only of the nuclear powers.[99] He once said: "The hydrogen bomb is a greater evil than any evil it is intended to meet."[100] Thant believed that the United Nations' new majority of developing countries had an important role to play in promoting progress in disarmament. He featured disarmament issues prominently in virtually all of his *Reports on the Work of the Organization*, though he was never satisfied with the United Nations' progress in the field, saying in his 1966 report that the United Nations "has devoted a great deal of time and discussion to disarmament. The results so far are extremely meagre."[101]

Thant was perhaps the first Secretary-General to call for the "reduction and elimination of vehicles for the delivery of nuclear weapons"[102] and to call for steps to "halt the proliferation of nuclear Powers and weapons."[103] He successfully proposed that the General Assembly declare the 1970s a "Disarmament Decade."[104] He asked the Assembly to request "a comprehensive international expert study be undertaken of the economic and social consequences of the arms race and massive military expenditures."[105] He stated that "[t]he time has come to inquire whether the United Nations should not be officially informed about the progress of the arms limitation discussions."[106] Before leaving office, he said he had "often felt the need for more scientific advice and assistance" on nuclear disarmament issues.[107]

Thant has received little credit for his contributions in helping to resolve the Cuban missile crisis. As documented by Walter Dorn, Thant advanced the idea of trading a US no-invasion pledge in exchange for the withdrawal of the Soviet missiles. Dorn argues persuasively that Thant "helped the superpowers to pull back from nuclear annihilation."[108]

Kurt Waldheim

The long-term reason for the necessity of disarmament ... is that without it our Organization will not be able effectively to play its primary role – a role which in the present circumstances is vital to the survival of organized life on our planet.
Kurt Waldheim, *Introduction to the Report of the Secretary-General on the Work of the Organization* (1975)

Kurt Waldheim is seldom recognized for his efforts to promote disarmament, but he made many such efforts – it would scarcely be fair to portray the expansion of nuclear arsenals in the 1970s as somehow his fault.

Waldheim consistently devoted vast portions of his annual *Reports on the Work of the Organization* to disarmament. He once observed: "Disarmament ... has from the outset been a major objective of the United Nations and has represented, in terms of effort, perhaps the most continuous activity of the United Nations."[109] Waldheim believed that "[t]he maintenance of international peace and security, which is the primary objective of the United Nations, depends to a great degree on major progress in the field of disarmament."[110] He said that "the United Nations cannot hope to function effectively on the basis of the Charter unless there is major progress in the field of disarmament."[111] He stressed that "the interest of the United Nations, and the international community as a whole, in these issues is not merely that of a passive spectator."[112]

He expanded the United Nations' role in undertaking research, in providing information to the public on disarmament (including through publication of the *United Nations Disarmament Yearbook* and the periodical *Disarmament*), and in promoting public education in disarmament.[113] He sent numerous reports to the General Assembly on many disarmament issues, ranging from the social and economic effects of the arms race to weapons in outer space.

Waldheim also contributed to the institutional development of the United Nations in disarmament. He persuaded the General Assembly to create an "advisory board" to provide counsel to the Secretary-General. He elevated the status of the DPSCA's Disarmament Affairs Division to a Centre for Disarmament headed, for the first time, by an Assistant Secretary-General. Waldheim persistently advocated a comprehensive nuclear test ban and was the first Secretary-General to stress the dangers of plutonium recovered from power reactors.[114] He was also the first to propose the establishment of regional or international fuel cycle centers.[115]

By 1980, his concern grew over the lack of progress in disarmament after the historic SSOD-I in 1978. At the United Nations, he said, "disarmament activities seem to remain largely confined to organizational and procedural matters rather than substantive ones."[116] In his last year in office, he called for greater attention to the fears and suspicions that stand as obstacles to disarmament.[117] He was one of the few secretaries-general to write at length on disarmament in his memoirs, devoting a chapter to the subject, which concluded:

> The lack of success in the disarmament process is not due to the occasionally cumbersome UN machinery or the often emotional and protracted debates in its fora. The United Nations is as good or bad as its members permit it to be. The lack of success is due simply to the attitude of the major parties, which currently lack the political will to take advantage of the international machinery at their disposal for the disarmament process.[118]

Javier Pérez de Cuéllar

It is my belief that nothing poses a greater threat to the international community than the continuing arms race, above all, the nuclear arms race.
Javier Pérez de Cuéllar,
Address to the General Assembly, 12 December 1984

In the history of disarmament at the United Nations, Pérez de Cuéllar will perhaps be most remembered for his role in converting the DPSCA's Centre for Disarmament into the Department of Disarmament Affairs. He was Secretary-General during two Special Sessions of the General Assembly on disarmament (in 1982 and 1988). He stated in 1986: "As long as they exist, nuclear weapons will entail the risk of totally unacceptable destruction to life and to human achievement."[119] In his first annual report to the General Assembly on the work of the organization, he said that the world is "perilously near to a new international anarchy" and that "it is imperative for the United Nations to dispel that sense of insecurity through joint and agreed action in the field of disarmament, especially nuclear disarmament."[120]

Like Thant and Waldheim, Pérez de Cuéllar often stressed the impact of arms races on social and economic development. He opened SSOD-II by observing that "it is ironic that the accumulation of arms is one of the few expanding industries in a period of economic depression and gloom," adding that "the arms race represents an abdication of our responsibilities for human welfare, a perversion of ingenuity and an offence against the dignity of man."[121]

He often stressed the potential role of the United Nations in the field of verification. In his opening address to SSOD-III, he identified verification as "an area in which the United Nations might be able to make an important contribution," and he added that it might be "possible in the future to create, under its auspices, verification machinery."[122] In 1990, he submitted to the General Assembly a major study on verification.[123] He also highlighted this issue in his reports on the work of the organization from 1985 through 1988.

Like Waldheim, Pérez de Cuéllar submitted many other studies to the Assembly – all together, he submitted 24 such reports during his tenure on nuclear-related subjects ranging from issues in specific countries (e.g. Israel and South Africa) to options for unilateral nuclear disarmament. He stressed the importance of the World Disarmament Campaign in raising public awareness, and once proposed the establishment of a "multilateral nuclear alert centre."[124]

Also like Waldheim, Pérez de Cuéllar believed that real progress on nuclear disarmament required progress in détente and in nuclear reductions by the United States and the Soviet Union. He said in his 1983 annual report on the work of the organization that "the key to its solution is in the hands of the two major nuclear Powers," a theme repeated in his 1984 report.[125] Yet he also said that "a durable improvement in international relations depends on the success of the United Nations in discharging its mandate in this field [of disarmament]."[126]

In his last year, and anticipating changes to come during the tenure of Boutros-Ghali, he said the United Nations must "weave collective approaches in this field more tightly into the fabric of peace-making and conflict control."[127] He also noted the important role of the Secretariat in organizing regional and interregional meetings on disarmament issues.[128]

It is curious that, despite his great interest in the issue, he never discussed any disarmament issues in his memoirs.[129]

Boutros Boutros-Ghali

It is my belief ... that the full array of hazards posed to humanity by these weapons cannot be adequately dealt with until we have crossed the threshold of the post-nuclear-weapon age.
Boutros Boutros-Ghali, *New Dimensions of Arms Regulation and Disarmament in the Post-Cold War Era* (1992)

Boutros-Ghali came to office in 1992 with two very distinct goals in mind with respect to disarmament, one organizational, the other substantive. His organizational goal was achieved in 1992 when he downgraded the Department of Disarmament Affairs to an Office within the DPA, as described earlier in this chapter. His substantive goal was essentially to re-conceptualize disarmament, by framing it as an issue that was subordinate to the larger problem of the peaceful resolution of disputes, which may help to explain why he failed to mention disarmament in his first annual report on the work of the organization.

His early focus was clearly on administrative reforms; as he said in his memoirs, the United Nations was in a "financial crisis" and the Secretariat was "bloated, slack, and out of touch."[130]

He recognized, however, that arms have their own destabilizing effects. In his *New Dimensions* report, he observed: "The relentless accumulation of armaments by States is not only a symptom of political tension; it can also cause and heighten such tensions and increase the risk of conflict."[131] He said that "the international community can aim for no less a goal than the complete elimination of nuclear weapons."[132] He also called for stronger nuclear non-proliferation efforts, and particularly for controls over "long-range delivery systems" and "dual-use technology."[133] He repeated this emphasis on non-proliferation in his 1996 annual report on the work of the organization, saying that "efforts towards the ultimate goal of total nuclear disarmament go hand in hand with efforts to ensure the non-proliferation of other weapons of mass destruction."[134]

His memoirs, however, scarcely mention disarmament.

Kofi Annan

The continued existence of nuclear stockpiles leaves the shadow of nuclear war hanging over our world – particularly given the existence of clandestine networks dealing in nuclear materials and the prospect of terrorists with extreme ambitions gaining access to these materials.

Kofi Annan, Message presented at the
Peace Memorial Ceremony in Hiroshima, 6 August 2004

Kofi Annan was certainly not the first Secretary-General to emphasize the close relationship between disarmament and non-proliferation as multilateral policy objectives, but he devoted more effort than the others to elaborating on this theme.

He also concluded that the NPT is facing a twin "crisis of confidence" stemming from insufficient progress on both disarmament and non-proliferation. More than any previous Secretary-General, he framed the "compliance" issue as applying to not just non-proliferation but also disarmament – the world was, he feared, "sleepwalking" toward a nuclear disaster.[135] He warned that the chronic stalemate in multilateral nuclear diplomacy has resulted in "mutually assured paralysis."[136] Paralleling such concerns, a group of seven middle-power states called the New Agenda Coalition (NAC) pressed forward in both NPT settings and the First Committee with specific disarmament proposals.[137]

Annan's legacy in this field will also be shaped by his role in raising the priority of other related issues, most notably missile proliferation[138] and

WMD terrorism, especially in implementing the UN Global Counter-Terrorism Strategy adopted by the General Assembly in 2006 (resolution 60/288, 8 September 2006) and in underscoring the reality of the threat of nuclear terrorism.[139]

Annan stressed the importance of the UN disarmament machinery, but warned that it was showing signs of "rust," which he called "a problem due not to the machinery itself but to the apparent lack of political will to use it."[140] As for the Secretariat, he defended his decision to re-establish the Department of Disarmament Affairs, saying in 1997 that "I think it was a mistake to have downgraded disarmament. I think disarmament is one of the crucial issues of our day and I am correcting that mistake."[141]

Annan viewed the "essential role" of the United Nations in disarmament as "one of norm-setting and of strengthening and consolidating multilateral principles for disarmament."[142] His tenure reflected the intention to strengthen those norms and the role of the United Nations in advancing them.

Ban Ki-moon

[R]evitalizing the international disarmament agenda, and the United Nations' own effectiveness in this area, has been a personal priority of mine from my very first day in office.

Ban Ki-moon, Remarks to the Advisory Board
on Disarmament Matters, 18 July 2007

There is much continuity apparent in the approach to disarmament taken by Kofi Annan and his successor, Ban Ki-moon, as well as some nuances of change. Annan's valedictory speech on disarmament referred to nuclear weapons as presenting "a unique existential threat to all humanity,"[143] and Ban stated in one of his inaugural addresses that "weapons of mass destruction ... present a unique existential threat to all humanity."[144] Both came to office intent on "revitalizing" the disarmament agenda and the United Nations' role in advancing it. Both voiced their concerns over the "crisis of confidence" facing the NPT.

In terms of their vision of the role of the Secretariat, Ban is much closer to Annan than to Boutros-Ghali, who downgraded disarmament by cutting its staff and budget, ending its institutional autonomy, and even omitting the issue from key publications. By contrast, the 2008 Office for Disarmament Affairs had the same budget, personnel, mandates, and institutional autonomy as the former Department; its High Representative retained the rank of Under-Secretary-General, with a position on the United Nations' high-level Policy Committee; and the Secretary-General repeatedly voiced his personal determination to give disarmament a higher priority.

Some preliminary conclusions and a look ahead

The conclusions of this analysis are only preliminary, since the role of the United Nations in disarmament is continuing to evolve, virtually on a daily basis.

There is clearly no single, dominant agent of change in the way the Secretariat goes about addressing nuclear weapons issues. There is an intuitively appealing argument that the great powers are in total control of the United Nations' agenda in disarmament, but there is surprisingly little corroborating evidence for this assumption, and many cases where other states (developing countries or middle powers) or even NGOs have had their own significant effects upon the work of the entire UN disarmament machinery.

The New Agenda Coalition has played an important role in advancing the norms of nuclear disarmament and non-proliferation both in the NPT and in the First Committee. The Secretariat's record of issuing publications, promoting disarmament and non-proliferation education, and expanding its networking with groups in civil society is due as much to the Secretariat's recognition of the value of such initiatives as to rising demands from civil society for greater information and access.

There is some reason to believe that administrative reforms in the Secretariat are driven largely by parochial internal concerns over efficiency and effectiveness, rather than by power politics. Every Secretary-General has had to deal with the problem of setting priorities in an environment of limited resources. Sometimes strong personal policy preferences of the Secretary-General can make a difference (for example, Annan's determination to re-establish the DDA even over the opposition of the United States). Yet there are enormous limitations on what the Secretary-General or the Secretariat can accomplish in disarmament, given that the most fundamental decisions are made by the United Nations' sovereign member states.

Perhaps the Secretariat's greatest contributions to the cause of disarmament are in helping to raise it as an international priority, to sustain and strengthen its basic legitimacy, to explain it to the public, to provide a forum for the public to make its own contributions, to serve as a kind of global "town hall" for debating relevant initiatives, and – above all – to create, build, sustain, and adjust international norms or standards of conduct concerning the possession, proliferation, or possible terrorist use of all weapons of mass destruction, in particular nuclear weapons. The Secretariat's independent contribution to these abstract goals is of course difficult to measure, though the sheer persistence of the United Nations' fundamental goals of WMD disarmament and conventional arms regulation owes a lot to the work of the Secretariat, year after year.

The tools used by the Secretariat are quite familiar: public statements, publications, assistance to delegations involved in the UN disarmament machinery and multilateral treaty conferences, research and analysis, and coordinating liaison relationships with other intergovernmental, regional, and non-governmental organizations. The Secretariat is more than just a document repository; it is also the institutional memory of the United Nations in the field of disarmament. Its experts are careerists, not political dilettantes; their loyalties are to the global institution rather than to the interests of only specific states.

A disarmament function has continued in the Secretariat since 1946 despite often strong resistance from the nuclear weapons states. It has survived varying priorities of the secretaries-general. Its work is influenced by broader trends in international relations – including the end of the Cold War, the age of decolonization, strains between the great powers, wars in the Middle East, and other such conditions. Yet it has also made its own contributions in promoting deeper public understanding of disarmament issues, advancing its norms in multilateral settings, and strengthening standards that constrain the behavior of states.

All the secretaries-general recognized the importance of disarmament, yet each has had his own approach. Lie, Hammarskjöld, and Thant drew attention to the role of science and technology in advancing disarmament. Thant and Pérez de Cuéllar stressed the social and economic costs of the arms race and rallied support for disarmament among developing countries. Waldheim and Thant both presided over a wave of new disarmament-related publications by the Secretariat. Pérez de Cuéllar often called for the United Nations to play a greater role in verification. Boutros-Ghali tried to integrate disarmament into the broader process of peace-building. Annan raised the priority of disarmament and added a new emphasis on non-proliferation and counter-terrorist themes. And Ban has indicated his intention to give the issue even a higher priority.

The work of the Secretariat in disarmament has also been affected by influential, opinion-leading states and blocs of states. Sweden's efforts to create a Centre for Disarmament Affairs in 1976 and Norway's 1982 resolution to elevate the Centre to a department are good examples, as was the role of the NAM and the G-77 states in the establishment of an independent Office for Disarmament Affairs in 2007, with help from NGOs. This history does not provide much evidence at all for any dominance by the great powers of the Secretariat's work in disarmament.

It is fair to conclude that secretaries-general have found it easier to reorganize the United Nations' work in disarmament than actually to achieve this goal, which is not surprising, given the extent to which progress in disarmament still depends on decisions by the member states. Moreover, the reorganizations that have occurred in disarmament have neither saved the United Nations much money nor significantly "streamlined" the Secretariat. The issue is one of scale. In 2007, for example, the United Nations spent more on procurements relating to "cleaning and waste disposal services" (US$10.1 million) than it budgeted for disarmament (less than US$9.9 million). For decades, the Secretariat employed only about a couple of dozen officials to work on disarmament issues, and its current staff – consisting of about 50 employees – still constitutes a minuscule part of the Secretariat staff of 8,900.

Although the work of the Secretariat in disarmament is not a significant drain on UN resources, its work remains very important in the eyes of member states – both large and small – whose political and financial support will be crucial for the future of this work. This support, combined with the leadership and priorities of the Secretary-General, will determine what the future will hold for disarmament in the Secretariat.

Looking ahead over the next few decades, this analysis points to at least three possible futures for the Secretariat in the field of disarmament: revolution; evolution; and devolution.

- *Revolution* would entail a comprehensive reform of the structures and functions of the UN disarmament machinery. If member states so desire, the Secretariat could gradually acquire new mandates, as well as consolidate and integrate many of the diverse multilateral activities under way in disarmament. This could lead to the creation of new global institutions, including a disarmament organization, a verification agency, and a disarmament academy, along with global organizations to deal with peaceful uses of outer space, to promote renewable energy and energy conservation, or to conduct various sensitive nuclear fuel cycle activities. Significant increases in budgets, staff, and the scope of mandates would provide some indicators of the emergence of a revolutionary course.
- *Evolution* suggests a future based on incrementalism. An evolutionary approach stresses the importance of doing existing tasks better – more effectively and efficiently – rather than overhauling existing institutions or mandates. Budgets would remain largely flat. Priorities would essentially remain unchanged, or evolve slowly in response to international events and shifting coalitions of political support. Whereas a tendency to incremental evolution is easy to predict, its consequences are not, especially if the evolution is away from disarmament toward more regulatory approaches to dealing with nuclear weapons. Evolutionary change has its highest potential when nuclear disarmament and nonproliferation progress together, rather than at each other's expense.
- *Devolution* encompasses a future in which global norms and institutions lose their relevance in the day-to-day activities of states. In this vision, global institutional structures and functions would increasingly

operate on regional, sub-regional, or local levels. The creation and enforcement of the global norms of nuclear disarmament and non-proliferation would increasingly emerge as activities undertaken by coalitions of states rather than by institutions of universal membership. Devolution could occur as a result of public and governmental frustrations with the slow rate of progress in existing multilateral institutions, or from growing perceptions of the limitations of global norms and institutions in alleviating immediate threats to security. States may also come to conclude that they have a greater voice or influence over decisions made in more restrictive arenas.

In all probability, the global nuclear regime and its associated machinery will continue to "muddle through" until an unusual configuration of forces – which might include dynamic leadership among key member states or elsewhere within the United Nations, a catalytic event, a historic breakthrough in US/Russian strategic relations, or some other such unpredictable circumstance – creates conditions that will lead to more fundamental changes. As long as weapons stockpiles keep declining and proliferation risks remain stable or decline, this may be the most practical route to a safer world for all.

Whichever route the world chooses to take (except in the most extreme case of devolution), there will be important roles for the Secretary-General and the Secretariat to play. In their own way, they have proven to be indispensable.

Acknowledgements

The views expressed herein are mine and do not necessarily reflect the views of the United Nations. I wish to thank Ye Joon Rim and Renata Zaleska for their assistance in undertaking background research for this chapter.

Notes

1. Inis Claude, *Swords into Plowshares*, 4th edn (New York: Random House, 1971), 211.
2. Ibid., 211, quoting from Trygve Lie, *In the Cause of Peace* (New York: Macmillan, 1954), 88.
3. Dag Hammarskjöld, *Introduction to the Annual Report of the Secretary-General on the Work of the Organization, 16 June 1960–15 June 1961*, General Assembly document A/4800/Add.1, 1.
4. Article 11 establishes the disarmament mandate of the General Assembly, and Articles 26 and 47 concern the mandates of the Security Council and its Military Staff Committee.

5. The General Assembly expanded this mandate by adopting decision 54/418 on 1 December 1999.
6. Kurt Waldheim, *Introduction to the Report of the Secretary-General on the Work of the Organization*, General Assembly document A/10001/Add.1, 11 August 1975, 4.
7. Ibid.
8. General Assembly resolution 3484[B], 12 December 1975.
9. General Assembly document A/AC.181/3, 9 June 1976.
10. *Report of the Ad Hoc Committee on the Review of the Role of the United Nations in the Field of Disarmament*, General Assembly document A/31/36, 1976.
11. The *United Nations Disarmament Yearbook* was first published in 1976 and has appeared annually ever since. It is also available at ⟨http://disarmament.un.org/e-yearbook.html⟩ (accessed 5 November 2008). The Secretariat also published a periodical, *Disarmament: A Periodic Review by the United Nations*, from 1978 through 1997.
12. The first Assistant Secretary-General for the Centre was Rolf Björnerstedt of Sweden.
13. General Assembly resolution 34/87[E], 11 December 1979.
14. *Study of the Institutional Arrangements Relating to the Process of Disarmament, Report of the Secretary-General*, General Assembly document A/36/392, 11 September 1981.
15. Ibid., 30. This is probably the first official reference to the notion of creating a "department" for disarmament affairs in the Secretariat.
16. Ibid., 28.
17. *Report of the Ad Hoc Committee of the Twelfth Special Session* of the General Assembly, General Assembly document A/S-12/32, 9 July 1982, 101.
18. Ibid., 104.
19. The first Under-Secretary-General for Disarmament Affairs was Jan Martenson of Sweden.
20. As summarized in the *United Nations Disarmament Yearbook* (New York: United Nations, 1982), 130.
21. *Secretary-General's Bulletin*, Secretariat document ST/SGB/199, 17 December 1982.
22. *Secretary-General's Bulletin*, Secretariat document ST/SGB/Organization, Section AA, 1 June 1983.
23. General Assembly resolution 41/60[J], 3 December 1986. The name change occurred pursuant to General Assembly resolution 43/76[H], 7 December 1988.
24. General Assembly resolution 42/39[D], 12 December 1987. The name change occurred pursuant to General Assembly resolution 44/117[F], 15 December 1989.
25. Secretariat document ST/SGB/Organization, Section: DDA, 2 August 1988.
26. *Report of the Group of High-level Intergovernmental Experts to Review the Efficiency of the Administrative and Financial Functioning of the United Nations*, General Assembly document A/41/49, 15 August 1986.
27. Official Records of the General Assembly, Forty-fifth Session, Supplement No. 42, General Assembly document A/45/42, para. 32. A full text appears also in General Assembly document A/51/182, 20 June 1990.
28. *United Nations Disarmament Yearbook 1991* (New York: United Nations, 1991), 396.
29. Security Council resolution 687, 3 April 1991.
30. Ibid., para. 9(b).
31. *United Nations Disarmament Yearbook 1991*, 397.
32. For a further description of the function of UNMOVIC's College of Commissioners, see ⟨http://www.un.org/Depts/unmovic/new/pages/commissioners.asp⟩ (accessed 5 November 2008).
33. "UN Leader Fires 14 Senior UN Officials in Reorganization Plan," *United Press International*, 7 February 1992.

THE SECRETARY-GENERAL AND THE SECRETARIAT   103

34. "UN Chief Announces Major Reorganization, No Layoffs, Savings Unknown," *Associated Press*, 7 February 1992.
35. *Note by the Secretary-General*, General Assembly document A/46/882, 21 February 1992.
36. *Secretary-General's Bulletin*, Secretariat document ST/SGB/248, 16 March 1992.
37. General Assembly resolution 46/232, 2 March 1992.
38. Vladimir Petrovsky, "Petrovsky on Disarmament," *Disarmament Times*, May 1992, 1.
39. *An Agenda for Peace, Report of the Secretary-General*, General Assembly document A/47/277 and S/24111, 17 June 1992. The reference is in paragraph 22, which cites disarmament as one of several initiatives that have "contributed immeasurably to the foundations for a peaceful world."
40. *Review of the Efficiency of the Administrative and Financial Functioning of the United Nations, Report of the Secretary-General*, General Assembly document A/C.5/47/2, 31 July 1992, 12 and 13.
41. "SG Reports on UN's Future," *Disarmament Times*, 8 October 1992, 2.
42. Ibid.
43. *New Dimensions of Arms Regulation and Disarmament in the Post-Cold War Era, Report of the Secretary-General*, General Assembly document A/C.1/47/7, 27 October 1992.
44. *Verbatim Record of the 29th Meeting, 11 November 1992*, General Assembly, First Committee, General Assembly document A/C.1/47/PV.29, 22 December 1992.
45. General Assembly decision 47/422, 9 December 1992.
46. *Verbatim Record of the 43rd Meeting, 9 March 1993*, General Assembly, First Committee, A/C.1/47/PV.43, 20 April 1993, 7.
47. General Assembly resolution 47/54 G, 28 April 1993. During the debate on this resolution, many delegations voiced their concern over the adequacy of funding for the ODA, including Japan, Indonesia, Iran, Mexico, and Nigeria, and others (including the United States) voiced opposition to any move of the ODA to Geneva. For further discussion, see "Comm I Debates Future of Disarmament Machinery, ODA," *Disarmament Times*, April 1993, 1, 4.
48. "NGOs Seek More Active Role," *Disarmament Times*, April 1993, 2.
49. *Report of the Secretary-General*, General Assembly document A/48/358, 20 September 1993, 2.
50. *Secretary-General's Bulletin*, Secretariat document ST/SGB/Organization, Section: DPA, 15 February 1996.
51. *Renewing the United Nations: A Programme for Reform, Report of the Secretary-General*, General Assembly document A/51/950, 14 July 1997. The quotes in this paragraph are from pages 40 and 41 of the report.
52. *Report of the Secretary-General*, General Assembly document A/52/303, 11 September 1997. The expenditure figure for 1996–1997 is found in "Proposed Programme Budget for the Biennium 2000–2001," General Assembly document A/54/6/Rev.1, Volume II, 19 July 1999, 148.
53. "NGOs Support Secretary-General's Bid to Create UN Disarmament Dept.," *Disarmament Times*, 25 September 1997, 1.
54. Ibid.
55. *Report of the Secretary-General*, General Assembly document A/51/950/Add.3, 14 October 1997.
56. Thalif Deen, a keen observer of politics at the United Nations, has offered the following explanation for the name change: "some countries feared that 'arms regulation' was a codeword to pursue a hidden agenda: nuclear non-proliferation. As a result of protests from several countries, including Pakistan and Egypt, 'arms regulation' was

dropped from the mandate of the department." Thalif Deen, "Sri Lankan Named to Head Department," *India Abroad*, 23 January 1998, 14.
57. *Report of the Secretary-General on the Work of the Organization, 1998*, General Assembly document A/53/1, 27 August 1998, 5.
58. *Report of the Secretary-General on the Work of the Organization, 2000*, General Assembly document A/55/1, 30 August 2000, 13.
59. *Note by the Secretary-General*, Economic and Social Council document E/AC.51/1999/2, 31 March 1999.
60. Ibid., 5.
61. *Secretary-General's Bulletin*, Secretariat document ST/SGB/2004/12, 11 August 2004.
62. In 1999, Kofi Annan had issued a statement drawing international attention to the lack of multilateral norms for missiles (UN Press Release SG/SM/6960, 15 April 1999).
63. *Statement by the Ministers of Foreign Affairs of the Republic of Kazakhstan, the Kyrgyz Republic, the Republic of Tajikistan, Turkmenistan and the Republic of Uzbekistan*, Press Release, 8 September 2006, available at ⟨http://www.cns.miis.edu/stories/pdf_support/060908_ministers_statement.pdf⟩ (accessed 5 November 2008). Although welcome at the United Nations, the praise is not entirely accurate. UN staffer William Epstein made significant contributions in the drafting of the Tlatelolco Treaty, which created a nuclear-weapon-free zone in Latin America and the Caribbean, as documented in William Epstein, "The Making of the Treaty of Tlatelolco," *Journal of the History of International Law* 3, no. 2 (2001): 153–179.
64. Security Council resolution 1540, 28 April 2004.
65. "Reform Should be Highest Priority for Next UN Chief, Front-Runner Says," *Associated Press*, 3 October 2006.
66. "New UN Chief Speeds Plans to Reshape Bureaucracy," *Reuters*, 4 January 2007.
67. Thalif Deen, "UN: Move to Downgrade Disarmament Triggers Protests," *Inter Press Service*, 16 January 2007.
68. Ibid.
69. All quotes in this paragraph are from *Inter Press Service*, 16 January 2007.
70. "Disarmament to Survive – Under an ASG?" *Terra Viva*, 18 January 2007.
71. "UN Chief to Drop Merger Plan," *Associated Press*, 19 January 2007.
72. Edith M. Lederer, "UN Chief to Drop Merger Plan," Associated Press, 19 January 2007.
73. "A SRSG for Disarmament?" *Inter Press Service*, 19 January 2007.
74. Thalif Deen, "U.N. Chief Moves to Restructure World Body," *Asian Tribune*, 24 January 2007.
75. "Reps. Markey, Shays Urge U.N. Secretary-General Ban to Strengthen Arms Control Depart., Not Downgrade It," *US Fed News*, 24 January 2007.
76. "UN Chief Wants to Split Peacekeeping Department," *Reuters*, 26 January 2007.
77. "Ban's U.N. Reform Plans Make Developing States Wary," *Reuters*, 30 January 2007.
78. "UN Chief's Reform Plans May be Stalled in Meetings," *Reuters*, 5 February 2007.
79. Thalif Deen, "South Rejects Deadline for UN Restructuring," *Inter Press Service*, 31 January 2007.
80. *Address to the General Assembly by Secretary-General Ban Ki-moon*, 5 February 2007.
81. Thalif Deen, "UN Chief Tries to Avoid Roadblocks on Path to Reform," *Inter Press Service*, 6 February 2007.
82. Edith M. Lederer, "UN Chief to Drop Merger Plan," *Associated Press*, 19 January 2007.
83. Michèle Montas, Regular News Briefing, UN Headquarters, 6 February 2007.
84. Thalif Deen, "Anti-war Groups Reject Move to Downgrade DDA," *Inter Press Ser-*

vice, 7 February 2007. The full text of the letter is available at ⟨http://www.lcnp.org/disarmament/dda-letter.htm⟩ (accessed 6 November 2008). Jonathan Granoff, president of the Global Security Institute, sent his own six-page letter to the president of the General Assembly and all the permanent missions on 1 February 2007.

85. *Letter Dated 15 February 2007 from the Secretary-General Addressed to the President of the General Assembly*, General Assembly document A/61/749, Annex II, 15 February 2007.
86. Edith M. Lederer, "UN Chief Picks up Support for Reforms after Some Compromise," *Associated Press*, 17 February 2007.
87. UN Press Release SG/A/1075, 2 July 2007.
88. *Note by the Secretary-General*, General Assembly document A/1304, 26 June 1950.
89. Dag Hammarskjöld, *Introduction to the Report of the Secretary-General on the Work of the Organization, 1958*, General Assembly document A/3844/Add.1, 1.
90. Press Conference by Dag Hammarskjold, New York, 19 May 1955.
91. Brian Urquhart, *Hammarskjold* (New York: Alfred A. Knopf, 1972), 317.
92. Ibid., 318.
93. Ibid., 322.
94. "The Uses of Private Diplomacy," Address to a Meeting of Members of both Houses of Parliament under the auspices of the British Group of the Inter-Parliamentary Union, London, 2 April 1958.
95. Urquhart, *Hammarskjold*, 324.
96. Brian Urquhart, *Ralph Bunche: An American Life* (New York: W. W. Norton, 1993), 257.
97. Urquhart, *Hammarskjold*, 327.
98. The McCloy–Zorin statement of 20 September 1961 is accessible at ⟨http://www.nuclearfiles.org/menu/key-issues/nuclear-weapons/issues/arms-control-disarmament/mccloy-zorin-accords_1961-09-20.htm⟩ (accessed 6 November 2008).
99. He made this point in his *Introduction to the Report of the Secretary-General on the Work of the Organization, 1962* (1962), 2.
100. U Thant, "Progress toward Peace," Address at the University of Warsaw, Poland, 31 August 1962.
101. *Introduction to the Report of the Secretary-General on the Work of the Organization, 1966*, General Assembly document A/6301/Add.1, 3.
102. *Introduction to the Report of the Secretary-General on the Work of the Organization, 1964*, General Assembly document A/5801/Add.1, 2.
103. *Introduction to the Report of the Secretary-General on the Work of the Organization, 1965*, General Assembly document A/6001/Add.1, 2.
104. *Introduction to the Report of the Secretary-General on the Work of the Organization, 1969*, General Assembly document A/7601/Add.1, 6.
105. *Introduction to the Report of the Secretary-General on the Work of the Organization, 1970*, General Assembly document A/8001/Add.1, 4. The General Assembly granted his request and he submitted his report (General Assembly document A/8496/Rev.1) in 1971.
106. *Introduction to the Report of the Secretary-General on the Work of the Organization, 1971*, General Assembly document A/8401/Add.1, 6.
107. Ibid.
108. A. Walter Dorn and Robert Pauk "He Saved the World," *Ottawa Citizen*, 22 October 2007, A11; and A. Walter Dorn, "Unsung Mediator: U Thant and the Cuban Missile Crisis," *Diplomatic History* (accepted for publication).
109. *Introduction to the Report of the Secretary-General on the Work of the Organization, 1975*, General Assembly document A/10001/Add.1, 2.

110. Kurt Waldheim, "Foreword," *United Nations Disarmament Yearbook* (New York: United Nations, 1976), iii.
111. *Report of the Secretary-General on the Work of the Organization, 1977*, General Assembly document A/32/1, 5.
112. Ibid., 6.
113. *Introduction to the Report of the Secretary-General on the Work of the Organization, 1976*, General Assembly document A/31/1/Add.1, 31 August 1976, 5. Here he called on the General Assembly "to discuss various ways in which public concern about disarmament could be stimulated and channeled in constructive ways."
114. *Introduction to the Report of the Secretary-General on the Work of the Organization, 1974*, General Assembly document A/9601/Add.1, 7.
115. *Introduction to the Report of the Secretary-General on the Work of the Organization, 1975*, General Assembly document A/10001.Add.1, 4.
116. *Report of the Secretary-General on the Work of the Organization, 1980*, General Assembly document A/35/1, 6.
117. *Report of the Secretary-General on the Work of the Organization, 1981*, General Assembly document A/36/1, 6.
118. Kurt Waldheim, *In the Eye of the Storm* (Bethesda, MD: Adler and Adler, 1986), 263.
119. *Report of the Secretary-General on the Work of the Organization, 1986*, General Assembly document A/41/1, 4.
120. *Report of the Secretary-General on the Work of the Organization, 1982*, General Assembly document A/37/1, 1, 2.
121. *Statement by the Secretary-General at the Opening of SSOD-II*, 7 June 1982; available in *Disarmament* 5, no. 2 (1982): 10, 12.
122. *Statement by the Secretary-General at the Opening of SSOD-III*, 31 May 1988; available in *Disarmament* 11, no. 3 (1988): 5.
123. *Study on the Role of the United Nations in the Field of Verification*, General Assembly document A/45/435, 28 August 1990.
124. *Report of the Secretary-General on the Work of the Organization, 1986*, 4.
125. *Report of the Secretary-General on the Work of the Organization, 1983*, General Assembly document A/38/1, 2; also *Report of the Secretary-General on the Work of the Organization, 1984*, General Assembly document A/39/1, 3.
126. *Report of the Secretary-General on the Work of the Organization, 1988*, General Assembly document A/43/1,14 September 1988, 7.
127. *Report of the Secretary-General on the Work of the Organization, 1991*, General Assembly document A/46/1, 6 September 1991, 5.
128. Ibid., 6.
129. Javier Pérez de Cuéllar, *Pilgrimage for Peace: A Secretary-General's Memoir* (New York: St. Martin's Press, 1997).
130. Boutros Boutros-Ghali, *Unvanquished* (New York: Random House, 1999), 15, 16.
131. Boutros Boutros-Ghali, *New Dimensions of Arms Regulation and Disarmament in the Post-Cold War Era* (New York: United Nations, 1992), 10.
132. Ibid., 14.
133. Ibid., 16.
134. *Report of the Secretary-General on the Work of the Organization, 1996*, General Assembly document A/51/1, 20 August 1998, 149.
135. Kofi Annan, Address delivered at University of Tokyo, UN Press Release SG/SM/10466, 18 May 2006.
136. Kofi Annan elaborated this theme in a major speech at Princeton University in 2006. Lecture by UN Secretary-General Kofi Annan at Princeton University, UN Press Release SG/SM/10767, 28 November 2006.

137. For a concise description of the NAC, see ⟨http://en.wikipedia.org/wiki/New_Agenda_Coalition⟩ (accessed 6 November 2008).
138. UN Press Release SG/SM/6960, 15 April 1999. On missile defense and proliferation, see also *Report of the Secretary-General on the Work of the Organization, 2001*, General Assembly document A/61/1, 6 September 2001, 13.
139. He addressed this theme in his remarks to the Security Council's Counter-Terrorism Committee, UN Press Release SG/SM/8624, 6 March 2003. He elaborated the United Nations' role in countering terrorism in a major speech in Madrid on 10 March 2005, UN Press Release SG/SM/9757.
140. *Remarks by the Secretary-General at the Opening of the 2000 NPT Review Conference*, UN Press Release SG/SM/7367, 24 April 2000.
141. *Transcript of Press Conference by Secretary-General Kofi Annan at United Nations Headquarters on 16 July*, UN Press Release SG/SM/6285, 16 July 1997.
142. *Report of the Secretary-General on the Work of the Organization, 1998*, 6.
143. Lecture by UN Secretary-General Kofi Annan at Princeton University, 28 November 2006.
144. "Secretary-General's Remarks at the Security Council Meeting on Threats to International Peace and Security," UN Press Release SG/SM/10833, 8 January 2007.

Part II
Actual and potential tools

5
United Nations sanctions and nuclear weapons

George A. Lopez and David Cortright

Since the new sanctions era of the 1990s began, the Security Council has imposed economic sanctions for a number of purposes, including bringing an end to war, restoring democratic governance, halting human rights abuse, controlling the spread of terrorism, and ending the development of nuclear weapons programs.[1] Council sanctions intended to eliminate nuclear weapons development programs and existing weapons stocks have proven reasonably successful, especially when used in collaboration with other techniques and if managed with considerable diplomatic skill. The most significant mechanism predicating such success blends the carrot of economic incentives with the sanctions stick. But recent history demonstrates that coercive sticks and inducement carrots can help disarm a nuclear state only if the confrontation between the United Nations and the target unfolds as a diplomatic engagement for shared problem-solving among sovereign states, rather than as a showdown with a pariah state, where harsh punishment and isolation tactics are the norm. Finally, emerging nuclear states rarely disarm without considerable security guarantees from major powers and contentious rivals.

Recent cases reveal that this combination of factors emerges not as a carefully crafted UN diplomatic offensive but as a framework derived from trial and error and using existing institutions, such as the International Atomic Energy Agency (IAEA), smartly. Moreover, the only real element of the equation that the Security Council controls – and then not exclusively – is the imposition of sanctions. Of course, ending sanctions can always be considered an inducement, even if in a limited sense.

The United Nations and nuclear orders, Boulden, Thakur and Weiss (eds),
United Nations University Press, 2009, ISBN 978-92-808-1167-4

Thus, UN-prompted denuclearization is very much a combination of Council sanctions that begin and undergird a process that may depend heavily on powerful member states of the permanent five (P-5) to forge and sustain a final deal. As the cases of Libya, Iran, and North Korea illustrate, a significant backdrop to such sanctions episodes and their accompanying diplomacy has been (and will continue to be) the claims by target states that the United Nations tolerates a double standard for nuclear weapons states, not criticizing those nations that hold such weapons, but imposing sanctions on those that attempt development.[2]

Confidence in a UN process involving sanctions, inducements and critical diplomacy emerges from an analysis of lessons from sanctions cases since 1990. For sanctions to contribute in any meaningful way to ending a nuclear program, they should not aim to punish and isolate but instead be used to establish dialogue, keep the target within the Non-Proliferation Treaty (NPT) guidelines, encourage IAEA or other monitoring, and complement economic incentives. The positive nuclear reduction decisions taken by Ukraine, Kazakhstan, South Africa (not related to Security Council action), and, most recently, North Korea (which was Council generated) clearly followed this pattern. Libya's disavowal of both the bomb and support for terrorism was the result of years of direct diplomacy and mutual conciliatory gestures tied to the lifting of coercive sanctions. Conversely, long-time punitive trade and technology sanctions mixed with inconsistent incentives – imposed primarily by the United States without Council involvement – failed to persuade either Pakistan, India, or, thus far, Iran to forgo the bomb.

In this chapter we attempt to capture the subtleties and nuances of sanctions use in the limited number of times the Security Council has taken action to control nuclear weapons. The analysis takes shape around four case studies. The chapter begins by examining the Iraq case, which rightly predominates and illustrates the risks of misusing and then rejecting Council involvement. We then examine the nuclear turnabout in Libya between 1992 and 2008, a period illustrating the effectiveness of combining sanctions and American diplomatic engagement. Next, the chapter investigates the Iran and North Korea cases. The manner in which the North Korean case appears finalized and the Iranian case stalled helps us to posit where sanctions imposition and accompanying innovations may occur to lead to effective disarmament in the future. Finally, we present a study of failed non-proliferation in South Asia, a case that highlights the critical importance of coherence and consistency of policy. The chapter concludes by taking stock of the lessons derived from the individual case studies and points to current and future issues of concern.

The bitter irony of Iraq

United Nations sanctions imposed on Iraq in August 1990 after its invasion of Kuwait were the longest, most comprehensive, and most controversial in the history of the organization. The massive trade, aid, arms, and financial embargo was the thorn in the side of Iraq, pressuring it to accept (however grudgingly) weapons inspections and monitoring, which, in turn, led to Iraq's disarmament.[3] Maintaining these tough sanctions helped to extract important concessions from Iraq in permitting inspector access to key weapons sites. By drastically reducing the revenues available to Saddam Hussein to purchase materials on the black and gray arms and technology markets and blocking vital imports needed for producing weapons of mass destruction, trade sanctions also ensured a stranglehold on and military containment of Iraq.[4]

The tragic irony of this case was that despite the embargo being the most effectively imposed, monitored, and enforced UN embargo in history – sanctions that took a devastating social and economic toll on the nation – it had only partial success politically. Skepticism about sanctions began when they did not achieve the original objective of forcing Iraqi withdrawal from Kuwait. Nor were sanctions successful in persuading Iraq to comply with the full range of demands in the Gulf war ceasefire agreement of Security Council resolution 687 (3 April 1991). The sanctions were a source of constant political friction between Baghdad and Washington. Iraq repeatedly demanded an end to the embargo and exploited the humanitarian crisis to win international sympathy for revising and then lifting sanctions.[5]

Quickly, the United States moved from using sanctions as bargaining leverage over Iraq to using them as a punitive instrument. Washington refused to consider even a partial lifting of sanctions in exchange for partial Iraqi compliance. As early as May 1991, President George H. W. Bush stated, "my view is we don't want to lift these sanctions as long as Saddam Hussein is in power."[6] This policy continued under Bush's successor, Bill Clinton, who remarked in November 1997 that "sanctions will be there until the end of time, or as long as he [Hussein] lasts."[7] This position was contrary to resolution 687, which stated explicitly that sanctions were to be lifted when Iraq complied with UN disarmament obligations. The United States rejected this view and used its position on the Security Council to block any easing of punitive pressures.

This moving of the "political goalposts" from achieving disarmament to regime change generated considerable controversy throughout the 1990s, undermining the ongoing sanctions, tainting assessments of their success, and ultimately preventing the disarmament crisis between Iraq and the West from being resolved via UN diplomacy and action. The failings of sanctions were owing not to the limitations of the instrument itself but to the flaws in the overall US/UN policy toward Iraq. Continuing political animosities between Iraq and the West (including ongoing US and UK bombing raids) prevented the redevelopment of a bargaining dynamic in the late 1990s and unnecessarily prolonged both the political crisis and the agony of the Iraqi people.[8]

The US decision to launch the March 2003 invasion of Iraq – a war of choice not endorsed by the Security Council, after the latter had been the venue for disarmament sanctions for over a decade – has had serious and substantial implications for global security that are likely to continue into the future. In particular, if nations perceive that Council sanctions become a "trap door for war," they will not accept anything like the combination of inspection by the IAEA and the United Nations Special Commission on Iraq (UNSCOM, later replaced by the United Nations Monitoring, Verification and Inspection Commission, or UNMOVIC) that was so essential to Iraqi disarmament. The logic of national security dictates that other regimes will be unlikely to accept disarmament without very costly and intricate security assurances that they will not be attacked.[9]

UN inspections: Eliminating Iraq's nuclear arsenal

The intrusive weapons monitoring efforts of UNSCOM (1991–98) and UNMOVIC (November 2002–March 2003) combined to decapitate both Iraq's banned weapons programs and its infrastructure for maintaining clandestine programs. The inspection system proved to be far more successful than was generally recognized before the war.[10] As Hans Blix wrote in his book *Disarming Iraq*, "the UN and the world had succeeded in disarming Iraq without knowing it."[11] In nearly eight years of operation UNSCOM identified and dismantled nearly all of Iraq's vast store of prohibited weapons. In its brief four-month effort UNMOVIC thoroughly monitored and confirmed the depleted state of Iraq's capabilities.

Most of the headlines of the early 1990s focused on Baghdad's attempts to stall, evade, and obstruct the work of UN weapons monitors. Yet the record shows that UNSCOM and UNMOVIC mounted a highly successful disarmament effort. Even the US Vice President Dick Cheney called the UN disarmament program "the most intrusive system of arms control in history," although he dismissed its utility.[12] During the 1990s UNSCOM and the IAEA conducted hundreds of inspection missions, surveying more than 1,000 potential and actual weapons sites and documentation centers. In the process, they systematically uncovered and eliminated Iraq's nuclear weapons program and destroyed most of its chemical, biological, and ballistic missile systems. The UK government reported in its September 2002 dossier on Iraqi weapons that "UNSCOM and the IAEA Action Team have valuable records of achievement in discovering and exposing Iraq's biological weapons programme and destroying very large quantities of chemical weapons stocks and missiles as well as the infrastructure for Iraq's nuclear weapons programme."[13]

The greatest success of the UN disarmament mission occurred in the nuclear realm. Because of the grave danger posed by these weapons, UN officials gave priority attention to eliminating Iraq's nuclear capabilities. IAEA inspectors found an extensive and alarming nuclear program when they entered the country in 1991, and they systematically eliminated all weapons-related activity. Inspectors destroyed all known facilities relating to the nuclear weapons program and verifiably accounted for the entire inventory of nuclear fuel.[14] In 1998 the IAEA and UNSCOM concluded that "there are no indications that any weapon-useable nuclear material remains in Iraq" and no "evidence in Iraq of prohibited materials, equipment or activities."[15]

The IAEA resumed inspections in late November 2002 and in the four months before war began conducted 237 inspections at 148 sites. IAEA director general Mohamed ElBaradei reported to the Security Council in March 2003 that inspectors found "no indication of resumed nuclear activities ... nor any indication of nuclear-related prohibited activities at any inspected sites." The IAEA report observed that "during the past four years, at the majority of Iraqi sites, industrial capacity has deteriorated substantially." The inspectors examined documents related to alleged Iraqi attempts to import uranium from Niger and found them to be "not authentic." The UN officials saw "no indication that Iraq has attempted to import uranium since 1990." Responding to claims about the import of specialized aluminum tubes, the inspectors reported "no indication that Iraq has attempted to import aluminium tubes for use in centrifuge enrichment."[16] All indications were that Iraq had no nuclear weapons and had no program or capacity for redeveloping them.

UN weapons inspectors also destroyed and accounted for Iraq's once substantial ballistic missile capability. UNSCOM reported "significant results" from its efforts to identify and dismantle missile capabilities.[17] All but two of the 819 proscribed Scud missiles known to have existed in Iraq prior to 1990 were accounted for by 1997. Although UN inspectors discovered evidence that Iraq failed to declare some dual-use equipment and that it attempted to import Russian ballistic missile guidance systems, they found no indication of the actual development or flight testing of prohibited missiles. Anthony Cordesman of the Center for Strategic and International Studies told the US Senate Foreign Relations Committee in July 2002 that "Iraq has not fired any Scud variants in nearly twelve years."[18]

When UN inspectors returned to Iraq in late 2002 they discovered "a surge of activity in the missile technology field," although no evidence of actual long-range missiles.[19] Iraq claimed that this activity involved a shorter-range (150 kilometers or less) missile permitted under UN resolutions. UNMOVIC officials determined that the missile in question, the Al Samoud II, exceeded the permissible range by 30 kilometers and had to be destroyed. Baghdad yielded, and destruction of missiles was under way when the invasion began in March 2003. UNMOVIC inspectors also discovered large chambers that could be used to produce missile rocket motors. These too were destroyed in March 2003. UNMOVIC chairman Blix reported to the Security Council that "the destruction undertaken constitutes a substantial measure of disarmament."[20]

Despite these advances on the technical side of weapons dismantlement, the political assessments of these accomplishments were muted. In Washington during the 1990s each new weapons report was taken as confirmation of the regime's perfidy, rather than as a measure of UN success in disarmament. There was a lingering belief among Americans – fueled by Saddam Hussein's recalcitrance – that lying behind each new discovery lay more hidden contraband. In the atmosphere after the attacks of 11 September 2001, the prior successes of UN disarmament were ignored and Saddam's defiance was seen as confirmation that deadly stockpiles remained.

Sanctions played a significant role in the success of weapons inspections. According to former UNSCOM director Rolf Ekéus, sanctions were "very important" in pressuring Iraqi officials to accept UN weapons inspections.[21] Although it is impossible to separate the role of economic sanctions from that of military pressure and other factors influencing the Iraqi government, it is safe to say that the continuing weight of sanctions had at least some impact in pressuring Baghdad to accept some of the weapons inspections provisions of resolution 687.

The expulsion of UNSCOM and the end of weapons inspections following the December 1998 bombing created a new dilemma for the Security Council that further delayed a resolution of the crisis. US officials initially expressed concern that Iraq would take advantage of the hiatus in monitoring to rebuild its weapons of mass destruction, but intelligence reports found no evidence of a major rearmament program. According to a US official quoted in the *Washington Post*, "We have seen no evidence of reconstruction of weapons of mass destruction."[22]

The critical role of inspections and monitoring

Monitoring borders, domestic goods, and the humanitarian impact of sanctions is the key to their success. The UN inspection program included the establishment of an Ongoing Monitoring and Verification (OMV) system, mandated by Security Council resolution 715 (11 October 1991). One of Iraq's most important concessions forced by the sanctions was its acceptance of the OMV system outlined in resolution 715. Iraq initially resisted the resolution but eventually yielded in November 1993. The installation of monitoring equipment began in early 1994 and was completed a few months later. The OMV system was designed to detect any future attempts to redevelop weapons of mass destruction. It included the installation of an elaborate array of radiological and chemical sensors, cameras, ground penetrating radar, and other detection systems at numerous locations throughout Iraq. The system also included procedures for monitoring Iraqi waterways and conducting aerial surveillance to detect traces of prohibited nuclear or chemical weapons activity. These capabilities were supplemented by the right of UN inspectors to conduct no-notice visits to any designated facility. The OMV system was reauthorized by the Security Council in resolution 1284 (17 December 1999) as an open-ended monitoring program.

UN officials emphasized the deterrent value of this monitoring system. According to the IAEA, "the presence in Iraq of inspectors with broad investigative and monitoring authority serves as a deterrent to, and insurance against, the resumption by Iraq of proscribed nuclear activities."[23] ElBaradei emphasized that "verification activities serve ... as an important deterrent to the resumption of such activities by Iraq."[24] The presence in Iraq of more than 100 highly trained weapons inspectors, equipped with the world's most advanced monitoring technology, provided unprecedented capability to detect any significant weapons activity. In the aftermath of war, Blix concluded: "it is becoming clear that inspection and monitoring by the IAEA, UNMOVIC and its predecessor UNSCOM, backed by military, political and economic pressure, had indeed worked for years, achieving Iraqi disarmament and deterring Saddam from rearming."[25] The UN inspection and monitoring system provided substantial security guarantees against any Iraqi attempt to develop or use prohibited weapons of mass destruction.

Sanctions-based diplomacy and weapons inspections

During discussions of Security Council resolution 715 in 1992, Iraqi leaders told UN officials that they wanted concrete assurances that sanctions would be lifted before agreeing to accept the OMV system.[26] Russian and French diplomats were sympathetic to this demand, noting that paragraph 22 of resolution 687 specified that sanctions were to be lifted when the disarmament mission was completed. They believed that the Iraqi desire to escape sanctions could be used as an inducement for compliance. Iraqi diplomats expected and hoped that their decision to accept monitoring would bring a reciprocal response from the Security Council. UNSCOM chair Rolf Ekéus encouraged this belief and told Iraqi officials that sanctions pressures could be eased once the OMV system was up and running.[27]

When Iraq accepted resolution 715, Russia and France proposed a presidential statement from the Security Council taking note of Iraqi compliance. This was intended as a diplomatic signal that further Iraqi compliance could lead to the lifting of sanctions.[28] The United States and the United Kingdom blocked the statement, however, and refused to consider any easing of coercive pressure. Rolf Ekéus adjusted his message accordingly, telling the Iraqis that the lifting of sanctions would be an all or nothing proposition, and that the end of the embargo would depend on full compliance with every element of the disarmament mandate.[29]

Once the ongoing monitoring system was in place, sanctions continued to play a role in exerting pressure on the regime to cooperate with the disarmament process. During the long history of the inspections, there were numerous disputes between UN officials and the Iraqi government – ranging from David Kay's famous 1991 standoff with Iraqi officials in a Baghdad parking lot, to the final confrontations in 1998 that prompted the withdrawal of UNSCOM. Baghdad played a constant cat-and-mouse game of denying access, then yielding to UN pressure, then resuming its obstruction. On several occasions during this dreary diplomatic dance, UNSCOM chairman Ekéus had to step in personally to cajole Iraqi leaders into granting access. Without question, the primary tool Ekéus used to gain Iraqi compliance was the pressure of sanctions and the hope that the embargo might be lifted. In 1995, for instance, Ekéus and his deputy Charles Duelfer used the threat of continuing sanctions to pressure Iraqi officials into disclosing previous efforts to produce VX nerve agents. Without further revelations, they warned, the "chances of Iraq achieving its objective of getting the sanctions lifted would be much reduced."[30] In 1997, as Iraqi harassment of inspectors increased, UNSCOM again used the threat of continuing sanctions, and the prospect that they would be lifted, to overcome resistance. Ekéus told Iraqi officials that compliance would result in the lifting of sanctions in the near future.[31] When Iraqi obstruction continued, the Security Council adopted resolution 1115 in June 1997, temporarily suspending regular sanctions reviews (thereby preventing any action to lift sanctions) and threatening additional unspecified measures unless the harassment of inspectors ceased.

Ekéus described the role of sanctions in a 2000 interview:

> Sanctions were the way to convince Iraq to cooperate with inspectors.... In this case it was a combined carrot-and-stick approach. Keeping the sanctions was the stick, and the carrot was that if Iraq cooperated with the elimination of its weapons of mass destruction, the Security Council would lift the sanctions. Sanctions were the backing for the inspections, and they were what sustained my operation almost for the whole time.[32]

According to former UNSCOM adviser Tim Trevan, Iraqi foreign minister Tariq Aziz told UN inspectors that "the only reason Iraq was cooperating with UNSCOM was that it wanted to be reintegrated into the international community. Chief among the benefits was the lifting of the economic sanctions."[33] Then Brookings Institution analyst Meghan O'Sullivan observed that "sanctions were a key element in coercing Iraq to initially accept weapons inspectors and in extracting Iraqi cooperation with UNSCOM throughout much of the 1990s."[34]

Blocking WMD imports

The sanctions system was dramatically successful in preventing the import of specific items that could be used for the development of nuclear, chemical, and biological weapons and long-range ballistic missiles. Intelligence, military, and police officials in many countries mounted a massive effort to interdict prohibited weapons shipments to Iraq. The United States led and made the largest commitment to this vast effort, but other countries also participated. In the State Department and other federal agencies, dozens of non-proliferation specialists vetted every oil-for-food contract to screen possible weapons imports. The US Navy established the Maritime Interception Force, a multinational operation that over a 10-year period searched more than 12,000 vessels in the northern Persian Gulf.[35] This unprecedented international dragnet was highly effective in denying Saddam Hussein the means to redevelop weapons of mass destruction.

This is not to suggest that sanctions blocked all prohibited imports. Some military supplies slipped through, as Saddam's smuggling operations offered lucrative rewards for arms traffickers. But the sanctions were generally successful in preventing the most high-grade and illegal weapons imports. This was accomplished through a series of high-profile interdictions over the years, which far too few analysts considered validation that the system of constraining Iraq was working. Ironically, the interdiction of prohibited items, rather than bolstering the case for sanctions success, was often interpreted, especially in Washington, as a sign of sanctions failure. The successful thwarting of attempts to import prohibited weapons – as evidenced by their capture – was read as the failure of the constraining means to prevent such imports. Inflated intelligence assumptions equated Iraq's supposed intentions with real capabilities, even in the face of evidence showing how deteriorated the latter actually were.

In reality, a successful policy of military containment had been achieved through UN sanctions and weapons dismantlement and monitoring. The combination of sanctions and inspections led to the elimination of Iraq's weapons of mass destruction. UN sanctions denied the regime the financial means to rebuild its war machine and contributed to the political and diplomatic isolation of Saddam Hussein.

Nuclear turnabout in Libya

The 16-year period (1992–2008) of UN and US sanctions against Libya illustrates that coercive sanctions can sometimes exert bargaining leverage that may help to influence regime behavior beyond even their issue area of original intent. This case also joins the issue of dismantling nuclear weapons with that of halting support for terrorism, a potential union that comprises a major, contemporary concern within the UN system.

In the years preceding the 1992 imposition of sanctions against it, Libya was convincingly implicated in the bombings of Pan Am flight 103 in 1988 and Union des Transports Aériens flight 772 in 1989. After sanctions were imposed for terrorist support and activity, Libya ceased its attacks against international aviation, prompting the US State Department's 1996 report on global terrorism to note: "Terrorism by Libya has been sharply reduced by UN sanctions."[36] Although the targeted UN sanctions did not cause major economic disruption in Libya, they provided sufficient damage to prompt a reconsideration of policy and a diplomatic settlement of the Pan Am bombing case. In 1998 Libya agreed to turn over suspects wanted in connection with the airline bombing to an international tribunal in The Hague. The Security Council responded by suspending and later lifting sanctions. The United States maintained its sanctions, however, demanding that Tripoli take further steps to compensate the victims of terrorist attacks and to cooperate in counter-terrorism and non-proliferation efforts.

Via a series of complex negotiations spanning nearly a decade, Libya subsequently agreed to pay full compensation to the families of victims of both flights. It also maintained diplomatic dialogue with US officials in the hopes of convincing Washington to lift sanctions and normalize commercial and diplomatic relations. For their part, from 1998 until 2004, US officials made clear that the lifting of sanctions would depend on the dismantlement of Libya's weapons programs.

In June 2004, Libyan leader Muammar Qaddafi surprised many observers by announcing his government's decision to disclose and dismantle its nuclear, chemical, and biological weapons programs and to allow international inspectors to verify compliance. Various officials of the George W. Bush administration immediately credited the war in Iraq with forcing Libya's hand. Vice President Cheney said Qaddafi "watched what we did in Afghanistan and Iraq, and he decided maybe he might want to reconsider what he was all about. Five days after we arrested Saddam Hussein, Colonel Qaddafi went public and said, I give it up, come and get it, it's all yours."[37] In reality, Libya's turnaround had nothing to do with the war in Iraq.

To the extent that there was a direct, proximate catalyst for Qaddafi's decision, it was not the capture of Hussein but rather a sanctions success: the interdiction by a US/UK team of a German ship heading for Libya carrying nuclear weapons-making equipment purchased from the nuclear supply network of Pakistani nuclear chief Abdul Qadeer Khan. This discovery provided the proof of bad intentions and the search for capabilities inconsistent with Libya's quest to be an accepted norm-abiding actor in the international community of states as it was attempting to negotiate the resolution of its culpability in the terrorism issue.

But the longer-term explanation lies in the process of sanctions-based diplomacy and dialogue with the United States and other Western nations that began years before, resulting from UN sanctions imposed against the regime because of its support for international terrorism. This conclusion is supported by various sources, most notably the former US Assistant Secretary of State Thomas E. McNamara, who was responsible for US policy toward Libya under the first Bush administration.[38] Similarly, Seif Al-Islam Qaddafi, influential son and heir apparent to Qaddafi, told *Le Monde* that the US–Libyan dialogue began years before and had nothing to do with the attack on Iraq. In the classic case of the promise of lifting sanctions becoming an incentive, the desire to be reintegrated with the world economy was a powerful inducement for Libya's change of policy. Over time, under the weight of sanctions, Libya acquiesced to international norms and ended its support for terrorism and the development of weapons of mass destruction. For its part, the United States made good on its pledge to normalize relations with Libya.

Sanctions and denuclearizing Iran

If the Libyan case can be considered a success for the reasons noted above, then the attempt by Western states through the Security Council and their own sanctions and incentive policies to halt the suspected march of Iran to the creation of nuclear weapons has been a dismal failure. The Council imposed the first of three sets of sanctions on Iran in 2003 when Iran admitted to a breach of its promises and obligations under the NPT by not disclosing to the IAEA nearly 18 years of planning and nuclear bomb development. Shortly thereafter Iran declared its right to enrich uranium under the NPT and its intention to do so post-haste to meet its growing energy needs. Thus began a major disagreement between the Iranian authorities and Council powers regarding Iranian intentions and actions. This disagreement played out within the Council, where new counter-proliferation sanctions were imposed again in May 2006 and March 2008. A coalition of states (primarily European) offered a major economic incentive package to Tehran to halt its enrichment program in November 2004, in early 2007 and again in spring of 2008. Meanwhile, the United States and Iran remained locked in a posture of deep hostility towards one another.

The ineffectiveness of US and UN efforts to restrain the Iranian nuclear program stems from several factors. First, the UN sanctions must be viewed in light of the longer history of the US-imposed unilateral comprehensive sanctions on Iran in the wake of the 1979 hostage crisis. This has been the cornerstone of a consistently hostile policy in Washington toward Tehran ever since. Iran has been at the top of the State Department list of states sponsoring terrorism for decades, and its steadily expanding nuclear program has become a source of major concern. In 1996, the US Congress passed the Iran and Libya Sanctions Act, placing additional restrictions on US interactions with Iran and imposing secondary sanctions on other companies, primarily European, that invest in Iran. With the possible exception of the US-imposed banking sanctions of October 2007, these efforts have not significantly weakened the Iranian economy. More essentially, they have not contained the regime and have failed to change its policies regarding support for terrorist groups and continued nuclear development. Sanctions have been counterproductive, strengthening nationalist and conservative forces within Iran.

The history of flawed sanctions against Iran illustrates the complexity of using economic policy across diverse issue areas, and the folly of relying on sanctions that have little support from other significant actors. It also points to the need for dialogue and incentives-based diplomacy as means of influencing Iranian behavior. The imposition of a multiple array of sanctions for a wide range of issues has limited the prospect of obtaining concessions from Iran on specific proliferation-related concerns. Unilateral US sanctions have not prevented Iran from developing commercial and diplomatic ties with the rest of the world and thus have had little effect economically or politically.

The lack of direct dialogue and joint formulation of security guarantees in dealing with Iran has significantly limited US influence. Officials in Tehran have demanded a lifting of US sanctions and face-to-face negotiation as an equal security partner as conditions for improving relations and addressing Washington's non-proliferation and counter-terrorism concerns. US unwillingness either to accept the Iranian position or to ease coercive pressure left the inducements to a coalition of European countries. France, the United Kingdom, and Germany engaged in a series of high-level negotiations that persuaded the Iranian government to accept some temporary, partial limits on its nuclear program in 2004. But these were not sustained and Tehran has since proceeded with its nuclear enrichment activities.

The danger remains that Iran may be in the process of acquiring full-scale nuclear weapons capability. Given the worsening insecurities in the region and Iran's hostile political relations with the United States and Israel, Iran is likely to continue to feel the need for greater deterrent capabilities – perhaps including a nuclear option. Until these underlying political insecurities and tensions are addressed, progress toward denuclearization will be uncertain. Washington seemed open to playing a more direct, influential role in sitting as an equal with Iran in the summer of 2008 when the Bush administration sent Under Secretary of State Nicholas Burns to direct talks with Iran and the Europeans. These steps could open a dialogue with Tehran aimed at building a new political relationship and laying the foundations for greater cooperation on non-proliferation and counter-terrorism.

Achieving denuclearization in North Korea

The North Korean case also illustrates the futility of unrelenting sanctions that are accompanied only by political hostility and security tensions, in contrast to the value of diplomatic engagement and incentives-based bargaining. In the 1994 agreed framework negotiated between the United States and North Korea, the latter halted its nuclear production and reprocessing activities and permitted on-site monitoring to confirm compliance. In exchange, the United States, South Korea, and Japan agreed to provide Pyongyang with fuel oil, new nuclear power reactors that were less proliferation prone, and the beginnings of diplomatic recognition. The agreed framework was successful initially, as international monitors verified the freeze on Pyongyang's plutonium production program. The agreed framework was constructed as a sequence of conciliatory steps and consequent reciprocal actions that, it was hoped, could create a pattern of sustained cooperation between the two sides. North Korea was "punctilious in observing the letter of the agreement," according to Leon Sigal,[39] but the United States fell behind in its deliveries of fuel oil. As the Clinton administration became bogged down in various other crises – some of its own – the construction of new reactors promised by Washington lagged, and a political backlash in the United States undermined support for incentives.

New crises developed in 1998–1999, in response to North Korea's failed test of a long-range ballistic missile. In 1999, the Clinton administration announced limited steps to open commercial trade relations and attempted to negotiate a new non-proliferation agreement, but it left office without completing a settlement, as an eleventh hour effort was stifled by the incoming Bush administration. From the outset, the following Bush administration showed no interest in bargaining directly with Pyongyang and ended fuel deliveries under the agreed framework. In the panicked political climate of 2002, when evidence surfaced of Pyongyang's undisclosed uranium enrichment program, North Korea's response was to withdraw from the NPT, expel international inspectors, and resume the reprocessing of spent fuel.

In seeking a new forum for engagement of North Korea on these issues, the United States created the "Six-Party Talks" as a half-way point in the direction of face-to-face dialogue between Washington and Pyongyang. The mixed success and slowness of this process were pre-empted by the North Korean test blast on 9 October 2006 of what appears to have been an atomic bomb. This resulted in North Korea feeling the full weight of Security Council sanctions soon after, as the Council adopted resolution 1718 (14 October 2006), which embargoed a wide range of technologies, materials, and missiles that would contribute to a nuclear North Korea.

The Korean test and immediate sanctions were followed by a sober assessment on all sides, partly stimulated by the work of IAEA director general Mohamed ElBaradei, as to where future options and goals led. To the surprise of most observers, the North Koreans not only re-entered the Six-Party mechanism, but they did so with greater frankness and energy. But this did not end the melodrama that both Washington and Pyongyang brought to the crisis. The United States played dual-track diplomacy by first adopting its own financial sanctions package, which went considerably beyond UN action, and then confronting Pyongyang directly via the deft negotiating of Under Secretary of State Christopher Hill. Both in the Six-Party framework and in bilateral dialogues, Hill wielded carrots and sticks to achieve what seemed impossible just 18 months earlier. The result was an agreement in 2007 – fully actualized in June 2008 – whereby the United Nations and the West lifted the vast majority of sanctions against North Korea in exchange for documentation by Pyongyang of the history of its nuclear program and the destruction of the cooling tower at the Yongbyon nuclear reactor, thus rendering it dysfunctional.

The 2007 agreement was stalled and nearly scrapped by North Koreans when they complained that the United States did not deliver as promised on unfreezing Korean financial assets. When Washington finally remedied this situation by late spring of 2008, the North Koreans were willing to permit IAEA inspectors back into their country. But they soon developed a final salvo against the United Nations and the Americans in claiming that they would not complete their side of the agreement until the United States removed North Korea from the American list of state sponsors of terrorism. By mid-October 2008, the Bush administration yielded to this demand and the final steps for denuclearization of North Korea under UN auspices were put in place.

India and Pakistan

The challenge of attempting to stifle nuclear materials and weapons production in India and Pakistan highlights the inadequacy of US non-proliferation policies that lie outside of the NPT and Security Council action. This South Asia case also illustrates how, in a post-9/11 world, the large powers, especially the United Kingdom and the United States, have been willing to have counter-terrorism policy concerns take priority over consistency of sanctions application for offenses against nuclear development. In terms of the first challenge, it may seem simplistic but nonetheless accurate to assert that, because both states remained outside of the NPT, the Council had limited jurisdictional authority to challenge nuclear developments. Thus the United Nations lacked the structural connection with these nations' behavior that was necessary to insert the IAEA into an inspections and monitoring role, which had proven so crucial to the success of disarmament in the Iraq case. By a combination of default and design, whatever influence was to be exercised over the development of (only somewhat clandestine) nuclear programs in South Asia would come from the actions of large powers (i.e. the United States) acting alone.

The pattern of US policy action in South Asia, however, offers the classic case of how not to use sanctions and incentives to achieve non-proliferation. Washington's attempts to keep South Asia non-nuclear over the course of three decades were erratic, inconsistent, and ultimately ineffective. Not only did India and Pakistan test and develop nuclear weapons, but A. Q. Khan's network emerged as a global proliferation entrepreneur invulnerable to any economic and legal constraint or accountability. US policy attempted to combine denial strategies – blocking exports to India and Pakistan of sensitive equipment and materials – and various economic and security assistance programs. Technology sanctions made nuclear development more difficult and costly and perhaps slowed it down, but they could not stop it.

From its beginning in the 1970s through the Bush administration's controversial nuclear reactor deal with India in 2007, US policy in South Asia has featured conflicting agendas and sometimes unclear purposes. Non-proliferation goals often clashed with other economic or strategic interests in the subcontinent. In the end, the United States was unable to influence political forces within India that pursued the nuclear option as a symbol of national pride. Nor did Washington recognize how its own inconsistencies in preaching nuclear abstinence to others, while clinging to these weapons for itself, undermined the credibility of its non-proliferation policies in a region where global disarmament goals were taken seriously.

By law, the United States was required to impose sanctions when India, then Pakistan, tested nuclear weapons in 1998. The sanctioning effort was half hearted and short lived, however. It conflicted with other US policies in the region, including growing commercial engagement with India and continued strategic partnership with Pakistan. Soon after sanctions were imposed in May and June 1998 – banning loans, military assistance, investment, and technology transfers – US senators from farming states gained an exemption for grain export credits and guarantees. Congress soon granted President Clinton waiver authority, which he promptly exercised to suspend sanctions that November. The many interests in the United States and South Asia supporting continued engagement made any substantial US sanctions effort toward the two countries extremely difficult.[40]

Similar dilemmas undermined earlier non-proliferation efforts. When Pakistan's help was needed in the mujahideen war against Soviet forces in Afghanistan, earlier non-proliferation restrictions were tossed aside. The floodgates swung open and lavish US assistance poured in, passing through the hands of senior Pakistani military and intelligence officials who in some cases were supporters of Khan and the country's nuclear program. The huge US aid program was a kind of perverse incentive, rewarding the centers of power in Pakistan that were least sympathetic to Western non-proliferation interests and to the broader goal of promoting democracy, human rights, and equitable development.[41] The same pattern emerged in the aftermath of 9/11. The United States relied heavily on Pakistan's military government as a principal ally in overthrowing the Taliban regime in Afghanistan and continuing the fight against al-Qaeda. This made Washington reluctant to challenge Islamabad's nuclear policies or press for more accountability and transparency in shutting down the Khan network. Aspirations for encouraging nuclear responsibility and a functioning democracy in Pakistan were once again cast aside.

Several lessons can be gleaned from the failed history of non-proliferation efforts in South Asia. Coherence and consistency of policy are crucial. Sanctions and incentives can be effective, but they must be strategically targeted. Pressure must be applied on decision-making elites responsible for violating non-proliferation norms, while assistance must be provided to pro-reform groups, strengthening and empowering constituencies that are most likely to support nuclear restraint. When US practice differs dramatically from what it preaches – that is, when it fails to take steps to reduce its own reliance on nuclear weapons while it attempts to dissuade others from acquiring such weapons – states aspiring to power status will seldom listen and change their own behavior. Now that India and Pakistan have become de facto nuclear states, the United States and the United Nations have no choice but to live with the result. Any hopes for denuclearization in the future will hinge on linking nuclear restraint in the subcontinent to broader regional and global disarmament efforts.

Conclusion: Current and future issues of concern

A comparison of the cases in which the United Nations has imposed sanctions to achieve denuclearization demonstrates what is possible in this complex nuclear world. Without question, targeted sanctions have an important and continuing role to play in controlling the spread of weapons of mass destruction. Strong sanctions begin the process and form its cornerstone, with inducements critical at later stages for achieving complete non-proliferation objectives. If incentives are to be offered, however, they must be applied consistently, linked to concrete reciprocal acts of restraint, and targeted to constituencies that are most likely to support denuclearization policies.

Sanctions succeed when the member states needed to enforce them have mobilized a mix of diplomatic engagement and security guarantees to complement the sticks and carrots. Moreover, the stronger the monitoring of prohibited material – often involving the inspections work of the IAEA – the more likely it is sanctions will succeed. There is little question that, had the Security Council not had the work and reports of the Agency on which to rely, then sanctions and related diplomacy would not have achieved their objectives in Libya, Iraq, and North Korea. In fact, one of the sub-themes regarding UN success that warrants more detailed study is the role played by the IAEA and its executive director in the past decade in breaking impasses and moving the disarmament process forward when it has stalled.

The effective use of these tools has helped to reverse nuclear weapons development in such diverse cases as Iraq, Libya, and North Korea. Similar processes, though not under UN auspices, prompted denuclearization in other nations, such as Ukraine. In South Asia, however, carrot-and-stick diplomacy failed to stem the development and testing of nuclear weapons. In the case of Iran, a sanctions-only policy proved ineffective at the outset of the crisis. But poor diplomatic engagement over time, combined with Iranian distrust and intransigency, meant that considerable incentives offered first by the European Union and then by these nations along with the United States, did not produce the shutting down of the Iranian enrichment program. This possibility was not out of reach by the summer of 2008, but short of major changes in the Iranian position it was unclear how it would be achieved.

Amidst these sanctions successes, current real world challenges and tough policy situations remain unresolved. Despite the Iraq case, we know little regarding how sanctions placed on nuclear weapons states that violate their NPT disarmament obligations will alter their behavior. Nor, as the Iranian case illustrates, has the UN system done well in recognizing and reacting to the dilemma built into the structure of the NPT, namely that states have a right to develop nuclear reactors for use in civilian energy. The crux of the matter is not just inspections, but how the system develops sanctions once weapons-grade material crosses the line from civilian to military use.

Even as the most prevalent cases of proliferation control focus on nations, the post-9/11 world poses a particular challenge to the United Nations regarding the spread of nuclear weapons to and by non-state actors. The February 2004 revelation of A. Q. Khan's nuclear supply network intensified concerns about possible terrorist acquisition of nuclear weapons materials. In response, the Security Council approved resolution 1540 (28 April 2004), prohibiting countries from providing support for non-state actors seeking to develop weapons of mass destruction.

At that time the Council also strengthened financial sanctions and other targeted measures against designated members of al-Qaeda and the Taliban. This solidified recognition at the Council level that the acquisition of nuclear weapons by terrorists was an issue joined to the risks posed by the spread of nuclear weapons to South Asia, so-called "loose nukes" in Russia, and the nuclear ambitions of Iran and North Korea. These actions reflect that denuclearization is defined more by counter-proliferation than by disarmament. And that tension – whether Security Council sanctions will be focused on counter-proliferation, or non-proliferation, or disarmament – will continue for the foreseeable future.

A very difficult set of larger questions regarding the longer-term adequacy of sanctions also looms. The important "moral authority" of the Security Council in the counter-proliferation and disarmament arenas is central to and must precede the political efficacy of sanctions. Here again the double standard of the weapons-dominant P-5 states continues to undermine the potential strength of the system. The United Nations' authority and potential success to change the behavior of horizontal proliferators will always be weakened by its unwillingness to impose sanctions on the vertical proliferators in its own club.

That noted, sanctions will continue to be a tool of first choice in the nuclear issue, not the least of the reasons being that they also have proven to be reasonably effective in containing recalcitrant regimes. They can provide bargaining leverage for engaging regimes in non-proliferation compliance. Since the early 1990s, carrot-and-stick diplomacy has offered the best strategy for establishing the foundations of improved political relations and building cooperation for non-proliferation under UN auspices.

Notes

1. For a detailed discussion of these cases, see David Cortright and George A. Lopez, *Sanctions and the Search for Security: Challenges to UN Action* (Boulder, CO: Lynne Rienner Publishers, 2002).
2. This double standard dilemma, which shapes a non-proliferation, rather than disarmament, agenda within the United Nations, is discussed with sharp frankness by Rebecca Johnson, "'Do As I Say, Not As I Do': From Nuclear Non-Proliferation to Counter-Proliferation," in *Arms Control After Iraq: Normative and Operational Challenges*, ed. Waheguru Pal Singh Sidhu and Ramesh Thakur (Tokyo: United Nations Press, 2006), 57–79.
3. See George A. Lopez and David Cortright, "Containing Iraq: Sanctions Worked," *Foreign Affairs* 83, no. 4 (2004): 90–113.
4. Sanctions against Iraq also had devastating humanitarian consequences. For the first six years, comprehensive sanctions cut off all trade and shut down oil exports, which shattered Iraq's economy and society. The combination of sanctions and bombing caused a severe humanitarian crisis, resulting in hundreds of thousands of preventable deaths among children. Infant and child mortality rates in south/central Iraq more than doubled, according to a study from the London School of Hygiene and Tropical Medicine published in *The Lancet*. See Richard Garfield, *Morbidity and Mortality among Iraqi Children from 1990 to 1998: Assessing the Impact of Economic Sanctions*, Occasional Paper Series 16:OP:3 (Goshen, IN: Joan B. Kroc Institute for International Peace

Studies at the University of Notre Dame and the Fourth Freedom Forum, March 1999). For further humanitarian impact data, see Mohamed M. Ali and Iqbal H. Shah, "Sanctions and Childhood Mortality in Iraq," *The Lancet* 355 (May 2000): 1837–1857.
5. This revision, given the multiple structural difficulties of Security Council resolution 687, and the need to reverse the negative humanitarian impact, can be considered an effective adaptation of the sanctions approach to Iraq. But history now reveals that the United States' changing policy goals and intent in relation to the sanctions made every revision and humanitarian decision a political lever that ultimately complicated the success of sanctions. See Cortright and Lopez, *Sanctions and the Search for Security*, 21–46.
6. George H. W. Bush, "The President's News Conference with Chancellor Helmut Kohl of Germany," transcript, Washington, DC, 20 May 1991.
7. As quoted in Barbara Crossette, "For Iraq: A Dog House with Many Rooms," *New York Times*, 23 November 1997.
8. We have explored this dilemma at various points. See David Cortright and George A. Lopez, "Are Sanctions Just? The Problematic Case of Iraq," *Journal of International Affairs* 52, no. 2 (1999): 735–755; George A. Lopez and David Cortright, "Trouble in the Gulf, Pain and Promise," *Bulletin of the Atomic Scientists* 54, no. 3 (1998): 39–43; and in Lopez and Cortright, "Containing Iraq."
9. For a far-reaching discussion of the countless technical, political, and economic issues at stake in this challenge, see Sidhu and Thakur, *Arms Control After Iraq*.
10. Joseph Cirincione et al., *WMD in Iraq: Evidence and Implications* (Washington, DC: Carnegie Endowment for International Peace, January 2004), 8.
11. Hans Blix, *Disarming Iraq* (New York: Pantheon Books, 2004), 259.
12. *Remarks by Vice President Richard Cheney to the Veterans of Foreign Wars 103rd National Convention*, Nashville, TN, 26 August 2002.
13. *Iraq's Weapons of Mass Destruction: The Assessment of the British Government* (London: The Stationery Office, September 2002), 39.
14. *Fourth Consolidated Report of the Director General of the International Atomic Energy Agency Under Paragraph 16 of Security Council Resolution 1051 (1996)*, Security Council document S/1997/779, New York, 6 October 1997, para. 72.
15. *Emergency Session of the United Nations Special Commission Established Under Paragraph 9(b)(i) of Security Council Resolution 687 (1991)*, Security Council document S/1997/922, 24 November 1997, para. 5.
16. *The Status of Nuclear Inspections in Iraq: An Update*, Report of the Director General of the International Atomic Energy Agency to the United Nations Security Council, New York, 7 March 2003, 5; available at ⟨http://www.un.org/News/dh/iraq/elbaradei-7mar03.pdf⟩ (accessed 7 November 2008).
17. *Report of the Executive Chairman on the Activities of the Special Commission Established by the Secretary-General Pursuant to Paragraph 9(b)(i) of Resolution 687 (1991)*, Security Council document S/1998/332, 16 April 1998, para. 31.
18. *Hearings to Examine Threats, Responses, and Regional Considerations Surrounding Iraq*, 107th Cong., 2nd sess., 31 July and 1 August 2002, testimony of Anthony H. Cordesman.
19. United Nations Monitoring, Verification and Inspection Commission, *Unresolved Disarmament Issues: Iraq's Proscribed Weapons Programmes* (New York: United Nations, 2003); available at ⟨http://www.un.org/Depts/unmovic/documents/cluster6mar.pdf⟩ (accessed 7 November 2008). See also Cirincione et al., *WMD in Iraq*, 40.
20. *Statement by Hans Blix to the Security Council*, 7 March 2003; available as "Oral Introduction of the 12th Quarterly Report of UNMOVIC. Executive Chairman Dr. Hans Blix," at ⟨http://www.un.org/Depts/unmovic/SC7asdelivered.htm⟩ (accessed 7 November 2008).

21. "Remarks by Rolf Ekéus to the Carnegie Endowment for International Peace, Conference on Nuclear Nonproliferation and the Millennium: Prospects and Initiatives," Washington, DC, 13 February 1996.
22. Karen de Young, "Baghdad Weapons Programs Dormant; Iraq's Inactivity Puzzles U.S. Officials," *Washington Post*, 15 July 1999.
23. *IAEA Update Report for the Security Council Pursuant to Resolution 1441 (2002)*, Security Council document S/2003/95, 27 January 2003, para. 71.
24. "The Status of the Agency's Verification Activities in Iraq as of 8 January 2003," United Nations Security Council Briefing by Mohamed ElBaradei, Director General, International Atomic Energy Agency, 9 January 2003; available at ⟨http://www.iraqwatch.org/un/IAEA/iaea-elbaradei-unscbriefing-010903.htm⟩ (accessed 7 November 2008), para. 16.
25. Blix, *Disarming Iraq*, 272.
26. Tim Trevan, *Saddam's Secrets: The Hunt for Iraq's Hidden Weapons* (London: Harper-Collins, 1999), 159 and 217.
27. Ibid., 311.
28. Sarah Graham-Brown, *Sanctioning Saddam: The Politics of Intervention in Iraq* (London: I. B. Tauris, 1999), 78–79.
29. Trevan, *Saddam's Secrets*, 311.
30. Ibid., 321.
31. Ibid., 352 and 356.
32. "Shifting Priorities: UNMOVIC and the Future of Inspections in Iraq: An Interview with Ambassador Rolf Ekéus," *Arms Control Today* 30, no. 2 (2000): 6.
33. Quoted in Trevan, *Saddam's Secrets*, 323.
34. Meghan O'Sullivan, *Shrewd Sanctions: Statecraft and State Sponsors of Terrorism* (Washington, DC: Brookings Institution Press, 2003), 140.
35. *Statement of General Anthony C. Zinni Commander in Chief US Central Command Before the U.S. Senate Committee on the Armed Services*, 106th Cong., 2nd sess., 15 March 2000.
36. US Department of State, "Overview of State-Sponsored Terrorism," in *Patterns of Global Terrorism, 1996*, April 1997; available at ⟨http://www.hri.org/docs/USSD-Terror/96/overview.html⟩ (accessed 7 November 2008).
37. Office of the Vice President, The White House, "Vice President Participates in a Q&A at the Boone County Lumber Company in Columbia, Missouri," 19 July 2004; available at ⟨http://www.whitehouse.gov/news/releases/2004/07/20040719-12.html⟩ (accessed 7 November 2008).
38. See Thomas E. McNamara, "Unilateral and Multilateral Strategies against State Sponsors of Terror: A Case Study of Libya, 1979–2003," in *Uniting Against Terror*, ed. David Cortright and George A. Lopez (Cambridge, MA: MIT Press, 2007), 83–122.
39. Leon Sigal, "Averting a Train Wreck with North Korea," *Arms Control Today*, 28, no. 6 (1998): 12.
40. We detail these sanctions in George A. Lopez and David Cortright, "Bombs, Carrots, and Sticks: The Use of Incentives and Sanctions," *Arms Control Today* 35, no. 2 (2005): 19–24.
41. See David Cortright and Samina Ahmed, *Pakistan and the Bomb* (Notre Dame, IN: University of Notre Dame Press, 1998).

6

The use of force

Ian Johnstone

The Iraq war and hints of pre-emptive strikes against North Korea and Iran, combined with the growing fear of nuclear terrorism since the attacks of 11 September 2001, mean that the possibility of military action against nuclear proliferation is real. This chapter considers that possibility primarily from a legal perspective, looking at both self-defense on the basis of Article 51 of the UN Charter and action authorized by the Security Council under Chapter VII. My central argument is that the system governing collective action by the Council can and should be strengthened to deal with proliferation threats, up to and including the use of force. In making that case, I look first at the existing law of self-defense and attempts by the George W. Bush administration to expand it to encompass preventive action. I consider whether the "accumulation of events" theory is a helpful way of elaborating the concept of an "imminent" threat, the accepted threshold for anticipatory self-defense. I conclude that this is a slippery slope and, although helpful in respect of threats from terrorist organizations, is too open to abuse for dealing with acts of nuclear proliferation by states. The theory does, however, provide a starting point for developing criteria for Council-authorized action.

The chapter is divided into main two sections. In the first section, I examine the doctrine of pre-emption and make the argument that "anticipatory self-defense" is permissible in response to truly imminent threats, but not preventatively against more remote threats. I then elaborate the test of imminence with reference to the accumulation of events theory,

The United Nations and nuclear orders, Boulden, Thakur and Weiss (eds),
United Nations University Press, 2009, ISBN 978-92-808-1167-4

applying it to both state and non-state actors. The section concludes by considering a state of necessity as an alternative basis for unilateral action. In the second section, on UN-authorized military action, I briefly review the sources of the Council's legal authority before making the case that the political will to act against nuclear threats – even with force – can probably be generated given the shared interests of the five permanent members of the Security Council (the P-5). I conclude with three proposals designed to ensure a more systematic, less selective approach in the Council: reaffirmation of positive and negative security assurances; adoption of a Chapter VII resolution on interdiction; and criteria to guide Council deliberations on preventive action. The proposals are designed to both stimulate Council action when appropriate and constrain it when not, while enhancing the legitimacy of this flawed institution without imagining that politics can be taken out of decisions about the use of force.

Self-defense

The doctrine of pre-emption and anticipatory self-defense

The most significant contemporary controversy surrounding the law of self-defense concerns the right of anticipatory self-defense: when, if ever, can a state act against a threat of attack before it materializes? President Bush raised the specter of pre-emptive action in June 2002 when he said in a speech that the Cold War doctrines of deterrence and containment do not work against new threats posed by "shadowy terrorist networks with no nation or citizens to defend" and "unbalanced dictators [who can deliver] weapons of mass destruction on missiles or secretly provide them to terrorist allies."[1] The 2002 *National Security Strategy* (NSS) was released three months later, claiming that Article 51 of the UN Charter permits "anticipatory self-defense," including pre-emptive strikes against terrorists potentially armed with weapons of mass destruction (WMD). The most telling parts of the NSS read as follows:

> For centuries.... [l]egal scholars and international jurists often conditioned the legitimacy of preemption on the existence of an imminent threat – most often a visible mobilization of armies, navies, and air forces preparing to attack.... We must adapt the concept of imminent threat to the capabilities and objectives of today's adversaries.... The greater the threat, the greater is the risk of inaction – and the more compelling the case for taking anticipatory action to defend ourselves, even if uncertainty remains as to the time and place of the enemy's attack. *To forestall or prevent such hostile acts* by our adversaries, the United States will, if necessary, act preemptively.[2]

Similarly, the *National Security Strategy to Combat Weapons of Mass Destruction* foresees the use of pre-emptive measures "to detect and destroy an adversary's *WMD assets* before these weapons are used."[3]

There is a long history to the doctrine of "anticipatory self-defense," going back to the *Caroline* case of 1837. In claiming that a British attack on a ship used to transport insurgents fighting British rule in Canada was illegal, US Secretary of State Daniel Webster stated that self-defense is permissible only when the threat of attack is "instant, overwhelming and leaving no choice of means and no moment for deliberation." Most international lawyers see the *Caroline* test as still good law; indeed, the argument for anticipatory self-defense is even stronger in the nuclear age, when common sense dictates that a state should not be required to wait passively for the bombs to start falling before it can defend itself.

Yet what the NSS seems to contemplate is not *pre-emption* of a truly imminent attack, but rather *prevention* of some future, not well-specified, threat from materializing. If accepted in its most expansive form, the doctrine stretches the term "armed attack" so far it collapses the distinction between the threshold for Security Council-authorized military action in Article 39 of the Charter ("threat to the peace") and the threshold in Article 51 ("armed attack"). It would allow for unilateral military action against virtually any threat, even if – as Vice President Dick Cheney put it – the chance of attack was only 1 percent.[4] British Attorney-General Lord Goldsmith rejected the doctrine of pre-emption in the secret advice he gave to Prime Minister Tony Blair in March 2003:

> I am aware that the USA has been arguing for recognition of a broad doctrine of a right to use force to pre-empt danger in the future. If this means more than the right to respond proportionately to an imminent attack (and I understand that the doctrine is intended to carry that connotation), this is not a doctrine which, in my opinion, exists or is recognised in international law.[5]

The Secretary-General's High-level Panel on Threats, Challenges and Change (HLP) agreed that *pre-emptive* military action against imminent threats is permissible in self-defense, but that *preventive* action against "non-imminent, non-proximate" threats is not.[6] The line between the two is hard to draw and the Iraq case does not shed much light because, despite the timing of the release of the NSS in 2002, self-defense was not the official justification for the war – enforcement of Security Council resolutions was.[7] Scholars have spilled a good deal of ink trying to draw the line by elaborating the concept of "imminence." John Yoo, for example, argued that the Iraq war could be justified as self-defense, based on a test of imminence that looks beyond the temporal dimension to the probability of an attack and the magnitude of harm.[8] Michael Reisman speaks of "palpable and imminent threats" as opposed to "conjectural and contingent threats of possible future attacks."[9] Jordan Paust would restrict anticipatory self-defense to "incipient" attacks, based not "on the ground of expectations, anticipations and fear," but rather when the other side "is already embarked on an inevitable course of action."[10] Niaz Shah stresses the degree of "certainty" that the attack will happen,[11] while T. D. Gill and Kristen Eichensehr equate imminence to "immediacy."[12]

Accumulation of events

As this long list suggests, ever-refined definitions of the term "imminence" are not likely to make its application to particular cases any easier. However, a legal theory with some pedigree – the "accumulation of events" theory – does seem to get at the problem with a rigid application of the *Caroline* test to threats of nuclear terrorism, if not nuclear proliferation more generally. The theory holds that, if a state has been attacked in the past and can present compelling evidence of both the source of the attacks and a genuine threat of future attacks from the same source, then a self-defensive response would be legal. The International Court of Justice (ICJ) endorsed it implicitly in the *Nicaragua* (1986) and *Iran Platforms* (2003) cases. Neither is about nuclear weapons or terrorism, but there is language in both to suggest that a *series* of attacks can be justification for a self-defensive response, even if a single incident in the series is not.[13] A more difficult legal situation arises when there has been only one past attack, or no attack at all. Can an accumulation of *events* justify anticipatory self-defense? Here it is worth separating the discussion of nuclear terrorism from nuclear threats posed by so-called rogue states.

Evidence that the threat of nuclear terrorism is real includes the determined efforts of Osama bin Laden to acquire nuclear weapons, which he called a "religious duty."[14] Just weeks before 9/11, two Pakistani nuclear scientists reportedly handed him a rough sketch of a nuclear bomb design; documents recovered in Afghanistan reveal a significant research effort; and in 2002 and 2003 the CIA received reports that al-Qaeda was negotiating to purchase three Russian nuclear weapons.[15] Similarly, Aum Shinrikyo (the group responsible for the sarin attack in Tokyo in 1995) and Chechen rebel groups have tried to get their hands on nuclear weapons and/or material.[16] None of these efforts bore fruit, but the evidence of intent is alarming.

The language of the Charter does not preclude self-defense against non-state actors and the widespread support for US military action against al-Qaeda in Afghanistan suggests that, whatever the state of the law before 9/11, it is now permissible.[17] It is not hard to imagine a

pattern of events that would justify pre-emptive action against the threat of nuclear terrorism. Consider, for example, the following scenario:
- A terrorist group has attempted to steal a nuclear weapon, or the group has attempted to steal fissile materials and has the equipment and know-how to build a nuclear device
- The group has close ties to a state of proliferation concern
- Statements threatening a nuclear attack have emanated from the group
- Detailed plans for attacks against specific targets have been discovered

None of the "events" is entirely far-fetched and, together, they could well lead a state to conclude that waiting any longer would be too late to thwart the attack. The threat is not quite "instant and overwhelming" but, as Michael Doyle argues, the *Caroline* standard of imminence is simply too rigid when applied to terrorists who are able to hide their intentions and then strike a devastating blow – such as 9/11 – without any obvious signs of an impending attack.[18]

The considerations are somewhat different for nuclear threats posed by states, partly because deterrence is more likely to work and therefore the case for relaxing the test of imminence is weaker. The issue tends to get framed in terms of the legality of strikes against nuclear facilities in order to prevent a state from acquiring *the capacity* to develop nuclear weapons. Israel claimed that its destruction of the Osirak nuclear reactor before it became operational was legal on the grounds that Iraq was "coldly planning [Israel's] nuclear obliteration" and that it had a right to halt the potentially "fatal process before it reaches completion."[19] Although at least one commentator argued that the strike was not a violation of the Article 2(4) prohibition against the use of force,[20] the Security Council unanimously denounced it as a "clear violation of the Charter of the United Nations and norms of international conduct."[21] The incident had echoes in September 2007 when Israeli warplanes bombed what Israel suspected was a nuclear site in Syria being built with assistance from North Korea.[22] Several scholars have considered whether a preemptive strike against Iran's nuclear facilities would be legal, most concluding that it would not.[23]

Although one can imagine a highly alarming "accumulation of events" (North Korea's withdrawal from the Nuclear Non-Proliferation Treaty (NPT), removal of the weapons inspectors, ballistic missile and then nuclear tests, for example), to permit unilateral self-defense leads down a slippery slope. The same or a similar set of events could be invoked by "unbalanced dictators" to make a claim against those seeking to prevent proliferation. North Korea, in withdrawing from the NPT, cited a long list of grievances against the United States, including nuclear war exercises, a 1999 joint US–South Korean statement threatening "strong retaliation ... with nuclear weapons," President Bush's "axis of evil" speech in January 2002, and what North Korea called "a nuclear attack plan" unveiled later that year.[24] The list of grievances may not sound credible, but it does highlight the risk in leaving it to each state to decide whether "the accumulation of events" is such as would amount to an imminent threat justifying pre-emptive action. That decision would be subject to collective judgment after the fact, in the form of the reactions of other governments through diplomatic channels and in the political organs of international organizations, but evidentiary considerations will render cohesive judgment by the international community almost impossible.

In sum, the accumulation of events is a useful way of fleshing out the concept of imminence as it applies to terrorist threats, but is less useful in dealing with state-based threats. The latter lend themselves to the use of more traditional tools of statecraft, from diplomacy to economic sanctions, and more time for deliberation. This is to say not that preventive action against states (action that does not meet the threshold test of imminence) will never be necessary, but that action should be taken by the Security Council.

Plea of necessity

Before turning to Council-authorized action, an alternative theory for unilateral action is worth considering briefly: the plea of necessity. The simple idea is that, in some extreme circumstances, states are driven to violate the law and should in effect be pardoned for their transgression. The ICJ has twice acknowledged that this defense exists in international law, although in neither case was the plea successful.[25] The International Law Commission (ILC), in endorsing it in its articles on state responsibility, described the defense of necessity as a "safety valve" by means of which states can escape the harmful consequences of rigid adherence to a rule of law in all circumstances.[26] It leaves the law intact while acknowledging that in certain circumstances violations are excusable.

It is tempting to argue that necessity may be invoked to excuse preventive action against nuclear threats after the fact, even if a claim of self-defense before the fact would not be persuasive.[27] However, there are problems with that line of argument. To begin with, the ILC's own criteria for a successful plea of necessity include a "grave and imminent peril," essentially the same standard as self-defense. Second, the defense of necessity has migrated from its original roots in the notion of "self-preservation" to the protection of "the essential interests of a state," and more recently to community interests that are not otherwise well protected by the law.[28] Thus the *Gabcikovo-Nagymaros* case and many of the examples cited by the ILC in its commentaries are about environmental and humanitarian concerns, where the necessity "safety valve" is needed because existing law provides inadequate protection and the Council's mandate does not naturally extend to these areas. The law of self-defense, on the other hand, applies directly to nuclear threats and they fall squarely within the Council's competence. To complicate matters by introducing necessity as an alternative defense could cast this whole area of law into even deeper uncertainty, requiring fine distinctions – i.e. between acts that are legal, acts that are illegal but excusable, and acts that are both illegal and inexcusable – that may be impossible to make in a decentralized legal system.[29]

That being said, whether or not the defense of necessity makes sense in theory, it corresponds to political reality. Some states, seeing a nuclear threat, will simply act without worrying about the legal niceties. The necessity defense is designed to deal with those situations. Whether the excuse is accepted in a particular case will depend on many factors, but for reasons given above it is hard to imagine circumstances in which the plea would be successful when a claim of self-defense would not.

The role of the Security Council

There is no shortage of ways by which the Security Council may become seized of a nuclear proliferation matter – ranging from referral by the International Atomic Energy Agency (IAEA) to the inherent authority based in the Charter itself. Whether the Council has the political will to act is a separate question, as is the legitimacy of action it does take, given the dominance of that body by the five declared nuclear powers (N-5). In this section, I briefly review the legal authority of the Council, then turn to a discussion of the prospects of the five permanent members agreeing on coercive action, and conclude with a set of proposals designed to improve those prospects while legitimizing Council action.

The legal authority of the Security Council

Both the NPT and the Treaty of Tlatelolco assign the Security Council the task of enforcement, the former indirectly through the Statute of the IAEA. The Statute and all Safeguards Agreements required by the NPT stipulate that its 35-member board of governors *must* report violations of the agreements to the Council.[30] In addition, the agreement defining the relationship between the IAEA and the United Nations requires the Agency to assist the Council in fulfilling its responsibilities, and the director general may be invited to Council meetings to supply it with information.³¹ The Treaty of Tlatelolco imposes an obligation on the General Conference of the Agency for the Prohibition of Nuclear Weapons in Latin America (OPANAL) to report to the Council, although the relevant provision limits the requirement to violations "which might endanger peace and security." OPANAL also has the authority to conduct challenge inspections of suspect sites at the request of members that believe a party is engaged in a prohibited activity, the results of which must be transmitted to the Council, regardless of whether a violation of the treaty is uncovered.

Both treaties entitle a party to withdraw with three months' notice, provided they send a statement to the Council informing it that "extraordinary events, related to the subject matter of the treaty, have jeopardized the supreme interests of the country." When North Korea (DPRK) announced its withdrawal from the NPT in 1993, the United States, the United Kingdom, and Russia – the three depositories of the treaty – issued a statement "questioning whether DPRK's stated reasons for withdrawing ... constitute extraordinary events relating to the subject-matter of the Treaty."³² After the DPRK tested a nuclear device in 2006, the Council adopted a resolution that could be read as implying North Korea's withdrawal in 2003 was legally invalid.³³ Whether the right to withdraw is unfettered as long as the procedural requirements are met is an interesting legal question; as a practical matter, however, there is no doubt that the Council can determine that the circumstances surrounding a withdrawal threaten international peace and security, justifying a response under Chapter VII.

In addition to the non-proliferation treaties, the Charter provides that the General Assembly (Article 11), the Secretary-General (Article 99) and any member of the organization (Article 35) can bring a threat to the attention of the Council. The Council also has inherent authority to deal with nuclear threats – it need not wait for a referral from a verification agency or other UN organ. Nor must it wait for the threat to materialize; it can act preventatively, as specified in Article 1(1) of the Charter (the first purpose of the United Nations is "prevention and removal of threats to the peace"). This was reinforced by a statement issued at the Security Council Summit meeting in January 1992 declaring "the proliferation of all weapons of mass destruction constitutes a threat to international peace and security." Though not legally binding, this statement signals that a specific act of proliferation *in itself* might justify coercive action under Chapter VII.³⁴

There are institutional implications if the Council chooses to act on its own authority. If the matter falls outside the scope of the non-proliferation treaties (for example, a nuclear test by a non-signatory to the NPT or the stockpiling of nuclear material by a signatory), no question of legal competence arises, though, with no established "trigger list" of prohibited action, the Council does throw itself open to charges of double standards. More problematic are situations where a treaty seems to have been violated but the relevant authorities do not bring the matter to the attention of the Council (perhaps because the requisite votes could not be mustered in the governing board). The Council is not bound by the procedures laid down in the treaties but, from an institutional point of view, this has the potential of undermining the integrity of the nuclear non-proliferation regime. In joining the treaties, the parties agree to the verification and enforcement mechanisms embodied therein. If the Council were to determine violations and enforce the treaties while casually by-passing the mechanisms the treaties create, states might be less inclined to join in the first place or more inclined to withdraw.

The General Assembly: Uniting for peace resolution

Before turning to the prospects of the Security Council acting in particular cases, a quick word about the authority of the General Assembly is in order. To avoid a Soviet veto of action on Korea in 1950, the United States orchestrated the Uniting for Peace (UFP) resolution in the Assembly, which in effect declared that if the Council is paralyzed the Assembly can act. When the resolution was later invoked to authorize two peacekeeping missions, it was challenged in the ICJ. The Court ruled that the Assembly could establish peacekeeping missions, creatively interpreting Article 11(2) of the Charter to mean that the Assembly cannot take "coercive" action but, because peacekeeping is consent based, the Assembly has competence.

To some, the Assembly is a more legitimate body than the Council and thus ought to play a greater role in non-proliferation. However, it is unlikely that the UFP resolution would ever be invoked to authorize military action against nuclear threats. To begin with, the logic of the ICJ opinion applies only to consent-based action. More to the point, the chances of obtaining the required two-thirds majority in the Assembly are slim because none of the P-5 has an interest in reviving the resolution, even if they would benefit from the legitimacy it could bring in a particular case. There was talk of activating UFP to bless the intervention in Kosovo by the North Atlantic Treaty Organization (NATO), but not only would Russia and China have opposed it on substantive grounds, the United States and the United Kingdom would have as well. From their perspective, acting on the basis of existing Council resolutions was preferable to doing an end run around the veto. The same logic would almost certainly apply to nuclear threats.

Prospects for Council action

The Council has legal authority to act against nuclear threats, but does it have the political will? While the unity of the P-5 is showing signs of strain – as evidenced by the recent vetoes of resolutions on Myanmar and Zimbabwe, and by tension over Georgia – there is reason to believe they have enough common interest in stemming the spread of weapons of mass destruction and countering terrorism that agreement on coercive action is a distinct possibility.[35]

To begin with, all five permanent members have suffered from acts of terrorism and – to varying degrees – have put counter-terrorism high on their list of foreign policy priorities. Russia sees the Chechen insurgency as a terrorist threat and China's 2002 National Defense white paper declares that China "has always resolutely opposed and condemned all forms of terrorism, and has actively adopted effective measures to fight against terrorism," including through the Council.[36] Although one may object that the P-5 employ vastly different conceptions of terrorism, it is noteworthy that the Council came close to adopting a definition after the Beslan school tragedy in Russia.[37]

This common interest in countering terrorism has been matched by a converging interest in preventing the spread of WMD. Although the evidence of cooperation in this area is slimmer, the European Union has adopted a strategy against proliferation that includes the possibility of force, and a new willingness on the part of Russia, China, and the United States to work through the Council has produced some rather striking developments. Even the legacy of Iraq is not altogether negative in terms of Council unity. After all, the discovery that the IAEA and the UN Special Commission on Iraq (UNSCOM) had effectively neutralized Iraq's WMD programs demonstrates that sanctions combined with the threat of force can work. Moreover, the events leading to military action in March 2003 do not signify as great a breakdown of the Council as commonly thought. The differences in the Council were not over whether Saddam Hussein's WMD programs posed a threat, but rather over the urgency of the threat and how best to deal with it. When Security Council resolution 1441 (8 November 2002) was adopted, each side of the debate over whether it authorized the use of force (the United States and the United Kingdom on the one hand, France and Russia on the other) knew how the other would interpret it.[38] As the French ambassador to Washington put it, the P-5 "agreed to disagree."[39] Moreover, the French advised Washington not to table a second resolution on the use of force that France would have vetoed, but rather to act on the basis of its own interpretation of existing resolutions and preserve some credibility of the

Council for another day. Even more to the point, British Ambassador Jeremy Greenstock insists that, with a little more patience, the United States and the United Kingdom could have obtained the votes needed for an explicit authorization.[40] Arguably the failure was as much one of US diplomacy as it was the result of radical differences of opinion about the utility of force. Admittedly, this is speculative but it does suggest that the Iraq episode should not be read as conclusive evidence that the P-5 will never agree on military action to deal with nuclear threats.

The Iraq episode was preceded and followed by a substantial body of Council practice on WMD proliferation. In the immediate aftermath of 9/11, the Council adopted resolution 1373 (28 September 2001) on the financing and other forms of support for terrorism, an unprecedented act of "legislation."[41] The resolution drew a connection between terrorism and proliferation, and was followed by resolution 1540 (28 April 2004), aimed at stopping WMD from falling into the hands of terrorists. All P-5 members but China have joined the Proliferation Security Initiative (PSI), and China has pledged its cooperation. The Six-Party Talks on North Korea, as well as resolutions imposing limited sanctions after the ballistic missile test in 2006 and nuclear test in 2007, are signs of P-5 unity. The ratcheting up of pressure on Iran, including through increasingly severe economic sanctions, is also revealing.

It is tempting to dismiss the Council as dysfunctional but, compared with the Cold War, it is better able to deal with threats posed by terrorism and WMD proliferation, precisely because there is some common ground among the P-5. Chastened by Iraq, the United States is displaying greater willingness to work through the Council and because the other four members do not want Washington to by-pass the Council they have not categorically rejected the use of force.

Collective action through the Security Council

The politics of the Council are driven mainly by the P-5 but, on WMD and terrorism, divisions among them maybe less pronounced than divisions between them and the rest of the UN membership. This ties in to the broader theme of the legitimacy of the Council as the supreme body for enforcing the non-proliferation regimes. I argued above that unilateral military action may be lawful in exceptional circumstances – against terrorists or in the face of truly imminent threats. But in cases where preventive action is contemplated, turning to the Council is the better course as a matter of both law and policy. That assumes, however, that the Council is seen and acts as something more than a cabal of the P-5 seeking to protect their unilateral and joint interests. A discussion of Council reform is beyond the scope of this chapter, but below are a three politically feasible proposals tied directly to counter-proliferation that would enhance the Council's legitimacy.

Security assurances

A first step would be for the P-5 to reaffirm the positive and negative security assurances made in past years. Positive security assurances – the first of which was made by the United States, the United Kingdom and the Soviet Union in 1968 when signing the NPT – are promises by those states to assist non-nuclear states attacked with nuclear weapons.[42] Negative security assurances, made in 1995 and welcomed by the Council in resolution 984 (11 April 1995) that same year, are commitments by the N-5 not to use nuclear weapons against non-nuclear states.[43] However, the United States, with France, Russia and the United Kingdom, all qualified their negative security assurances by claiming they did not apply "in the case of an invasion or any other attack on the US ... its allies or on a state towards which it has a security commitment, carried out or sustained by a non-nuclear-weapon state in association or alliance with a nuclear weapon state."[44] And, since then, the United States and the United Kingdom have backed even further away, making statements that they reserve the right to use nuclear weapons in response to biological or chemical attacks.

Reaffirming these assurances would be a small but significant step towards righting the perceived imbalance of a nuclear order in which the states that control the Council are entitled to retain nuclear weapons, whereas those required to forgo them may find themselves on the receiving end of Council-authorized military action. Picking up on the ICJ's opinion that the NPT and associated security assurances foreshadow a future general prohibition on the use of nuclear weapons,[45] reaffirming NPT and associated security assurances and removing any qualifications would signal that the P-5 take seriously their responsibilities – and special privileges – under the NPT and the Charter.

Interdiction

When resolution 1540 was adopted, the United States sought to include a provision on the interdiction of ships, aircraft, or trucks suspected of carrying weapons of mass destruction or related material. The prospect of a Chinese veto led to the deletion of that paragraph. Instead, the Bush administration launched the PSI – an agreement among 11 countries, the most important feature of which is a set of interdiction principles designed to stop weapons of mass destruction from falling into the hands of state and non-state actors. More than 80 countries have since expressed their support, but the PSI rests on uncertain legal grounds. Even within the territorial sea of a participating state, the right to board and seize items from traversing ships may conflict with the "right of innocent passage" guaranteed by the Law of the Sea Convention.[46] Interdiction on the high seas is almost certainly illegal unless the interdicting country has the permission of the flag state (Washington has made bilateral agreements with Panama, Liberia, and five other countries granting it that permission). A 2005 Protocol to the Suppression of Unlawful Acts against the Safety of Maritime Navigation would allow for interdiction on the high seas but, if and when it comes into force, the protocol will bind only states that sign and ratify it.

In addition to the legal uncertainties, the PSI lacks clear standards as to when an interdiction would be warranted – which states and non-state actors are "of proliferation concern" (terminology used in the statement of PSI principles), when to interdict the ships of other states, how much proof is necessary to justify an interdiction, who gets to see the evidence, and what redress there is when an interdiction proves not to have been justified.[47] Because the United States has considerable leverage over many of the states participating in the PSI, it has inordinate say over whether and how to interdict particular ships.

Enshrining the PSI in a Chapter VII resolution would serve three purposes: it would remove any uncertainty as to the authority to interdict in territorial seas; it would allow for interdiction on the high seas; and it would enable some collective oversight of how the regime is implemented. As another legislative-style resolution, it could be seen in some quarters as an illegitimate power grab by an "imperial" Council. But almost half of UN member states are already participating and so a critical mass may have been reached. Moreover, on the spectrum of uses of force, interdiction of ships is relatively mild. It is a form of pre-authorized preventive military action for a specified purpose, over which the Council as a whole would have some control. Diluting the disproportionate influence of the United States by institutionalizing the arrangement in this way may give the PSI the legitimacy it needs to succeed as an effective counter-proliferation tool.

Criteria

Finally, the Council should adopt a set of criteria to guide deliberations on the use of force to counter proliferation and nuclear terrorism. The International Commission on Intervention and State Sovereignty proposed such criteria for humanitarian intervention (the responsibility to protect), and the HLP and Secretary-General converted them into a set of considerations that would apply to decisions on the use of force generally: How serious is the threat? What is the purpose of the intervention? Is the use of force a last resort? Are the means proportional? What are the chances of success?[48] The 2005 World Summit, while acknowledging the responsibility to protect, did not endorse the criteria.

Although *the UN membership as a whole* was not ready to sign on to generic criteria, an effort to get the Council to announce criteria focused more directly on nuclear proliferation and nuclear terrorism could bear fruit. The shared interests of the P-5 in seeing action on this front, combined with a concern about the slippery slope of unilateral pre-emptive action, create a window of opportunity. A "trigger list" of acts that would give rise to an automatic response is not realistic: the P-5 do not want to tie their hands in that way, and it would necessarily require making distinctions among the four non-NPT nuclear states (India, Israel, North Korea, and Pakistan), or between them and other potential proliferators. But, as with the generic criteria proposed by the HLP, the Council could come up with a list of factors it would take into account in considering whether and how to react to a threatening situation.

Michael Doyle has proposed four standards for preventive action that would apply to both anticipatory self-defense and Council-authorized enforcement: lethality, likelihood, legitimacy, and legality.[49] My proposed criteria are more narrowly focused on nuclear threats and would not apply to unilateral action. A non-exhaustive list of considerations, informed by the accumulation of events theory, would include:

- Whether the state or organization involved is "of proliferation concern," based on an agreed understanding as to what that means[50]
- Whether the state or organization involved has used weapons of mass destruction in the past
- Whether the state or organization involved has engaged in aggression or terrorism in the past
- Whether the acts in question are approaching a threshold that, if crossed, would make it difficult to thwart a future attack
- Whether the evidence of the threat comes from reliable sources, confirmed through objective, third-party assessments
- Whether there are external checks that might deter the state from using nuclear weapons or transferring them to terrorists

The criteria would not distinguish between types of regimes, as Lee Feinstein and Anne-Marie Slaughter propose in articulating a "duty to prevent."[51] But the nature of the regime might affect consideration of some of the explicit standards, such as the viability of deterrence.[52]

What purpose would such criteria serve? They would send a signal to states and organizations that the Council takes the threat seriously and is prepared to act forcefully if necessary; they would provide a framework for threat assessment and decision-making that would lend legitimacy to the enterprise; and they would change the parameters for negotiation with target states and among Council members and others involved.[53] The signal that the Council is prepared to act might not only deter potential proliferations, but also dissuade counter-proliferators from acting unilaterally. The enhanced legitimacy would come from the felt need to deliberate on the basis of set standards, justifying decisions to act or not to act in terms that all have agreed in advance are relevant, as opposed to entirely self-serving, arbitrary, or beside the point.[54] The most important lesson of Iraq is not that military action was taken despite the weak case for it, but that the United States and the United Kingdom have paid a significant price because the case for it was weak – at the time and even more so in hindsight.

Conclusion

In this chapter I have considered some of the legal issues associated with the use of force to prevent or counter nuclear threats, from either terrorists or states. The use of force, of course, is never the only option available to policy-makers. Experience is limited, but there is reason to believe that forcible counter-proliferation is more likely to undermine than strengthen the nuclear non-proliferation regime because the grand bargain that underpins it is hanging by a thread. That being said, the use of force cannot and should not be ruled out as an option. This does not necessarily mean full-scale invasion and regime change; the spectrum of possible forcible action is broad, from interdiction and sanctions enforcement to pin-prick airstrikes at terrorist bases or nuclear facilities.

Are existing law and institutions adequate to address these threats in a manner that will be seen to enhance rather than undermine international security? In this chapter, I have considered the circumstances in which self-defensive action would be legal and I have argued for relaxing the test of imminence slightly by applying the accumulation of events theory. The case for that is stronger with respect to nuclear terrorism than to threats posed by so-called "rogue states" because impending danger from the former is harder to detect than the latter and so waiting until it is "instant and overwhelming" may be too late. Moreover, acting against terrorist threats – especially from terrorist organizations that have struck in the past – does not require nuanced calculations about intentions or the capacity to deter. When it comes to state-based threats, the same accumulation of events (for example, the development of enrichment capacity, the acquisition of a delivery device, war games, bellicose statements) can look very different depending on the state engaged in the action. Leaving it to each state to decide unilaterally whether the use of force would be justified in self-defense is an invitation to lower the "armed attack" threshold so far that it becomes essentially meaningless as a legal concept.

Though not the most impartial institution, the requirement of collective decision-making in the Council imposes a check on arbitrary action. This check would be reinforced by the adoption of criteria to guide deliberations. The Council is not likely to be able to agree on a trigger list, nor is it clear that such a trigger list would be wise, given that it would inhibit context-specific judgments and signal to would-be proliferators how far they can go before crossing the line. But even general considerations of the sort outlined above would structure the debates, open Council decision-making to some public scrutiny (truly "secret" consultations are impossible in a political body such as the Council), and therefore compel those involved in a decision to make good arguments in support of it.[55] Is it politically realistic to expect the Council to agree on such criteria? Yes, because they would enhance the legitimacy of the Council, and effectiveness depends in part on legitimacy. To the extent that the P-5 value the Council as an instrument for countering proliferation threats, they have an incentive to ensure that their collective power is used for collective – not entirely self-serving – purposes.

Notes

1. George W. Bush, "Commencement Address to the United States Military Academy in West Point," 1 June 2002; 38 *Weekly Comp Pres Doc* 944, 946 (10 June 2002).
2. *The National Security Strategy of the United States of America*, September 2002, Part V, 15 (emphasis added); available at ⟨http://www.whitehouse.gov/nsc/nss.pdf⟩ (accessed 10 November 2008). The thrust of the NNS 2002 was repeated in the National Security Strategy of 2006.
3. *National Security Strategy to Combat Weapons of Mass Destruction*, December 2002, 3 (emphasis added); available at ⟨http://www.whitehouse.gov/news/releases/2002/12/WMDStrategy.pdf⟩ (accessed 10 November 2008).
4. Ron Suskind, *The One Percent Doctrine: Deep Inside America's Pursuit of Its Enemies Since 9/11* (New York: Simon & Schuster, 2006), 62.
5. Lord Goldsmith, "Iraq: Resolution 1441," secret memo to the Prime Minister, 7 March 2003; available at ⟨http://www.ico.gov.uk/upload/documents/library/freedom_of_information/notices/annex_a_-_attorney_general%27s_advice_070303.pdf⟩ (accessed 10 November 2008).
6. *A More Secure World: Our Shared Responsibility. Report of the Secretary-General's High Level Panel on Threats, Challenges and Change*, General Assembly document A/59/565, December 2004, paras 188–189.
7. See *Letter by the Permanent Representative of the US to the President of the UN Security Council*, Security Council document S/2003/351, 21 March 2003. See also William Howard Taft IV and Todd Buchwald, "Pre-emption, Iraq and International Law," *American Journal of International Law* 97, no. 3 (2003): 557–563.
8. John Yoo, "International Law and the War in Iraq," *American Journal of International Law* 97, no. 3 (2003): 563–576, at 571–574.

9. Michael Reisman, "Self-Defense in an Age of Terrorism," *American Society of International Law Proceedings* (2003): 141–152, at 142.
10. Jordan Paust, "Post 9/11 Overreaction," *Notre Dame Law Review* 79 (2004): 1335–1363, at 1343.
11. Niaz Shah, "Self-Defence, Anticipatory Self-Defence and Preemption," *Journal of Conflict and Security Law* 12, no. 1 (2007): 95–126, at 111.
12. T. D. Gill, "The Temporal Dimension of Self-Defence: Anticipation, Pre-emption, Prevention and Immediacy," *Journal of Conflict and Security Law* 11, no. 3 (2006): 321–369, at 369; Kristen Eichensehr, "Targeting Tehran: Assessing the Lawfulness of Preemptive Strikes against Nuclear Facilities," *UCLA Journal of International Law and Foreign Affairs* 11 (2006): 59–98, at 95.
13. "Military and Paramilitary Activities in and against Nicaragua, Merits," 1986 *ICJ Rep.* 14 (Judgment of June 27), para. 231; *Case Concerning Oil Platforms (Islamic Republic of Iran v. U.S.)*, 2003 *ICJ* 90 (6 November), para. 50. See also Mary Ellen O'Connell, "The Myth of Pre-emptive Self-Defense," *American Society of International Law Task Force on Terrorism* 7 (2002).
14. Cited in Matthew Bunn, *Securing the Bomb 2007* (Cambridge, MA, and Washington, DC: Project on Managing the Atom, Harvard University, and Nuclear Threat Initiative, September 2007), 3; available at ⟨http://www.nti.org/e_research/securingthebomb07.pdf⟩ (accessed 10 November 2008). See also Weapons of Mass Destruction Terrorism Research Program, "Chart: Al-Qa'ida's WMD Activities," available at ⟨http://cns.miis.edu/pubs/other/sjm_cht.htm⟩ (accessed 10 November 2008).
15. Bunn, *Securing the Bomb*, 4–5.
16. Matthew Bunn, "The Demand for Black Market Fissile Material," at ⟨http://www.nti.org/e_research/cnwm/threat/demand.asp#_ftnref19⟩ (accessed 10 November 2008). On the threat of nuclear terrorism generally, see Charles Ferguson and William Potter, *The Four Faces of Nuclear Terrorism* (New York: Routledge, 2005) and Graham Allison, *Nuclear Terrorism: The Ultimate Preventable Catastrophe* (New York: Times Books, 2004).
17. A short passage in a recent ICJ Advisory Opinion may suggest otherwise. See *The Legal Consequences of the Construction of a Wall in the Occupied Palestinian Territory*, International Court of Justice, 9 July 2004, para. 139. But the context of the case and the strong dissents of three judges suggest that it is not the final word. See Ian Johnstone, "The Plea of Necessity in International Legal Discourse," *Columbia Journal of Transnational Law* 43, no. 2 (2005): 337–388. See also Sean Murphy, "Terrorism and the Concept of 'Armed Attack' in Article 51 of the UN Charter," *Harvard International Law Journal* 43 (2002): 41–50.
18. Michael Doyle, *Striking First: Pre-emption and Prevention in International Conflict* (Princeton, NJ: Princeton University Press, 2008), 18.
19. *Statement of the Israeli Permanent Representative before the SC*, UNSCOR, 36th Sess, 228th mtg, 44, UN Doc. S/PV.2288, 19 June 1981. See, generally, Mary Ellen O'Connell and Maria Alevras-Chen, "The Ban on the Bomb – and Bombing: Iran, the US and the International Law of Self-Defense," *Syracuse Law Review* 57 (2007): 497, at 506.
20. Anthony D'Amato, "Comment: Israel's Air Strike upon the Iraqi Nuclear Reactor," *American Journal of International Law* 77 (1983): 584–589.
21. Security Council resolution 487, 19 June 1981.
22. *The Economist*, 3–9 May 2008, 69.
23. See, for example, O'Connell and Alevras-Chen, "The Ban on the Bomb"; David Sloss, "Is International Law Relevant to Arms Control? Forcible Arms Control: Pre-emptive Attacks on Nuclear Facilities," *Chicago Journal of International Law* 4 (2003): 39–57.

24. "KCNA 'Detailed Report' Explains NPT Withdrawal," Korean Central News Agency, P'yongyang, 22 January 2003; available at ⟨http://www.fas.org/nuke/guide/dprk/nuke/dprk012203.html⟩ (accessed 10 November 2008).
25. *Case Concerning the Gabcikovo-Nagymaros Project (Hungary v. Slovakia)*, 1997 *ICJ* 92 (25 September); *The Wall* (see above, n17), paras 140–142.
26. The final articles, as well as prior drafts and commentaries, appear in James Crawford, *The International Law Commission's Articles on State Responsibility: Introduction, Text and Commentaries* (New York: Cambridge University Press, 2002). Article 25 is at 66.
27. See e.g. Harold Koh, "Comment," in Doyle, *Striking First*, 101–103.
28. Johnstone, "Plea of Necessity," 387–388.
29. For a fuller development of this argument, see Johnstone, "Plea of Necessity."
30. See Article XII.C. of the Statute of the International Atomic Energy Agency, 1957; available at ⟨http://www.iaea.org/About/statute_text.html⟩ (accessed 10 November 2008); and Article 15 of the model Safeguards Agreement (*The Structure and Content of Agreements Between the Agency and States Required in Connection with the Treaty on the Non-Proliferation of Nuclear Weapons*, INFCIRC/153 (corrected), Vienna: IAEA, 1972), on which all agreements are based.
31. *Agreement Governing the Relationship Between the United Nations and the International Atomic Energy Agency*, IAEA document INFCIRC/11, 30 October 1959.
32. Masahiko Asada, "Arms Control Law in Crisis? A Study of the North Korean Nuclear Issue," *Journal of Conflict & Security Law* 9, no. 3 (2004): 331–355, at 350.
33. Security Council resolution 1718, 14 October 2006, paras 3 and 4. For an analysis of resolution 1718, see Andreas Paulus and Jorn Muller, "Security Council Resolution 1718 on North Korea's Nuclear Test," *ASIL Insight* 10, no. 3 (2006). On the right to withdraw generally, see George Bunn and John Rhinelander, "The Right to Withdraw from the NPT: Article X Is Not Unconditional," *Disarmament Diplomacy* 79 (2005). http://www.asil.org/insights/2006/11/insights061103.html-author#author
34. United Nations Security Council, *Provisional Verbatim Record of the Three Thousand and Forty-Sixth Meeting*, S/PV.3046, 31 January 1992, 146.
35. For a similar analysis, see Allen Weiner, "The Use of Force and Contemporary Security Threats: Old Medicine for New Ills?" *Stanford Law Review* 59 (2006): 415–504.
36. *China's National Defense in 2002*, Office of State Council, 9 December 2002, Section VI. See Weiner, "The Use of Force and Contemporary Security Threats," 452–464. See also Jack Garvey, "A New Architecture for the Non-Proliferation of Nuclear Weapons," *Journal of Conflict and Security Law* 12, no. 3 (2008): 339–357, at 353–356.
37. Security Council resolution 1566, 8 October 2004, para. 3.
38. See Ian Johnstone, "US–UN Relations after Iraq," *European Journal of International Law* 15 (2004): 831 and references in footnote 73.
39. Jean-David Levitte, Address at the Council on Foreign Relations, "France, Germany and the U.S.: Putting the Pieces Back Together," 25 March 2003; available at ⟨http://www.cfr.org/publication.php?id=5774⟩ (accessed 10 November 2008); see also James Rubin, "Stumbling Into War," *Foreign Affairs* 82, no. 5 (2003): 54; Michael Byers, "Agreeing to Disagree: Security Council Resolution 1441 and Intentional Ambiguity," *Global Governance* 10, no. 2 (2004): 165–186, at 173.
40. Joseph Nye, "US Power and Strategy after Iraq," *Foreign Affairs* 82, no. 4 (2003): 60–73. See also Fareed Zakaria, "I Needed Evidence," *New York Times*, 11 April 2004, Section 7, p. 8.
41. Ian Johnstone, "Legislation and Adjudication in the Security Council: Bringing Down the Deliberative Deficit," *American Journal of International Law* 102, no. 2 (2008): 275–308.
42. The Security Council took note of these with satisfaction in Security Council resolution 255 (1968).

43. The security assurances of the five nuclear weapons states are embodied in S/1995/261, S/1995/262, S/1995/263, S/1995/264, S/1995/265. Negative security assurances are also embodied in the Protocols to the treaties establishing nuclear-weapon-free zones in Latin America, South Pacific, Southeast Asia, Africa, and Central Asia.
44. Resolution S/1995/263.
45. ICJ, Advisory Opinion, *Legality of the Threat or Use of Nuclear Weapons, I.C.J. Reports*, 8 July 1996, para. 62.
46. On the legal issues surrounding the PSI, see Douglas Guilfoyle, "Maritime Interdiction of Weapons of Mass Destruction," *Journal of Conflict and Security Law* 12, no. 1 (2007): 1–36; Walter Gary Sharp Sr, "Proliferation Security Initiative," *Transnational Law and Contemporary Problems* 16 (2007): 991–1028; Daniel Joyner, "The Proliferation Security Initiative: Nonproliferation, Counterproliferation and International Law," *Yale Journal of International Law* 30 (2005): 507–548.
47. Jack Garvey, "The International Institutional Imperative for Countering the Spread of WMD: Assessing the PSI," *Journal of Conflict and Security Law* 10, no. 2 (2005): 125–147, at 137.
48. *A More Secure World: Our Shared Responsibility*, para. 207; *In Larger Freedom: Towards Development, Security and Human Rights for All. Report of the Secretary-General*, UN Doc. A/59/2005, 21 March 2005, para. 126.
49. Doyle, *Striking First*, 46.
50. Weiner, "The Use of Force," 500; Sharp, "Proliferation Security Initiative," 1004.
51. Lee Feinstein and Anne-Marie Slaughter, "A Duty to Prevent," *Foreign Affairs* 83, no. 1 (2004): 136–150.
52. Doyle factors the character of the regime into his "likelihood" criteria, on the grounds that liberal democratic states do not wage war with each other, whereas dictatorial regimes are subject to fewer internal constraints. Doyle, *Striking First*, 50–51.
53. These three purposes are similar to those offered by Garvey to support "proliferation benchmarks." See Garvey, "A New Architecture," 346.
54. See, generally, Johnstone, "Legislation and Adjudication," 275–308.
55. Ian Johnstone, "Security Council Deliberations: The Power of the Better Argument," *European Journal of International Law* 14, no. 3 (2008): 437–480.

7

Verification and compliance

Harald Müller

This chapter discusses verification, compliance issues, and compliance policy as part of broader disarmament and non-proliferation agreements,[1] with a focus on the Treaty on the Non-Proliferation of Nuclear Weapons (NPT) and the role of the International Atomic Energy Agency (IAEA). It is not primarily concerned with enforcement – the effort to bring a non-compliant party back into compliance by sanctions and/or military action; yet it touches upon this issue repeatedly because verification is an essential part of compliance policy, and the application of compliance policy may, eventually, require enforcement action.

The chapter opens with definitions of verification and compliance. The need for verification as a tool of conflict management is then emphasized. Next, the distinction between verification and compliance policy in routine circumstances and in crisis situations is elaborated. The existing or desirable functions of the institutional apparatus – the IAEA, regional bodies, and the UN machinery (the Security Council, the General Assembly, the Secretary-General, and the International Court of Justice) – are screened with particular emphasis on the forensic phase of the verification/compliance process.

Definitions

Verification

Verification serves to create transparency in the implementation of undertakings to which states have committed under international treaties or other agreements.² For this purpose, verification uses a variety of technical methods to check whether the real actions of a state correspond to its reported actions. Verification needs benchmarks – the commitments themselves and their translation into standards of observation and measurement. It also needs persons and organizations authorized to make these standardized observations and to transform them into precise assessments of whether or not the observed party has lived up to its undertakings. Given the technical nature of the issues involved (in addition to the political and legal ones), the individuals involved must be experts and the organizations charged with the mission must comprise an expert staff. Critically, these organizations and the people who staff them must enjoy high authority among relevant publics (including the political leadership of the countries involved); authority is the necessary antidote to conversion of the verification process into power politicking.

Such authorized people or organizations might belong to the states parties as national verification organizations and their staff (as is the case in many bilateral arms control agreements, but also in the multilateral Treaty on Conventional Forces in Europe). Alternatively, they could belong to an international organization, where the nationalities of its civil servants (should) play no role, as in the case of the nuclear non-proliferation regime, where the IAEA is entrusted with the task of conducting verification measures. Inspections are a part of most verification schemes. Routine inspections serve to make sure that what inspected parties have reported is correct. Special inspections are designed to uncover clandestine activities: inspectors go to sites not reported by the inspected party as relevant to its treaty obligations, and to spots at declared sites in a non-routine, unannounced way.

Compliance

Compliance is the correct conduct of a state party to an agreement. *Compliance policy* is the set of procedures used when doubts about compliance arise, and when the measures contemplated in the event that well-founded doubts are financial, technical, or diplomatic, and not (yet) of a sanctioning nature (be it in the economic or even the military realm). Once the threshold of a sanctions debate is passed, we talk about enforcement rather than compliance policy.³ Positive incentives to comply – rewards, promises of material or symbolic benefit – fall within compliance policy, and negative incentives to comply – sanctions, armed action – are within the realm of enforcement.

Compliance policy and verification are closely related. Verification reveals whether states comply with relevant agreements or whether a compliance problem exists. In the latter case, compliance policy will start forthwith. At the outset, the state party suspected of being in non-compliance, the IAEA, and/or other interested parties will strive to clarify the situation cooperatively; here, verification is the tool of compliance policy towards a particular target state. The first step in compliance policy should be cooperative because concerns about possible non-compliance can arise from quite innocent causes.

These causes can arise from measurement errors, from false interpretations of correctly observed data, from reporting mistakes or failures by the state concerned, from a lack of technical, financial, or administrative capacity, which prevents the non-compliant state from fulfilling its duty (out of ignorance or against its own will), or from ambiguities in the legal documents that lead to different readings and, consequently, to different understandings of what compliance entails. Each of these problems requires a different approach. None asks for the harsh measures embodied by enforcement. In some cases, taking new data or revisiting old information will clarify the matter. In other cases, financial, technical, or administrative assistance will help delinquent states comply. Sometimes a procedure to clarify ambiguous meaning will help to decide whether non-compliance exists in the first place, and, if so, may induce the non-compliant state to change its behavior. All these steps fall well within the realm of the IAEA (some may be taken by inspectors on the spot) or of the community of states parties, notably when interpretations of the treaty are concerned, as this is the legitimate realm of the NPT Review Conferences. None requires action at a higher level of authority, namely the Security Council.[4]

The meaning of verification under the security dilemma

The verification/compliance nexus is of pivotal political meaning. Nation-states – apart from pacified regions such as the European Union or the members of the North Atlantic Treaty Organization – still operate in an environment characterized by the security dilemma.[5] There is a basic uncertainty for decision-makers about whether other states are partners, rivals, or threatening enemies. Arms control agreements are meant to mitigate this security dilemma, rendering states more secure and thereby opening the opportunity to enter further welfare-enhancing cooperation. For it is unlikely that states will envisage such cooperation if they fear that the gains accruing from it might be turned against them by an implacable predator.[6]

Arms control, however, will not achieve this effect if it does not tackle the uncertainty problem, which is at the root of the security dilemma. Commitments under agreements – for example, those compelling states not to develop nuclear weapons – are just promises. Uncertainty remains the dominant obstacle to developing more peaceful and cooperative relations as long as states have no good reasons to believe that these promises will be kept. It is this function that verification is supposed to fulfill:[7] to provide states parties with sufficient certainty that one's own compliance with the agreed rules is reciprocated by the other parties to the agreement. In that function, verification is indispensable for arms control not only as a stabilizer but also owing to its potential for transforming state relations from anarchy and distrust into a rule-bound, trust-based system.[8]

The relationship between information and uncertainty, however, is tricky. Information is never complete, but always selective. If a verification agency comes up against a crafty perpetrator whose efforts at concealing and deceiving compete with the agency's efforts at uncovering, the outcome is by no means assured. The information necessary for a decent verification job involves systematic selection of the specific mission of the verification tasks that would lead to a conclusion that undeclared, illegal activities were going on. Such tasks might include mapping the nuclear and nuclear-related facilities in a country, calculating the necessary number of measurements and samples at a facility to draw reliable conclusions, and analyzing random probes drawn from buildings and the environment to gain an indication as to the presence or absence of isotopes. Apart from the systematic selection of information, being open to receive random data (such as supplied by domestic opposition groups in suspect countries), incidental information gathered during an inspection visit (such as catching sight of an unknown building), or intelligence information supplied by friendly states has proven indispensable in the hunt for undeclared activities. Such information leads back to a systematic approach (such as buying satellite photographs of sites where such activities may be suspected on the basis of randomly gathered data). Eventually, however, data must be interpreted and conclusions drawn. This procedure is not completely determined by scientific rules, but permits some leeway for artful interpretation. In this process, the inspection agency must sail the treacherous waters between complacency and false alarms. Either extreme can be fatal. Complacency built upon a verification system not up to the task of uncovering clandestine activities proved almost disastrous in the Iraqi case before 1991. False alarms (not by the IAEA but by some member states) precipitated the war of 2003.[9]

In the light of these dilemmas, reducing uncertainty for states that commit to the non-proliferation regime requires not only verification as such, but a neutral, reliable, reputable body that discharges this job with professional credibility. This, in turn, rests on the quality of both the professional staff and the top leadership of the agency. These virtues can be built and maintained only if it enjoys the loyal support of major actors and the unrestricted flow of resources needed to do the job well. The IAEA has not always enjoyed either asset and therefore it is all the more remarkable how well it has weathered the storms it has gone through.[10]

Verification and compliance in routine operations

Verification/compliance policy can be envisaged as a routine system that functions smoothly and continuously. From the perspective of the participating states, it offers the chance to prove to their partners that they are complying with the rules, therefore engendering the trust that provides social capital in external relations. From the point of view of the partners, it serves to enhance their security by learning about the strict compliance of those who might otherwise be perceived as threats, or to give them confidence that small compliance problems will be resolved by the measures discussed above. In the nuclear field, this routine system consists of the reporting by states parties to the NPT on their nuclear activities and the naming of all facilities that contain fissile material[11] and all facilities that are related to the nuclear sector.[12] In addition to this baseline inventory (which is added to only when new facilities are constructed), annual reports or, for certain facilities, more frequent reports inform the IAEA about changes in the fissile material inventory. Inspectors check these reports against evidence – including material probes that will be analyzed in the Agency's own laboratory at Seibersdorf, Austria – and report back to the Agency. The IAEA, on the basis of all available data, draws conclusions about each state party's compliance in the comprehensive annual country report.

The question has been frequently discussed of whether the extraordinary verification tools contained in both the old and the new verification system, such as "special inspections," access to non-reported sites, and environmental sampling, should be part of the *routine* or should be reserved for extraordinary circumstances. Not the least because of industrial concerns, the latter alternative has been chosen. Only sweep samples within facilities have been added to the regular inspection cycles, with some effect (e.g. in North Korea in 1992), because new analytical methods permit conclusions to be drawn from astonishingly small numbers of isotopes gathered in such samples. This de-routinization automatically means that special inspections are politically charged.

Looking at the routine tools and envisaging the expansion of the IAEA's role to a future process of multilateral nuclear disarmament, the one missing capability is verification competence for issues closely related to nuclear weapons themselves, such as design, neutron trigger development, implosion experiments, development of fast and slow conventional explosives, and reflector and boosting material. The IAEA encountered this problem during the post-1991 inspections of Iraq. The mission is delicate because inspectors obtain weapons-relevant knowledge. If they are citizens of a non-nuclear-weapon state and will return to their home country on the expiration of their contract, a technology transfer will take place that is profoundly undesirable in the perspective of the NPT. If applied to nuclear disarmament, it would compromise the obligation of the inspected nuclear weapons states not to assist non-nuclear-weapon states in illegal activities. After 1991, the IAEA solved this problem by requesting the nuclear weapons states to second expert personnel to the Agency. This could be repeated on a larger scale in a systematic disarmament process. To have such staff permanently at IAEA headquarters would also make sense in light of the Additional Protocol, with its stipulations for enhanced access. If the Agency finds evidence that a nuclear weapons facility is hidden in a country, it will request access and then will need staff who can do the inspection without broadcasting proliferation-relevant information.[13]

However, the experience of the United Nations Special Commission on Iraq (UNSCOM) shows that these experts must move from national to IAEA payrolls. Unknown to the UNSCOM leadership, personnel seconded from national intelligence agencies continued to work for their masters. That these people conducted target-acquisition tasks in the inspected country undermined the credibility of UNSCOM, and not just in the eyes of the Iraqi leadership.[14] When the United Nations Monitoring, Verification and Inspection Commission (UNMOVIC) was installed in 1999, every UNSCOM officer legally became an international civil servant.[15] This might not completely prevent a person from serving two masters, but it makes it riskier and strictly illegal. In the sensitive area of nuclear weapons verification, this formal detachment from continuing national instructions would be particularly important.

Multilateral verification of disarmament will have to break through the shrouds of secrecy enveloping nuclear weapons activities, including the isotopic composition of fissile material (even though the thresholds are known and the precise data on specific weapons pose little harm either to a state's national security or to proliferation risks at large).[16] Since isotopic composition is important for determining weapons grade, and since measurement is hardly possible without revealing the isotopic content, refusing to be transparent on this item is a showstopper for verification. There is, however, a silver lining: the inclination to prefer transparency is linked to an uncertain, vulnerable deterrent posture and to political tradition. If, and when, all nuclear weapons states develop confidence in their second-strike capabilities (which is a function partially of a reduction in the offensive capabilities of the two large arsenals, and partially of a limitation on missile defenses), and as all develop experience in multilateral arms control agreements, these two obstacles will be incrementally removed. In the process, interest in knowing in more detail what others possess – the *interest in transparency* – is bound to rise.

Verification and compliance in crisis (short of enforcement)

The situation is much more serious when a party is suspected of being in material breach of its core undertakings. In the case of the NPT, this would be a non-nuclear-weapon state suspected of working towards the development, production, or acquisition of nuclear weapons. It can be asked with some justification whether the refusal of nuclear weapons states to work faithfully towards disarmament is not an equally serious failure to fulfill treaty obligations. For the rest of the chapter, however, I focus on the first type of nuclear crisis.[17]

In this situation, one of the parties to the NPT is identified as suspect, from its own behavior or because of others' suspicions. From this moment on, the verification system changes from an instrument of trust-building to a forensic tool. Indeed, the closer compliance policy moves to the enforcement threshold, the more the relationship between the verification agency, the inspected state, and the decision-making body (the IAEA board of governors, later the Security Council) becomes a relation of prosecutor, defendant, and judge; the procedure becomes similar to a court trial, although some differences remain.

First, the burden of proof on the "defendant" is higher than in a court. The accused state has to make considerable efforts to prove its innocence; it is not completely up to the other side to prove its guilt. This burden is all the heavier if this state evinces an enduring hostility to internationally influential parties, notably the five permanent members of the Security Council (the P-5).

Secondly, and especially in this latter condition, the process is (unfortunately) highly politicized. The accused country has its friends and foes in "the court." Its friends defend the assumption of innocence and dismiss the alleged proof; its foes cry "guilty" and do their best to promote the conviction of the defendant. The watching public (for example, non-committed states, or non-members of the particular decision-making body) approach the case with their own situation and their relationships with the protagonists in mind: Could I stumble into the same situation as the suspect? Do I share interests with the suspect? Am I allied to, or dependent on, its friends or its foes? The stronger the group that is skeptical about the accusation and hostile to the accusers, the more evidence will be needed to get a critical mass for achieving a decision to enter the enforcement stage. On the other hand, the greater the number of countries that are hostile, suspicious, or fearful of the defendant, the harder it will be for that country to supply convincing proof of its innocence, such that a pro-enforcement coalition is prevented.

It is this politicking at the decision-making stage of compliance policy that raises doubts that there is any fairness in considerations of non-compliance, a concern that has been reinforced by the partisan way some members of the Council have handled the Iraqi case. These doubts are damaging both to the integrity of the non-proliferation regime in particular and to the prospects for enlarging the rule of law in general. At worst, they may lead to additional countries considering the need for a national nuclear deterrent.[18]

The IAEA Secretariat, with its inspectorate, is thus walking a thin tightrope in this phase. The parties try to (ab)use it for their own political ends, while at the same time watching the Agency with complete distrust to detect whether it is leaning towards their foe's position. If so, they will quickly be on hand with accusations of incompetence and political partisanship. In recent years, the IAEA has suffered from repeated accusatory salvos by US officials who were dismissive of the utility of international organizations as such, and who even led a campaign to prevent the re-election of Mohamed ElBaradei as director general.[19]

These accusations and ensuing pressures have proven unfounded and unsuccessful, most recently in the wake of the Iraq war, when allegations by the United States and the United Kingdom of a continued Iraqi nuclear weapons program were proven baseless. Being in the line of fire in any serious case of compliance policy, the Agency, if not forced outright by the circumstances, must stick to the principle of good forensics at the highest professional standard if it is to survive in its mandated mission: it must present only convincing evidence strictly in line with scientific standards, remain transparent about the degree of uncertainty and the gaps in information, and base its assessments on impeccable proof. Indeed, it is remarkable how Hans Blix, as director general of the IAEA and also as chair of UNMOVIC, and Mohamed ElBaradei lived up to this demanding challenge.

The verification apparatus: The IAEA and regional bodies

The IAEA is the decisive verification body in the nuclear field. Regional organizations – EURATOM in the European Union[20] and the Brazilian-Argentine Agency for Accounting and Control of Nuclear Materials

(ABACC)[21] – play a role, but the Agency's supreme function for the NPT gives it pride of place. Nevertheless, an economic division of labor between the regional and universal organizations is reasonable because it is cost and labor saving – an important consideration given the years of zero budget growth at the IAEA and the constantly increasing missions heaped on it (which will grow when, eventually, nuclear disarmament progresses). Such a division of labor has been negotiated between EURATOM and the IAEA, though not without difficulties owing to their overlapping missions and the bureaucratic self-interest of both bodies. EURATOM verifies civilian uses of all fissile material and facilities in the territory of EU states, including the nuclear weapons states (which can withdraw material for military use if they so decide) pursuant to the Rome treaties, while the IAEA verifies NPT commitments by the EU non-nuclear-weapon states. Tellingly, EURATOM is better equipped and financed. The European Union is a community of wealthy nations that gives its supranational bodies sufficient money to do their job. The IAEA is a universal body with all members jealously watching (and always suspicious) lest the international bureaucracy spends their money uneconomically. Consequently, EURATOM looks on the IAEA with condescension, and the IAEA views EURATOM not without envy. Nevertheless, a viable system of divided as well as overlapping tasks has still emerged.

The central role of the IAEA applies to both routine and crisis verification activities. It makes no sense to divide the two functions between two different bodies. The Agency inspectorate, owing to its technical expertise, its knowledge of countries' nuclear infrastructure, and its organization and equipment, can combine both missions economically. As a neutral international body in the UN family, it is responsible to its members and their organs – the General Conference and the board of governors – and to the Council, which can task the Agency with missions unconnected to the NPT, such as after the first and before the second Gulf war. The Agency's activities under these mandates were different from the NPT system, even though Iraq remained a party to the NPT. The authority of the inspectors and the intrusiveness of the inspections went beyond NPT safeguards, even as amended by the Additional Protocol. The missions included not only verifying Iraq's reports and searching for undeclared facilities and materials, but also the dismantling and removal of facilities, equipment, and material.[22]

The combination of both functions in one organization and the connection between IAEA and Council procedures – as foreseen by the combined stipulations of the NPT, the Safeguards Agreement and its Additional Protocol, and the IAEA Statute – imply a systematic relationship between the nuclear non-proliferation regime, on the one hand, and the global security system with the Council at the center, on the other hand. The regime relieves the Council of the impossible task of micromanaging the nuclear policy field. The Council, in its role as the ultimate guarantor and enforcer of the integrity of the regime, relieves the regime organization of the impossible mission of putting a specific case in the perspective of global security, which encompasses much more than assessing whether certain findings indicate an NPT party to be in non-compliance. In this relationship, IAEA verification is the linkage. This mechanism triggers the board of governors' decision to refer a serious case to the Council, and it provides the Council with the facts on which it will base its own deliberations. The authority of the Council, notably to act under Chapter VII of the UN Charter, in turn gives the IAEA more leverage vis-à-vis the inspected state, and may empower the Agency to use methods of verification, scope of access, and activities that would be *ultra vires* under the NPT.

The IAEA has often been criticized for combining the twin tasks of verifying the absence of military abuse of fissile material and promoting civilian uses of nuclear energy. Anti-nuclear non-governmental organizations never tire of perpetuating the myth that the IAEA spreads weapons-related technology around. The facts prove differently. The bulk of the IAEA's technical assistance goes into agriculture, medicine, material sciences, and basic research. From critical assemblies through research reactors to hot cells, power reactors, heavy water plants, and other items related to nuclear energy, it is advanced member states that render assistance to less developed countries, most of the time at commercial prices. When it comes to weapons technology, for the past two decades it has been private traffickers who have done the job.[23] The support closest to both energy and weapon uses that the IAEA has rendered is assistance for uranium prospecting, and this is far from a true proliferation activity. It can safely be said that the mission of promotion has not impeded the verification work of the IAEA in practice.[24]

The role of the United Nations

In this deliberation on the relationship between the regime organization and the global security organization, two important functions of the United Nations,[25] both entrusted to the Council, have been mentioned and need only brief repetition.

The first is that the Council guarantees the integrity of the regime by taking over compliance policy in serious non-compliance crises with a view to bringing the deviating party back into good standing.[26] This is

presently being tried in the Iranian case. The Council has a broad range of instruments at its disposal. All these instruments relate back to the verification activities of the IAEA:
- The Council can just take note of the verification results and invite the IAEA and the state in question to continue cooperation in order to clarify the situation. In the North Korean case, most of the time it has acted in this manner.
- It can express concern and call on the state to improve cooperation and come back into good standing, as it did initially in the Iranian case.
- It can invoke sanctions, as against Iran, it can enhance the authority of the IAEA, as in resolution 687 and its corollaries at the end of the Gulf war in 1991, and it can impose a variety of military means.
- The Council can also refer the case to particular parties or to regional organizations or processes, such as the Six-Party Talks in East Asia.

It is up to the Council to decide when the transition from compliance policy to enforcement is due. But even in the dangerous field of enforcement, verification activities continue to be needed. It is precisely after military action that the world community has a keen interest in learning about the state of nuclear affairs in the attacked country, and in ensuring that whatever is left of nuclear technology is rendered useless for military purposes or removed completely.

The second function of the Council is to develop case-specific verification systems not related to the NPT. It did this in the Iraqi case. The post-war situation in 1991 triggered specific measures not covered by the NPT in order to clarify the situation and eliminate all traces of a nuclear weapons program. This task was valiantly implemented by the IAEA after 1991 and in the period between resolution 1441 and the beginning of the war in 2003. In one of the characteristic blunders by the occupying powers, they refused to give the Agency access, thereby renouncing the utilization of the enormous amount of knowledge it had assembled on the Iraqi nuclear infrastructure; only a US team should find the suspected nuclear weapons activities. This attitude betrayed a remarkable defiance of the duty of accountability to the world community that should have been self-evident to the invaders. However, the Iraq Survey Group could only confirm the pre-war findings of the IAEA: there were no weapons activities, no weapons, no facilities. The nuclear weapons scare invoked in the multimedia show by US Secretary of State Colin Powell at the United Nations on 5 February 2003 was a hoax.[27]

The Secretary-General, under Article 99 of the Charter, has the authority to inquire into cases that appear to affect international peace and security and, if the Secretary-General is convinced that this is indeed the case, bring them to the attention of the Council. It is likely – though it has never happened – that in the course of such an inquiry the Secretary-General might call on the IAEA for a briefing. It would be interesting to have an informed legal opinion as to whether the IAEA would have to respond to a call by the Secretary-General under Article 99 in the same way that it has to respond to a call by the Council under Chapter VII, even outside of NPT procedures. If so, verification would assume an additional function in relation to the United Nations. It goes without saying that use of the Secretary-General's authority under Article 99, which has lain dormant for many years, would create controversy, notably among the P-5 oligarchs, which, much too often, give the impression that they own the Council. Nevertheless, it could be an instrument to steer the United Nations onto more neutral, less politicized ground, an ironic consequence of the Secretary-General's taking a political stance! It is also obvious that, in order to make good use of this authority, the Secretary-General would need, not a verification agency under his authority, but qualified technical advice to assist him in translating technical reports into political assessments.[28] Alternatively, the Secretary-General might decide, after being briefed about rumors of non-compliance, to urge the Council to use its authority to request information from the IAEA.[29] It would likely depend on the political constellation in the Council (and on the personality of the Secretary-General) which path he or she would choose.

Among the UN organs, the General Assembly appears to be less involved in verification issues. The Assembly has, of course, the opportunity to adopt resolutions asking for changes in verification systems. A more daring thought would be the Assembly debating assessments by the Council based on verification. Since Article 12(1) of the Charter prohibits the Assembly from taking up a security issue as long as the Council remains seized of it, this would be, in fact, a breach of the Charter that could turn into new law only by constant practice. It is difficult to conceive, however, that the Assembly would take initiatives of this kind as long as the Council – and the P-5 in particular – remains united. If, however, the abuse, or blatant ignoring, of verification data by individual members prevents the Council from exerting its proper authority, as in the Iraqi case of 2003, the Assembly might be within its rights to express its own opinion. Using the Uniting for Peace procedure (UFP), the Assembly could even call upon member states to take the necessary steps in order to enable the IAEA to obtain information needed to clarify the situation. Choosing an easier path, the Assembly could wrap the debate on a specific issue in a broader agenda topic in a regular session, thereby circumventing Article 12(1) and the politically charged (and costly) convening of a Special Session. Indeed, the Assembly has done this on several occasions.[30]

Using Article 99 or the UFP to break a Council deadlock is not without risks. If the Secretary-General fails repeatedly in an Article 99 approach, or if he or she pursues this path on the basis of insufficient information, not only would this strategy quickly be disavowed and thus not be available in future contingencies, but the Secretary-General as a person and as an office would suffer. Since Article 99 proceedings are politically charged, any Secretary-General would be well advised to consider the case in question thoroughly before going down this path. Likewise, the Assembly has to use the UFP instrument with care. The veto power of the P-5 is not just a blatant injustice at the UN level; it also serves the purpose of maintaining peace and support for the United Nations by preventing the organization from confronting the vital interests of a great power head on. It can be presumed that in nuclear weapons matters such interests are involved most of the time. The frivolous use of the blocking power of a P-5 state can never be excluded but, if crucial interests are at stake, the Assembly should probably not interfere. A simple example illustrates the point: if the question of military sanctions against North Korea were at stake with a view to preventing the further accumulation of nuclear weapons and forcing access by IAEA inspectors to all nuclear facilities in that country, and if China in such a case were to use its veto, the Assembly would be ill advised to overturn the Chinese objection and invite member states to "take all actions necessary." In the murky area between verification, compliance policy, and enforcement, sound political judgment is needed to prevent the best from becoming the enemy of the good.

Nevertheless, it might be not the use of these instruments but the mere *possibility* of use that might suffice to produce the desired political effect. The P-5 cherish their privileges. The possibility that either the Secretary-General or the Assembly could cut into these beloved prerogatives might be incentive enough for them to behave acceptably. If the P-5 have a clear understanding that the Secretary-General could put issues on the table that they want to keep off it, or that the Assembly might move to deal with the most important issues of war and peace and sideline the Council because of a lack of action, they might deem it the better alternative to get their act together and do what is necessary to persuade the Secretary-General and the Assembly to stay quiet. The political dialectics between a doubtlessly risky gamble by these two actors to intrude into what is generally seen as the fiefdom of the Council and the incentives of the mere possibility that this risky gamble might be realized are not easy to disentangle. Yet they might be reasonably effective anyway. Nevertheless, it should be noted that the Assembly also has the problem that any UFP resolution needs a two-thirds majority, and these are harder to get today than in the glory days of the G-77.

UN Security Council forensics: Verification versus national intelligence and the need for independent assessment

Whenever the Council debates proliferation crises, IAEA verification data confront data supplied by national intelligence. The IAEA provides its data-based assessment as a neutral international agency at the service of the Council. National intelligence data, in contrast, are presented in a partisan way, selected according to the national interests and political objectives as defined by the presenting government. The experiences of 2003 are too salient to be forgotten in the near future: the international community will be hesitant, for the time being, to rely, without checking thoroughly, on any "proof" that individual governments might supply. The passionate selectivity of the US and UK governments in this regard has devalued – to the detriment of the international community and the two perpetrators – whatever national governments may have to contribute to improving the assessment capabilities of the Council. The credibility of national intelligence agencies has been compromised for some time to come.

However, these agencies may be in a position to contribute valuable information to the full picture of a situation. They may have access to sources not available to the international verification agency, just as the Agency will collect information not accessible to intelligence. These differences lie in the nature of the beast. The IAEA has open access within the limits of its mandate, and (meanwhile) quite a few measures to tell deception and lies from the truth; but it cannot work against the law in the inspected countries. Intelligence agencies by definition work outside the law (in addition to using open sources) because they are tasked with acquiring information the host country would not want them to have. If used wisely, their information can enhance the knowledge of the international community in crisis decision-making.

There is thus the dilemma between the risk of obtaining and using biased information supplied by states, and the equally deplorable disadvantage of refusing to use data that might be useful in the decision-making process because their sources are national governments. The only way out of this dilemma is to interpose a neutral and trusted filter between the national source and the international utilization of the information by the Council.

For this purpose, it would be appropriate to provide such information to the Agency promptly, so that it could check data reliability and validity and include them, if appropriate, into its assessment of the case.[31] If intelligence is presented only in the Council, however, two possibilities exist. First, the Council as a whole refers it back to the IAEA for an assessment (the most appropriate way). Second, the Council refers it to a UN technical assessment unit tasked with advising the UN organs on technical aspects of weapons of mass destruction. Such a unit could be placed in the Disarmament Department and could consist just of liaison expert staff in the chemical and nuclear sectors, because it should always draw on the specialized agencies (the Organisation for the Prohibition of Chemical Weapons and the IAEA) in these fields, while more in-house expertise would be needed for biological weapon and missile issues. The information referred to this unit, then, would be expeditiously conveyed to the IAEA for in-depth assessment.[32]

Whether the need for such a unit is widely seen or whether the status quo continues, the important point is that, if national intelligence data are added to information from the IAEA, they must pass through a neutral filter before they can be processed by the Council and before the Council moves to take decisions. Politicking will enter the decision-making process at this stage anyway; it should be kept away from the stage of technical assessment as far as possible.

A role for the ICJ?

An interesting question relating to the future world order concerns the role of the International Court of Justice (ICJ). The Court has proven its competence in the nuclear field in issuing its landmark Advisory Opinion on the legality of the use of nuclear weapons in 1996, the most balanced and authoritative interpretation of this issue (including the obligation of the nuclear weapons states under Article VI of the NPT to disarm).[33] It is worth considering whether the ICJ could play any role in the verification/compliance interface.

As stated before, compliance policy, once the level of the Council is reached, assumes the character of a criminal trial. As such, the findings of the Council should be submitted to review, as appropriate, if the idea of applying the rule of law in international relations is to progress further. It is precisely because of the self-interested voluntarism that the P-5 (and the United States and the United Kingdom in particular) have shown in dealing with proliferation cases that the opportunity to submit Council decisions to juridical review looks attractive. Enabling the ICJ to address such issues would be a step towards revolutionizing international relations. Eventually, decisions by the most powerful countries would undergo the scrutiny of international judges. Given the difficult task of assessing proliferation cases, and the serious consequences engendered by such assessment, an independent review might serve a law-based world order well.

There is a problem of timing, though. If the Council acts in a preventive mode, there might be time for the ICJ to do a review before the Council decisions are implemented. If the time span between decision and action is short, a second court chamber acting on a "fast track" might be worth considering. If action has to follow decision immediately because the Council sees a clear and present danger, post-action court review could still make sense to lend legitimacy to forceful action or to give the victim of an unjustified action access to damage compensation.

If the ICJ is to play such a role, it would have to rely on independent technical expertise. The IAEA would necessarily be the supplier of such expertise. The Court would thus enjoy the expert opinion of the most authoritative body in the nuclear realm without the interpretative interference of the Council, and could thus call into question (or confirm) findings by the Council that had been made beyond the expertise supplied by the data from IAEA verification.

Conclusion

Verification is indispensable in the nuclear weapons sector. Matters connected with these powerful arms impact too heavily on national and international security to permit trust without verification. Verification and compliance are thus intertwined, and verification activities remain relevant when the threshold between compliance policy and enforcement is crossed, and also in a post-enforcement environment.

The IAEA has grown into a capable, trusted, robust organization for this purpose and has proven its capacity to learn from past shortcomings. Its performance in the Iraqi, North Korean, and Iranian cases is satisfactory. Member states need to recognize the Agency as an indispensable asset and provide it with the resources needed to deal with its growing missions. The Agency, in turn, must ensure that routine never overwhelms vigilance, and that it does its best to remain abreast of ever-moving technical developments.

At the same time, further changes in verification rules must be approached with care. The time has passed when it was possible to increase the burden on the civilian nuclear industries of non-nuclear-weapon states (and these states in general) without compensatory concessions by the nuclear weapons states. The inherent asymmetry of the NPT is creating increasing misgivings among the non-nuclear-weapon states, notably the non-aligned ones. During the 2005 NPT Review Conference, the united front of the non-aligned against any improvement in the non-proliferation instruments of the NPT as long as the nuclear "haves" do not move on disarmament was a serious warning. The IAEA Expert Group on Multilateral Approaches to the Nuclear Fuel Cycle concluded in its report to the director general that the time had passed when further discriminatory burdens could be heaped on the have-nots, and that additional requirements for the sake of non-proliferation must be universal or would not be accepted at all.[34] This dictum applies in full force to the IAEA's verification activities.

If nuclear disarmament were to start in earnest, verification would become complicated. There would be vast areas that could be entrusted to the IAEA, such as verifying that former military facilities were no longer used for weapons purposes (which would be a primary task under a comprehensively verified Fissile Material Cut-off Treaty)[35] or that fissile material from dismantled warheads was safely stored and/or transferred to the civilian fuel cycle. Other aspects of the disarmament process relating to weapons and their primary components would possibly be verified jointly by the nuclear weapons states in order to prevent the spread of proliferation-relevant technical knowledge or by a special IAEA unit composed of nuclear weapons states' citizens. This special regime, however, would end with the disarmament process, since no weapons and components would be left but only facilities and fissile materials.

Among the UN bodies, the Security Council is most important in the verification/compliance/enforcement continuum. The IAEA plays an essential role not only in alerting the Council to cases of non-compliance and in supplying the necessary technical information for decision-making in such cases, but also in relieving the process of technical assessment of political undertones as much as possible. The Council, in turn, not only is the recipient of information from the Agency but provides the Agency with extraordinary powers and the necessary authority if it comes to enforcement against an agitated culprit. The Secretary-General may act as a facilitator, but rarely as an instigator or a mediator between Council and Agency. The General Assembly is largely restricted to the role of an observer and, it is to be hoped, an efficient watchdog if needed. The ICJ could complement the system to bring it closer to the rule of law. It goes without saying that these revolutionary roles for the Council, the Assembly, and the ICJ carry the risk of abuse and, thus, damage to the United Nations without helping with the compliance problem. But this is the case with all proposals for reform: they work well only if those who are empowered by change use the new authority well. That political wisdom is a rare virtue, unfortunately, holds all too true.

Notes

1. Serge Sur, ed., *Verification of Arms Limitations or Limitation of Armaments: Instruments, Negotiations, Proposals* (New York: United Nations, 1992).
2. Nancy W. Gallagher, *The Politics of Verification* (Baltimore, MD: Johns Hopkins University Press, 1999).

3. Abram Chayes and Antonia Handler Chayes, *The New Sovereignty: Compliance with International Regulatory Agreements* (Cambridge, MA: Harvard University Press, 2000); Harald Müller, "Compliance Politics: A Critical Analysis of Multilateral Arms Control," *Nonproliferation Review* 7, no. 2 (2000): 77–90.
4. For much detail on this issue, see Chayes and Chayes, *The New Sovereignty*.
5. Charles L. Glaser, "The Security Dilemma Revisited," *World Politics* 50, no. 1 (1997): 171–201.
6. Joseph M. Grieco, *Cooperation among Nations: Europe, America and Non-Tariff Barriers to Trade* (Ithaca, NY: Cornell University Press, 1990); Randall L. Schweller, "Neorealism's Status-Quo Bias: What Security Dilemma?" *Security Studies* 5, no. 3 (1996): 90–121.
7. Zachary S. Davis, "The Realist Nuclear Regime," *Security Studies* 2, nos 2&3 (1993): 79–99.
8. Harald Müller, "The Future of Nuclear Weapons in an Interdependent World," *Washington Quarterly* 31, no. 2 (2008): 63–76.
9. See, particularly, the enlightening contributions of Hans Blix, *Disarming Iraq* (New York: Pantheon, 2004).
10. David A. V. Fischer, *History of the International Atomic Energy Agency: The First Forty Years* (Vienna: IAEA, 1997); Dirk Schriefer, Walter Sandtner, and Wolfgang Rudischhauser, eds, *50 Jahre Internationale Atomenergie-Organisation IAEO. Ein Wirken für Frieden und Sicherheit im nuklearen Zeitalter* (Baden-Baden: Nomos-Verlag, 2007).
11. Under the old safeguards document INFCIRC/153 (IAEA, *The Structure and Content of Agreements between the Agency and States Required in Connection with the Treaty on the Non-Proliferation of Nuclear Weapons*, June 1972). For a discussion, see David A. V. Fischer and Paul Szasz, *Safeguarding the Atom: A Critical Appraisal* (London: Taylor & Francis, 1985).
12. Under INFCIRC/540, the "Additional Protocol" (IAEA, *Model Protocol Additional to the Agreement(s) between State(s) and the International Atomic Energy Agency for the Application of Safeguards*, September 1997). Theodor Hirsch, "The Additional Protocol. What It Is and Why It Matters," *Nonproliferation Review* 11, no. 3 (2004): 140–166.
13. James Acton and Carter Newman, *IAEA Verification of Military Research and Development* (London: Vertic, 2006).
14. David Malone, "Goodbye UNSCOM: A Sorry Tale in US–UN Relations," *Security Dialogue* 30, no. 4 (1999): 393–412.
15. Blix, *Disarming Iraq*.
16. Annette Schaper, *Looking on the Demarcation between Nuclear Transparency and Nuclear Secrecy*, PRIF Reports 68 (Frankfurt: HSFK, 2004).
17. This is an opportunistic decision, since these cases are prone to trigger dangerous international crises. I remain convinced, however, that the refusal of the nuclear weapons states to abide by their undertakings risks precipitating the erosion of the NPT; see also Harald Müller, "The Future of Nuclear Weapons in an Interdependent World."
18. Nina Srinivasan Rathbun, "The Role of Legitimacy in Strengthening the Nuclear Nonproliferation Regime," *Nonproliferation Review* 13, no. 2 (2006): 227–252.
19. Dafna Linzer, "IAEA Leader's Phone Tapped, U.S. Pores over Transcripts to Try to Oust Nuclear Chief," *Washington Post*, 12 December 2004, A01.
20. Darryl A. Howlett, *EURATOM and Nuclear Safeguards* (London: Palgrave Macmillan, 1990).
21. See ⟨http://cns.miis.edu/inventory/pdfs/abacc.pdf⟩ (accessed 11 November 2008).
22. Trevor Findlay, "Lessons of UNSCOM and UNMOVIC for WMD Non-proliferation, Arms Control and Disarmament," in *Arms Control After Iraq: Normative and Operational Challenges*, ed. Waheguru Pal Singh Sidhu and Ramesh Thakur (Tokyo: United Nations University Press, 2006), 140–159.

23. Gordon Corera, *Shopping for Bombs: Nuclear Proliferation, Global Security, and the Rise and Fall of A.Q. Khan's Nuclear Network* (New York: Oxford University Press, 2006).
24. Fischer, *History of the International Atomic Energy Agency*.
25. In addition, the United Nations is involved in the development of general principles for verification in its various deliberating bodies. See *The Role of the United Nations in the Field of Verification*, Study Series 20 (New York: United Nations, 1991).
26. Tsumotu Kono, "The Security Council's Role in Addressing WMD Issues: Assessment and Outlook," and Harald Müller, "Dealing with WMD Crises: The Role of the United Nations in Compliance Politics," in *Arms Control After Iraq*, 83–113 and 114–139.
27. *Iraq Survey Group Final Report*, 30 September 2004, available at ⟨http://www.globalsecurity.org/wmd/library/report/2004/isg-final-report/⟩ (accessed 11 November 2008).
28. Una Becker, Harald Müller, and Carmen Wunderlich, "While Waiting for the Protocol: An Interim Compliance Mechanism for the Biological Weapons Convention," *Nonproliferation Review* 12, no. 3 (2005): 541–572.
29. I thank M. J. Peterson for calling my attention to this alternative.
30. Again, I am indebted to M. J. Peterson for drawing my attention to this possibility.
31. The IAEA Secretariat was authorized by the board of governors in 1992 to integrate information provided by member states into its assessment of states' compliance with their treaty obligations.
32. "Multilateral Disarmament and Non-Proliferation Regimes and the Role of the United Nations: An Evaluation," in *Contribution of the Advisory Board on Disarmament Matters to the High-Level Panel on Threats, Challenges and Change*, DDA Occasional Paper 8 (New York: United Nations Department of Disarmament Affairs, October 2004).
33. International Court of Justice, *Legality of the Threat or Use of Nuclear Weapons*, Advisory Opinion, 8 July 1996, *I.C.J. Reports 1996*; available at ⟨http://www.icj-cij.org/docket/files/95/7495.pdf⟩ (accessed 11 November 2008).
34. IAEA, *Multilateral Approaches to the Nuclear Fuel Cycle: Expert Group Report Submitted to the Director General of the International Atomic Energy Agency* (Vienna: IAEA, 2005).
35. Annette Schaper, *A Treaty on the Cut-off of Fissile Material for Nuclear Weapons: What to Cover? What to Verify?* PRIF Reports 48 (Frankfurt: HSFK, 1997).

8
Codification and legal issues

Lori Fisler Damrosch

After the Cuban missile crisis, former Secretary of State Dean Acheson asserted:

> I must conclude that the propriety of the Cuban quarantine is not a legal issue. The power, position and prestige of the United States had been challenged by another state; and law simply does not deal with such questions of ultimate power – power that comes close to the sources of sovereignty ... The survival of states is not a matter of law.[1]

Acheson's challenge to the relevance of law for nuclear weapons did not go unanswered:[2] international lawyers in the present generation continue to engage with it.[3]

With the superpowers having pulled back from the brink in 1962, codification of legal instruments controlling nuclear weapons began in earnest. Within a year, a partial test ban treaty had entered into force;[4] within the decade, major elements of a legal architecture for nuclear weaponry were in place, with the Treaty on the Non-Proliferation of Nuclear Weapons (NPT) as their centerpiece. Together with the NPT, US–Soviet/Russian arms control treaties have occupied center stage.[5] Although these treaties are legally binding, non-binding initiatives have also transformed nuclear weapons control.[6] The General Assembly cannot create binding law,[7] but it exerts influence as a forum for agenda-setting, political debate, and approval of the outcome of other processes.

The United Nations and nuclear orders, Boulden, Thakur and Weiss (eds), United Nations University Press, 2009, ISBN 978-92-808-1167-4

CODIFICATION AND LEGAL ISSUES 171

This chapter examines efforts in several arenas to develop law that could constrain nuclear weaponry. As a predicate to UN-centered processes, in the first section I survey humanitarian law prior to the nuclear age, before turning in the second section to efforts to control nuclear testing through law. Following this survey of attempts to codify nuclear restraint, I look at UN legal initiatives, focusing on the General Assembly's request to the International Court of Justice (ICJ) – the United Nations' principal judicial organ – for an Advisory Opinion on the legality of nuclear weapons. I then take up the controversial subject of Security Council "legislation" on the nuclear issue and beyond. Finally, I reflect on the changing nature of these law-making processes.

Codification of constraints on weapons prior to the nuclear age

Antinuclear activists waged a major legal campaign in the 1980s and 1990s, culminating in an Advisory Opinion of the ICJ,[8] in an effort to establish that any use or threat of use of nuclear weapons would violate international law. Central to this campaign was the position that customary international law and treaties already obliged states to refrain from using or threatening to use weapons that by their nature could not discriminate between combatants and noncombatants or that would cause unnecessary suffering. As a predicate for considering the Advisory Opinion, I trace briefly here the evolution of international law governing the conduct of warfare, focusing on efforts to codify principles of international humanitarian law (IHL) in the nineteenth and twentieth centuries.

Histories of the law of war often begin with the code of conduct for the Union Army in the American Civil War, drafted by Francis Lieber.[9] Its progeny figured prominently in the arguments made to the ICJ almost a century and a half later that long-established humanitarian principles already barred resort to excessively harmful weapons. As the ICJ observed in the *Nuclear Weapons* Advisory Opinion:

> The "laws and customs of war" – as they were traditionally called – were the subject of efforts at codification undertaken in The Hague (including the Conventions of 1899 and 1907), and were based partly upon the St. Petersburg Declaration of 1868 as well as the results of the Brussels Conference of 1874. This "Hague Law" and, more particularly, the Regulations Respecting the Laws and Customs of War on Land, fixed the rights and duties of belligerents in their conduct of operations and limited the choice of methods and means of injuring the enemy in an international armed conflict. One should add to this the "Geneva Law" (the Conventions of 1864, 1906, 1929 and 1949), which

protects the victims of war and aims to provide safeguards for disabled armed forces personnel and persons not taking part in the hostilities. These two branches of the law applicable in armed conflict have become so closely interrelated that they are considered to have gradually formed one single complex system, known today as international humanitarian law. The provisions of the Additional Protocols of 1977 give expression and attest to the unity and complexity of that law.[10]

Nuclear weapons states (NWS) presenting arguments to the ICJ accepted the applicability of IHL as a general proposition but denied that they had committed themselves through the Geneva Conventions of 1949 (to which they are all parties) or any other IHL instrument to refrain from all resort to nuclear weapons.[11]

Attempts to codify restraints on nuclear testing

One strand of efforts to control nuclear weaponry through treaties has focused on restricting nuclear tests. These efforts include the Limited Test Ban Treaty (1963), the US–Soviet Threshold Test Ban Treaty,[12] and the Comprehensive Nuclear-Test-Ban Treaty (CTBT), which was opened for signature in 1996 but is not in force.[13]

Non-participation in test-ban treaties (at least for long periods) by certain nuclear-capable states, particularly France, motivated resort to other legal strategies between the 1970s and 1990s, including applications by Australia and New Zealand to the ICJ in an effort to obtain a determination that French atmospheric testing was unlawful. In the *Nuclear Tests* cases, the ICJ found it unnecessary to reach the merits of these contentions; during their pendency, France publicly declared that it had ended its testing program and did not intend to resume testing. The Court thus concluded that no further judicial action was required.[14] More than 20 years later, upon resumption by France of nuclear testing, New Zealand sought to reopen its ICJ case. Because the original case had concerned atmospheric testing and the resumed program was for underground testing, the Court did not consider that the conditions for reopening the matter had been met.[15]

Efforts toward a comprehensive test ban reached a new level with the adoption of the CTBT at the 1996 General Assembly session; 71 states, including all five declared nuclear weapons states (N-5), signed the CTBT then. The total number of signatories is now 178, with 144 having completed ratification through 2008. By its terms, however, the treaty cannot enter into force until it has been ratified by 44 states listed in an annex, which includes all states with nuclear power or research reactors on their territories; 35 of those 44 ratifications have been obtained. Until the remaining ratifications by China, Egypt, India, Indonesia, Iran, Israel, North Korea, Pakistan, and the United States are secured, the CTBT cannot enter into force.

Upon signing the CTBT on behalf of the United States, President Bill Clinton declared that the signatures of the N-5 and many other countries "will immediately create an international norm against nuclear testing even before the treaty formally enters into force."[16] Students of international law could debate whether an unratified treaty might have such a law-generating effect,[17] but events in the real world soon dashed the hopes for Clinton's proposed norm. Less than two years after the CTBT was opened for signature, India and Pakistan carried out nuclear tests (in May 1998), and North Korea did so in October 2006. The year after the Indian and Pakistani tests, the US Senate voted down a resolution of advice and consent to the CTBT. The vote of 48–51 was substantially lower than the two-thirds required for approval of a treaty under Article II of the US Constitution, and it would require a very significant change in political conditions for the treaty to be sent forward again.[18]

ICJ Advisory Opinion on the legality of the use or threat of use of nuclear weapons

On 15 December 1994, the General Assembly asked the ICJ for an Advisory Opinion under Article 96(1) of the Charter, on the question: "Is the threat or use of nuclear weapons in any circumstance permitted under international law?" On 8 July 1996, the Court gave its response,[19] together with its decision not to answer a corresponding question referred to it by the World Health Organization (WHO).[20] Because a variety of states had urged the Court to decline to render the requested opinion, the Court's first order of business was to decide in favor of proceeding to the merits. To do so, the Court rejected a range of objections to its exercise of jurisdiction, including the argument that the question was more political than legal. Turning to the merits, the Court first inquired into the relevant applicable law, both by surveying a large number of potentially applicable treaties (in the fields of human rights and humanitarian law and environmental protection as well as arms control, among others) and also by examining the matter under international customary law.

In the dispositive provisions of the opinion, the Court found unanimously that there is in neither customary nor conventional international law any specific authorization of the threat or use of nuclear weapons, and by 11 votes to 3 that neither customary nor conventional international law contains "any comprehensive and universal prohibition of the threat or use of nuclear weapons as such." In two unanimous paragraphs, the Court found that any threat or use of force by means of nuclear weapons would have to comply with Article 2(4) and Article 51 of the Charter and with international law requirements applicable in armed conflict, especially IHL rules. Then, by a vote of 7 to 7, with President Mohammed Bedjaoui of Algeria casting the tie-breaking vote, the Court adopted the following dispositive paragraph:

> It follows from the above-mentioned requirements that the threat or use of nuclear weapons would generally be contrary to the rules of international law applicable in armed conflict, and in particular the principles and rules of humanitarian law;
>
> However, in view of the current state of international law, and of the elements of fact at its disposal, the Court cannot conclude definitively whether the threat or use of nuclear weapons would be lawful or unlawful in an extreme circumstance of self-defence, in which the very survival of a State would be at stake.[21]

Finally, the Court unanimously ascertained "an obligation to pursue in good faith and bring to a conclusion" negotiations leading to nuclear disarmament.

The fact that the Court was unanimous (or largely unanimous) on several aspects of its opinion, and equally divided on the critical paragraph, has elicited voluminous commentary.[22] Each of the 14 participating judges also appended a separate or dissenting opinion, reflecting a wide range of views on jurisprudential theory as well as on the substance of the issues.

Whether the Advisory Opinion has influenced the policies of the states that matter for nuclear arms control may well be doubted. Soon after its issuance, the deputy legal adviser of the US Department of State began and ended an essay on the Advisory Opinion with the proposition that nothing in the ruling suggested a need for any change in the nuclear posture and policy of the United States or the North Atlantic Treaty Organization (NATO) alliance.[23] It is unlikely that the other NWS saw the matter differently. It would be difficult to identify any policy shift attributable directly to the Advisory Opinion and equally difficult to ascertain whether its reception in global public opinion shaped the terms of debate in any arena with concrete authority over nuclear decision-making. At the margins, the perception that the opinion tended toward delegitimation of most potential uses of nuclear weapons may have strengthened antinuclear advocacy in some countries, thereby conceivably affecting the political calculus for national leaders in weighing their stances toward such matters as willingness to tolerate such weapons on their territories or admit vessels carrying them into port.

There is another, more troubling, hypothesis about the impact of the Advisory Opinion on the real world in which the nuclear threat has to be addressed. As previously noted, quite a few states – several nuclear weapons states and a considerable number of states sheltering under their umbrella – urged that the Court should not opine on the legality of nuclear weapons because of the intensely political nature of the matter. Behind these arguments about justiciability lurked a fear – perhaps overstated, but neither disingenuous nor trivial – that a judicial opinion on the legality of nuclear weapons could have the counterproductive effect of making the task of negotiating disarmament even more intractable (for example, by removing the flexibility needed for compromise).[24] Some perceive that what the Court actually did was proof that it never should have answered the General Assembly's question. Writing shortly after the issuance of the Advisory Opinion and before events could prove them right or wrong, some scholars found in the opinion's perplexing treatment of "extreme self-defence" a possible validation for the proliferationist tendencies of states that might perceive themselves so threatened. The claim is that the Court's formulation may have strengthened "nuclearist" factions in political deliberations within states facing a choice whether to pursue or forgo such weapons.[25] If more than one state in today's world – North Korea after being branded part of an "axis of evil"; Israel in the face of Iranian threats to wipe it from the face of the earth – could plausibly claim that possession and credible threat of use of nuclear weapons are their only safeguards in "an extreme circumstance of self-defence, in which the very survival of a State would be at stake," the Advisory Opinion might have unwittingly lent some legitimacy to that claim. Of course, the paragraph as drafted is not a decision in favor of the lawfulness of nuclear weapons in such circumstances but rather an acknowledgment of inability to reach a definitive conclusion in the abstract. Still, it would be necessary to rule out the hypothesis of inadvertent support for pro-nuclear advocacy as part of an inquiry into whether the opinion's effects have been benign, neutral, or counterproductive.

Some perceive an influence from the ICJ Advisory Opinion in encouraging the General Assembly to insist on genuine progress from NWS toward the elimination of these weapons. With the Advisory Opinion having contributed to the mobilization of pressure toward this objective, statements emanating from the 2000 NPT Review Conference may have gone further than the NWS had previously been willing to do in making their first real commitments in this regard.[26] Whether there has been any change in the actual positions of nuclear weapons states in response to the aspect of the opinion dealing with negotiated disarmament (or the Assembly's further pressures in response to the opinion) is not easy to discern.

Other effects, especially as refracted through evolving jurisprudence on IHL, human rights law, and environmental law, are more noticeable. The Advisory Opinion is now discussed in every textbook on international law, both for its doctrinal contributions and for its treatment of fundamental problems in the theory of international law, such as the significance of state consent (or lack thereof) to changes in legal rules. A notable example concerning sources of international law is its consideration of General Assembly resolutions: the Court examined a long series in which large majorities condemned nuclear weapons and characterized them as illegal, yet the Court correctly found those resolutions to "fall short of establishing the existence of an *opinio juris* on the illegality of the use of such weapons."[27] On substantive law, the Court's conclusions on the applicability of human rights and humanitarian law in armed conflict are frequently cited as authoritative. Not only the ICJ itself but also other tribunals at the international, regional, and national levels have made use of these holdings.

A final observation concerns the effects of the Advisory Opinion on the ICJ's constituencies, which include the General Assembly (as well as other bodies in the UN family), and ultimately states, which must weigh their evaluations of the opinion along with other data in considering whether to resort to the ICJ to resolve their disputes. The Assembly soon turned to the Court again for legal advice on another intensely political question – the construction by Israel of a wall in the occupied Palestinian territory – which the Court answered as expected,[28] leading some critics to decry the ICJ for serving as a rubberstamp for the political preferences of the Assembly's majority.[29] As for potential effects on states' attitudes toward ICJ dispute settlement, one commentator has observed that the *Nuclear Weapons* advisory procedure opened up the Court for unprecedented access by a wide range of states and other actors and achieved a result that "uncannily, was almost universally welcomed." Ultimately, then, the effect of the Advisory Opinion may be judged less by whether it helped shape the defense strategies of nuclear states than by whether it helped shape the conflict-resolution strategies of those states that were first-time users of the Court's services.[30] Several of those first-time users, apparently gratified by exposure to this formerly underutilized judicial body, later returned to the Court to resolve disputes over boundaries, treaty rights, and other matters.[31]

The Security Council as a law-making forum

Since other chapters address Security Council actions in various contexts, this part focuses only on legal aspects of its powers under Chapter

VII of the Charter, in particular the constitutional controversies over the Council's recent "legislative" initiatives.[32] International lawyers and scholars have taken particular notice of the new ground broken with the adoption of Security Council resolution 1540 (28 April 2004). Resolution 1540 joined the problem of the proliferation of weapons of mass destruction with the risk that such weapons could fall into the hands of terrorists. Although both proliferation and terrorism had been treated as threats to the peace for the purposes of the Council's compulsory powers under Chapter VII,[33] resolution 1540 was qualitatively different. It followed in the footsteps of resolution 1373 (29 September 2001), adopted after the attacks of 11 September 2001, in which the Council required states to take specified measures against terrorist threats.

As legal commentators have observed, in contrast to other actions that have had the character of enforcement against specific targets, the Council in resolution 1540 was embarking on a wholly new kind of activity, which is essentially legislative in character.[34] The international law community is divided concerning the constitutional competence of the Security Council to establish general obligations for all states, as contrasted to enforcing obligations that are already in existence or addressing threats to peace in specific contexts. Some support the authority of the Council in principle to create new rules of conduct, with a range of positions on conditions that could make the exercise of such authority more or less legitimate. Others insist that the Council exceeded its constitutional powers by purporting to legislate as it did in resolution 1540 and that the resolution should be treated as invalid.[35]

These questions of a constitutional character are bound up with the broader agenda for reform of the Security Council and demands to open up its processes for fuller participation by those required to abide by its dictates. Pending resolution of those larger issues, continued resistance to expansive law-making claims on the Council's part can be expected. It remains the case, however, that such legislative capacity is sorely needed to address urgent threats to peace, which are the Council's primary responsibility.

Specific legal issues relating to the NPT regime

Pressures on the NPT have focused attention on legal questions concerning the obligations of parties while the treaty is in force and in connection with potential withdrawal. Without attempting an exhaustive treatment, tentative thoughts can be offered on a few such questions.

Prohibition on aiding the acquisition of nuclear explosive devices (Article I)

The first and most critical requirement of the NPT is the prohibition on any transfer by an NWS "to any recipient whatsoever" of any nuclear weapons or other nuclear explosive devices or control over such weapons or devices directly or indirectly. Moreover, no NWS may "in any way ... assist, encourage, or induce" any non-nuclear-weapon state to manufacture or otherwise acquire such weapons or devices or control over them. These seemingly clear words have given rise to various interpretive issues, most recently in the context of the 2007 US–Indian agreement on civilian nuclear cooperation.[36] A full exploration of legal issues relevant to the US–Indian agreement is beyond the scope of this chapter,[37] but it may be noted that a central premise of the agreement is a strict separation of India's civilian and military nuclear programs, as well as the conclusion of a Safeguards Agreement with the International Atomic Energy Agency (IAEA), which would be applicable to India's separated civilian nuclear sector.[38] On this basis, the US government has concluded that the agreement is fully compatible with US obligations under the NPT and under US law.[39] The Congress is expected to scrutinize conformity of the agreement with the NPT and US legislation governing nuclear cooperation, in connection with the vote that is a prerequisite to entry into force of the agreement.

Selectivity in cooperation (Article IV)

Article IV of the NPT leaves less than optimally clear the nature and scope of the obligations "to facilitate ... the fullest possible exchange of equipment, materials and scientific and technological information for the peaceful uses of energy" and to cooperate "to the further development of the applications of nuclear energy for peaceful purposes."[40] It has been suggested elsewhere in this volume that these provisions might entail an obligation to grant access to nuclear technology, components, and material on a most-favored-nation basis, thereby putting in question whether parties can be selective in choosing how and with whom to cooperate. It is doubtful, however, that the legal obligation under Article IV of the NPT should be interpreted as foreclosing states from exercising discretion in this regard. More plausibly in view of the text, context, and history of the treaty, all parties (including the NWS) are legally entitled to choose their partners in cooperation, whether from among existing treaty parties or from states outside the treaty framework.

The concept of nondiscrimination does indeed find expression in Article IV, but only in the context of the "inalienable right of all the Parties to the Treaty to develop research, production and use of nuclear energy for peaceful purposes without discrimination" under paragraph (1) of that article, thus evidently referring only to the unilateral rights specified under that paragraph and not to the cooperative activities indicated under paragraph (2). Nowhere in the text of paragraph (2)'s provisions on cooperation is a comparable explicit reference to nondiscrimination to be found. Rather, the terms of that paragraph offer parties various options, including the possibility of "contributing alone or together with other States or international organizations" and "with due consideration for the needs of the developing areas of the world." Paragraph (2) thus envisions a considerable measure of flexibility in implementation. There is no indication that the NPT's drafters meant to require states to cooperate with states that they might view as hostile, or to exclude them from favoring states with which they prefer to cultivate cooperative relationships. Indeed, given the circumstances of the Cold War prevailing in 1968 when the NPT was negotiated, its drafters could hardly have contemplated mandatory cooperation across bloc lines, or to have ruled out strategic choices of partners for cooperation. Translated to today's circumstances, under the more plausible legal interpretation, the United States is not foreclosed from engaging in civilian nuclear cooperation with a non-NPT party such as India, nor is it required to share sensitive technology with or provide fuel to states with potentially inimical interests.

Obligations to negotiate disarmament (Article VI)

Article VI of the NPT provides in full:

> Each of the Parties to the Treaty undertakes to pursue negotiations in good faith on effective measures relating to cessation of the nuclear arms race at an early date and to nuclear disarmament, and on a treaty on general and complete disarmament under strict and effective international control.

The ICJ dealt with this obligation in the final paragraph of its *Nuclear Weapons* Advisory Opinion – one on which the 14 participating judges were unanimous – which reads in full: "There exists an obligation to pursue in good faith and bring to a conclusion negotiations leading to nuclear disarmament in all its aspects under strict and effective international control."[41] The Court characterized Article VI as going beyond "a mere obligation of conduct" to entail "an obligation to achieve a precise result – nuclear disarmament in all its aspects."[42] The Court found confirmation of this view in unanimous resolutions of the General Assembly, in at least one resolution of the Security Council, in the final document of the 1995 NPT Review Conference, and in general international law on treaties and good faith.[43]

In view of the gloss that the Court placed on Article VI – not only to "pursue negotiations in good faith" but also to bring them to a conclusion – and the fact that more than a decade has elapsed since the Court's exhortation, there is understandable frustration that the goal of complete nuclear disarmament seems no closer and perhaps further away than in 1968 or 1996.[44] Still, in considering whether any state has been or is currently in violation of Article VI, it is important to bear in mind the vast numbers of US and ex-Soviet nuclear weapons that have been physically eliminated or otherwise defanged. Although this record may not satisfy the yearning for speedier and fuller progress toward "complete disarmament," it nonetheless goes a long way to show that the leading nuclear powers have acted "in good faith" toward Article VI's ultimate objective, which requires negotiated and not unilateral disarmament. The commitment of considerable sums toward tangible assistance to other states in reducing, securing, or eliminating their nuclear weapons is also relevant to evaluation of compliance.

The legal meaning of NPT Review Conferences (Article VIII)

Article VIII of the NPT provides for several kinds of actions to be taken by the parties to the treaty acting collectively. These include the consideration and adoption of proposed amendments,[45] as well as the convening of conferences to review the operation of the treaty "with a view to assuring that the purposes of the Preamble and the provisions of the Treaty are being realized."[46] Article X(2) provides for a collective decision to be taken by a majority of parties 25 years after entry into force of the treaty, concerning its extension indefinitely or for a fixed period. Agreement on indefinite extension was reached at a Review and Extension Conference held in 1995. In general, consensus procedures rather than the majority decision-making rules specified in the NPT have governed most actions taken in Review Conferences.[47]

NPT Review Conferences could provide an important vehicle for the promulgation of authoritative interpretations of the treaty. In international law, "any subsequent agreement between the parties regarding the interpretation of the treaty or the application of its provisions" is to be taken into account in its interpretation.[48] The authority of such interpretive decisions could depend on whether they are adopted unanimously (e.g. under consensus procedures), by analogy to the kinds of declarations approved by unanimity in the General Assembly that can constitute authoritative interpretations of the Charter. The fact that the NPT allows majority voting on some but not all aspects of the substantive treaty regime supports the view that an interpretation not embraced by unanimity (or not explicitly accepted by all the states whose consent is required to amend the treaty) would not be authoritative in this sense.

The ICJ's *Nuclear Weapons* Advisory Opinion took note of the final decision of the 1995 Review and Extension Conference, underscoring that it had endorsed the "importance of fulfilling the obligation expressed in Article VI" of the NPT.[49] The Court treated the Review Conference as having confirmed the priority attached to an existing obligation, rather than as having any new law-making significance.

Withdrawal (Article X)

Article X(1) of the NPT provides for withdrawal if a party "in exercising its national sovereignty" decides "that extraordinary events, related to the subject matter of this Treaty, have jeopardized the supreme interests of its country." Withdrawal is conditioned upon giving three months' advance notice to all other parties and to the Security Council, together with a statement of the events the state regards as having jeopardized its supreme interests. These procedural conditions have given rise to legal questions about whether complete compliance is a prerequisite to effective withdrawal and whether the Council could block such a notice from taking effect. The actions of North Korea (the DPRK) in 1993–1994 and from 2002 forward present a test case.

On 12 March 1993, in the same month in which the IAEA director general reported that North Korea was in continuing non-compliance with its Safeguards Agreement, Pyongyang gave notice of withdrawal from the NPT. Before the three months required by Article X had elapsed, the Council passed a resolution calling for compliance.[50] Intensive diplomacy culminating in high-level talks held 2–11 June 1993 produced an announcement that North Korea had suspended its notice of withdrawal and would consider itself in "special status" under the NPT. An "agreed framework" for resolving the crisis was reached in 1994, with commitments by North Korea on one side and by the United States and other states on the other. In the ensuing decade, each side claimed that the other had not fulfilled its part of the bargain. By 2002, another crisis over suspected violations was in full swing, and in January 2003 Pyongyang announced that it would withdraw from the NPT effective immediately.[51]

Although numerous media reports and even some governmental sources characterize North Korea as having withdrawn from the NPT, it appears that the parties to the NPT and the Security Council have not accepted North Korea's legal position on withdrawal. North Korea has been continuously carried as a party to the NPT on status lists maintained by the official depositaries of the treaty,[52] as well as in the lists carried on the records of the UN Department of Disarmament Affairs and the IAEA.[53] The Council has "deplor[ed] the DPRK's announcement of withdrawal" from the NPT[54] and, acting in its enforcement capacity under Chapter VII of the Charter, has "[d]emand[ed] that the DPRK immediately retract its announcement of withdrawal" and "return to the Treaty on the Non-Proliferation of Nuclear Weapons and [IAEA] safeguards,"[55] and it has imposed economic sanctions to induce this result.

The difference of positions between the DPRK and the rest of the NPT and UN communities manifests itself as a technical legal dispute over treaty formalities, when what is at stake could not be of greater consequence to peace and security. Whether the Security Council could require a state that has never been party to the NPT to comply with the substantive obligations of that voluntary treaty raises issues of a constitutional character comparable to those concerning resolution 1540. In relation to North Korea, which had voluntarily accepted NPT obligations yet apparently violated their substance while in party status, the legal issue is whether the Council can authoritatively determine that the DPRK's putative notice of withdrawal either never became effective or in any event cannot be legally recognized. Given the Council's Charter-based responsibilities for dealing with "threats to peace" and its specific role in receiving notices relevant to such threats, there seems little doubt that the Council could be the decision-maker of last resort in a dispute over NPT withdrawal.

Conclusion

Echoing Acheson's skepticism about whether international law could meaningfully constrain states in pursuing nuclear weapons policies out of self-preservation or self-interest, the present generation of international law scholarship includes prominent denials that international law could induce states to change behaviors that they otherwise adopt out of interest.[56] The challenge for those convinced of international law's potential is to demonstrate that enmeshment of states in a network of binding legal commitments can exercise a restraining influence even in the face of potential proliferation of weapons of mass destruction. That the regimes may not elicit perfect compliance does not mean that they are ineffectual.

International law depends on perceptions of legitimacy, which in turn depend on beliefs that rules have come into being through fair procedures, apply equally to like cases, and resonate with deeply grounded principles.[57] Well-known features of the nuclear weapons regime fall short of an ideal program for international law-making. Problems include differential levels of obligation between nuclear and non-nuclear-weapons states and differential capacity of the permanent members of the Security Council (not, incidentally, the only "nuclear weapons states" under the NPT) to impose their preferred policy positions as rules of conduct obligatory on others. Still, international law-making, like all legislative endeavors, can make reasonable distinctions between categories of conduct or between categories of actors whose conduct ought to be controlled in different ways, without necessarily impairing the legitimacy of the enterprise.

The consensual foundations of the treaty framework for nuclear arms control may be insufficient in the current era and in the future. Whether legislative initiatives such as resolution 1540 will be welcomed or resisted remains to be seen. Treaty provisions allowing unilateral exit after short notice unquestionably made it possible for many states to join arms control treaties such as the NPT, states that would not necessarily have done so if their consent had been irrevocable.[58] But, as the North Korean example shows, the Security Council may need to exert its lawful competence to ensure that free exit is not available to parties that are not demonstrably in compliance with their previously assumed obligations.

The United Nations, as a quintessentially state-centered body and one whose law-making capabilities are embryonic and contested, has mixed prospects as a principal locus of legislative activity in the non-proliferation domain. The major powers have resisted ceding significant authority in the United Nations' direction in this sphere, and indeed have retained control even of what otherwise might be considered legal technicalities (such as recording and regulating party status in the NPT). Crucial elements of the international legal architecture for controlling weapons of mass destruction fall outside the UN system at the present time. Even so, the fact of decades of UN-centered legally oriented activities addressed to nuclear disarmament has created some measure of autonomous capability for this legally significant international institution. It is necessary to build on the achievements to date by strengthening the effectiveness of the legal tools at hand.

Notes

1. Dean Acheson, "The Cuban Quarantine," *Proceedings of the American Society of International Law* 57 (1963): 13–14.
2. Louis Henkin, *How Nations Behave* (New York: Columbia University Press, 1979), 279–302; Abram Chayes, *The Cuban Missile Crisis: International Crises and the Role of Law* (Lanham, MD: University Press of America, 1974).

3. Marcelo G. Kohen, "The Notion of 'State Survival' in International Law," in *International Law, the International Court of Justice and Nuclear Weapons*, ed. Laurence Boisson de Chazournes and Philippe Sands (Cambridge: Cambridge University Press, 1999), 293–295, 312; Pierre-Marie Dupuy, "Between the Individual and the State: International Law at a Crossroads?" in *International Law, the International Court of Justice and Nuclear Weapons*, 449.
4. Treaty Banning Nuclear Weapons Tests in the Atmosphere, in Outer Space and Under Water (Limited Test Ban Treaty) (1963).
5. E.g., Treaty on the Limitation of Anti-Ballistic Missile Systems (1972) (no longer in force); Intermediate-Range Nuclear Forces Treaty (1987); Treaty on the Reduction and Limitation of Strategic Offensive Arms (START I) (1991); Treaty on the Further Reduction and Limitation of Strategic Offensive Arms (START II) (1993).
6. The history of US–Soviet/Russian arms control negotiations includes agreements reached in other than legally binding form. Furthermore, certain agreements that were intended to be binding never entered into force but nonetheless were observed by both sides for many years.
7. UN Charter Article 13(1)(a) charges the General Assembly to "initiate studies and make recommendations for the purpose of: ... encouraging the progressive development of international law and its codification." The Assembly's record is addressed elsewhere in this volume.
8. International Court of Justice, *Legality of the Threat or Use of Nuclear Weapons*, Advisory Opinion, 8 July 1996, *I.C.J. Reports 1996*, 226 (hereafter "Advisory Opinion").
9. John Fabian Witt, professor of law and history at Columbia University, finds irony in the invocation of Lieber's principles in the nuclear age. Article 29 of the Lieber Code stated that "[t]he more vigorously wars are pursued, the better it is for humanity. Sharp wars are brief." The theory underlying those words led Secretary of War Henry Stimson to recommend the use of atomic bombs against Hiroshima and Nagasaki. John Fabian Witt, "Lieber's Lectures: Law and the Usages of War," unpublished manuscript, 3 December 2007, 11.
10. Advisory Opinion, para. 75.
11. See Advisory Opinion, paras 22, 85–86; see also Pierre-Marie Dupuy, "Between the Individual and the State," 453; Christopher Greenwood, "*Jus ad Bellum* and *Jus in Bello* in the *Nuclear Weapons* Advisory Opinion," in *International Law, the International Court of Justice and Nuclear Weapons*, 247, 249, 252.
12. Treaty on the Limitation of Underground Nuclear Weapons Tests (1974) (entered into force 1990).
13. Comprehensive Nuclear-Test-Ban Treaty, General Assembly document A/50/1027, 24 September 1996, Annex.
14. *Nuclear Tests* (Australia v. France; New Zealand v. France), *I.C.J. Reports 1974*, 253, 457.
15. Ibid. International Court of Justice, *Request for an Examination of the Situation in Accordance with Paragraph 63 of the Court's Judgment of 20 December 1974 in the* Nuclear Tests (New Zealand v. France) Case, 22 September 1995, *I.C.J. Reports 1995*, 288.
16. Alison Mitchell, "Clinton, at UN, Signs Treaty Banning All Nuclear Weapons," *New York Times*, 25 September 1996, A1, A6.
17. Unratified treaties can contribute to customary international law if they are of norm-creating character, intended for broad multilateral participation, and widely observed. Furthermore, states that have signed a treaty that is not yet in force may be obliged to refrain from acts that would defeat its object and purpose. Lori Fisler Damrosch et al., eds, *International Law: Cases and Materials*, 4th edn (Eagan, MN: West Publishing Co., 2001), 86, 477, 1085.

18. The CTBT continues to be carried on the treaty docket of the Senate Foreign Relations Committee, under the category of treaties as to which the administration does not support action.
19. Advisory Opinion, para. 75.
20. International Court of Justice, *Legality of the Use by a State of Nuclear Weapons in Armed Conflict*, Advisory Opinion, 8 July 1996, *I.C.J. Reports 1996*, 66. Charter Article 96(2) limits the authority of UN specialized agencies to request an Advisory Opinion to "legal questions arising within the scope of their activities." The Court found this condition not to have been met in the WHO's request. The General Assembly, by contrast, is authorized under Article 96(1) to request an Advisory Opinion on "any legal question."
21. Advisory Opinion, para. 105 (2) E.
22. See, generally, Boisson de Chazournes and Sands, eds, *International Law, the International Court of Justice and Nuclear Weapons*; Ved Nanda and David Krieger, *Nuclear Weapons and the World Court* (Ardsley, NY: Transnational Publishers, 1998); Symposium, "Nuclear Weapons, the World Court, and Global Security," *Transnational Law and Contemporary Problems* 7 (1997): 313–457.
23. Michael J. Matheson, "The Opinions of the International Court of Justice on the Threat or Use of Nuclear Weapons," *American Journal of International Law* 91, no. 1 (1997): 417–434. For a favorable view, see Richard A. Falk, "Nuclear Weapons, International Law and the World Court: A Historic Encounter," *American Journal of International Law* 91, no. 1 (1997): 64.
24. The United States urged that an opinion "has the potential of undermining progress already made or being made on this sensitive subject." The United Kingdom, France, Finland, the Netherlands, and Germany made similar points. Australia argued that the rendering of an Advisory Opinion "may have the effect of impeding future and beneficial developments of international law" (*Verbatim Record*, International Court of Justice, 30 October 1995, CR 95/22, 38).
25. Reisman, "The Political Consequences of the General Assembly Advisory Opinion," 486–487. As Rein Müllerson has observed, none of the five nuclear weapons states would find their "very survival" threatened short of resort to nuclear weapons; rather, it is other states that might believe they need something stronger than their current arsenal to defend themselves against existential threats. Rein Müllerson, "On the Relationship between *Jus ad Bellum* and *Jus in Bello* in the General Assembly Advisory Opinion," in *International Law, the International Court of Justice and Nuclear Weapons*, 267, 270.
26. This suggestion was offered by M. J. Peterson in comments on this chapter.
27. Advisory Opinion, para. 71. Judge Schwebel's dissenting opinion elaborates: "When faced with continuing and significant opposition, the repetition of General Assembly resolutions is a mark of ineffectuality in law formation as it is in practical effect."
28. *Legal Consequences of the Construction of a Wall in the Occupied Palestinian Territory*, Advisory Opinion, 9 July 2004, *I.C.J. Reports 2004*, 136. See "Agora: ICJ Advisory Opinion on Construction of a Wall in the Occupied Palestinian Territory," *American Journal of International Law* 99, no. 1 (2005): 1–141.
29. Michla Pomerance, "The ICJ's Advisory Jurisdiction and the Crumbling Wall between the Political and the Judicial," *American Journal of International Law* 99, no. 1 (2005): 26–42.
30. Thomas M. Franck, "Fairness and the General Assembly Advisory Opinion," in *International Law, the International Court of Justice and Nuclear Weapons*, 511, 519.
31. First-time users Indonesia, Malaysia, and Mexico (ibid., 518) subsequently brought contentious cases to the ICJ.

32. Lori F. Damrosch, "The Permanent Five as Enforcers of Controls on Weapons of Mass Destruction: Building on the Iraq 'Precedent'?" *European Journal of International Law* 13, no. 1 (2002): 305–321.
33. Country-specific Chapter VII resolutions against suspected proliferators include resolution 687 (3 April 1991) on Iraq; resolutions 748 (31 March 1992) and 883 (16 November 1993) on Libya; resolutions 1696 (31 July 2006), 1737 (23 December 2006), and 1803 (3 March 2008) on Iran; and resolution 1718 (10 December 2007) on North Korea. The Council has also adopted resolutions without specifically invoking Chapter VII in other instances involving nuclear weapons, including resolutions 885 (16 November 1993) and 1695 (31 July 2006) on North Korea and resolution 1172 (6 June 1998) condemning the Indian and Pakistani nuclear tests. Other Security Council actions include resolution 984 (11 April 1995) on security assurances to non-nuclear-weapon NPT parties (cited in the Advisory Opinion).
34. José E. Alvarez, *International Organizations as Law-Makers* (Oxford: Oxford University Press, 2005), 197–198, 318–319; Stefan Talmon, "The Security Council as World Legislature," *American Journal of International Law* 99, no. 1 (2005): 175; Ian Johnstone, "Legislation and Adjudication in the UN Security Council: Bringing Down the Deliberative Deficit," *American Journal of International Law* 102, no. 2 (2008): 275.
35. Daniel H. Joyner, "Non-proliferation Law and the United Nations System: Resolution 1540 and the Limits of the Power of the Security Council," *Leiden Journal of International Law* 20, no. 2 (2007): 489–518.
36. Agreement for Cooperation between the Government of the United States of America and the Government of India Concerning Peaceful Uses of Nuclear Energy, 3 August 2007; available at ⟨http://www.state.gov/r/pa/prs/ps/2007/aug/90050.htm⟩ (accessed 11 November 2008). The agreement is anticipated in the Henry J. Hyde United States–Indian Peaceful Atomic Energy Cooperation Act of 2006, 22 USC sec. 8001 (2006), and requires approval of the US Congress. Political developments on the Indian side have cast the future of the agreement into some doubt.
37. Kate Heinzelman, "Towards Common Interests and Responsibilities: The U.S.–India Civil Nuclear Deal and the International Nonproliferation Regime," *Yale Journal of International Law* 33, no. 2 (2008): 447–478.
38. R. Nicholas Burns, "America's Strategic Opportunity with India," *Foreign Affairs* 86, no. 6 (2007): 131–146.
39. "On-the-Record Briefing on the Status of the U.S.-India Civil Nuclear Cooperation Initiative and the Text of the Bilateral Agreement for Peaceful Nuclear Cooperation (123 Agreement)," by R. Nicholas Burns, Under Secretary of State for Political Affairs, 27 July 2007; available at ⟨http://www.state.gov/p/us/rm/2007/89559.htm⟩ (accessed 11 November 2008). "We think that the U.S.-India agreement strengthens the international nonproliferation regime.... India will open up its system to international inspection and it puts the majority of its civilian reactors under IAEA safeguards."
40. Article IV(2).
41. Para. 105 (2) (F).
42. Para. 99.
43. Paras 100–103. The Court referred to Security Council resolution 984 (11 April 1995), which characterizes Article VI of the NPT as "a universal goal."
44. Ramesh Thakur in this volume insists that the nuclear weapons states "must be deemed to be in violation of their solemn obligation to disarm, reinforced by the Advisory Opinion of the International Court of Justice in 1996 that Article VI requires them to engage in *and bring to a conclusion* negotiations for nuclear abolition."
45. Art. VIII(1), (2). The NPT does not authorize amendments without consent; any state that does not ratify an amendment cannot be bound.

46. Art. VIII(3).
47. It is frequently noted that consensus procedures produce lowest-common-denominator results and that this feature has impeded progress at the NPT Review Conferences. See Miguel Marin Bosch, "The Non-Proliferation Treaty and Its Future," in *International Law, the International Court of Justice and Nuclear Weapons*, 375, 378–379.
48. Vienna Convention on the Law of Treaties (1969), 1155 UNTS 331, art. 31(3)(a).
49. Advisory Opinion, para. 103.
50. Security Council resolution 825 (11 May 1993).
51. IAEA, "Fact Sheet on DPRK Nuclear Safeguards," May 2003, ⟨http://www.iaea.org/NewsCenter/Focus/IaeaDprk/fact_sheet_may2003.shtml⟩ (accessed 11 November 2008).
52. Pursuant to Article IX(2) of the NPT, the United Kingdom, the Soviet Union, and the United States are the designated depositaries. See US Department of State, *Treaties in Force: A List of Treaties and Other International Agreements of the United States in Force on January 1, 2007* (Washington, DC, 2007), 136 (showing DPRK as an NPT party without qualification, based on information said to be "authoritative as of July 27, 2007").
53. For the UN Department of Disarmament Affairs listing, see ⟨http://disarmament.un.org/TreatyStatus.nsf⟩ (accessed 12 January 2009). The DPRK is shown as having acceded to the NPT on 12 December 1985, without change in party status.
54. Security Council resolution 1695 (15 July 2006), Preamble; Security Council resolution 1718 (14 October 2006), Preamble.
55. Security Council resolution 1718, paras 3–4.
56. E.g., Jack Goldsmith and Eric Posner, *The Limits of International Law* (New York: Oxford University Press, 2005). Even those who do not share Goldsmith and Posner's world-view could sympathize with the proposition that establishing rule-based systems under conditions of high risk and low trust has to be difficult.
57. Thomas Franck, *The Power of Legitimacy among Nations* (New York: Oxford University Press, 1990).
58. In addition, legal requirements of formal notice in advance of major policy changes can be stability enhancing in the security realm.

Part III

Looming threats, new challenges

9

Technology proliferation, globalization, and the role of the United Nations

Brian Finlay and Rita Grossman-Vermaas

If the United Nations is to be a useful instrument for its Member States and for the world's peoples ... it must be fully adapted to the needs and circumstances of the twenty-first century.
  Report of the Secretary-General of the United Nations, 2005[1]

On 8 December 1953, President Dwight Eisenhower stepped to the podium at the United Nations General Assembly in New York City as the nuclear arms race was in full motion. The United States had already produced nearly 1,500 warheads,[2] and the Pentagon was equipping each of the military services with nuclear weapons. Also, the Soviet Union and the United Kingdom were testing and deploying atomic weapons. Eisenhower hinted at America's rapidly declining nuclear hegemony, cautioning that "the knowledge now possessed by several nations will eventually be shared by others – possibly all others." He also warned about the perils of proliferation: "let no one think that the expenditure of vast sums for weapons and systems of defence can guarantee absolute safety for the cities and citizens of any nation. The awful arithmetic of the atomic bomb doesn't permit of any such easy solution."[3]

Eight years later, the nuclear club expanded yet again as France conducted its first nuclear test, leading then-Senator John Kennedy to criticize Vice President Richard Nixon for his inattention to the growing proliferation threat. Kennedy asserted that "there are indications, because of new inventions, that ten, fifteen, or twenty nations will have a nuclear capacity – including Red China – by the end of the Presidential office in 1964."[4] As it turned out, China would go nuclear that year and

Italy, Sweden, and other industrialized European countries were also pursuing weapons programs.

Together with the superpower standoff, the entry into force of the Treaty on the Non-Proliferation of Nuclear Weapons (NPT) in 1970 tempered overt pursuit of the bomb beyond the original permanent five (P-5) members of the UN Security Council for the next decade. But it did little to stem the race between the United States and the Soviet Union, which chased each other up the ladder of escalation. By the 1980s, however, experts were sounding similar alarms heard 20 years earlier: the non-proliferation regime was under siege. This time, the locus of concern was not the developed states in the North but developing states, particularly in the Global South. Up to 18 developing countries were thought to be harboring nuclear ambitions – including Argentina, Brazil, Syria, Iraq, Nigeria, and Libya.[5] By the 1990s, Israel, Pakistan, India, and South Africa were being joined by Iran, North Korea, and Taiwan as potential breakout states. And, by 2000, the Pentagon was warning: "In virtually every corner of the globe, the United States and its allies face a growing threat from the proliferation and possible use of nuclear, biological, and chemical weapons and their delivery systems."[6]

Other chapters in this volume examine the existing mechanisms both in the United Nations' toolkit and at the disposal of the international community to address the nuclear threat. From the existing treaty regime (based on the NPT) and sanctions, to the option of using force, it is clear that a multi-layered strategy is needed to address the nuclear threat environment.

This chapter examines how technology proliferation – defined as the spread of weapons, fissile material, and weapons-applicable technologies of mass destruction to state and sub-state actors – is being fomented by the forces of globalization in ways that are rendering the traditional non-proliferation toolkit inadequate for managing evolving nuclear threats. It argues for a new innovative partnership among the United Nations, national governments, and sub-national actors – most notably, the private sector. And it stresses the need to develop these partnerships beyond the traditional supply-side approaches to proliferation prevention by engaging the development community in designing integrated mechanisms to manage the demand side of proliferation, while promoting the buy-in of all potential proliferators and sustainability for the long term.

"Back to the future?"

Since the nuclear era began, the proliferation debate has assumed a macabre character. Looking back at its 60-year history, the future always seemed to be more terrifying than the past. But despite apocalyptic projections about the demise of the non-proliferation regime, such alarms have been mostly unfounded. The success in containing nuclear weapons to just four countries beyond the original P-5 testifies to the NPT's effectiveness, the broader non-proliferation regime, the ability and willingness of most governments to control the diffusion of dangerous technologies and materials, and the relative stability provided by the prevailing world order.

During the Cold War, international norms grew against the possession and use of weapons of mass destruction (WMD). The world was expecting at least some reduction in stockpiles, even if the elimination of such weapons seemed a distant hope. Although the number of nuclear-armed states has grown from five to nine since China's entry into the nuclear club, many more countries have abandoned their nuclear ambitions and arsenals, including Argentina, Brazil, South Africa, Ukraine, Belarus, and Kazakhstan. In comparison with today, the supply of weapons, materials, and technologies was tightly controlled by a limited number of governments, while demand was comparatively minimal and more easily tempered under superpower influence. Global trading patterns were predictable and commerce, while still international, was relatively modest. Although the forces of globalization and trade liberalization were gathering toward the end of the Cold War, they had not matured to the point where diverse networks of licit and illicit middlemen facilitated access to the nuclear market for thousands of newly independent producers, as is true today.[7] Moreover, the scientific community capable of marrying weapons components to fissile material was limited in size and strictly governed by the nuclear powers.

In hindsight, state governance of materials and technologies, along with little upward pressure on breakout to additional countries because of superpower suasion, meant that proliferation was mostly manageable. With a limited number of nuclear states, with know-how and materials under the nearly exclusive control of the P-5, and with downward pressure from superpowers on their allies to go nuclear, restriction of supply was the best strategy to prevent wider proliferation. One analyst describes this as the doctrine of the three no's: no unsecured weapons and materials and no new domestic capabilities to enrich uranium or reprocess plutonium meant no expansion of the nuclear club.[8]

By the 1980s, the simplicity of that equation began eroding. Globalization, privatization, technological innovation, and ease of communications and transport all collided with the end of bipolar stability to challenge the non-proliferation regime. The focus on states as potential proliferators and the bulwark of the proliferation regime was in doubt as new forces began shaping social, political, and economic interactions. New sub-state actors emerged, including a more independent private sector with control over sensitive technologies and dual-use products, and terrorists intent on acquiring WMD – both acting to substantially diminish state sovereignty. Governmental controls of their nuclear arsenals thus became insufficient in a global economy where states could not exert absolute control over their territory. In many cases, the transfer of equipment and technologies once under the management of national authorities moved to private hands. Innovation brought to market new dual-use and commercial technologies just as the pace of global commerce was reaching once unimaginable heights.[9] In retrospect, although the dire predictions of the past regarding the future of the nuclear-armed world may have been overstated, they may yet come to pass in an environment where the emphasis on using supply-side instruments to prevent proliferation is insufficient.

In a time when many of the privileges of sovereignty are turning into burdens, governments have proven to be lethargic, unimaginative competitors to a growing array of state and non-state actors intent on dual-use sales and/or nuclear acquisition. Until the international community begins using the same resources that would-be proliferators have exploited for 20 years now, the non-proliferation regime may buckle under the immense weight of the new challenges being posed.

The post–World War II non-proliferation regime: Supply side and state centric

America's use of atomic bombs on Japan in 1945 forever changed military strategy and political posturing in both war and peace. With the Soviet display of its nuclear capability in 1949, one to three years earlier than the timing predicted by the West,[10] the arms race was on. By the NPT's conclusion in 1968, five states – the United States, the Soviet Union, China, France, and the United Kingdom – had acquired arsenals. For 40 years, these states have enjoyed special rights and privileges under international law, which are still debated today. Their weapons confer on them a status to which more than a dozen other nations aspire.

But, since the NPT's signing, more countries have abandoned nuclear weapons programs than started them. In the 1960s, six nations abandoned developing or conceptual nuclear weapons programs: Egypt, Italy, Japan, Norway, Sweden, and West Germany. Since the 1970s, 16 nations have abandoned nuclear programs or weapons or both: Argentina, Australia, Belarus, Brazil, Canada, Iraq, Kazakhstan, Libya, Romania, South Africa, South Korea, Spain, Switzerland, Taiwan, Ukraine, and Yugoslavia.[11]

The international community's approach was to create a non-proliferation architecture using an overlapping series of treaties and agreements obligating states to prevent proliferation. Little thought was given to the implications of proliferation by non-state actors because the technical barriers and practical obstacles to nuclear terrorism were considered insurmountable by anyone but a government. Today, there are 25 multilateral, regional, and bilateral agreements on nuclear weapons and energy, of which the 1968 NPT is the cornerstone. The premise of these was that the state is the main repository of weapons technology and can thus prevent access to it by illegitimate states.

Testifying to the success of the state-centric, supply-side focus of the non-proliferation regime, a relatively small number of nuclear-armed states exists today. Conventional wisdom during the Cold War held that the traditional nuclear exporters were parties to the NPT, as well as subscribers to codes of conduct for international nuclear exports, including the Zangger Committee, the London Club, and the Nuclear Suppliers Group. These countries included those with and without nuclear weapons, such as Belgium, Canada, Germany, Italy, the Netherlands, Norway, Sweden, and Switzerland. Countries such as Argentina, Brazil, India, Japan, Pakistan, South Africa, and South Korea, although considered potential second-tier suppliers, were not believed to have had the technical and financial capabilities, or the incentives, to impact the international marketplace.[12]

But there have been serious cases of non-compliance and ultimate breakout. In addition to the P-5, India, Pakistan, and Israel have developed nuclear weapons – although Israel neither confirms nor denies this. Iraq had violated its NPT and safeguards obligations up to the first Gulf war. The international community has repeatedly warned and tried to verify the extent to which Iran and North Korea are pursuing weapons programs; North Korea even withdrew from the NPT in 2003.[13] Significantly, no non-state actor is known to have a nuclear capability. But, to be effective in preventing this occurrence, we must understand what has gone right and why, and how the environment may be changing.

Globalization and the post–Cold War world: An evolving proliferation challenge

The end of the Cold War coincided with growing state demand – and some would say non-state demand – for nuclear capability.[14] As demand for peaceful and potentially offensive capacities increased, so too did supply. The end of the superpower standoff unleashed an unprecedented era of demobilization, shifting knowledge and capacity from state-governed institutions and a limited number of regulated partners to a broader swath of private actors. With a rapidly globalizing world economy, the 1990s were even more transformational than the demobilization following World War II. The emerging nuclear powers of the 1940s and 1950s orchestrated the production and procurement of dual-use technologies in their efforts to build their nuclear weapons capabilities.[15] But these efforts were bound by transportation and communication limitations, as well as by the P-5's strict governance.

In the 1990s, demobilization was fundamentally different. In the former Soviet Union, new companies emerged from state-owned manufacturing enterprises. For instance, the government in Moscow became eager to capitalize on its long history and expertise in civilian nuclear power generation. In 1999, exports of nuclear fuel cycle goods and services topped US$2 billion, comprising US$500 million in fuel assemblies and US$1.6 billion in other goods and services. Two years later, exports rose to US$2.5 billion, and by 2004 they topped US$3.5 billion.[16] In addition, the number of companies serving this global market – particularly dual-use items – expanded.

Superpower demobilization also unleashed the proliferation of technical expertise. Thousands of scientists who had been the brains behind the Soviet weapons complex lost their place in society, and subsequently sought opportunities to lend their dual-use talents to the private sector in Russia and abroad. Many ended up in the United States and Western Europe, but others found lucrative work in North Korea, Iran, and other countries of proliferation concern.[17]

The end of the Cold War also coincided with new economic forces that would put dual-use nuclear technologies in the hands of more non-state actors, including legitimate industries and, potentially, terrorists and other criminal organizations. This dynamic spread well beyond the former Soviet Union. During most of the post–World War II era, foreign investment in the developed economies of the North and the developing economies of the South was resisted by developing state governments.

By the 1990s, however, mainstream economic thinking had concluded that foreign investment yielded not only short-term financial gains but long-term economic benefits. The global development community joined economists and state development agencies in promoting models of export-oriented growth to the governments of less developed countries. Lower labor costs and often lax government regulation attracted massive new sources of foreign investment. Barriers to imports and exports lowered worldwide. In 1981, the worldwide average tariff on imports was 29.7 percent. By 2006, that dropped to 9.5 percent.[18] As companies from the developed world began moving their manufacturing and even

R&D to developing nations because of cheaper labor and fewer legal restrictions, the corresponding transfer of information, processes, and technology led to the generation of local enterprises that collaborated with or competed for market share. By the late 1990s then, more companies in more countries than ever could produce dual-use products.[19] Intelligence agencies the world over recognized that the locus of proliferation concern was expanding from the developed North – Germany, Russia, France, and the United States – to far-flung places such as Malaysia, Burma, and Sudan.[20]

In addition to trade liberalization and off-shoring, transportation technology development enhanced the capacity of companies – including dual-use technology manufacturers – to ship products in an unhampered, undetected manner. Larger and more efficient ships, roll-on/roll-off cargo container vessels, new loading and unloading tools, more efficient port management, and satellite navigation and tracking accelerated the pace at which goods flowed. An unprecedented volume of goods began moving through international mega-ports linked to maritime networks around the globe. Just as developed countries began expanding their port facilities to meet burgeoning demand, so too did developing countries capitalize on the growing industry of transit, transhipment and re-export services. The United Arab Emirates (UAE) alone invested billions of dollars during the 1990s to become a global trading hub. By 2007, more than US$12 billion worth of US goods were flowing through the UAE annually.[21] In 2007 alone, DP World, one of the largest marine terminal operators, announced that it had recorded growth of 19 percent in throughput with the handling of 11 million TEUs (twenty-foot equivalent container units) at its marine terminals in the UAE.[22] The sheer volume of trade through many of these ports imposed limitations to oversight and regulation.

Inspection of goods was further inhibited by some countries' reluctance to prioritize controlling the production and trade of dual-use items over developing their economies.[23] As export-oriented economic models were adopted in countries across the developing world, officials were reluctant to sacrifice financial gains to prevent proliferation. Joined by trade experts, many of these governments blamed the developed world for overstating the potential dangers of many dual-use items passing through their ports. In some cases, intense diplomatic and economic pressures led countries to adopt domestic supply-side, export control regulations, as the UAE did in 2005. Regulators have since learned, however, that domestic enforcement of the new standards was lacking on some occasions. Furthermore, differing legal restrictions in various countries give criminals the chance to "forum shop," driving shady operations to vulnerable locations. In many cases, financial incentives – not non-proliferation – were the prime motivators among private companies, port authorities, and national governments.

At its root, the perceived unwillingness of many states of the South to embrace tight non-proliferation standards was a conflict over technology itself. The controls demanded by the North were seen as a gambit to stymie competition and keep the developing world in a secondary economic tier. In response, the developing countries formed the Group of 77, which subsequently demanded a New International Economic Order (NIEO) in the 1970s. This was based on neo-Marxist political economy theory, which argued that the international trading system was condemning South America and other developing countries to poverty. Specifically, the NIEO called for technology transfer to the South and the negotiated redeployment of some developed countries' industries to developing nations.[24] With this backdrop, restrictions on technical transfers southward were not viewed favorably by developing countries.

Finally, the information revolution has hastened the ease of transmitting sensitive data to more countries, and thus technology has democratized access to information in ways that both benefit and potentially harm humanity. Countries once thought to lack the expertise to perform complex manufacturing operations are developing competitive industrial sectors that challenge traditional suppliers in Western Europe, for example. Now, suddenly, it seems that companies anywhere can build centrifuges and other components.

In addition to the increase in states with the capacity to move dual-use technologies, the growing number of weak and failing states threatens to invite wider proliferation by providing havens to sub-state proliferators. Weakened or non-existent law enforcement, porous borders, ineffective judicial institutions, and a general lack of capacity in state security are making these states attractive as either bases or havens for terrorists.

The nexus of failed states, criminal activities, and terrorism is perhaps most acute across Africa. Al-Qaeda and other terrorist movements have been active in a number of countries there, with known cells in Egypt, Tunisia, Algeria, Kenya, Tanzania, Uganda, South Africa, Côte d'Ivoire, Mauritania, and elsewhere. Criminal networks have developed across the continent, with money from the lucrative trade in diamonds, narcotics, and other illicit products being used to support terrorist activities.[25] Moreover, the prevalence of poor, disillusioned youth and other persons whose dire situations have nurtured religious or ethnic grievances provides fertile ground for criminal or terrorist recruitment.[26] Terrorist and criminal groups have also used Africa in their quest to obtain WMD, including uranium and other precious minerals from Niger, Congo, and Sierra Leone and chemical weapons components from Sudan. The expertise to fabricate dual-use hardware and weapons materials into WMD has been sought from the scientific communities of the former Soviet Union and South Asia, as well as from Libya and South Africa.[27]

Today, the conventional arms trade is a case study in the dark side of globalization and offers lessons vis-à-vis the potential for dual-use and nuclear acquisition. During the Cold War, the arms trade was dominated by a limited number of wealthy states and private companies. Markets were identified and developed, not for financial gain, but to secure the loyalty of "client states" in the superpower game of chess. Although these activities continue without superpower influence, they are joined by a growing private trade in small arms and light weapons. It can no longer be assumed that suppliers are governments or state-sanctioned companies. Criminal networks are capitalizing on the reduction in border controls and increased flow of goods.[28] Unlike past decades, proliferation by a shadowy network of criminal organizations and quasi-legitimate businesses is more difficult to identify and control. Although less is known about the growing trade in dual-use nuclear items or the potential trade in WMD materials and expertise, the lessons of the conventional arms trade should stand as a warning of the potentially catastrophic consequences of globalization.[29]

Gaps in the international non-proliferation toolkit

The previous sections have outlined the evolution of a regime conceived in the context of a superpower confrontation and expanded to meet the realities of a collapsing Soviet empire. Increasing anxiety about the clandestine proliferation of unsecured nuclear weapons, materials, and know-how from the former Soviet republics to unscrupulous states or even non-state actors led to the conclusion that traditional arms control tools, although necessary, were insufficient to stem weapons and technology dispersal. Governments' ability to prevent proliferation became questioned – not merely on the basis of ideology, but also on the basis of capacity. In one innovative response, "threat reduction" programs were launched between the United States and former Soviet republics and then expanded to all G-8 partners and beyond.[30]

Meanwhile, the growing impact of second-tier proliferation from countries such as Pakistan became a more broadly recognized threat. As with the collapse of the Soviet Union, strategies to address this phenomenon became more focused on technology denial, such as export controls, strengthened safeguards, sanctions, and even regime change. Little thought was given to the need for comprehensive outreach to an array of new actors having a potential role in proliferation prevention, including industry and developing governments. Strategies to stem supply were limited by governments' lack of coordinated effort to curtail demand. Little thought was given to the notion of integrating hard-security, supply-side programming with soft-security, demand-side incentives to build buy-in and ensure sustainability.

Generally, governments' non-proliferation toolkits are limited by stove-piped policy structures and bureaucratic obstacles that stifle innovative approaches. The policy-making process in national security agencies is often sequestered and segmented, rarely forcing departments to coordinate their activities. The United States has become the classic case study in the challenges of inter-agency collaboration, particularly in regard to the intelligence failure preceding the invasion of Iraq. But this dysfunction is not limited to intelligence nor is it strictly a symptom of large governments. Governments in Australia, Canada, Denmark, Finland, and Sweden have joined France, Germany, and the United Kingdom in identifying the need to dissolve stove-pipes across and within government departments to achieve their foreign policy goals.[31]

In the face of this, governments have still responded with state-centric, supply-side controls, including tighter export controls, technology access restrictions, and rigorous regulation enforcement. Ironically, these tend to put governments in confrontational relationships with the constituency with which they should develop collaborative partnerships – the private sector and the developing world. Unless this changes, proliferation challenges will continue to grow.

While scouring the Iraqi desert in 1991, UN weapons inspectors stumbled on several vacuum pumps that were traceable to Oerlikon Leybold Vacuum, a German firm that produces vacuum technologies for use in air-conditioning and television tubes and in automotive applications and processes. At the time, none of the items discovered were on any export-control or dual-use item list. But, on closer study, the inspectors realized that the pump was attached to a cyclotron, which can be used to enrich uranium through electromagnetic isotope separation. Thus, Oerlikon and its competitors had supplied the pumps to the Iraqi government and unwittingly advanced its weapons program. As news of this spread, the resulting damage to Oerlikon prompted it to re-think the filling of a growing number of suspicious requests for technology.[32] The incident also highlighted the ease with which proliferators can exploit legitimate companies to obtain weapons technologies, the inability of supply-side measures to contain the threat, and the potential impact of illicit networks on legitimate businesses and global security. Oerlikon is an example of many public prosecutions of companies that have been willingly complicit in proliferation or victimized by illicit traders, illustrating the need for governments to share information collaboratively with both Western businesses and those in the developing world.

While even advanced governments remain challenged by technology proliferation, developing nations face much greater difficulties in proliferation prevention. Not only are these governments targets for criminal networks and would-be proliferators, but many face systemic economic and social challenges with serious implications for their national budgets. Convincing governments to invest more in counter-proliferation or treaty compliance, while their infrastructures suffer from gross neglect, is not easy or even reasonable.

All of this indicates the need to better understand the motives behind the proliferation chain to prevent the diffusion of technologies. Whereas an extensive literature was generated during the Cold War examining states' decisions to go nuclear, no analysis has evaluated the incentives for non-state actors to proliferate – either private companies or terrorist organizations. Understanding demand and motivations to meet it is a critical challenge for the non-proliferation community.

One way to tackle this might be to untangle the web of assistance dollars given to states worldwide. It should be acknowledged that aid for judicial sector reform, disaster management, public health, and other capacity-building initiatives could also support the overall infrastructure needed to counter proliferation. At a minimum, donors should at least be assured that stove-piped investments made in one area are not offset in another; for example, is aid for rule of law and democratization undermined by counter-terror assistance to law enforcement agencies? Ideally, coordinated assistance across the security/development divide could promote mutual goals. For example, port modernization assistance could support both economic development goals as well as non-proliferation objectives.

Although national non-proliferation efforts remained dominated by supply-side strategies, global mechanisms at least tilt toward more holistic approaches. For instance, the 1999 International Convention for the Suppression of the Financing of Terrorism set the stage for conceptually merging conventional terrorism, nuclear terrorism, drug-trafficking, corruption, and misuse of financial systems. Recognizing that existing measures failed to address proliferation challenges, the Security Council went further by passing resolution 1540 in 2004 – the first UN action to recognize the role of non-state actors in nuclear proliferation. The resolution mandates that UN member states implement a set of supply-side controls and criminalize proliferationist activities within their territories. As groundbreaking as 1540 was itself, equally significant was the profile accorded to proliferation. After the announcement of resolution 1540 with great fanfare, even the Bush administration, long criticized for its unilateralist approach to foreign policy, seized on it as a critical component of its security agenda.

The adoption of 1540 marked the most significant opportunity since the attacks of 11 September 2001 to provide states at risk of contributing to the proliferation threat with the capacity to meet global non-proliferation norms. If considered more broadly, the resolution could help bridge the security/development divide by linking mandated non-proliferation standards to in-country development needs. It also provides an avenue through which states in need may request assistance by recognizing that "some States may require assistance in implementing the provisions of this resolution within their territories and invit[ing] States in a position to do so to offer assistance as appropriate in response to specific requests to the States lacking the legal and regulatory infrastructure, implementation experience and/or resources for fulfilling the above provisions."[33] After decades of refining a state-centric regime, UN member states had an opportunity to combine strategies that were considered distinct from nuclear issues – i.e. capacity-building, strengthening institutions, border security, and counter-terrorism mechanisms – in support of the common goal to prevent the spread of WMD and their delivery systems.[34]

Similarly, a new initiative to study proliferation financing is an uncomfortable issue vis-à-vis international diplomacy. Members of the Financial Action Task Force (FATF) have been charged to study the issue based on Iran and North Korea's illicit financing activities,[35] but there is political debate regarding whether FATF is the appropriate place for such discussions. The FATF focuses primarily on countering money laundering and other operations that could be linked to funding terrorism. Although strategies to address terrorism and proliferation-related financial networks overlap – and FATF could exploit them to understand both challenges better – the response to the proliferation finance initiative has been similar to 1540. The general inaction of FATF members to address proliferation finance may signify a burden of implementing targeted financial measures, a lack of political prioritization, or that the FATF initiative is repetitive. It may be unclear to members how the FATF initiative fits in with or differs from other obligations in existing WMD-related treaties, resolutions, or their historical focus on money laundering and terrorism. Proliferation finance received higher priority in the new FATF mandate issued in February 2008,[36] but whether the initiative can gain traction is uncertain.

In sum, supply-side efforts – although a critical component of the nonproliferation regime – must be leveraged by complementary demand-side efforts to prevent the illicit transfer of potentially lethal technologies to governments or groups of proliferation concern. Strategies that stymie the conditions driving legitimate governments and businesses to look the other way or that propel disaffected persons toward criminal activities must become equal layers in global efforts to prevent technology diffusion. This approach must also integrate a range of actors from the security and development communities and the public and private sectors. Furthermore, to achieve the greatest possible buy-in among rich and poor states and non-state actors, these efforts must be motivated by a strong sense of enlightened self-interest on the part of all parties.

Closing the gaps: The United Nations' role in a new nuclear age

As globalization continues to present new challenges to the non-proliferation community, innovative approaches that capitalize on its opportunities are also necessary. National governments have largely proven to be unwilling or unable to adapt to these challenges; and national security organs seldom intersect constructively with development agencies.

At the same time, the United Nations has suffered from the same compartmentalized approach to its mission. To the extent that there has been any collaboration, it has occurred across the economic and social development missions and within the post-conflict peace-building and peace-keeping roles. But the intersections between these issues and arms control, disarmament, and non-proliferation are negligible. Despite this, there is evidence that the United Nations could lead more innovative approaches to managing the spread of potentially deadly technologies.

The global challenges emerging after the Cold War brought a new impetus for the United Nations to reach out to civil society, businesses, and governments at the sub-national level. This trend grew exponentially in the late 1990s for many of the same reasons driving other international changes. As with criminal networks, globalization forged a new awareness of transnational opportunities that the United Nations attempted to shape and manage. The Internet and other communications technologies have also made global coordination and information- and resource-sharing – a core activity of the United Nations – easier. In addition, the end of the superpower standoff created a climate in which UN agencies could reach beyond their traditional government partners to civil society, businesses, and local and state governments. At the same time, the propagation of these partnerships has been driven by the realization that individual states, or even a consortium of states, can no longer address many of the transnational challenges facing the world. From environmental degradation to public health, new problems are challenging traditional state actors and their conventional toolkit. The result is a plethora of new partnerships that include sub-state and non-state actors such as those found in the business community.

For example, the UN Global Compact has been a vehicle for the world organization's outreach to the business community, engaging companies in advancing broader UN goals. Specifically, the Compact provides a set of best practices to better align business strategies with the universally accepted principles involving human rights, labor, the environment, and anti-corruption. It also engages the private sector in policy dialogues and partnerships,[37] which have taken various forms serving often overlapping goals, from developing codes of conduct to sharing expertise. Examples include the Global Alliance for Improved Nutrition, the Stop TB Partnership, the Global Reporting Initiative, and UN coordination of relief efforts following the Indian Ocean tsunami in 2004.[38] Despite the success of these efforts, a similar partnership has not formed to enhance global security. Given the serious proliferation threat, the breadth of resources needed to address it, and the limitations on governments, the timing appears ripe for the United Nations to refine its toolkit in innovative new ways that complement and promote the efforts of governments.

In key ways then, the United Nations is a logical focus for addressing nuclear technology diffusion and know-how. Its geographical scope is suited to addressing transnational challenges and its convening powers are unparalleled. Therefore, the United Nations may be ideal for approaching aspects of technology diffusion and underdevelopment that could provide solutions to nuclear proliferation.

The Security Council has already taken a significant step through resolution 1540 and the formation of the committee charged with its implementation. Unfortunately, the committee is under-resourced and restricted to monitoring, without detailed analysis of correlated needs and resources. Nonetheless, the 1540 Committee, in conjunction with the Global Compact and UN development agencies, could form the basis of a partnership to address the potential for technological innovation leading to WMD proliferation. Effective 1540 implementation requires outreach not just to countries but to local and regional governments, non-governmental organizations, and the private sector. It also requires building traditional, development-oriented capacities in states and regions of concern. Thus, 1540 is tailor-made for linking – across functional areas – supply-side security objectives with demand-side development instruments.

By supporting key underlying development needs in-country, the capacity for implementing 1540 will be reinforced as well. There is little sense in allocating resources for drafting new export control measures in a country with limited judicial and legal capacity that cannot even enforce border control or prosecute transgressions. Thus, linking 1540's security goals with the development lessons learned from this aspect of the mandate may expose where the absence of capacity engenders prolif-

eration. Also constructive, this linkage could transform the perception of the Global South of 1540 as a burden to an opportunity in the Global South. If used and financed appropriately, the 1540 Committee could also lead development of an innovative partnership with the business community, whose activities could include:
- Reaching out to civil society to attract the resources for addressing the underlying capacity needs connected with 1540 implementation
- Pushing for greater involvement of governments and non-state actors to create sustainable efforts that meet the needs of all partners from development and security perspectives
- Strengthening codes of conduct and norms not only among governments but among technology manufacturers, exporters, shipping companies, port operators, and domestic middlemen who are vulnerable targets for criminals and illicit networks
- Providing a mechanism for coordinating resources and expertise on both the supply and the demand sides of the proliferation threat

Conclusion

The technological advances of the 1990s empowered a new spectrum of government and non-governmental actors to capitalize on globalization for the common good – yielding unprecedented advances in global development. As a result, the world is a better place to live than ever before. Although the so-called "bottom billion" continue to lag far behind, the number of people in extreme poverty is falling – in some cases dramatically. Between 1990 and 2004, the share of people in the Asia-Pacific region (comprising 61 percent of the global population) living in extreme poverty fell from over 1 billion to 641 million. According to the World Bank, if projected growth rates remain on track, global poverty rates will fall to 12.5 percent by 2015 – less than half of the 1990 level. Although not as dramatic, the number of undernourished people in developing countries is also falling. Today, more students than ever before are completing a full course of primary education, and infant mortality rates have fallen by 12 percent since 1990 in low-income countries and by 36 percent in middle-income states.[39]

On the down-side, the 1990s also fomented the growth of criminal networks bent on exploiting the globalized economy for nefarious purposes. Bolstered by an environment rich in opportunities, illicit traffickers in human beings, narcotics, pharmaceuticals, and, increasingly, small arms and light weapons built global decentralized businesses to serve global markets. The movement of their goods was easily masked by the explosion of legitimate goods making their way around the world.

In 2007, reflecting on his years as director of the Central Intelligence Agency, George Tenet noted: "In the new world of proliferation, nation states have been replaced by shadowy networks like [A.Q.] Khan's, capable of selling turnkey nuclear weapons programs to the highest bidders. Networks of bankers, lawyers, scientists, and industrialists offer one-stop shopping for those wishing to acquire the designs, feed materials, and manufacturing capabilities necessary for nuclear weapons production. With Khan's assistance, small, backward countries could shave years off the time it takes to make nuclear weapons."[40]

The apocalyptic projections of the future are not new to proliferation analysts. But, in the post-9/11 era, the world may have greater reason than ever to fear a new era of unchecked proliferation. The stability of the past has given way to an uncertain future that is increasingly beyond the capacity of one state, or even a group of states, to control.

Considering the new threats to the non-proliferation regime and the dramatic shifts in global politics and economics, two conclusions can be drawn. First, an effective non-proliferation strategy can no longer rely exclusively upon the traditional mechanisms of prevention. Although these tools remain critical to preventing unchecked proliferation, they are no longer sufficient in a world where stringent controls over supply are no longer possible. A new, multi-level strategy must be used to coordinate the supply-side efforts of the security community with the demand-side programs of the economic development and democratization communities. Second, we must focus more attention on the role of non-state actors as potential proliferators, consumers, and middlemen for technology, materials, and WMD know-how. This will require the formation of innovative partnerships that transcend the traditional state and leverage the capacities of non-state actors, including civil society and the business community.

As we better understand the implications of globalization for technology proliferation threats, we must simultaneously begin to promote and develop a more comprehensive set of solutions. This will involve identifying a common purpose among actors having a vested interest – most notably, the security and development communities and private industry. The United Nations is ideally poised to serve as a broker of these interests. We can start with existing mandates, such as resolution 1540, which provide the foundation for building partnerships to meet the challenges posed to the non-proliferation regime by modern technologies and globalization. When this happens, the only question that would remain is whether the United Nations and its member states will overcome the long-ingrained barriers to cooperation and muster the will to launch and carry out this important endeavor to its full conclusion.

Notes

1. *In Larger Freedom: Towards Development, Security, and Human Rights for All. Report of the Secretary-General*, General Assembly document A/59/2005, 21 March 2005, para. 153.
2. Natural Resources Defense Council, Archive of Nuclear Data, "Table of US Nuclear Warheads 1945–75," ⟨http://www.nrdc.org/nuclear/nudb/datab9.asp⟩ (accessed 12 November 2008).
3. "Address by Mr. Dwight D. Eisenhower, President of the United States of America, to the 470th Plenary Meeting of the United Nations General Assembly," 8 December 1953, available at ⟨http://www.iaea.org/About/history_speech.html⟩ (accessed 12 November 2008).
4. "Face-to-Face, Nixon-Kennedy," Vice President Richard M. Nixon and Senator John F. Kennedy, Third Joint Television-Radio Broadcast, 13 October 1960, John F. Kennedy Presidential Library and Museum.
5. Lewis A. Dunn, *Controlling the Bomb: Nuclear Proliferation in the 1980s* (New Haven, CT: Yale University Press, 1982), 1–94.
6. "Proliferation: Threat and Response," Office of the Secretary of Defense, US Department of Defense, January 2001, 1.
7. For a summary of the post–Cold War economic trends that facilitated proliferation, see International Institute for Strategic Studies (IISS), *Nuclear Black Markets: Pakistan, A.Q. Khan, and the Rise of Proliferation Networks. A Net Assessment*, IISS Strategic Dossier (London: IISS, 2007); see ⟨http://www.iiss.org/publications/strategic-dossiers/nbm/⟩ (accessed 12 November 2008).
8. Graham Allison, "How to Stop Nuclear Terror," *Foreign Affairs* 83, no. 1 (2004): 64–74.
9. For an overview of the rise of global trafficking in the new economy, see Moises Naim, *Illicit: How Smugglers, Traffickers, and Copycats are Hijacking the Global Economy* (New York: Anchor Books, 2006).
10. Torrey C. Froscher, "Anticipating Nuclear Proliferation: Insights from the Past," *Nonproliferation Review* 13, no. 3 (2006): 468.
11. Joseph Cirincione, Jon Wolfsthal, Miriam Rajkumar, *Deadly Arsenals: Nuclear, Biological and Chemical Threats* (Washington, DC: Carnegie Endowment for International Peace, 2005), 8, 24.
12. William C. Potter, "The New Proliferation Game," paper prepared for the Weapons of Mass Destruction Commission, No. 12, June 2004; available at ⟨http://www.wmdcommission.org/files/No12.pdf⟩ (accessed 12 November 2008).
13. Security Council resolution 1803, S/RES/1803, 3 March 2008; Security Council resolution 1747, S/RES/1747, 24 March 2007; Security Council resolution 1737, S/RES/1737, 27 December 2006; IAEA Board of Governors, *Report by the Director General on the Implementation of the NPT Safeguards Agreement and Relevant Provisions of Security Council Resolutions 1737 (2006), 1747 (2007) and 1803 (2008) in the Islamic Republic of Iran*, GOV/2008/15, 5 June 2008; Security Council resolution 1718, S/RES/1718, 14 October 2006; IAEA Board of Governors General Conference, *Report by the Director General on the Application of Safeguards in the Democratic People's Republic of Korea*, GOV/2007/45-GC(51)/19, 17 August 2007.
14. Today, up to 32 countries are considering or have long-term plans under way to develop nuclear power. See US Department of State, International Security Advisory Board, *Report on Proliferation Implications of the Global Expansion of Civil Nuclear Power*, Washington, DC, 7 April 2008; available at ⟨http://www.state.gov/documents/organization/105587.pdf⟩ (accessed 12 November 2008).

15. As recent cases involving China, North Korea, and Pakistan suggest, state regulation or even ownership of an industry does not necessarily insulate against illicit trading practices.
16. World Nuclear Association, "Nuclear Power in Russia," Information Paper, October 2008, ⟨http://www.world-nuclear.org/info/inf45.html⟩ (accessed 12 November 2008).
17. Authors' interview with private sector energy companies and US government officials.
18. The World Bank, "Table 1: Trends in Average Applied Tariff Rates in Developing and Industrial Countries, 1981–2006 (Unweighted in %)," ⟨http://siteresources.worldbank.org/INTRES/Resources/469232-1107449512766/tar2006.xls⟩ (accessed 12 November 2008).
19. IISS, *Nuclear Black Markets*.
20. See Douglas Frantz and Catherine Collins, *The Nuclear Jihadist: The True Story of the Man Who Sold the World's Most Dangerous Secrets ... And How We Could Have Stopped Him* (New York: Hachette Book Group, 2007), and Mark Schapiro and Michael Montgomery, "Business of the Bomb: The Modern Nuclear Marketplace," American RadioWorks documentary, American Public Media, available at ⟨http://americanradioworks.publicradio.org/features/nukes/⟩ (accessed 12 November 2008).
21. Eric Lipton, "U.S. Alarmed as Some Exports Veer Off Course," *New York Times*, 2 April 2008, ⟨http://www.nytimes.com/2008/04/02/washington/02UAE.html⟩ (accessed 12 November 2008).
22. DP World, "UAE Records 19% Growth in 2007," 28 February 2008, ⟨http://www.dpworld.ae/news.asp?catid=1&id=78&PageId=21⟩ (accessed 12 November 2008).
23. Authors' interviews with UN and national government officials.
24. Stephen Krasner, *Structural Conflict: The Third World against Global Liberalism* (Berkeley: University of California Press, 1985), 7–13.
25. Thomas J. Biersteker and Sue E. Eckert, eds, *Countering the Financing of Terrorism* (London and New York: Routledge, 2008), 11, 104, 140–141, 193–202, 300.
26. Co-chairmen's report, "Implementing the UN General Assembly's Counter-Terrorism Strategy: Addressing Youth Radicalisation in the Mediterranean Region. Lessons Learned, Best Practices and Recommendations," Brainstorming Conference organized by Istituto Affari Internazionali and Center on Global Counter-terrorism Cooperation, Rome, Italy, 11–12 July 2007; available at ⟨http://www.iai.it/pdf/DocIAI/iai0730.pdf⟩ (accessed 12 November 2008).
27. See Susan E. Rice, "U.S. Foreign Assistance and Failed States," The Brookings Institution, 25 November 2002, available at ⟨http://www.brookings.edu/papers/2002/1125poverty_rice.aspx⟩ (accessed 12 November 2008); Lisa D. Cook, "Africa: The Next Battleground in the Terror War," *Hoover Digest*, No. 1, 2004, available at ⟨http://www.hoover.org/publications/digest/3043311.html⟩ (accessed 12 November 2008); Princeton N. Lyman and J. Stephen Morrison, "The Terrorist Threat in Africa," *Foreign Affairs*, 83, no. 1 (2004): 75–86; Sara Daly, John Parachini, and William Rosenau, "Aum Shinrikyo, al-Qaeda, and the Kinshasa Reactor: Implications of Three Case Studies for Combating Nuclear Terrorism," RAND Corporation, 2005; and John V. Parachini, David E. Mosher, John C. Baker, Keith Crane, Michael S. Chase, and Michael Daugherty, "Diversion of Nuclear, Biological, and Chemical Weapons Expertise from the Former Soviet Union: Understanding an Evolving Problem," RAND Corporation, 2005, available at ⟨http://www.rand.org/pubs/documented_briefings/2005/RAND_DB457.pdf⟩ (accessed 12 November 2008).
28. See Misha Glenny, *McMafia: A Journey Through the Global Criminal Underworld* (New York: Alfred A. Knopf, 2008).
29. Sonia Ben Ouagrham-Gormley, "An Unrealized Nexus? WMD-Related Trafficking, Terrorism and Organized Crime in the Former Soviet Union," *Arms Control Today* 37, no. 6 (2007); available online at ⟨http://www.armscontrol.org/epublish/1/108⟩ (accessed 15 January 2009).

30. For a comprehensive assessment of the cooperative threat reduction programs, see Brian Finlay and Elizabeth Turpen, *Cooperative Nonproliferation: Getting Further, Faster* (Washington, DC: Henry L. Stimson Center, 2007).
31. Stewart Patrick and Kaysie Brown, "Greater Than the Sum of Its Parts? Assessing 'Whole of Government' Approaches in Fragile States," CGD Brief, Center for Global Development, Washington DC, June 2007; available at ⟨http://www.cgdev.org/doc/weakstates/Fragile_States.pdf⟩ (accessed 12 November 2008).
32. Carnegie Endowment for International Peace, Carnegie International Nonproliferation Conference, "Finding Innovative Ways to Detect and Thwart Illicit Nuclear Trade," Comments by Ralf Wirtz of Oerlikon Leybold Vacuum, 26 June 2007, Washington DC; available at ⟨http://www.carnegieendowment.org/files/detect_thwart.pdf⟩ (accessed 12 November 2008).
33. See Security Council resolution 1540, S/RES/1540, 28 April 2004. Similarly, in 2005 the International Convention for the Suppression of Acts of Nuclear Terrorism was agreed upon. It

- Covers a broad range of acts and possible targets, including nuclear power plants and nuclear reactors
- Covers threats and attempts to commit such crimes or to participate in them, as an accomplice
- Stipulates that offenders shall be extradited or prosecuted
- Encourages States to cooperate in preventing terrorist attacks by sharing information and assisting each other in connection with criminal investigations and extradition proceedings
- Deals with both crisis situations (assisting States to solve the situation) and post-crisis situations (rendering nuclear material safe through the International Atomic Energy Agency)

Summary available at UN Action to Counter Terrorism, International Instruments to Counter Terrorism, ⟨http://www.un.org/terrorism/instruments.shtml⟩ (accessed 12 November 2008).
34. In February 2007, the G-7 finance ministers even defined a new area of "proliferation finance" to be examined, which cuts across facets of counter-proliferation, counter-terrorism, and development to understand the role of witting and unwitting actors in the transfer and export of technology, goods, software, services, or expertise that could be used in nuclear, chemical, or biological weapon-related programs.
35. Financial Action Task Force, "Chairman's Summary," Paris Plenary, 10–12 October 2007; available at ⟨http://www.fatf-gafi.org/dataoecd/0/23/39485130.pdf⟩ (accessed 12 November 2008).
36. Financial Action Task Force, "FATF Revised Mandate 2008–2012," 12 April 2007; available at ⟨http://www.fatf-gafi.org/dataoecd/3/32/40433653.pdf⟩ (accessed 12 November 2008).
37. United Nations Global Compact, "Overview of the UN Global Compact," ⟨http://www.unglobalcompact.org/AboutTheGC/index.html⟩ (accessed 12 November 2008).
38. *Business UNusual: Facilitating United Nations Reform Through Partnerships*, commissioned by the United Nations Global Compact Office, produced by the Global Public Policy Institute, August 2005; available at ⟨http://www.unglobalcompact.org/docs/news_events/8.1/bun_part1.pdf⟩ (accessed 12 November 2008).
39. The World Bank, *Millennium Development Goals*, ⟨http://web.worldbank.org/WBSITE/EXTERNAL/EXTABOUTUS/0,,contentMDK:20104132~menuPK:250991~pagePK:43912~piPK:44037~theSitePK:29708,00.html⟩ (accessed 12 November 2008).
40. George Tenet with Bill Harlow, *At the Center of the Storm: My Years at the CIA* (New York: HarperCollins, 2007), 287.

10

Dealing with extra-NPT actors and non-state actors

Waheguru Pal Singh Sidhu

In the post–Cold War world the United Nations has witnessed the emergence of three challenges related to nuclear weapons. First, there is the challenge posed by states within the existing Nuclear Non-Proliferation Treaty (NPT) regime.[1] The second set of challenges comes from states outside the NPT regime, what this chapter refers to as the "extra-NPT regime actors." The third and perhaps most formidable challenge emanates from non-state actors, including but not limited to terrorist groups. This chapter will focus on the role of the United Nations in effectively addressing the challenges posed by these new actors – state and non-state – presently outside the NPT regime.

The international community of states – either individually or collectively – has followed at least three different approaches to address these challenges: technological; military; and political and diplomatic. Technological approaches primarily seek technical fixes to deal with nuclear challenges and include civil defense measures to protect populations against nuclear attacks as well as missile defense systems to prevent nuclear-capable missiles and aircraft from reaching their intended targets.[2] This approach does not normally involve the United Nations. Military approaches that seek to use force to address the threat of nuclear weapons are also referred to as counter-proliferation.[3] The Israeli attacks against the Osirak reactor in 1981 and against the suspected nuclear reactor in Syria in 2007, as well as the various limited strikes against Iraq launched by the United States and its allies in the 1990s followed by the full-scale invasion in 2003, fall into this category. The United Nations has

The United Nations and nuclear orders, Boulden, Thakur and Weiss (eds),
United Nations University Press, 2009, ISBN 978-92-808-1167-4

been involved only to the extent that such attacks have been either endorsed or condemned by the world organization. Political and diplomatic approaches to address the nuclear challenges of extra-NPT and non-state actors have ranged from negotiations to sanctions and have often (though not always) occurred within the UN system.

Although the three above-mentioned approaches are all distinct, there is clearly a considerable degree of overlap between them. For instance, the technological fixes, especially missile defense systems, can also have military doctrinal implications. Similarly, military options (both the actual use of force and the threat of the use of force) have sometimes been used to buttress political and diplomatic efforts. On the other hand, a particular emphasis on only one approach could end up undermining another equally important approach. This chapter will consider all three approaches but will specifically focus on the political and diplomatic approach. After all, the UN system is most conducive to political and diplomatic deliberations.

The chapter begins by defining extra-NPT actors, then surveys the historical record of such actors in world politics. It then assesses three distinct approaches to extra-NPT actors. The chapter next turns its attention to the salience of non-state actors in international nuclear orders. After defining non-state actors for the purposes of this investigation, the chapter analyzes two approaches employed to deal with these actors. The chapter concludes with a discussion of the implications of extra-NPT and non-state actors for the United Nations.

Defining extra-NPT actors of concern

Defining the extra-NPT actors that pose nuclear challenges is problematic. Conventional wisdom suggests that the three states that acquired nuclear weapons after the conclusion of the NPT on 1 July 1968 – either overtly and explicitly by declaring themselves to be nuclear weapons states (India and Pakistan) or covertly and implicitly by not confirming the existence of nuclear weapons (Israel) – and that are the only states not to have signed the NPT are the obvious extra-NPT actors of concern. However, states that signed the NPT but developed nuclear weapons (South Africa, Iraq) and conducted nuclear tests (the Democratic People's Republic of Korea, DPRK) defy this neat categorization. Indeed, the DPRK, which has been a non-nuclear-weapon state member of the NPT since 1985, is reported to have started a nuclear weapons program soon thereafter, announced its withdrawal from the NPT in 2003, and subsequently conducted a nuclear test on 6 October 2006.[4] Similarly, both France and China, which conducted nuclear tests before 1 July

1968 but joined the NPT only as late as 1992, could also be regarded as extra-NPT actors for the interim period. Moreover, if the NPT regime is understood to include the Comprehensive Nuclear-Test-Ban Treaty (CTBT), then both China and the United States, which have signed but not ratified this treaty, could be considered to be extra-NPT actors.

Nonetheless, for the purposes of this chapter, Israel, India, and Pakistan will be considered as the new state actors that are outside the existing NPT regime since the end of the Cold War, although both Israel and India, clearly, became nuclear weapons states much earlier. Iraq and the DPRK, though they posed a significant challenge to the United Nations, will not be considered here at length for two reasons: first, both of these cases and their implications for the United Nations have already been studied in great detail.[5] Second, Iraq is now back in the fold and efforts have begun to ensure that the DPRK will also eventually return to the non-proliferation regime. Similarly, the NPT nuclear states, particularly China, France, and the United States, will also not be considered because as veto-wielding members of the Security Council they have an implicit immunity against any UN efforts to ensure their compliance.

Historical overview

This section provides a brief overview of how the UN system dealt with the three extra-NPT actors. Its objective is to identify the pattern of approaches followed by UN members to address the cases of Israel, India, and Pakistan.

Israel

On 12 June 1968 Israel voted in favor of the NPT in the General Assembly and was expected to sign the treaty even though it had already developed a nuclear weapons program and, possibly, even nuclear weapons by then. This approach was not dissimilar from that of other states, notably Sweden and Switzerland, which too had pursued nuclear weapons programs but eventually gave them up and joined the NPT. However, Israel did not sign the NPT and still remains outside the regime. Israel's reasons for staying out of the NPT are primarily security related.[6]

The first tentative UN response to the Israeli position came in the form of a 1974 General Assembly resolution, originally mooted by the shah of Iran and the League of Arab States, on the Establishment of a Nuclear-Weapon-Free Zone in the Region of the Middle East. This resolution came in the wake of the 1973 Yom Kippur War, during which it was widely reported that Israel, facing a possible conventional defeat, had seriously considered using its nuclear option before the tide turned in its favor. This resolution does not explicitly mention Israel but implicitly refers to it by calling on "all parties concerned in the area" to "refrain ... from producing, testing, obtaining, acquiring or in any other way possessing nuclear weapons."[7] The resolution also calls on all parties concerned in the area to accede to the NPT. This resolution, which was regularly repeated, was expanded in 1990 to create a "zone free of weapons of mass destruction in the Middle East" (WMDFZ). The same resolution was also a key element in the 1995 deal between non-nuclear Arab states and the United States, which allowed for the NPT to be extended indefinitely.[8] The Middle East WMDFZ (and the tacit reference to Israel's nuclear program) was also reiterated in Security Council resolution 687 (3 April 1991) dealing with Iraq's annexation of Kuwait.

In 1978, a General Assembly resolution specifically called upon the Security Council to issue a resolution under Chapter VII that would call upon all states to "end all transfer of nuclear or fissionable material or technology to Israel." Although the resolution refers to all states, it makes particular mention of the "military and nuclear collaboration with South Africa."[9] However, the Council did not oblige. Nonetheless, the Assembly resolution is particularly noteworthy because it came just months before the suspected nuclear explosion reported in the south Indian Ocean in September 1979 which was alleged to have been jointly conducted by South Africa and Israel.[10] Since then the Assembly has regularly passed resolutions that call upon Israel to "renounce possession of nuclear weapons" and accede to the NPT, noting that Israel is now the "only State in the Middle East that has not yet become party to the Treaty."[11] This persistence on the part of the Assembly is in contrast to the reticence of the Council on the subject of Israel's nuclear weapons.

Following the Israeli attack on the Iraqi nuclear reactor at Osirak on 7 June 1981, both the General Assembly and the Security Council responded with resolutions. The Assembly resolution not only condemned the attack but also requested the Council to "investigate Israel's nuclear activities and collaboration of other states and parties in those activities."[12] However, this resolution, which came months after the attack and was dependent on the Council for enforcement, did not have the same weight as the Council resolution issued within weeks of the attack.

Security Council resolution 487 (19 June 1981) passed unanimously and marked the first instance of Council action dealing with Israel's nuclear program despite evidence of the program's existence for more than a decade. Even here, although the Council strongly condemned the Israeli military action, it merely called upon Israel to "place its nuclear facilities under the safeguards of the International Atomic Energy

Agency." The Council did not call for Israel to dismantle its nuclear weapons program or to sign the NPT. Nor did it call on member states to impose sanctions or end the transfer of nuclear material and technology to Israel. Significantly, this resolution was not passed under Chapter VII of the Charter. Since then, no Council resolution has made a specific effort to deal with Israel's nuclear weapons program.

Interestingly, neither the General Assembly nor the Security Council has taken up the issue of Israel's attack of 6 September 2007 on a suspected nuclear facility deep within Syria. This was partly because initially neither Israel nor Syria admitted to the incident. However, subsequently, the United States released information asserting that the site hit in Syria was a nuclear reactor built with the assistance of North Korea. These revelations, made seven months after the Israeli attack, led the director general of the International Atomic Energy Agency (IAEA), Mohamed ElBaradei, to criticize both the United States for not revealing the presence of an unsafeguarded nuclear reactor in Syria and Israel for taking unilateral action against it and preventing a proper IAEA inspection.[13] This admonishment notwithstanding, the Council is unlikely to pass a resolution condemning Israel's action against Syria along the lines of resolution 487, especially given the tacit US approval.

On 25 September 1996, Israel signed the CTBT but has still to ratify it. In 2004, Israel also agreed to host monitoring facilities related to the International Monitoring System (IMS) of the CTBT, which might indicate that Israel has ruled out nuclear tests even though it has not ratified the treaty. Israel might be holding up the ratification of the CTBT as a bargaining chip against some of its neighbors, such as Syria and Iran, which have still not signed the treaty, or even Egypt, which has signed but not ratified the CTBT.

Significantly, ever since the case of Tehran's alleged violation of its NPT commitments was raised in the United Nations – most significantly, Security Council resolutions passed under Chapter VII that imposed sanctions on Iran – Israel has also been taking political and diplomatic initiatives within the United Nations to pressure the international community to ensure that Iran adheres to its obligations. Simultaneously, Israel has hinted at military action in the event that Iran is not prevented from developing nuclear weapons.[14] Israel's behavior implies that, even though it remains outside the regime, NPT norms are critical for managing the nuclear world order.

Perhaps this is why, in 2007, Israel made a pitch to the Nuclear Suppliers Group (NSG) and sought exemption from non-proliferation rules on two grounds: first on account of Israel's credentials in nuclear non-proliferation, safety, and security; and, second, to develop a "criteria based approach for nuclear collaboration with non-NPT states."[15] This approach is not dissimilar from the efforts being made by India to seek a similar exemption from the NSG.

India

India was among the first countries to propose the principles of an NPT in 1965 and took an active part in the negotiations at the Eighteen-Nation Disarmament Conference (ENDC) in Geneva.[16] It was the key author of Article IV, which ensured "the inalienable right" of all NPT parties "to develop research, production and use of nuclear energy for peaceful purposes without discrimination."[17] However, by the time of the crucial vote on the NPT in the General Assembly, India expressed its opposition to the treaty. Although it had not developed nuclear weapons by then, India did not want to foreclose this possibility in the future. India's non-accession was succinctly expressed by Prime Minister Indira Gandhi on the grounds that, "[w]ith China at her back, and Pakistan lurking on the sidelines, she foresaw no alternative but to keep open her option on the production of nuclear weapons."[18] Since then India has not signed, and is unlikely to sign, the NPT as a non-nuclear-weapon state.[19]

Subsequently, on 18 May 1974, India conducted a "peaceful nuclear explosion" and tested a nuclear device.[20] The UN response to the first Indian nuclear test was a General Assembly resolution declaring a nuclear-weapon-free zone in South Asia, though it makes no specific reference to India's nuclear test.[21] Curiously, although the resolution makes references to other nuclear-weapon-free zones, it makes no mention of the NPT, unlike a similar resolution on the Middle East, which was passed around the same time and which explicitly refers to the treaty. This lapse is probably because Pakistan, the sponsor of the resolution, was itself opposed to the NPT. This resolution was also regularly repeated right until 1997, even though Pakistan had itself developed nuclear weapons during this period.[22] The resolution was not introduced after Pakistan conducted its own nuclear tests in May 1998.

In contrast, the Security Council did not pass a single resolution in response to the first Indian nuclear test in 1974. However, a group of seven countries, including four veto-wielding permanent members (France, the Soviet Union, the United Kingdom, and the United States), established the NSG with the express objective of further curtailing the export of nuclear equipment, materials, or technology to countries such as India. With the exception of France, all the other NSG countries were also members of the NPT. China, another veto-wielding member of the Council, became a member of the NSG in 2004. Given the voluntary nature of the regime, NSG members could still export equipment, materials, or technology to non-NSG countries. For instance, Russia transferred nuclear fuel to India in 2001 "even though 32 of 34 NSG members earlier declared that the shipment would contradict Russia's NSG commitments."[23] That NSG members were some of the biggest violators became evident when Iraq presented its weapons-program dossier to the Council in December 2002 – it read like a who's who of the NSG.

As in the NPT negotiations, India was one of the prime movers in the negotiations at the Conference on Disarmament (CD) in Geneva leading to the CTBT in the 1990s. However, by the time the treaty was ready to be adopted in 1996, New Delhi, which was vehemently opposed to some of its key provisions, blocked it. The treaty was salvaged when an Australian proposal to move the CTBT to the General Assembly in New York was adopted. The reasons for India's reticence about the treaty became clear when two years later it conducted nuclear tests and declared itself to be a nuclear weapons state.

In the wake of the Indian and Pakistani nuclear tests of May 1998, the Security Council passed resolution 1172 (6 June 1998). China, in its capacity as president of the Council, actively sought and coordinated the consultation between the permanent five members (P-5) that led to the adoption of the resolution, which condemned the tests and demanded that India and Pakistan unconditionally sign the CTBT and the NPT and refrain from weaponization. In fact, China also unsuccessfully lobbied the other P-5 members to ban India from becoming a permanent member of the Council in future.[24] During US President Bill Clinton's visit to Beijing in June 1998, China and the United States issued a joint communiqué on South Asia that called on India and Pakistan to "stop all further nuclear tests and adhere immediately and unconditionally to the CTBT,... and to enter into firm commitment not to weaponize or deploy nuclear weapons or the missiles capable of delivering them."[25]

Ironically, despite resolution 1172 (or perhaps because of it), India and the United States embarked on an unprecedented and prolonged dialogue on security issues from 1998 to 2000. Although the mandate for this dialogue came ostensibly from the resolution and was primarily to preserve "the viability of the global nonproliferation regime," it led to the first serious and substantial engagement between the world's two largest democracies in the post–Cold War era.[26] The erudite foreign minister Jaswant Singh led the Indian side while the seasoned diplomat and accomplished arms control negotiator Strobe Talbott headed the US team. The discussion focused on five issues: de facto adherence to the CTBT; fissile material; strategic restraint; export controls; and an India–Pakistan dialogue.[27] In all, the Singh–Talbott dialogue lasted 12 rounds. This engagement culminated in Bill Clinton's visit to India in March 2000 and the signing of the joint Vision Statement, which moved the Indo-US relationship one notch up.[28] It could also be argued that the dialogue paved the way for the subsequent Indo-US nuclear deal announced in 2005 (known officially as the "US-India Civil Nuclear Cooperation Initiative"). Similarly, partly as a result of resolution 1172, India was successful in embarking on strategic dialogues with not only the other four "official" nuclear weapon states but also Germany, Japan, and even Australia. These dialogues inevitably provided a tacit endorsement of India's status as a state with nuclear weapons, clearly a consequence contrary to what resolution 1172 was intended to achieve.[29]

The proposed Indo-US nuclear deal illustrates this approach and reflects the touchy relationship between such ad hoc initiatives and the treaty-based regime. The Indo-US agreement calls, in the first instance, for a separation of the Indian civilian and military nuclear programs. This is to be followed by an agreement between New Delhi and the IAEA that would put all 14 Indian civilian nuclear reactors under IAEA safeguards, followed by another special arrangement with the NSG to allow its members to supply nuclear fuel for India's civilian reactors. Predictably, this effort to establish Indian exceptionalism has proved to be contentious both within India and outside. One school, pejoratively referred to as the "non-proliferation ayatollahs," argues that such a deal, which rewards actions that blatantly challenge the non-proliferation norm, would not only allow India to expand its nuclear arsenal but further undermine the already battered NPT regime.[30] Another equally vocal school asserts that the Indo-US deal is essential not only to facilitate India's participation in the global non-proliferation regime but also to ensure the relevance of the existing regime, strengthening it further.[31] In either case, what is evident is that ad hoc approaches, which promote the exceptional rather than the universal, are likely to be regarded with great suspicion and consequently are unlikely to be smoothly integrated with the global regime.

Pakistan

Pakistan supported the Irish proposal for the NPT and participated (although not as actively as India) in the ENDC. Pakistan also supported the NPT resolution in the General Assembly in 1968. However, once India refused to accede to the NPT, Pakistan also decided not to join the treaty and still remains outside the regime. Like India, Pakistan also chose not to sign the CTBT and is unlikely to do so.

Following the 1974 Indian nuclear test, Pakistan embarked on its own nuclear weapons program and simultaneously proposed the establishment of a nuclear-weapon-free zone in South Asia. There were no Pakistan-specific resolutions related to its nuclear program in either the General Assembly or the Security Council until its tests in May 1998.

However, Pakistan was the target of both the US Nuclear Non-Proliferation Act of 1978 and the NSG Guidelines.[32] Some scholars argue that "US policy toward Pakistan has been much less consistent [than towards India]."[33] For instance, Washington cut off economic and military assistance when Pakistan acquired uranium-enrichment technology in 1979 only to rescind its suspension a couple of years later in order to get Pakistan's support against the Soviet presence in Afghanistan. Throughout the 1980s, while Pakistan was a key US ally in the region, it was subject to the Pressler Amendment, which called for the US president to certify that Pakistan did not possess a nuclear device. Although Pakistan President Zia-ul-Huq boasted in 1987 that Pakistan had acquired nuclear weapons capability, US certification was nonetheless forthcoming. However, in 1990, as soon as the Soviets were ousted from Afghanistan, President George H. W. Bush could not certify that Pakistan did not possess a nuclear device, and this led to the reimposition of sanctions. Following the May 1998 nuclear tests, these sanctions were buttressed by prohibitions on US bank-backed loans or credits and the denial of the American Export-Import Bank's support for exports. In addition, Pakistan, like India, was the target of Council resolution 1172. However, soon after the events of 11 September 2001 and the US invasion of Afghanistan, all of these sanctions were lifted and Pakistan was reinstated as a strategic ally of Washington in the region.

Although the United States and Pakistan embarked on a nuclear dialogue in the wake of resolution 1172, the results were very different than those of the Indo-US dialogue. The US–Pakistan dialogue was focused more on the safety and security of Pakistan's nuclear arsenal. This dialogue and US concerns became more pointed following revelations of the activities of Dr A. Q. Khan and his alleged role in the proliferation of nuclear weapons technology to Iran, Libya, and North Korea. The Pakistani authorities argued that Khan was acting alone and had violated national laws, but these assertions are not borne out by the particulars. In the first instance, Pakistan passed a law controlling exports of goods, technologies, material, and equipment related to nuclear and biological weapons that entered into force only on 23 September 2004. Prior to that, Pakistan released export control regulations in July 1998, February 1999, and August 1999, as well as the Export Policy and Procedures Order of November 2000, all of which – according to experts – were full of loopholes.[34] These weak regulations, coupled with Khan's special status in Pakistan, meant that "Khan had a complete blank check. He could do anything. He could go anywhere. He could buy anything at any price."[35]

One possible explanation is that the Pakistani government knew of these proliferation activities and, perhaps, even acquiesced for the sake of the national nuclear arsenal. An equally worrying, but perhaps more unlikely, possibility is that the Pakistani authorities were unaware of the activities of Khan and had no oversight or control over them.[36] The Khan case scuttled any possibility of a US–Pakistan nuclear deal along the lines of that reached through the Indo-US dialogue, about which Islamabad had been keen.

Three approaches to extra-NPT actors

From the above overview, it is evident that the community of states has sought to address challenges posed by extra-NPT actors through three approaches. The first is the traditional multilateral institutional approach anchored in treaty-based regimes related to non-proliferation, such as the NPT, the CTBT, and the Fissile Material Cut-off Treaty (FMCT). The central idea is to enmesh the three extra-NPT actors into various elements of the evolving architecture so that in the not-too-distant future these states become de facto, if not de jure, members of the non-proliferation regime. However, this approach appears to be increasingly difficult to implement for a number of reasons and risks becoming a pipedream.

In the case of the CTBT, opened for signature in September 1996, it was hoped all 44 states mentioned in Article XIV, including Israel, India, and Pakistan, would sign and ratify the treaty. However, even 10 years later only 35 of the 44 Article XIV states (excluding China, Israel, India, North Korea, Pakistan, and the United States) had done so. Thus, even if Israel, India, and Pakistan sign the treaty it is unlikely to enter into force unless the others sign and ratify it as well.

Similarly, the FMCT is at risk of being still-born. It began its precarious life as a resolution prohibiting the production of fissile materials for nuclear weapons or explosive devices in December 1993. In March 1995, just before the NPT Review and Extension Conference, the Conference on Disarmament adopted a report agreeing to establish an ad hoc committee to negotiate the proposed fissile materials ban. Several delegations, particularly Pakistan, Iran, Egypt, and Algeria, pushed hard to include existing stocks (the product of past production). The nuclear weapons states and India rejected attempts to address stocks, arguing that the UN resolution was for a ban only on future production, i.e. a cut-off.

From 1995 until now, the FMCT issue has been blocked by two main issues: stocks and linkage with nuclear disarmament. Led by India, a number of non-aligned countries had been linking the commencement of FMCT negotiations to concurrent negotiations on a timetable for nuclear disarmament, which the five nuclear weapons states refused to take seriously. Subsequently, China also linked the FMCT to progress on the resolution to prevent an arms race in outer space. The FMCT pre-negotiations were ironically the only silver lining to an otherwise dismal record of the CD over the past decade. According to the September 1999 issue of the official newsletter of the United Nations Department for Disarmament Affairs, the CD "never reached agreement on the adoption of a programme of work for its 1999 session, and thus was not able to undertake substantive work."[37] With the CD paralyzed, the FMCT a non-starter, and the CTBT still to enter into force, there is little prospect of the de facto inclusion of the extra-NPT actors into the broader non-proliferation regime.[38]

Moreover, one major drawback of these treaties, even if they were successfully negotiated or entered into force, is that, although they tend to be strong in international law, their institutionalized compliance mechanisms are weak on enforcement. For example, the NPT is as ineffective in enforcing Article X (which deals with the withdrawal of states from the treaty) as it is Article VI (which calls for disarmament).

The second approach is through non-treaty-based multilateral statements, such as the various declarations and resolutions by the Security Council and the General Assembly. The first significant step to co-opt the three extra-NPT actors was the Council's presidential statement of 31 January 1992, which stressed that "proliferation of all weapons of mass destruction constitutes a threat to international peace and security" and, with specific reference to nuclear weapons, noted "the decision of many countries to adhere to the Non-Proliferation Treaty and emphasize the integral role in the implementation of that Treaty of fully effective IAEA safeguards."[39] This statement, which also highlighted the failure of the NPT nuclear weapons states (which are also the Council's unelected P-5) to keep their commitments to the treaty, was probably the price they were willing to pay for getting the elected members to accept the issuing of a presidential statement. Apart from this presidential statement, the Council has passed only four resolutions in the past 60 years related to the extra-NPT actors and nuclear proliferation: 487, 687, 1172, and 1540 (28 April 2004).

These resolutions also reveal several trends related to the Council itself. First, with the exception of the presidential statement of 1992 and resolution 1540 – to be discussed below – all these resolutions are country specific. Second, resolutions have been possible only when there is a consensus amongst the Council's P-5. Third, neither of the resolutions relating specifically to Israel, India, and Pakistan (487 and 1172) falls under Chapter VII of the UN Charter. This is in sharp contrast to those resolutions addressing NPT member states (Iraq, North Korea, and Iran), all of which are under Chapter VII. Thus, it would appear that the Council is unable or unwilling to pass resolutions under Chapter VII against non-NPT states. Fourth, even when it does manage to pass resolutions against the three extra-NPT states, the Security Council's implementation remains uneven and contentious, partly on account of the limited capabilities of the IAEA (often the implementing agency) and partly as a result of the reluctance of one of the P-5 to confront the country in question for political or strategic reasons. Finally, historically the P-5 have taken initiatives to address the issue of the extra-NPT states outside the Council, evident in the creation of the NSG, for example. However, Israeli, Indian, and Pakistani nuclear weapons bear testimony that initiatives outside the United Nations, such as the NSG, may have delayed nuclear weapons programs but they were unable to prevent these states from building nuclear weapons. Still, although these initiatives have not stopped the nuclear weapons programs of the three countries, they have, clearly, changed their behavior. For instance, both Israel and India have sought to adhere to NPT norms and are now seeking exemption from the NSG Guidelines based on their responsible behavior. Similarly, all three states have introduced legislation or made declarations to adhere to Council resolutions related to non-proliferation.

In contrast to the reluctant activism of the Security Council towards the extra-NPT actors, the General Assembly has been active in the sphere of nuclear non-proliferation ever since the 1950s. US President Dwight D. Eisenhower first presented the "Atoms for Peace" plan before the General Assembly in 1953. During the 1960s, the Assembly passed several resolutions supporting the NPT and after further revision – concerning mainly the Preamble and Articles IV and V – commended the draft text of the NPT, which is annexed to resolution 2373 (XXII). Similarly, it was the Assembly that resurrected the CTBT by adopting a resolution (A/RES/50/245) on 10 September 1996. In April 2005 the Assembly followed up by adopting an International Convention for the Suppression of Acts of Nuclear Terrorism, which specifically addresses non-state actors.[40]

Interestingly, unlike Security Council resolutions, General Assembly resolutions do not tend to be country specific (perhaps with the notable exception of Israel and of Mongolia, which has a one-state Assembly-endorsed nuclear-free zone). In addition, Assembly resolutions tend to be region specific – Middle East or South Asia, for instance. Moreover, they do not always deal with immediate crises and therefore lack both the immediacy and the functional focus of Security Council resolutions. Instead, by setting out broader sets of laws, the General Assembly contributes significantly to long-term norm-building. However, it would appear that the Assembly resolutions have the least impact on either the behavior or the programs of the extra-NPT actors.

The third approach consists of a set of ad hoc, non-treaty-based, non-UN-centered, non-institutional, non-conventional approaches to address the immediate challenges of nuclear proliferation. These include the Proliferation Security Initiative (PSI); negotiations by France, Germany, and the United Kingdom (EU-3) with Iran; the Six-Party Talks to address the DPRK's nuclear program; and the Indo-US nuclear agreement. All of these arrangements tend to be strong on the enforcement dimension but relatively weak in international law: they do not enjoy as much global legitimacy as the treaties and UN declarations, and they generally lie outside the remit of the United Nations. Nonetheless, as is evident from the Indo-US nuclear deal, such initiatives are likely to play an increasing role in the attempt to accommodate the extra-NPT actors within the broad non-proliferation architecture provided their behavior is responsible and normatively in line with the broad principles of the NPT regime.

Defining non-state actors of concern

There is no universally accepted definition of "non-state actors" among the community of states. According to Security Council resolution 1540, a non-state actor is an "individual or entity, not acting under the lawful authority of any State."[41] Although this definition is broad enough to make it relevant for most instances, it does not necessarily cover all contingencies. For instance, if the laws of a state do not explicitly ban proliferation (as was the case with Pakistan before 2004) then can an individual or entity that indulges in proliferation activities be considered a "non-state actor"? Moreover, how would a highly qualified, state-sponsored non-state actor (such as A. Q. Khan) fit into this puzzle? Resolution 1540's definition also begs the question of whether non-governmental organizations, such as Greenpeace, which often challenge the lawful authority of the state, might be considered "non-state" actors on a par with militant groups that also attack the authority of states. Moreover, because the definition focuses on individuals and entities, it does not take into consideration the existence of failed or non-functioning states. Nonetheless, this chapter will adhere to the definition laid out by resolution 1540 to consider the quest of transnational or sub-national armed groups (such as Aum Shinrikyo or al-Qaeda) to develop nuclear weapons as well as the antics of nuclear scientists and private or semi-official entities (such as Khan) to hawk their materials and expertise to new proliferators.

Although non-state actors used biological and chemical weapons as early as the mid-1980s and sought to acquire nuclear weapons thereafter, concerns about nuclear terrorism heightened following 9/11, when the phenomenon of mass terrorism became more apparent. Expert opinion is sharply divided over the threat posed by non-state actors, particularly armed non-state actors. According to Graham Allison: "In sum, my best judgement is that based on current trends, a nuclear terrorist attack on the United States is more likely than not in the decade ahead."[42] This alarmist view is challenged by other scholars who argue that "nuclear terrorism is a less significant threat than is commonly believed, and that, among terrorists, Muslim extremists are not the most likely to use nuclear weapons."[43]

To consider this threat realistically, the following factors would have to be taken into account: the motivations of the groups (whether they are apocalyptic groups or religious terrorists); their methods (whether they have a propensity for indiscriminate and mass killings); their access to nuclear material, and the necessary expertise to manufacture and use such weapons.[44] Given what we do know about transnational armed non-state actors, we can conclude that, although there is certainly a high risk of nuclear terrorism, the probability of its occurrence is low. However, there is a higher risk and probability of the use of a radiological dispersal device (popularly called a "dirty bomb" because it combines conventional explosives with other radioactive material, such as that used for medical or industrial purposes). Such a device when detonated would not cause a nuclear explosion but would cause radioactive material to scatter and fall over a large area, increasing panic and radioactive risk.

Two approaches to non-state actors

Unlike the challenges posed by extra-NPT actors, the international community of states has sought to address the challenges posed by non-state actors through two approaches: first, through UN-led, non-treaty-based multilateral approaches, such as the various declarations and resolutions made by the Security Council and the General Assembly; and second, through a set of ad hoc, non-UN-based, non-institutional, non-conventional approaches to deal with immediate threats. Indeed, since non-state actors (as defined in resolution 1540) cannot belong to any institutional or multilateral arrangement, there is little prospect of either involving them in treaty-based arrangements or expecting them to adhere to treaty-based regimes.

As part of the first approach, the Security Council resolutions 1373 (28 September 2001), 1540 (28 April 2004), 1673 (27 April 2006), 1735 (22 December 2006), and 1810 (25 April 2008) are all designed to strengthen the state against non-state actors. The General Assembly's International Convention for the Suppression of Acts of Nuclear Terrorism was adopted in April 2005 with a similar intent. These resolutions are particularly innovative for two reasons: first, they seek to deal exclusively with non-state actors; and, second, they seek to provide stopgap arrangements to plug existing loopholes in the present treaty-based regime. Resolution 1540 is particularly far-reaching because it calls on all UN member states to "adopt and enforce appropriate effective laws which prohibit any non-State actor to manufacture, acquire, possess, develop, transport, transfer or use nuclear, chemical or biological weapons and their means of delivery," as well as to "take and enforce effective measures to establish domestic controls to prevent the proliferation of nuclear, chemical, or biological weapons and their means of delivery." It also envisages cooperative action and calls upon all states to promote dialogue and cooperation, including assistance in the implementation of the resolution. The resolution established a Security Council Committee (the 1540 Committee), initially for a period of two years. The tenure of the 1540 Committee has been extended until 25 April 2011. Although the resolution has been generally welcomed, given that present treaty-based regimes do not address this aspect of proliferation, there is concern that this approach of using the Council to legislate, if exercised often enough, would circumvent the negotiated approach to developing treaty-based regimes. There is also concern about the ability of weak or poor states to implement these laws and enforce domestic control.[45]

The second approach comprises "carrots" – such as the Group of Eight Global Partnership, aimed primarily at preventing the leakage of nuclear material and expertise from the former Soviet Union as well as other nuclear states – and "sticks" – such as the so-called preventive non-proliferation war doctrine first invoked against Iraq in 2003 and the US-led. Although the PSI is aimed at states rather than non-state actors, the initiative is also likely to impact on the activities of non-state actors. This was evident in the case of the interception of the German-owned freighter *BBC China*, which was carrying Malaysian-built centrifuge parts to Libya via Dubai for the Khan network.[46] Similarly, although countries such as the United States have clearly planned for pre-emptive strikes against potential nuclear threats by non-state actors, successfully implementing such a strategy would be critically dependent on a higher level of intelligence than has been available up to now. In contrast, French President Jacques Chirac is the only one who publicly but tentatively raised the possibility of deterring non-state actors with nuclear weapons; no one else has seriously considered the relevance (or irrelevance) of deterring the potential nuclear weapons of non-state actors with the nuclear weapons of states.[47]

All of these non-UN arrangements tend to be strong in the enforcement dimension but have relatively weak international legitimacy. Indeed, all of these initiatives are discriminatory and, predictably, do not enjoy universal adherence. Although the states behind these initiatives – primarily the P-5 – have attempted to seek greater legitimacy for their actions by having these initiatives endorsed by the Security Council, there is concern that these initiatives might deal a fatal blow to the already weakened treaty-based non-proliferation regime. Nonetheless, given the focus of treaty-based regimes on compliance and their inability to address many of the proliferation challenges of today – especially enforcement – these ad hoc initiatives are likely to flourish.

However, no state has seriously contemplated the possible response in the event of the use of a nuclear weapon by non-state actors, and none is prepared for such an eventuality. As Secretary-General Kofi Annan noted, "a nuclear catastrophe in one of our great cities" would raise questions ranging from whether it was a terrorist act or aggression by a state or an accident. These scenarios "may not be equally probable, but all are possible,"[48] and yet no response has been prepared.

Conclusion: Implications for the United Nations

This overview of the nuclear challenges posed by new nuclear states and extra-NPT actors raises several key questions. Do these ad hoc and alternative approaches reflect the limits of the UN-led non-proliferation regime in addressing truly tough questions, such as the cessation of the arms race and disarmament within the regime, as well as the emergence of new actors outside the regime? Are we going to see a rise in the number of ad hoc and alternative initiatives and a relative decline or lack of initiative in the more multilateral, institutional approaches? Does the inactivity in the Geneva-based CD since 1996 reflect the limitations of formal multilateral structures and regimes? Do the 1995 NPT Review and the treaty's indefinite extension, combined with the 13 steps of the 2000 NPT Review and the subsequent inability of the 2005 NPT Review even to acknowledge (let alone operationalize) them, indicate a future trend? What are the prospects for the 2010 NPT Review?

Second, to what extent do these ad hoc and alternative approaches depend on the multilateral regime for their success? Are such approaches possible without the multilateral agreements? The relevant General Assembly and Security Council resolutions do certainly make pointed references to "multilateral treaties" aimed at eliminating or preventing the proliferation of nuclear weapons, as do some ad hoc approaches (e.g. the PSI, the EU-3, and Iran). However, it is not clear whether the Six-Party Talks or the Indo-US agreement do the same, although both make reference to agreements with the IAEA. In both cases, the efforts to operationalize the linkages have been uneven.

Third, how might the UN system best approach the question of nuclear challenges from new actors: through multilateral treaty-based instruments, through Council or Assembly resolutions, or through a series of ad hoc arrangements?

Although there are no clear answers to these questions, the following trends are evident and will affect the ability of the United Nations to address new nuclear challenges. First, in the foreseeable future new nuclear states and extra-NPT actors will continue to play an important part in proliferation and, therefore, also have an impact on international peace and security. Second, the present set of proliferation tools, especially the state-centric, treaty-based non-proliferation regime, are likely to remain inadequate to address the challenge posed by both non-state and extra-NPT actors. Third, and consequently, there will be a greater impetus to develop ad hoc short-term unilateral or plurilateral responses to addressing the immediate challenges posed by non-state and extra-NPT actors. Fourth, in the wake of this ad hoc trend, which seeks short-term and immediate solutions, there is a grave danger that the treaty-based non-proliferation regime might be inadvertently further weakened. This was apparent in the 2005 NPT Review Conference. One reason for its failure was that there were no deals to be made within the NPT setting (as was the case in the 1995 and 2000 Review Conferences); all of the action was happening outside the multilateral institutions (evident in the Indo-US nuclear negotiations and the EU-3's dialogue with Iran). Finally, efforts will continue to try to bridge the gap between the three pillars – the treaty-based regime; the non-treaty-based multilateral regime; and the ad hoc, non-institutional regime – by seeking to legitimize the ad hoc initiatives and also to link them to existing treaty-based regimes. This has been sought through endorsements by the General Assembly and the Security Council, efforts at universalization, and simply being more effective. However, these efforts have limited appeal and scope. In the long run, the existing non-proliferation regime, which already appears to be past its prime, will have to be revamped in a significant way to address the challenges posed by new actors.[49] This might be a more manageable prospect than the more pragmatic but daunting task of outlawing nuclear weapons.[50]

Notes

1. The nuclear non-proliferation regime is generally understood to include the Treaty Banning Nuclear Weapon Tests in the Atmosphere, in Outer Space and Under Water (Partial Test Ban Treaty, 1963), the Treaty on the Non-Proliferation of Nuclear Weap-

ons (1970), the Convention on the Physical Protection of Nuclear Material (1987), the Comprehensive Nuclear-Test-Ban Treaty (1996), and the various nuclear-weapon-free zones, as well as the Comprehensive Safeguards and Additional Protocol of the IAEA. More contentiously, the regime is also considered to include the various supply control regimes, such as the Nuclear Suppliers Group (1975).
2. On civil defense measures, see Watson Davis, Jane Stafford, Majorie Van de Water, Sam Matthews, and Wadsworth Likely, *Atomic Bombing: How to Protect Yourself* (New York: Wm. H. Wise & Co, 1950), and Steve Coll, "The Unthinkable: Can the United States Be Made Safe from Nuclear Terrorism?" *The New Yorker*, 12 March 2007. On missile defense, see Dean A. Wilkening, "A Simple Model for Calculating Ballistic Missile Defense Effectiveness," CISAC Working Paper, Center for International Security and Cooperation, Stanford University, August 1998; and Lisbeth Gronlund, David C. Wright, George N. Lewis, and Philip E. Coyle III, *Technical Realities: An Analysis of the 2004 Deployment of a U.S. National Missile Defense System* (Cambridge, MA: Union of Concerned Scientists, 2004).
3. Claire Rak, "The Role of Preventive Strikes in Counterproliferation Strategy: Two Case Studies," *Strategic Insights* 2, no. 10 (October 2003).
4. IAEA, "Fact Sheet on DPRK Nuclear Safeguards," available at ⟨http://www.iaea.org/NewsCenter/Focus/IaeaDprk/fact_sheet_may2003.shtml⟩ (accessed 13 November 2008).
5. See, for instance, Waheguru Pal Singh Sidhu and Ramesh Thakur, eds, *Arms Control After Iraq* (Tokyo: United Nations University Press, 2006), and Victor D. Cha and David C. Kang, *Nuclear North Korea: A Debate on Engagement Strategies* (New York: Columbia University Press, 2003).
6. See Avner Cohen, *Israel and the Bomb* (New York: Columbia University Press, 1998), 300–301.
7. General Assembly resolution 3263 (XXIX), 9 December 1974.
8. Rebecca Johnson, "Rethinking Security Interests for a Nuclear-Weapon-Free Zone in the Middle East," *Disarmament Diplomacy* 86, no. 2 (2007): 21–31.
9. General Assembly resolution 33/71, 14 December 1978.
10. Seymour M. Hersh, *The Samson Option* (New York: Random House, 1991), 272–273, 280.
11. See, for instance, General Assembly resolution 48/78, 16 December 1993; General Assembly resolution 49/78, 15 December 1994; General Assembly resolution 50/73, 12 December 1995; General Assembly resolution 51/48, 10 December 1996; and General Assembly resolution 60/92, 8 December 2005.
12. General Assembly resolution 36/27, 13 November 1981.
13. Ewen MacAskill and David Batty, "UN Censures US and Israel over Syria Nuclear Row," *The Guardian*, 25 April 2008.
14. Nicole Gaouette, "Israel: Iran Is Now Danger No. 1," *Christian Science Monitor*, 28 November 2003.
15. George Jahn, "Israel Seeks Exemption from Atomic Rules," *Associated Press*, 25 September 2007, and Nuclear Suppliers Group Point of Contact [Confidential] Note, NSG(07)13, 19 March 2007.
16. George Bunn, "The World's Non-Proliferation Regime in Time," *IAEA Bulletin* 46/2, 2005.
17. George Bunn and John B. Rhinelander, "Looking Back: The Nuclear Nonproliferation Treaty Then and Now," *Arms Control Today*, July/August 2008.
18. U.S. Embassy New Delhi Airgram A-540 to Department of State, "Canadians Warn GOI on NPT," 12 December 1967, Secret, The National Security Archive.
19. For details of the Indian position, see George Perkovich, *India's Nuclear Bomb* (Berkeley: University of California Press, 1999).

20. W. P. S. Sidhu, "India's Nuclear Tests: Technical and Military Imperatives," *Jane's Intelligence Review*, April 1996.
21. General Assembly resolution 3265 (XXIX), 9 December 1974.
22. See for example, General Assembly resolution 43/66, 7 December 1988; General Assembly resolution 47/49, 9 December 1992; General Assembly resolution 52/35, 9 December 1997.
23. "The Nuclear Suppliers Group (NSG) at a Glance," *Arms Control Today*, May 2006.
24. Therese Delpech, "Nuclear Weapons and the 'New World Order': Early Warning from Asia?" *Survival* 40, no. 4 (1998–1999): 62.
25. Sino-U.S. Joint Statement on South Asia, available at ⟨http://www.china-embassy.org/eng/zmgx/zysj/kldfh/t36228.htm⟩.
26. Strobe Talbott, "Dealing with the Bomb in South Asia," *Foreign Affairs* 78, no. 2 (1999), 120–121.
27. Ibid., 111.
28. See Rajeswari Pillai Rajagopalan, "Indo-US Relations in the Bush White House," *Strategic Analysis*, July 2001: 545–556.
29. See Michael Krepon, "Looking Back: The 1998 Indian and Pakistani Nuclear Tests," *Arms Control Today* 38, no. 4 (2008); available at ⟨http://armscontrol.org/act/2008_05/lookingback⟩ (accessed 15 January 2009).
30. See Kaushik Kapistalam, "Nuclear Hypocrisy and Hot Air Proliferation," *Bharat Rakshak Monitor* 6, no. 6 (2004); Praful Bidwai, "The 'Ayatollahs' Are Here," *Frontline* 22, Issue 23 (2005): 18; and A. Vinod Kumar, "Nobel Laureates Pitch in against the Indo-US Nuclear Deal," *IDSA Strategic Comments*, 19 June 2006.
31. Ashley J. Tellis, *Atoms for War? U.S.-Indian Civilian Nuclear Cooperation and India's Nuclear Arsenal*, Carnegie Endowment for International Peace, Washington, DC, 2006; C. Raja Mohan, "As Complicated as 1, 2, 3," *Indian Express*, 13 July 2007; and K. Subrahmanyam, "To PM, Sonia, Advani," *Indian Express*, 10 May 2008.
32. For NSG Guidelines, see ⟨http://www.nuclearsuppliersgroup.org/guide.htm⟩ (accessed 13 November 2008).
33. Marvin Miller and Lawrence Scheinman, "Israel, India, and Pakistan: Engaging the Non-NPT States in the Nonproliferation Regime," *Arms Control Today*, December 2003.
34. Shi-chin Lin, "The AQ Khan Revelations and Subsequent Changes to Pakistani Export Controls," NTI Issue Brief, October 2004, available at ⟨http://www.nti.org/e_research/e3_54a.html⟩ (accessed 13 November 2008); Ziad Haider and Souvik Saha, "Analysis of India and Pakistan's Export Control Laws," Henry L. Stimson Center, Washington, DC, 2007, available at ⟨http://www.stimson.org/print.cfm?SN=SA20050713866⟩ (accessed 13 November 2008).
35. William J. Broad, David E. Sanger, and Raymond Bonner, "How Pakistani Built His Network," *New York Times*, 12 February 2004.
36. Christopher Clary, "Dr. Khan's Nuclear Walmart," *Disarmament Diplomacy* 76 (March/April 2004): 31–36. See also David Albright and Corey Hinderstein, "Unraveling the A. Q. Khan and Future Proliferation Networks," *Washington Quarterly* 28, no. 2 (2005): 111–128; William Langewiesche, "The Wrath of Khan," *The Atlantic Online*, November 2005, available at ⟨http://www.theatlantic.com/doc/200511/aq-khan⟩ (accessed 13 November 2008); and Kenny Butler, Sammy Salama, and Leonard S. Spector, "Where Is the Justice?" *Bulletin of the Atomic Scientists* 62, no. 6 (2006): 25–62.
37. See United Nations Department for Disarmament Affairs, "Conference on Disarmament Concludes 1999 Session," *DDA 1999 Update*, September 1999, 2, available at ⟨http://disarmament.un.org/update/sep1999.pdf⟩ (accessed 13 November 2008).

38. On the state of the Conference on Disarmament, see Michael Hamel-Green, "New Impetus, Old Excuses – Report on the Conference on Disarmament in 2007," *Disarmament Diplomacy* 86 (Autumn 2007): 3–13; and John Borrie, "Cooperation and Defection in the Conference on Disarmament," *Disarmament Diplomacy* 82 (Spring 2006): 34–40. For Indian and Israeli views, see Gopalaswami Parthasarathy, "Nuclear Disarmament, Nuclear Proliferation and WMD Proliferation: An Indian Perspective," and Shlomo Brom, "Israel's Updated Perspective on WMD Proliferation, Arms Control, Disarmament and Related Threats from Non-State Actors," in Sidhu and Thakur, eds, *Arms Control After Iraq*.
39. "Statement by the President of the Security Council" at the conclusion of its 3046th Meeting, Security Council document S/23500, 31 January 1992; available at ⟨http://www.securitycouncilreport.org/atf/cf/%7B65BFCF9B-6D27-4E9C-8CD3-CF6E4FF96FF9%7D/UNRO%20S23500.pdf⟩ (accessed 13 November 2008).
40. The Convention was adopted on 13 April 2005 and is available at ⟨http://untreaty.un.org/English/Terrorism/English_18_15.pdf⟩ (accessed 13 November 2008).
41. Security Council resolution 1540, 28 April 2004.
42. Graham Allison, "Nuclear 9/11: The Ongoing Failure of Imagination," *Bulletin of the Atomic Scientists* 62, no. 5 (2006): 34–41.
43. Robin M. Frost, *Nuclear Terrorism after 9/11*, Adelphi Paper No. 378 (London: IISS, 2005).
44. See Rashed Uz Zaman, "WMD Terrorism in South Asia: Trends and Implications," *Journal of International Affairs* 7, no. 3 (2002): 134–139; and William C. Potter, "Nuclear Threats from Non-State Actors," in Sidhu and Thakur, eds, *Arms Control After Iraq*.
45. For contrasting views on resolution 1540, see Daniel Joyner, "UN Security Council 1540: A Legal Travesty?" CITS Briefs, Center for International Trade and Security, University of Georgia, August 2006; and Seema Gahlaut, "UN Security Council 1540: A Principled Necessity," CITS Briefs, Center for International Trade and Security, University of Georgia, August 2006.
46. For details of PSI, see Sharon A. Squassoni, Steven R. Bowman, and Carl E. Behrens, *Proliferation Control Regimes: Background and Status*, CRS Report for Congress, 10 February 2005, 15; and for details of the interception of the *BBC China*, see Albright and Hinderstein, "Unraveling the A. Q. Khan and Future Proliferation Networks."
47. See "Speech by Jacques Chirac, President of the French Republic, during his Visit to The Strategic Air and Maritime Forces at Landivisiau/L'Ile Longue," Brest (Finistère), 19 January 2006, available at ⟨http://www.elysee.fr/elysee/elysee.fr/anglais/speeches_and_documents/2006/speech_by_jacques_chirac_president_of_the_french_republic_during_his_visit_to_the_stategic_forces.38447.html⟩ (accessed 13 November 2008); and Ann MacLachlan and Mark Hibbs, "Chirac Shifts French Doctrine for Use of Nuclear Weapons," *Nucleonics Week*, 26 January 2006.
48. Secretary-General Kofi Annan's address to the Nuclear Non-Proliferation Treaty Review Conference, New York, 2 May 2005, UN Press Release SG/SM/9847DC/2956.
49. Rebecca Johnson, "Is the NPT Being Overtaken by Events?" *Disarmament Diplomacy* 87, no. 4 (2008).
50. George P. Schultz, William J. Perry, Henry A. Kissinger, and Sam Nunn, "A World Free of Nuclear Weapons," *Wall Street Journal*, 4 January 2007; and George P. Schultz et al., "Towards a Nuclear Free World," *Wall Street Journal*, 15 January 2008.

11

The international nuclear trade: Harnessing peaceful use while preventing proliferation

Nicole C. Evans

The analytical framework for this book is based on two interrelated questions: is the United Nations a viable or desirable actor in the nuclear realm; and, if it is, to what end? This chapter will argue that the United Nations, through the International Atomic Energy Agency (IAEA), is a viable actor in international nuclear trade. Indeed, the IAEA should have an enhanced role and should be given the resources to fulfill it properly.

This chapter will begin by discussing critical background issues, including the inherent tensions of the international nuclear trade, how nuclear material can be acquired for malicious uses, and the potential impact of the detonation of a nuclear device. It will then explain the framework for international nuclear trade by highlighting international legal and normative instruments, as well as relevant groupings that facilitate legal international nuclear trade. The chapter will next examine the role of the United Nations in international nuclear trade, including safeguards and other mechanisms. With the role of the United Nations in mind, the chapter will present the key challenges and threats posed by the international nuclear trade, such as the use of illicit networks (such as the A. Q. Khan network), the "free-rider" problem, and the potential impact of a nuclear power renaissance. Lastly, this chapter will turn to solutions. It will analyze the way in which the United Nations, states, and industry can work together to transform challenges and threats into opportunities.

The United Nations and nuclear orders, Boulden, Thakur and Weiss (eds), United Nations University Press, 2009, ISBN 978-92-808-1167-4

Background

Governments have two overarching objectives for international nuclear trade. The first objective is to harness nuclear technology for the benefit of humankind. Indeed, the promotion of the peaceful use of nuclear energy requires a thriving international nuclear trade. The second is to prevent the proliferation of nuclear weapons. These two objectives are in constant tension, because international trade for the peaceful use of nuclear technology necessarily opens the door to international trade for the development of nuclear weapons.

The main issue surrounding the international nuclear trade is concern about the development or acquisition of nuclear materials and technology for malicious use, either by non-nuclear-weapon states (NNWS) or by non-state actors such as terrorist organizations. The difficulty is that the same processes that are required to produce nuclear material for peaceful purposes can also be used to produce nuclear material for non-peaceful purposes.

Weapons-usable nuclear material can be acquired in one of two ways: producing it indigenously or obtaining it from an existing source.

Indigenous production of weapons-usable nuclear material

Weapons-usable nuclear material can be produced by uranium enrichment or by separating plutonium from spent fuel. In order to be weapons usable, uranium generally needs to be at least 90 percent enriched in the isotope U-235 (highly enriched uranium, or HEU). The technological sophistication and sheer size of such a production enterprise currently mean that this path can be pursued only by states. The required scientific, technical, and industrial resources are such that it would be extraordinarily difficult for a non-state actor to indigenously produce weapons-usable nuclear material. In addition, the indigenous production of weapons-usable nuclear material would rely heavily upon the import of various technologies. This is where international nuclear trade can both smooth the pathway and throw up obstacles for the development of indigenous production capabilities.

Given the extensive, long-term investment required to develop indigenous nuclear capabilities, why would states make such an investment? First, many states rely upon nuclear and other radiological materials for legitimate industries, including the generation of nuclear power, running research reactors, producing isotopes for medical use, and industrial uses such as mining. States may have legitimate concerns about the reliability of supply and worry that it may be interrupted for political or economic reasons. As such, states may believe that, in order to prevent such a potential danger, they must be able to produce their own nuclear and other radiological materials.

Second, on the other side of the spectrum lie more insidious motivations such as providing cover for the development of nuclear weapons.

Third, although states may not have a contemporary desire to produce nuclear weapons, they may wish to hedge their bets by developing the capability to do so in conjunction with developing capabilities for peaceful nuclear use. Such states may be motivated by the potential threat of an ally or foe developing nuclear weapons, or of a shift in a regional balance of power necessitating the development of nuclear weapons to be wielded as the ultimate geopolitical trump card.

Lastly, there are important political and prestige issues to be considered. In general, possession of a nuclear arsenal has remained the remit of the few and the influential. At the very least, possession of nuclear weapons is a sure-fire way to guarantee that the entire international community will sit up and take notice. In many ways, nuclear weapons capability can help ensure protection against a conventional attack, and can force states that are stronger economically, politically, and militarily to the negotiating table. A good example of such a case is North Korea. Despite fierce disagreements within academic, government, and military circles about the military utility of nuclear weapons, there is little doubt about their political utility. The bottom line is that many states want to be in the nuclear game and are working to develop indigenous nuclear capabilities.

Obtaining weapons-usable nuclear material from an existing source

The second way to acquire fissile material is to get it from an existing source, without developing an indigenous production capability. Nuclear material required for peaceful purposes can be purchased on the open market through legitimate trade.

However, if the objective is to acquire nuclear material for non-peaceful purposes, it can also be stolen or purchased on the black market. This is the route most likely to be pursued by non-state actors such as terrorist organizations. It can be surmised that, without the resources or territoriality of a state, such organizations are more interested in perpetrating one or a few high-impact nuclear incidents than in acquiring long-term nuclear capability.

The potential for non-state actors to acquire the capability to detonate a nuclear device is not as far-fetched as it might seem.[1] Terrorists have been formally charged with seeking nuclear weapons and the materials to make them, and a *fatwa* has been issued authorizing the use of nuclear weapons against civilians.[2] Open sources also reveal that several terrorist groups have the capabilities, if not the materials, necessary to construct at least a crude nuclear device.³ A relatively simple nuclear bomb can be built using open-source blueprints and only 15–20 kg of HEU, or 4–8 kg of weapons-grade plutonium for a slightly more sophisticated weapon.

The potential impact of the detonation of a nuclear device, in terms of casualties and injuries, highlights how high the stakes are with international nuclear trade. The potential short- and long-term environmental impact is also often mentioned. What is not as obvious is the potential economic impact. Taking into account the impact on trade, including the obliteration of agriculture in the radiation zone,[4] the detonation of a nuclear device could send the world economy spinning in a downwards spiral toward not only a global recession but a global depression. In recognition of this, in 2005 Secretary-General Kofi Annan stated that a nuclear terrorist attack would "thrust tens of millions of people into dire poverty."[5]

The international nuclear trade framework

The international nuclear trade framework was purposefully designed to facilitate the peaceful use of nuclear energy, while ensuring the non-proliferation of nuclear weapons as enshrined in the Nuclear Non-Proliferation Treaty (NPT). The "grand bargain" of the NPT is that NNWS will not seek to acquire nuclear weapons, in exchange for the promotion of the peaceful use of nuclear energy through technology transfer combined with good faith efforts by nuclear weapons states (NWS) towards nuclear disarmament.

Many NNWS argue that the grand bargain is unraveling at the seams and that, as a result, some NNWS are looking to break away from the norm of non-proliferation. Iran's apparent attempt to develop nuclear capabilities is often cited as an example, as is the continuing stalemate in arms control and disarmament, especially since the dissolution of the Treaty on the Limitation of Anti-Ballistic Missile Systems (ABM Treaty) in 2002 and the looming collapse of the Intermediate-Range Nuclear Forces Treaty. However, many voices have been arguing that the grand bargain has been eroding for some time.

In order to ensure that NNWS are not pursuing nuclear weapons capabilities, the NPT obligates NNWS states parties to submit to a nuclear verification system ("Comprehensive Safeguards") operated by the IAEA. Recently, the Additional Protocol was developed to ensure more robust safeguards by enabling the United Nations not only to verify the non-diversion of declared nuclear material but also to provide assurance as to the absence of undeclared nuclear material and activities in the state. The IAEA is charged with being the United Nations' nuclear inspector and verifying that all nuclear material is being used in peaceful pursuits.

Another component of the international nuclear trade framework is the Nuclear Suppliers Group (NSG). The impetus for the creation of the NSG was the 1974 explosion by India of a nuclear device, which concretely demonstrated that nuclear technology transferred to a state for peaceful use could nevertheless be employed for non-peaceful purposes. Unchecked and unmitigated, this could have threatened to undermine the legal international nuclear trade. The NSG "is a group of nuclear supplier countries which seeks to contribute to the non-proliferation of nuclear weapons through the implementation of Guidelines for nuclear exports and nuclear related exports."[6] NSG member countries evaluate export applications, in accordance with their own national export licensing requirements. It should also be noted that the Non-aligned Movement disputes the legitimacy of the NSG.

In order to help ensure consistency in this approach, close linkages between the IAEA and the NSG, as well as the NPT and the NSG, were developed. The 1995 NPT Review and Extension Conference endorsed the full-scope safeguards policy adopted by the NSG in 1992. This further solidified the already widely accepted view that nuclear supply policies for international nuclear trade are a critical component of a comprehensive strategy to prevent nuclear proliferation. The NSG has also made the link between international nuclear trade and the threat of nuclear terrorism and has strengthened the NSG Guidelines to prevent and counter the threat of nuclear exports to potential nuclear terrorists. The Zangger Committee, also known as the NPT Exporters Committee, is another important mechanism in the international nuclear trade framework. The committee is composed of certain NPT members that are nuclear suppliers, and maintains a trigger list of nuclear-related strategic goods that would "trigger" the application of safeguards.

A difficulty faced by the international nuclear trade framework is that some of the states that have nuclear capabilities and are involved in the international nuclear trade are not signatories of the NPT and are not members of the NSG. Two such examples are India and Pakistan. Finding a way to engage meaningfully with non-NPT states on the issue of the international nuclear trade in order to prevent the further proliferation of nuclear technology, without undermining the NPT or being seen as rewarding states that operate outside of international nuclear non-proliferation regimes and norms, remains a singular challenge.

A key stakeholder subject to the international nuclear trade framework is the nuclear industry and the companies that deal in nuclear-related technology. They are regulated through national means, such as domestic laws that are in compliance with export controls and sanctions. However, this is often not enough, because not all eventualities can be anticipated and spelt out in detailed national export control laws. In order to be truly comprehensive, individual companies must develop and implement their own internal mechanisms. To a large degree, such internal mechanisms are dependent upon an honor system drawing upon the good faith of companies.

The need for this relatively novel notion of companies going above and beyond domestic laws became especially apparent after the discovery of Saddam Hussein's pursuit of nuclear capability. As a result, one German company put in place an internal regulatory framework. The Leybold Charter is now the bar against which other German companies are measured. A key part of halting the proliferation of nuclear technology is ensuring buy-in from industry, not just in letter but also in spirit. It needs to be in companies' interests to comply with non-proliferation norms, and incentives for compliance must be financially based.

The role of the United Nations in the international nuclear trade

Since its inception, the United Nations was expected to play a major role in the nuclear arena. In this spirit, the IAEA was established in 1957 and now plays several important roles. Its best-known function is as a verification tool to ensure the implementation of Safeguards Agreements, especially those authorized under the NPT. These Safeguards Agreements require that states disclose civilian nuclear activities and allow the IAEA to monitor nuclear facilities to ensure that they are not used to produce nuclear weapons. Verification measures include on-site inspections, visits, and ongoing monitoring and evaluation – all activities that heavily consume both time and resources. The system of safeguards serves several purposes: confidence-building, an early warning mechanism, and the trigger that sets in motion other responses by the United Nations, such as sanctions, if and when the need arises. Safeguards have been complemented by the development and implementation of the Additional Protocol, which gives the IAEA expanded rights of access to information and sites.

A recent innovation is the establishment of the nuclear trade analysis unit (NUTRAN) within the IAEA.[7] This enterprising unit undertakes procurement outreach to nuclear-related industries by seeking to use "trash" information from industry to supplement information received via more traditional means. For example, in 2003 the number of rejected orders and inquiries that Oerlikon Leybold did not touch reached a volume of €25 million.[8] In other words, the orders that actually go forward for export licensing are the small tip of a very large iceberg. Sharing trash information is a win–win situation for industry, states, and the IAEA: "The first winner is the authority that gains precious information for its state analysis. The second winner is the enterprise that gains trust for a mouse click. It doesn't take more to forward an inquiry to an authority."[9]

The establishment of NUTRAN is representative of the reality that safeguards are no longer specific to a state or to a facility. They are global in nature, as is the threat they seek to address – the proliferation of nuclear material. It is important to recognize that this initiative is not a panacea. States that have volunteered to cooperate with Trade and Technology Analysis (TTA) are unlikely to be the states that have been problematic in the past. Similarly, companies that volunteer to participate are unlikely to be the troublesome and shady companies. Another issue is that the United States is not actively involved, which is problematic given the breadth and depth of the US nuclear industry and its involvement in international nuclear trade. It is likely that US reluctance stems from concerns about sharing information when the road goes only one way. This speaks to a larger issue that the IAEA faces: when the IAEA has relevant safeguards information, it is not able to forward it to states, even if it would lead to a significant enhancement in a state's ability to prevent illegal nuclear trade.

The IAEA's Office of Nuclear Security is also a key player. Under the leadership of Anita Nilsson, the Office is implementing the *Nuclear Security Plan for 2006–2009*.[10] The importance and stature of the Office rose after the tragic events of 9/11. The IAEA responded swiftly to the terrorist attacks by developing the first *Plan of Activities to Protect Against Nuclear Terrorism* and establishing the Nuclear Security Fund. The implementation of the *Plan of Activities* is predominantly funded through extra-voluntary contributions to the Nuclear Security Fund, and the Office has a very small staff given the magnitude of its tasks. Many countries, including Canada, are calling for these activities to be more securely funded from the regular IAEA budget and not left to the discretionary spending habits of member states.

The Office undertakes missions to recommend and implement physical protection measures. Moreover, it advises member states on the development of regulations and in some cases works to help establish regulatory bodies. It also maintains the IAEA Illicit Trafficking Database, which collects information on incidents of illicit trafficking and other unauthorized activities involving nuclear and radioactive material. The database, although useful, is dependent upon the voluntary reporting of incidents by participating states. It is widely assumed that states underreport incidents and/or do not have accurate knowledge of all incidents.

In July 2005, 88 of the states parties and Euratom agreed by consensus to amend the 1979 Convention on the Physical Protection of Nuclear Material (CPPNM). The "amended CPPNM will make it legally binding for States Parties to protect nuclear material and facilities in peaceful domestic use and storage, as well as in domestic and international transport."[11] It also includes provisions that will allow for and facilitate more extensive cooperation between states for the interdiction and recovery of stolen or smuggled nuclear material. The amended CPPNM is the first instance of a legally binding obligation for states to ensure the security of their nuclear and radioactive material. Another important development was the introduction by Russia of the International Convention for the Suppression of Acts of Nuclear Terrorism (Nuclear Terrorism Convention), which opened for signature in September 2005. The Convention requires states parties to adopt measures as necessary to criminalize the unlawful and intentional possession and use of radioactive material or a radioactive device, and the use or damage of nuclear facilities.[12] Put together, these mechanisms and tools of the United Nations offer an increasingly robust response to the threat of nuclear terrorism and disruption of legal international nuclear trade.

Challenges and threats

There are several challenges threatening the twin objectives of the international nuclear trade: the use of illicit networks for the illegal international trade of nuclear technology; and the possibility of unauthorized access to and malicious use of weapons-grade nuclear material and highly radioactive material.

Underlying these threats is the challenge posed by the "free-rider" problem. Security is an international collective good from which all countries benefit. The potential challenge is that, with some states carrying the burden and investing heavily in activities to ensure the prevention of nuclear proliferation, other states may make the calculation that they need not contribute meaningfully to ensure collective good. This is because, even if a state does not participate in activities to promote nuclear security, it nevertheless reaps the rewards of the efforts of others who do. This in turn could dissuade those states carrying the burden from continuing to shoulder more than their fair share of the load.

Although the free-rider challenge is ubiquitous to all arenas of international security, it can be especially acute in the realm of nuclear security. Because nuclear security is a threat that often appears distant to taxpaying publics and the politicians that serve them, the pressure to redirect precious resources to domestic issues such as education and health care can make it even more difficult for governments to argue effectively that resources should be invested in activities to strengthen nuclear security when other countries are not making the same sacrifice. This issue can also be seen in the area of nuclear exports, when companies may argue for relaxing domestic export controls when they see their competitors in other countries benefiting from less robust export controls. In order to ensure nuclear security internally and the continuing viability of the legal international nuclear trade, it is critical that all states are contributors to security, and not just consumers of security benefits.

The unveiling of the Khan network opened the world's eyes to the reality that there was a robust illicit demand for and supply of nuclear technology and that the system of state-operated export controls could be easily thwarted by both states and non-state actors. In October 2003, a German-registered ship was intercepted in an Italian port en route from Dubai to Libya. An inspection of the cargo revealed that the ship was carrying parts of a centrifuge enrichment plant. Two months later, Libya subsequently admitted that it had been involved in undeclared nuclear activities that were aimed at acquiring nuclear weapons capability. Libya also confessed that it had been engaged in clandestine nuclear cooperation with other countries. A. Q. Khan, the father of Pakistan's nuclear arsenal, was implicated, and shortly thereafter he was stripped of his cabinet rank and dismissed. Dr Khan issued a public apology, during which he accepted responsibility for past proliferation activities and absolved the Pakistani government of any complicity in his acts.

When the dust settled, it was apparent that this illicit international nuclear weapons proliferation network had operated in more than 40 countries and comprised multiple entities and individuals from various countries including Germany and South Africa. Known customers of the Khan network included not only Libya but also Iran and North Korea. Mark Hibbs, one of the world's leading experts on this subject, argues that the information needed to construct nuclear weapons is out there and can be bought by anyone with sufficient funds.[13] Others have argued that "today's black market suppliers are far less integrated than Khan's 'one-stop shopping'. His enterprise was unique in its ability to provide nearly the entire array of materials and services to produce highly enriched uranium."[14] The good news, however, is that South Africa was able successfully to prosecute a German citizen for contravening South African export control laws and for cooperating with the nuclear weapons programs of Libya and Pakistan. This demonstrates that positive steps are being taken to aggressively prosecute those involved in illicit nuclear trade.

The Khan network is an instance of quasi-non-state actors and non-state actors supplying state actors with the nuclear technology and knowledge necessary to develop nuclear weapons capabilities. There are considerable concerns that these illicit networks are constantly morphing from one entity into another by changing shell companies and by altering headquarters and moving their operations.[15] This can make it very difficult, if not impossible, to track the behavior of questionable companies over time and geography, and to gain a clear picture of the individuals involved with such behavior. There are also the intrinsic difficulties stemming from the fact that many nuclear technology items have a legitimate peaceful use. This leads to the challenge of discerning whether the intended end use is peaceful or military.

Another challenge for the IAEA, as for the United Nations more generally, is that of state sovereignty. Within this context, adherence to the notion of state sovereignty precludes the United Nations or other countries from "intervening" in the domestic affairs of a state without an explicit invitation to intervene being extended by the state in question. The IAEA can verify or provide assistance regarding nuclear security only at a state's request, which can often impede progress towards strengthening nuclear security to prevent illegal international nuclear trade. For example, the IAEA may be aware that a particular member state is lacking appropriate physical protection measures for weapons-grade nuclear material at one of its nuclear facilities. However, the IAEA cannot provide support to help remedy the situation – through the provision of technical advice as part of an International Physical Protection Advisory Service (IPPAS) mission, for example – unless the member state in question specifically requests an IAEA IPPAS mission. Similarly, states can use the guise of sovereignty to mask illicit nuclear activities.

Complicating matters further is the perception of many that the "grand bargain" of the NPT is in danger of collapse, caused in part by the perception of double standards. This accusation is most often lobbed regarding the nuclear situation in the Middle East. When asked about the morality of supplying Libya with nuclear technology, a South African scientist replied: "What justifies America having more than 10,000 nuclear devices and not others?"[16] A less discriminatory international security framework would help address this perception of double standards and would reduce the incentives for the acquisition of nuclear weapons. In addition, genuine movement towards a meaningful reduction in nuclear weapons under Article VI of the NPT by the NWS would take the wind out of the sails of states seeking nuclear weapons in order to protect themselves from perceived threats. This would go a long way towards solving the security dilemma that is currently plaguing the international nuclear non-proliferation regime.

It is important to recognize that although observers have been making doomsday predictions about the demise of the NPT for three decades the

NPT continues to survive. Indeed, important mechanisms supportive of the NPT such as Safeguards Agreements, the Additional Protocol, and the Zangger Committee are functioning well, despite a few high-profile cases. The NPT also remains a staunch purveyor of the international norm against nuclear non-proliferation.

A further potential challenge is the undermining of the international nuclear non-proliferation regime by working outside of the NPT. The foremost example of this is the nuclear cooperation agreement between the United States and India. The United States argues that other aspirant nuclear powers will learn the lesson that good behavior pays; others argue, however, that rewarding India could encourage other countries to strive even harder to acquire a nuclear bomb, thereby burning a huge hole in the global non-proliferation regime.[17] The fundamental question, however, is how the NPT can be adapted to deal with and recognize the existence of new nuclear powers outside of the NPT. This boils down to an oft-viewed dilemma in international relations: is it better to engage states and bring them inside the tent, or to estrange them and keep them outside of it?

Another challenge is the possibility of a nuclear power "renaissance" on the horizon. The US Department of Energy's Information Administration predicts that energy demand will increase by nearly 60 percent by 2030.[18] Nuclear power is seen by many as the answer to the problems of global warming and the looming energy crisis. Indeed, the United States has launched the Global Nuclear Energy Partnership in order to seek ways to have nuclear power actualized as an important component of a comprehensive response.

The challenge of a nuclear renaissance comes from three main areas: increased threat of theft and unauthorized access, increased threat to safety, and increased threat of diversion of nuclear materials and technology for a military program. Many experts believe that the proliferation of nuclear power will lead to the proliferation of nuclear weapons. William Cohen, US Secretary of Defense 1997–2001, recently stated: "Nuclear power is French for nuclear weapons."[19]

However, it should be noted that there is considerable debate as to whether a nuclear power renaissance is really in the making. There remain significant problems related to costs; there is not widespread confidence that nuclear power can be competitively priced or result in successful cost recovery.[20] It is also important to note that securing the future of nuclear energy is intrinsically tied to securing nuclear materials: "A major terrorist theft or diversion anywhere will reduce public confidence in nuclear power and fuel cycle activities everywhere."[21] One need only mention the Three Mile Island or Chernobyl accidents to encounter a strong, visceral, negative response to the notion of nuclear energy. If a weapons-based nuclear incident occurred, the impact would be felt even more acutely.

Solutions

The solutions to these threats lie with the United Nations, states, and industry. One possibility builds upon and coordinates the existing tools of the IAEA Trade and Technology Analysis and the NSG: "When NSG members deny nuclear-related license applications on non-proliferation grounds, they routinely notify other NSG members, who are obliged, under the NSG no-undercut rule, not to export the item to the same buyer themselves. Sharing these denial notifications with the IAEA as well would impose no additional burden."[22]

Part of this solution could include building on and allocating additional political, human, and financial resources to the TTA, as well as encouraging US participation. The Khan network demonstrated that there is an ongoing dynamic of sword and shield at play. Within this context, a powerful shield against the threat from non-state actors can be sharing and then analyzing information about all inquiries received. As the TTA becomes more fully integrated with the IAEA and other international efforts, the chances of identifying and thwarting attempts to perpetuate illicit nuclear trade activities increase. The IAEA Illicit Trafficking Database is also an important tool, but as always there is room for improvement. Most significantly, there is a clear need to be able to distinguish more readily between trivial events and significant events, which would allow analytical work to focus on the most dangerous and worrying events. The IAEA Office of Nuclear Security should also be allocated a larger permanent staff, and should receive stable funding from the regular budget to implement nuclear security activities.[23]

The NPT should continue to be seen as an integral part of the solution. The suggestion has also been made that the Additional Protocol be made mandatory for NPT states parties. However, this solution inevitably carries a heavier burden for the IAEA, which is already overburdened and struggles to fulfill its current mandate under Safeguards Agreements. The Additional Protocol can also be seen as a burden by states that already struggle to implement existing Safeguards Agreements. States should commit additional resources to the IAEA Department of Safeguards to help ensure effective implementation. The suggestion has also been made that states in non-compliance with safeguards commitments that subsequently withdraw from the NPT should have equipment and materials they received while under safeguards removed under IAEA supervision. In a similar vein, the NSG should make the Additional Protocol a condition of supply while remembering that the importance of engaging industry in voluntary controls and self-policing cannot be overstated. It also needs to be asked whether tighter export control or reporting actually prevents proliferation. The requirement for end-user certificates is not an insurmountable obstacle when the possibility of high-quality forgeries and very attractive large bribes is taken into consideration.

The Global Partnership Against the Spread of Weapons and Materials of Mass Destruction (led by the Group of Eight, G-8) is foremost amongst international activities to prevent the illegal international nuclear trade. Initiated in 2002 at the G-8 Kananaskis Summit under Canada's chairmanship, the Global Partnership works to secure weapons and materials of mass destruction, initially in Russia and other countries of the former Soviet Union. The Proliferation Security Initiative, on the other hand, works to interdict illicit movement of WMD materials and technology. The Global Initiative to Combat Nuclear Terrorism pulls all these elements together, providing a cradle-to-grave approach. The common feature of all these activities is that they offer principles of action, but it is up to partner countries to implement them as they see fit. As a result, gaps can appear in the program of activities, leaving some threats unaddressed.

The international community should not only continue to invest in cooperative threat reduction programs to address the threat of nuclear proliferation, but escalate them in both breadth and depth. By their nature, cooperative threat reduction programs such as the Global Partnership suffer from the difficulties inherent in trying to prove a negative. In the absence of a nuclear incident, it can often be difficult for policy-makers to justify continued funding. However, the cost associated with this preventive work is a mere fraction of what it would cost if a nuclear incident were to occur.

Although much good work has been done to strengthen the physical security of nuclear materials, even more work remains to be done. High-level US officials have confirmed that the production or acquisition of nuclear weapons material is the main "choke point" to prevent al-Qaeda from acquiring a nuclear weapon.[24] From the break-in at a South African nuclear facility housing weapons-grade HEU, to the seizure of HEU in Georgia, the international community continues to be confronted with the unfortunate reality that nuclear materials could be stolen and used for non-peaceful purposes. In order to ensure that these threats continue to be addressed, the Global Partnership should be extended beyond its current end date of 2012.

The threat of nuclear proliferation can also be addressed by using an open fuel cycle model. In the open fuel model, enriched fuel (uranium) passes through the nuclear reactor once and is then spent and sent for disposal. The closed cycle, in contrast, separates plutonium from spent fuel and recycles it to a nuclear reactor as fuel. The risk here is not so much from the reactors but from the reprocessing technologies. This risk could be partially mitigated by measures described above: providing increased funding for IAEA safeguards, and linking more robust safeguards to the supply of nuclear technologies.

A proposed solution for many of these problems is to develop an international fuel assurances mechanism. Several suggestions have been put forward by a variety of different countries, which at last count totaled 13 proposals, ranging from providing a back-up fuel supply to setting up an IAEA-controlled fuel reserve. If an appropriate fuel assurance framework was implemented, it could potentially mitigate the perceived vulnerability of supply that might create incentives for states to build their own enrichment or reprocessing capabilities.

A senior IAEA official stated: "The vision of the IAEA's director general is that all enrichment and reprocessing over time should be exclusively under multinational control."[25] However, it is unlikely that all member states will readily and happily agree to dilute their rights under the NPT to the full fuel cycle. As such, fuel assurance mechanisms need to allow for states to make sovereign choices within the framework of a multi-layered mechanism based on the market, which includes back-up assurance and an actual fuel reserve. A common thread through all the fuel assurance mechanism proposals is that the predominant role of any mechanism will be to continue to supply nuclear fuel during "political disruption," but not if the disruption in the fuel supply is caused by a state's failure to live up to non-proliferation obligations. However, this is a difficult concept to define, and many states have different views on the definition of political disruption.

Another solution to the challenges described above resides in international activities that help prevent the illegal international nuclear trade by eliminating the utility of nuclear material for weapons. This can be done either by "disposing of" or "down-blending" weapons-usable nuclear material by rendering it unsuitable for military use altogether, or by securing weapons-usable nuclear material until such time as it can be disposed of. Highly enriched uranium can be rendered unusable for nuclear weapons by relatively simply and inexpensively blending it with natural or depleted uranium. The product can then be used as fuel for nuclear power plants.

There are also methods for manufacturing nuclear fuel for the production of electricity that buttress non-proliferation efforts through the down-blending process described above. The US–Russian Megatons to Megawatts Program converts HEU from decommissioned Russian nuclear warheads to low-enriched uranium (LEU) to provide fuel for US civilian nuclear power plants. By down-blending HEU to LEU, the material is effectively put out of reach of military purposes, which reduces the amount of fuel that needs to be secured against theft. Unauthorized access is also reduced. To put this in perspective, 10 percent of US electricity is currently being generated by fuel from Russian ex-warheads. As of 30 September 2008, 345 metric tons of Russian ex-warhead HEU (the equivalent of 13,795 nuclear warheads) have been recycled into 10,010 metric tons of LEU.[26] In contrast, rendering weapons-grade plutonium unusable for nuclear weapons is a more complicated and expensive process.

Reducing the number of warheads could result in a significant amount of uranium and plutonium being freed to fuel an increasing number of reactors. It would simultaneously help the NWS live up to their Article VI commitments under the NPT to work towards eventual disarmament. One way to move towards such a goal would be extending the Megatons to Megawatts Program after the first 500 metric tons have been converted and used, rather than allowing the program quietly to sunset. This should go hand in hand with genuine movement towards significant, irreversible reductions in nuclear weapons by Russia and the United States, as well as other NWS, through meaningful and verifiable arms reduction treaties. In order to make meaningful, sustainable progress against the threat of the use of nuclear weapons, by either state or non-state actors, there need to be significant reductions in the nuclear arsenals of NWS. It is only through such a move that the political utility of nuclear weapons can be downgraded and existing stocks of nuclear weapons and materials properly secured.

Conclusion

Former US Secretary of Defense William Perry and former Assistant Secretary of Defense Graham Allison are among those who have estimated the chance of a terrorist nuclear attack at more than 50 percent over the next 10 years.[27] Meaningful progress has been made to reduce the threat of nuclear terrorism, but the threat has not evaporated and much work remains to be done.

It is extremely difficult to alter intent, whether of a state to acquire or develop a nuclear arsenal or of a terrorist group to acquire a nuclear or radiological device. It is also extremely difficult to contain knowledge and dual-use technologies. What is more realistic and feasible, however, is the goal of restricting access to the essential, necessary component of a nuclear device – the weapons-usable nuclear material itself.

The nuclear threat is global in nature, and the defense against nuclear terrorism is only as strong as its weakest link. The exposure of the Khan network should be recognized as a wake-up call compelling all states to take action to prevent illegal international nuclear trade. The tools and mechanisms that have been developed need to be collectively wielded in order to ensure that international nuclear trade is used to advance humanity and to capitalize upon its progress. Put together and used wisely, tools and mechanisms such as the NPT, the NSG, the IAEA Nuclear Security Plan, Security Council resolution 1540, and the Global Partnership can be stronger as a whole than as the sum of its parts.

As we work collectively to bolster legal international nuclear trade and to suffocate illegal international trade, it is worth revisiting the 1946 Baruch Plan: "Behind the black portent of the new atomic age lies a hope which, seized upon with faith, can work our salvation. If we fail, then we have damned every man to be the slave of Fear. Let us not deceive ourselves: We must elect World Peace or World Destruction."[28]

Acknowledgements

The views expressed in this chapter are mine alone and do not represent the opinions or policies of the Department of Foreign Affairs and International Trade Canada.

Notes

1. There are a few authors who believe that the risk of nuclear terrorism is overstated. For example, see Robin M. Frost, *Nuclear Terrorism After 9/11*, Adelphi Paper 378 (Oxford: Routledge for IISS, 2005).
2. "Text: US Grand Jury Indictment against Usama Bin Laden," United States District Court, Southern District of New York, 1998, available online at ⟨http://www.fas.org/irp/news/1998/11/98110602_nlt.html⟩ (accessed 13 November 2008); "Testimony of Attorney General John Ashcroft," US House of Representatives, Committee on the Judiciary, Department of Justice, 5 June 2003, available at ⟨http://www.usdoj.gov/ag/testimony/2003/060503aghouseremarks.htm⟩ (accessed 13 November 2008).
3. Matthew Bunn and Anthony Wier, "Terrorist Nuclear Weapon Construction: How Difficult?" *Annals of the American Academy of Political and Social Science* 607 (September 2006); Office of Technology Assessment Energy Program, *Nuclear Proliferation and Safeguards*, Report No. PB-275843 (Washington, DC: US Congress, Office of Technology Assessment, 1977), available at ⟨http://fas.org/ota/reports/7705.pdf⟩ (accessed 13 November 2008); National Commission on Terrorist Attacks upon the United States, *The 9/11 Commission Report: Final Report of the National Commission on Terrorist Attacks upon the United States* (New York: Norton, 2004); Commission on the Intelligence Capabilities of the United States Regarding Weapons of Mass Destruction, *Report to the President* (Washington, DC: WMD Commission, 2005), available at ⟨http://www.wmd.gov/report⟩ (accessed 13 November 2008).

4. The accident at Chernobyl in 1986 contaminated 150,000 km^2 in Belarus, Russia, and Ukraine, and the contaminated area stretched northward from Chernobyl for 500 km. IAEA, "Frequently Asked Chernobyl Questions," ⟨http://www.iaea.org/NewsCenter/Features/Chernobyl-15/cherno-faq.shtml⟩ (accessed 13 November 2008).
5. Kofi Annan, "A Global Strategy for Fighting Terrorism," Keynote Address to the Closing Plenary of the International Summit on Democracy, Terrorism and Security, Madrid, Spain, 10 March 2005; available at ⟨http://english.safe-democracy.org/keynotes/a-global-strategy-for-fighting-terrorism.html⟩ (accessed 13 November 2008).
6. "What Is the NSG?" at ⟨http://www.nuclearsuppliersgroup.org/testo_home.htm⟩ (accessed 13 November 2008).
7. In January 1997 the Department of Safeguards underwent international reorganization and NUTRAN was renamed Trade and Technology Analysis (TTA).
8. Ralf Wirtz is an executive in the export control department of Oerlikon Leybold Vacuum, a manufacturer of sensitive high-technology parts that are sometimes employed in the manufacture of gas centrifuge systems. Ralf Wirtz, Carnegie International Nonproliferation Conference, session on "Finding Innovative Ways to Detect and Thwart Illicit Nuclear Trade," 25 June 2007, Washington, DC (transcript by Federal News Service), 11; available at ⟨http://www.carnegieendowment.org/files/detect_thwart.pdf⟩ (accessed 13 November 2008).
9. Wirtz, "Finding Innovative Ways to Detect and Thwart Illicit Nuclear Trade," 11.
10. See ⟨http://www-ns.iaea.org/security/NSP_2009.htm⟩ (accessed 13 November 2008).
11. *Nuclear Security – Measures to Protect Against Nuclear Terrorism. Annual Report*, Report by the Director General to the 50th regular session of the IAEA General Conference, September 2006, GC/50/13, 6; available at ⟨http://www.iaea.org/About/Policy/GC/GC50/GC50Documents/English/gc50-13_en.pdf⟩ (accessed 13 November 2008).
12. Ibid., 6.
13. "Warning over Nuclear Black Market," *BBC News*, 27 June 2007; available at ⟨http://news.bbc.co.uk/2/hi/americas/6244708.stm⟩ (accessed 13 November 2008).
14. International Institute for Strategic Studies, *Nuclear Black Markets: Pakistan, A.Q. Khan and the Rise of Proliferation Networks. A Net Assessment*, IISS Strategic Dossier (London: IISS), 159.
15. David Albright, Carnegie International Nonproliferation Conference, session on "Finding Innovative Ways to Detect and Thwart Illicit Nuclear Trade," 4.
16. "Panorama: The Nuclear Walmart," BBC One, 12 November 2006; available at ⟨http://news.bbc.co.uk/go/pr/fr/-/2/hi/programmes/panorama/6135736.stm⟩ (accessed 13 November 2008).
17. Comment by US Congressman Markey at a meeting at the Federation of American Scientists, 18 October 2007; available at ⟨http://www.fas.org/press/_docs/Markey_TRANSCRIPT-1.pdf⟩ (accessed 13 November 2009).
18. Carnegie International Nonproliferation Conference, "Part I: A Conversation with Deputy Secretary of Energy Clay Sell on GNEP and Nonproliferation Policy. Hosted by Rose Gottemoeller," 26 June 2007, Washington, DC (transcript by Federal News Service), 2; available at ⟨http://www.carnegieendowment.org/files/sell.pdf⟩ (accessed 13 November 2008).
19. Secretary Cohen speaking at the Canadian Association of Defence and Security Industries Annual Conference, Ottawa, Canada, 9 April 2008.
20. Albright, "Finding Innovative Ways to Detect and Thwart Illicit Nuclear Trade," 4.
21. Corey Hinderstein, "Securing a Nuclear Future by Securing Nuclear Material: The Need for Collecting and Sharing Best Practices," PowerPoint presentation delivered to the 2007 Carnegie International Nonproliferation Conference, 26 June 2007; available at ⟨http://carnegieendowment.org/files/nuc_ren_hinderstein.pdf⟩ (accessed 4 December 2008).

22. Mark Fitzpatrick, "Nuclear Black Markets: Can We Win the Game of Catch-up with Determined Proliferators?" Testimony before a Joint Hearing of the House Committee on Foreign Affairs' Subcommittee on the Middle East and South Asia, and the Subcommittee on Terrorism, Nonproliferation and Trade, 27 June 2007; available at ⟨http://www.iiss.org/whats-new/iiss-in-the-press/press-coverage-2007/june-2007/mark-fitzpatricks-testimony/⟩ (accessed 13 November 2008).
23. Currently, the average annual budget of the Office of Nuclear Security for the implementation of the *Nuclear Security Plan* is approximately US$15.5 million, which is funded through the extra-voluntary Nuclear Security Fund. This is significantly less than the average annual budget allocated by Canada's Global Partnership Program for the implementation of international nuclear security activities, which is approximately US$175 million for 2007 through 2013 (annual average of US$35 million).
24. "Al-Qaeda Seeks Nuclear Weapons, U.S. Warns," Homeland Security Undersecretary Charles Allen speaking to the Senate Homeland Security and Governmental Affairs Committee, *Global Security Newswire*, 7 April 2008; available at ⟨http://www.nti.org/d_newswire/issues/2008_4_7.html⟩ (accessed 13 November 2008).
25. Tariq Rauf, Carnegie International Nonproliferation Conference, session on "Realizing Fuel Assurances: Third Time's the Charm?" 26 June 2007, Washington, DC (transcript by Federal News Service), 5; available at ⟨http://www.carnegieendowment.org/files/fuel.pdf⟩ (accessed 13 November 2008).
26. "Megatons to Megawatts: Recycling Nuclear Warheads into Electricity," ⟨http://www.usec.com/megatonstomegawatts.htm⟩ (accessed 13 November 2008).
27. Graham T. Allison, *Nuclear Terrorism: The Ultimate Preventable Catastrophe*, 1st edn (New York: Times Books/Henry Holt, 2004); Matthew Bunn, "The Risk of Nuclear Terrorism – And Next Steps to Reduce the Danger," Committee on Homeland Security and Governmental Affairs, United States Senate, Testimony, 2 April 2008, available at ⟨http://belfercenter.ksg.harvard.edu/publication/18187/risk_of_nuclear_terrorism_and_next_steps_to_reduce_the_danger.html⟩ (accessed 13 November 2008).
28. "The Baruch Plan," presented to the United Nations Atomic Energy Commission, 14 June 1946; available at ⟨http://www.atomicarchive.com/Docs/Deterrence/BaruchPlan.shtml⟩ (accessed 13 November 2008).

12

Nuclear proliferation and regional security orders: Comparing North Korea and Iran

Amitav Acharya

Three and a half months after the attacks of 11 September 2001, the Bush administration formally designated Iran and North Korea, along with Iraq, as an "axis of evil" – states governed by dictators who sponsor international terrorism and threaten global security with weapons of mass destruction. Seven years later, North Korea is part of a regional accord aimed at ending its nuclear weapons program, while Iran's nuclear program continues, despite signs of greater Iranian cooperation reported by the International Atomic Energy Agency (IAEA).

To be sure, the progress in North Korea is not irreversible[1] and Iran is by no means a lost cause.[2] But some important lessons are already emerging from the contrasting experiences of the two cases for managing regional non-proliferation.

Variations in the regional contexts of conflicts play a crucial role in addressing global security concerns, including non-proliferation issues. Although the United Nations can offer leadership and is indispensable to global peace and security, the involvement of regional actors in developing a cooperative security framework from the bottom up is crucial to the success or failure of the United Nations' efforts.

This is not simply a defense of the "subsidiarity" argument, or what might be more appropriately called regional subsidiarity theory (RST) – since the notion of subsidiarity has other usages – which holds that regional organizations are a stepping-stone to global order and must share some peace and security tasks of the United Nations to make them more achievable. This argument is already familiar to the epistemic community

---

The United Nations and nuclear orders, Boulden, Thakur and Weiss (eds), United Nations University Press, 2009, ISBN 978-92-808-1167-4

of scholars and policy-makers concerned with the United Nations' role in international peace and security. But the nexus between regional and global security problems and their management is more than a matter of giving regional institutions and coalitions a role in conflict management. It depends very much on local conditions and the approaches adopted by the local actors. The notion of subsidiarity is insufficient by itself in the absence of attention to how and why regional contexts differ and what local conditions and approaches are likely to facilitate conflict management. Hence, one must look at more general theories of regional security, such as regional security complex theory (RSCT) and regional cooperative security theory (RCST), to create a better framework for designing regional security arrangements for managing nuclear proliferation.

In the sections that follow, this chapter first outlines these three perspectives on regional order-making. Next, I identify the key and structural differences in the regional context between the North Korean and Iranian nuclear proliferation issues. I then explore the conditions and pathways for conflict management adopted by the international community in the case of both North Korea and Iran, highlighting factors that might illuminate the hitherto better prospects for "success" in North Korea and "failure" in Iran. Finally, the chapter concludes with some observations and policy guidelines on the role of regional actors and institutions in managing regional conflict in general and nuclear proliferation in particular.

Regional security orders: Three perspectives

The first wave of theorizing about regional orders[3] was a byproduct of the "universalist–regionalist debate" that accompanied the birth of the United Nations.[4] Although they were not labeled as such during this early period, the arguments of the regionalists at this time were to be incorporated into a theory of subsidiarity, which became prominent during the relatively optimistic environment after the end of the Cold War in the context of a wider re-examination of the role of the United Nations in international peace and security.[5]

The notion of subsidiarity derives from the belief that central bodies need not and should not perform tasks that can be adequately performed by local bodies. The RST makes the following assumptions, which draw from the universalist–regionalist debate:
1. excessive deference to the ideal of universal organization risks marginalizing the vital and legitimate role of local actors in regional conflict management;

2. neighbors may have a better understanding of the complexity of a local conflict and may be able to provide more timely and meaningful help to the victims of neighborhood conflicts; and
3. regional organizations are not competitors to the ideal of universal organization, but stepping-stones to universal peace and security.

These arguments have their critics. Neighbors are rarely objective in their assessment of local conflicts and may even be part of their cause. Regional groups often lack the resources to offer assistance, whether military or humanitarian, to contain a local conflict. Earlier arguments about the proximity advantage of regional actors have been compromised by the transport and communication revolution and the growing ability of nations to project power rapidly over long distances. And, finally, the record of regional mediation and intervention efforts in local conflicts has not been particularly encouraging to support the claims associated with the RST.

Yet no serious advocate of multilateralism today can deny a role to regional groups – whether formal institutions or informal or ad hoc coalitions – in conflict management in their neighborhoods. Like the United Nations itself, regional bodies perform a crucial legitimizing function, the absence of which could cripple the most efficient and most resource-endowed UN operation. Not all regional groups are without resources, especially with the transformation of the North Atlantic Treaty Organization from a military alliance to a more multipurpose security institution. Although they may not always take the initiative in conflict management – for instance, the Association of Southeast Asian Nations (ASEAN) in the Cambodia conflict – and offer "regional solutions to regional problems," regional actors singly or collectively have the ability to wreck solutions offered by outside or global actors. Global-level actors must also talk with regional groups to obtain timely and accurate information about the regional context within which conflicts are generated and sustained.

A second strand of theorizing about regional orders is the RSCT, initially offered by Barry Buzan and developed more fully in his book with Ole Wæver, *Regions and Powers*.[6] The RSCT is especially useful in understanding structural differences between regions and the power configurations that explain them. The RSCT argues that the international security order is increasingly regionalized. The regional level of analysis, or the intense security interdependence that exists among geographic neighbors and makes their national security concerns inseparable, is a crucial but often neglected factor behind the understanding of how conflicts arise and evolve. It further argues that regions are defined by powers at both the global and regional levels. The presence and role of these powers lead to different types of security complexes with different probabilities of conflict and cooperation. There are three main types of regional security complex (RSC). Some are "centered," either by a global-level power or by a strong supranational institution. In the second category are "great power RSCs," defined by the presence of more than one global-level power in them. A third is "standard" RSCs, which are bereft of any global-level powers, thereby leaving the space entirely to regional-level powers dealing with essentially local security issues. Applying this formula, the East Asian RSC, where North Korea is located, is a great power security complex, thanks to the presence of China and Japan. The Middle East, where Iran is located, is a standard RSC, since it does not have a resident great power.

It is possible to quibble with such categories. The absence of any resident global-level power in the Middle East did not make it immune to the intense impact of superpower rivalry during the Cold War or to the US presence and influence both during and after the Cold War. Whereas the wider Middle East and East Asia RSCs may be dissimilar in this respect, the sub-regions (or sub-complexes) of the Gulf and Northeast Asia are heavily penetrated by outside powers, especially the United States. But a more important question is how structural differences between the regions affect the prospects for conflict management,[7] including nuclear proliferation management. One might infer that an RSC centered by either a global-level power (e.g. North America) or a strong regional organization (e.g. the European Union) would be more amenable to the peaceful resolution of conflicts of all kinds, through coercion and consensus respectively. But what about the prospects for conflict management within great power and standard regional security complexes?

Although the RSCT helps us to understand differences between regions, it does not tell us much about how these variations affect the prospects for conflict management. Here, a third body of theoretical writings on regional orders assumes importance. The RCST, a body of writings that examines how local actors reduce conflict within the region through measures including confidence-building, preventive diplomacy, and mutual engagement of adversaries, is particularly relevant here. Whereas the RST points to the normative and functional division of labor between global and regional institutions, and the RSCT helps to differentiate regions in terms of their power configurations, the RCST is fundamentally a theory of conflict mitigation and management.

The RCST emerged towards the end of the Cold War, riding on the back of the success of the Conference and then the Organization for Security and Co-operation in Europe (CSCE/OSCE) in developing East–West security mechanisms that contributed significantly to bringing that period to an end. Despite the application of this term to describe global security regimes and cooperative mechanisms, the RCST is fundamentally a theory of regional security, emerging as it did from Cold War Europe and finding its most serious post–Cold War application in Asia (although regional institutions in Latin America and Africa have adopted aspects of it and proposals have been made for its application in the Middle East). The label "cooperative security" was actually the Pacific localization/adaptation of the European notion of "common security" outlined by the Palme Commission, whose central normative argument was that security is best achieved with, rather than against, one's adversary. Like common security, cooperative security emphasized the principle of inclusiveness, or the principle that ideological differences and regime types should not lead to the exclusion of any actor from a regional security framework. But, whereas the OSCE stressed rather formal measures of transparency and confidence-building to create mutual security, cooperative security – especially in the East Asian context – avoided formalistic and legalistic measures and institutions backed by verification and sanctions in favor of more informal processes of norm-setting and dialogue, guided by the norm of "process over the product" (known as the "ASEAN Way").[8] And whereas the OSCE made participation in the regional framework conditional upon the human rights performance of states and regimes, no such linkage was attempted in the East Asian case.

The three approaches are actually complementary: the RSCT tells us about why and how conflicts can be linked to structural variations among regions, while the RCST offers a pathway to conflict reduction and management, and the RST underscores the complementary relationship between the United Nations and regional actors and organizations (see Table 12.1). Together, they constitute a holistic understanding of regional orders and help to conceptualize the regional–global nexus (RST), inter-regional relations, including the relationship between regional actors and extra-regional powers (RSCT), and intra-regional relationships (RCST).

A tale of two regions?

I now consider the similarities and differences between the sub-regional contexts of North Korea and Iran as they affect the issue of nuclear proliferation. First, both regions have traditionally featured a defining local rivalry – North Korea and South Korea in the case of Northeast Asia, and Iran and Iraq in the case of the Gulf. This is the hallmark of any regional security complex, which according to its original formulation is marked more by an interdependence of rivalry than by one of shared interests.[9] Ideology is a key basis of this intra-regional rivalry, as manifested in the rivalry between Iran's Shiite Islam and Sunni Islam in the

Table 12.1 Theories of regional security orders

	Regional subsidiarity theory	Regional security complex theory	Regional cooperative security theory
Definition	Regional organizations are stepping-stones to global order, somewhat akin to neighborhood-watch mechanisms	A pattern of security interdependence where states "link together sufficiently closely that their securities cannot be considered separate from each other"[a]	Security with, not against, the enemy
Origin	Post-WWII period (revived in the post–Cold War period – Boutros-Ghali's Agenda for Peace)	Late Cold War period (revised to fit post–Cold War period by lessening the importance of the interdependence of rivalry and acknowledging the interdependence of shared interests)	Late Cold War Europe – Helsinki process (extended to other regions in post–Cold War era)
Main explanatory focus	Regional–global organizational nexus	Inter-regional differentiation and relationship between regions and extra-regional powers	Intra-regional relationships
International environment	Collective security	Anarchy	Cooperative security
Main agent	Universal organization plays central role in conflict management	Global and regional-level powers	Regional institutions and processes
Non-proliferation management	NPT, UN Security Council, IAEA, some regional NWFZs (Antarctica)	Supplier clubs, counter-proliferation regimes (e.g. Proliferation Security Initiative, Container Security Initiative)	Regional NWFZs (e.g. South Pacific NWFZ; Southeast Asia NWFZ), regional dialogues on conflict reduction to minimize incentives to proliferate

[a] Barry Buzan and Ole Wæver, *Regions and Powers: The Structure of International Security* (Cambridge: Cambridge University Press, 2003), 43.

Gulf and between centrally planned communism (however outdated) and liberal economics and politics in Northeast Asia (except in the case of China).

Second, as noted earlier, both North Korea and Iran are located in sub-regions with a high level of great power penetration. The implications of the fact that Iran's sub-region does not include a global-level power whereas North Korea's does should not be overstressed, given the high level of European, superpower and US interest and involvement in the Gulf during the colonial, Cold War, and post–Cold War periods respectively.

The differences between the two regions concern, first and foremost, the nature and role of regional organizations. Neither is a "centered" region or sub-region (here I am applying the RSCT to sub-regional level) in the sense of being dominated by either a single great power or a supranational organization. The Gulf has its Gulf Cooperation Council (GCC), but this excludes Iran (indeed, it was created as a bulwark against the threat of Iranian subversion in the wake of the 1979 Islamic revolution). Hence, the Gulf has no cooperative security mechanism, whether formal or informal. By contrast, although Northeast Asia has no permanent sub-regional organization (at least not as yet), its dialogue and negotiating forum, the Six-Party Talks, is more inclusive than any that exists in the Gulf, and efforts are being made to turn these talks into a permanent regional grouping. Moreover, Northeast Asia is embedded in wider regional organizations, especially the ASEAN Regional Forum, in which all the parties to the Six-Party Talks, North Korea included, are full and formal members. This makes cooperative security processes in Northeast Asia in managing proliferation easier to realize than in the Gulf.

A second difference between the two cases relates to the motivations behind their respective nuclear programs. Iran's nuclear program is rooted in its regional and international ambition; North Korea's is geared essentially to domestic concerns. Iran's nuclear program pre-dates the Islamic regime, as it was part of the shah of Iran's grand ambition to be the Gulf's superpower, a policy actively encouraged by successive US administrations under the "twin-pillar strategy" (the other pillar being Saudi Arabia). Among others, Gerald Ford administration functionary Dick Cheney was believed to have supported Iran's quest for civilian nuclear energy. This is a reminder of the fact that Iran's nuclear program is intimately linked to its quest for regional status. Indeed, the issue of status underscores a crucial difference between Iran and North Korea. While nuclear weapons help the internal legitimacy of the regimes in both cases,[10] nuclear weapons, as Sharam Chubin (director of research at the Geneva Center for Security Policy) put it, "provide Iran with status and influence in the region."[11] Iran is not content just with keeping its Islamic regime alive, but also wants to create a zone of influence in the neighborhood. By contrast, North Korea's regional posture is isolationist. Its ideology poses no threat to its neighbors, whereas Iran's religious fervor has put it at odds with its Sunni neighbors.

The third difference concerns the economic–security nexus. With the sole exception of North Korea, Northeast Asia is far more industrialized and integrated into the global economy than is the Gulf, which is critically dependent on a single resource. Both North Korea and Iran are relatively poorer states compared with their neighbors (Iran relative to the oil-rich GCC members), but the gap is especially severe in the case of North Korea. Intra-regional economic disparities have exacerbated conflict between North and South Korea, but economic interdependence among the other actors – China, Japan, South Korea, and the United States – has helped to mitigate geopolitical rivalries that might have otherwise made a coordinated approach to conflict management difficult, if not impossible. Intra-regional economic disparities also have an important bearing on conflict management strategies, as could be seen from the critical importance of economic demands and incentives in managing the Korean peninsula conflict. This is less the case in the Gulf, since Iran, thanks to the massive rise in oil prices, is less dependent on external aid.

Fourth, social forces affect regional conflict dynamics differently in the two sub-regions. Although both the Gulf and Northeast Asia are relatively homogeneous culturally (compared with Southeast Asia for example), sectarian differences of the kind that are found in the Gulf sub-region (e.g. the Sunni/Shiite split) are absent in Northeast Asia, despite Samuel Huntington's characterization of Japan and China as two distinct civilizations.[12] This has significant implications for regional order. North Korea cannot mobilize regional public opinion to legitimize its claim to nuclear weapons the way Iran can count on the Shia population of neighboring Iraq and other Muslim Middle Eastern states.

Fifth, Gulf security is linked to the Arab–Israeli conflict and to some extent embedded in it. After the overthrow of the shah of Iran, the Ayatollah Ruhollah Khomeini regime presented itself as a champion of the Palestinian cause. Iran is able to play both Arab and Muslim grievances against the West and Israel, a potent mobilizing and legitimizing factor in its quest for nuclear weapons. The fact that Israel is a de facto nuclear weapon power but is able to escape any sanctions because of Western support adds considerably to Iran's ability to draw sympathy from within the Middle East region and in the wider Islamic world for its claim to have nuclear technology. None of this applies to North Korea, which cannot turn to ideology in order to mobilize popular support beyond its borders for its nuclear program.

Last but not least, the US-led "war on terror" helped contain North Korean nuclear ambitions by creating a common ground between the United States and China (whose bilateral relations have improved significantly, if not permanently, since the 9/11 attacks). In the case of Iran, the war on terror and its corollary, the invasion and occupation of Iraq, have severely damaged the prospects for keeping the Gulf nuclear free. The war in Iraq not only removed a countervailing power from the scene. The collapse of the Taliban regime in Afghanistan and the rise of Shiite influence in post–Saddam Hussein Iraq, coupled with the dramatic rise in oil prices (which also helped the re-emergence of Russian power, along with its backing of Tehran), helped Iran's strategic position in the region. In attacking Iraq, notes Amin Saikal,

> the [George W.] Bush Administration failed to see that its approach could also achieve what it had never intended: the empowerment of the Iraqi Shiites, and the diluting of Iraq's national identity, which had historically been forged within the Sunni-dominated Arab world.
>
> [This] unquestionably strengthened the position of Iran, given the close sectarian ties between the two sides at both leadership and popular levels. This, together with Iran's support of the Lebanese Shiites in Hezbollah and close political relationship with Damascus, has now given rise to a Shiite-dominated strategic entity, enabling Tehran to influence not only the course of events in Iraq but also the geostrategic situation in the region as a whole.[13]

Added to this was the Bush administration's unthinking and arrogant dismissal of Iran's offer of negotiations and cooperation against al-Qaeda in the immediate aftermath of 9/11.

Approaches to conflict management

After having considered the similarities and differences in the sub-regional contexts, I now turn to an examination of the conflict management strategies adopted by the international community in the two cases. Table 12.2 summarizes the key elements of the conflict management dynamic. Four aspects are important: the negotiating framework and the actors involved; sanctions; the nature of the incentives offered; and direct negotiations with the United States.

The negotiating framework

In terms of the negotiating framework, perhaps the most important aspect of the conflict management process, the two cases are dramatically different. In North Korea's case, the Six-Party Talks constitute a genuinely regional multilateral framework. The George H. W. Bush administration had rejected multilateral approaches to security in East Asia as a "solution in search of a problem," but its willingness to accept an à la carte multilateralism through the Four-Party and Six-Party Talks was consistent with the notion of cooperative security.[14] The policy of seeking a multilateral solution – sometimes criticized as a camouflage for US unwillingness to engage in direct talks with North Korea – survived the general disdain of multilateralism by the neoconservative Bush administration.[15] It had the added benefit of bringing China into the game at a time when Beijing was keen to prove its multilateral credentials by joining other regional forums such as the ASEAN Regional Forum (ARF) and the ASEAN-Plus-Three framework.

In short, the fact that the wider Asia-Pacific region had an evolving multilateral framework did help to achieve a nuclear accord with North Korea. To be sure, North Korea, after having joined the ARF, has not played an active role. The ARF itself has shied away from concrete initiatives on the Korean peninsula problem, going only so far as issuing statements and declarations.[16] But the ARF has at least bestowed regional legitimacy on the Six-Party Talks. By contrast, negotiations with Iran cannot be deemed to be a regional affair. Although the talks are organized by the European Union, that regional group is external to the region and the autonomy of the European Union vis-à-vis the permanent five members of the Security Council (P-5) is substantially blurred. The European Union's mandate is to negotiate on behalf of the Council, all of whose members have a controlling influence on the terms of the talks.

According to the RSCT, geographic proximity induces the most intense pattern of security interdependence. This in turn can make regional actors, including the great powers in a region, more serious about resolving regional conflicts. China and Japan have a major stake in preventing war and instability in the Korean peninsula. Their security is directly and existentially challenged by North Korea's missile and nuclear weapons programs, as well as by the potential for refugee flows from a serious political crisis there. Lacking such direct physical linkage with the Gulf, the relatively distant European powers that have taken the lead in managing Iranian proliferation have less need to accommodate Iran's security needs, although they seem to have developed an irrational fear of Iran's regime. Unsurprisingly, the negotiating framework adopted in the two cases has had a greater potential to succeed in Northeast Asia than in the Gulf.

Moreover, the willingness of China, the pre-eminent regional power, to get involved in the Six-Party Talks was critical.[17] Beijing's participation was possible because Washington became willing to respect China's insistence on regime security, rather than regime change, in North Korea. Moreover, as North Korea's main lifeline, China was not using Pyongyang

Table 12.2 North Korea and Iran

	North Korea	Iran
When nuclear program started	Late 1980s through the acquisition of dual-use technology; summer 2002, suspicion of uranium enrichment activity	1957 under Atoms for Peace Program (interrupted by the Islamic revolution, 1979, and the Iran–Iraq War, 1980–1988); Iran's uranium enrichment program was detected by the IAEA in August 2003, although it may go back earlier
Status of nuclear program	Believed to possess a limited number of nuclear weapons	Believed to be years away from weapons-grade uranium enrichment capability
UN sanctions	July 2006: all member states banned from selling material or technology of missiles or WMD to North Korea, and from receiving missiles, banned weapons, or technology from North Korea October 2006: UNSC Resolution 1718 bans sale to, or export from, North Korea of military hardware; bans sale or export of nuclear and missile-related material; bans sale of luxury goods; freezes finances and bans travel of anyone involved in nuclear or missile programs; allows inspection of cargo to and from North Korea. But these sanctions cannot be enforced through military means	December 2006: sanctions on trade with Iran in sensitive nuclear materials and technology March 2007: intensification of the December 2006 sanctions by ban on the country's arms exports and freezing the assets and restricting the travel of individuals engaged in the country's proliferation-sensitive nuclear activities March 2008: ban on supply of nuclear-related technology; asset freeze on key individuals and companies; inspection of vessels and aircraft owned by certain Iranian companies. But Security Council resolution did not authorize the use of force
US national sanctions	Restrictions on travel, trade, and banking with North Korea imposed after Korean war, most of them lifted by the Clinton administration in 1999 October 2005: under Executive Order 133382 (WMD proliferators and their supporters), targets North Korean companies	Comprehensive sanctions imposed since the hostage crisis in 1979 In addition to US sanctions, the EU countries have their own sanctions on Iran. In August 2008, the EU imposed new sanctions on Iran in retaliation against Tehran's refusal to accept a new package of incentives offered by the EU.

		These sanctions go a little beyond existing UN trade sanctions and include denial of export credits or public loans to companies trading with Iran. In addition, EU governments will monitor financial companies doing business with Iranian banks and increase checks on ships and airplanes traveling to Iran
Membership in regional organizations	ASEAN Regional Forum, Council for Security Cooperation in the Asia Pacific (Track II)	Observer status in the Shanghai Cooperation Organization
Negotiating framework and actors	Six-Party Talks involving North Korea, South Korea, the United States, China, Japan, and Russia	EU–Iran dialogue, supported by the United States, Russia, China, France, Germany, and the EU
Incentives offered	2004: monthly supply of heavy fuel oil, a "provisional" guarantee not to attack the regime, lifting more sanctions imposed since the Korean war, retraining of nuclear scientists and long-term energy cooperation (Sanger 2004) 2007 Agreement: initial supply up to the equivalent of 50,000 tons of heavy fuel oil for North Korea, eventually amounting to 1 million tons. Bilateral talks between United States and North Korea to remove North Korea's designation as a state sponsor of terrorism and to unfreeze North Korean financial assets; cessation of US efforts to shut off North Korea's access to international finance; and lifting of the Trading with the Enemy Act provisions against North Korea. Energy and economic assistance to North Korea 2008: United States hinted at removal of North Korea from list of terror-supporting states	2006: civil nuclear cooperation, including a light water reactor, partial ownership of a Russian enrichment facility, five-year stock of enriched uranium stored under the supervision of the IAEA, trade in civil aircraft, energy, high technology, and agriculture in return for Iran's suspension of uranium enrichment. These incentives were "refreshed" in May 2008, but "political confidence-building measures" (Buckley 2008) suggested by China and Russia were rejected by the United States, which insisted that it was "always looking at tougher sanctions on Iran" (Pleming 2008) June 2008: the EU on behalf of the P-5+Germany offered a package of incentives that was an enhanced and updated version of the 2006 package, providing for civilian nuclear cooperation and for trade in civilian aircraft, energy, high technology, and agriculture

259

Table 12.1 (cont.)

	North Korea	Iran
Direct negotiations with the United States?	US refused to hold bilateral talks with North Korea in April 2006 (Pinkston 2006), but the February 2007 agreement "was really hammered out in large part in bilateral negotiations" between the two sides in Berlin in December 2006 (Feffer 2007). This did not prevent Bush from claiming disingenuously in March 2007 that refusal to talk bilaterally with North Korea was key to reaching the accord and hence would serve as a "model" for dealing with Iran (Reuters 2007)	The United States offered "wide-ranging talks should Iran suspend its enrichment-related and processing activities," not beforehand (US Department of State 2008). US Ambassador Nicholas Burns attended talks between the EU and Iran in Geneva on 18 July 2008. Iran expressed satisfaction
Outcome	February 2007: Initial Actions Agreement committing North Korea to abandon all nuclear weapons and nuclear programs and return to NPT and IAEA safeguards. Followed by October 2007 Second Phase Actions, which committed North Korea to disable all its existing nuclear facilities, beginning with the three core facilities at Yongbyon by 31 December 2007, and not to transfer nuclear materials, technology, and know-how. Most of the agreed disablement actions at Yongbyon completed by that date, but North Korea missed the agreed deadline for providing a "complete and correct declaration of all its nuclear programs" (Hill 2008) – in May 2008 it provided data on plutonium facilities but not on uranium-enrichment ones	Iran continues uranium enrichment, wants to negotiate directly with the IAEA, offers mixed signals on continuing with the dialogue with the EU. The P-5+1 powers are due to offer a revised set of incentives to Tehran.

Sources:

"Appeasing Iran, North Korea?" *Washington Times* (Editorial), 9 May 2008; available at ⟨http://www.washingtontimes.com/article/20080509/EDITORIAL/546180601/1013/editorial⟩ (accessed 14 November 2008).

Associated Press, "New EU Sanctions over Iran's Nuclear Program," 8 August 2008; available at ⟨http://www.msnbc.msn.com/id/26094872/⟩ (accessed 14 November 2008).

Bilefsky, Dan, "EU Plans 2nd Package of Incentives to Iran," *International Herald Tribune*, 15 May 2006,; available at ⟨http://www.iht.com/articles/2006/05/15/news/union.php⟩ (accessed 14 November 2008).

Bilefsky, Dan, "Europe to Offer Iran Conditional Incentives," *New York Times*, 16 May 2006; available at ⟨http://www.nytimes.com/2006/05/16/world/middleeast/16iran.html?_r=1&pagewanted=print&oref=slogin⟩ (accessed 14 November 2008).

Buckley, Chris, "Iran Nuclear Talks in China Fall Short," *Reuters*, 16 April 2008, available at ⟨http://www.reuters.com/article/latestCrisis/idUSPEK259323⟩ (accessed 24 November 2008).

"Clinton Eases North Korea Sanctions," *New York Times*/Associated Press, 17 September 1999; available at ⟨http://globalpolicy.igc.org/security/sanction/nkorea/99-09-17.htm⟩ (accessed 14 November 2008).

Feffer, John, "North Korean Nuclear Agreement: Annotated," FPIF Commentary, Foreign Policy In Focus, 14 February 2007; available at ⟨http://www.fpif.org/fpiftxt/3997⟩ (accessed 14 November 2008).

Friends Committee on National Legislation, "North Korea Nuclear Test: United Nations Sanctions – What's the Next Step?" 17 October 2006; available at ⟨http://www.fcnl.org/issues/item.php?item_id=2132&issue_id=34⟩ (accessed 14 November 2008).

Global Policy Forum, "Sanctions Against North Korea," available at ⟨http://globalpolicy.igc.org/security/sanction/indexkor.htm⟩ (accessed 14 November 2008).

Goodenough, Patrick, "North Korea's Allies Resist Action in Security Council," *Cybercast News Service*, 6 July 2006; available at ⟨http://globalpolicy.igc.org/security/sanction/nkorea/2006/0706allies.htm⟩ (accessed 14 November 2008).

Hill, Christopher, *Statement of Christopher R. Hill before the Senate Foreign Relations Committee on the Status of the Six-Party Talks for the Denuclearization of the Korean Peninsula*, 6 February 2008.

Labott, Elise, "U.S. Agrees to EU's Iran Nuclear Plan," CNN.com, 8 May 2008; available at ⟨http://edition.cnn.com/2008/WORLD/meast/05/08/iran.nuclear/index.html⟩ (accessed 14 November 2008)

Lederer, Edith M., "UN Imposes Limited Sanctions on N. Korea," Associated Press, 16 July 2006; available at ⟨http://globalpolicy.igc.org/security/sanction/nkorea/2006/0716limited.htm⟩ (accessed 14 November 2008)

Pinkston, Daniel A., "North Korea's Nuclear Weapons Program and the Six-party Talks," Nuclear Threat Initiative (NTI) Issue Brief, April 2006, Washington, DC; available at ⟨http://www.nti.org/e_research/e3_76.html⟩ (accessed 14 November 2008).

Pleming, Sue, "U.S. Says Iran Will Get Incentives 'Very Quickly'," *Reuters*, 5 May 2008; available at ⟨http://www.alertnet.org/thenews/newsdesk/N05394570.htm⟩ (accessed 14 November 2008).

Table 12.1 (cont.)

Reuters, "Bush Hails N. Korea Nuclear Accord as Possible Model for Iran," Haaretz.com, 3 October 2007; available at ⟨http://www.haaretz.com/hasen/spages/909529.html⟩ (accessed 14 November 2008).
Sanger, David E., "U.S. to Offer North Korea Incentives in Nuclear Talks," *New York Times*, 23 June 2004; available at ⟨http://query.nytimes.com/gst/fullpage.html?res=9C0DE5D61039F930A15755C0A9629C8B63⟩ (accessed 14 November 2008).
"Timeline: Iran Nuclear Crisis," *BBC News*, 24 September 2005; available at ⟨http://news.bbc.co.uk/1/hi/world/middle_east/4134614.stm⟩ (accessed 14 November 2008).
"UN Passes Iran Nuclear Sanctions," *BBC News*, 23 December 2006; available at ⟨http://news.bbc.co.uk/go/pr/fr/-/1/hi/world/middle_east/6205295.stm⟩ (accessed 14 November 2008).
United Nations Security Council, "Security Council Imposes Sanctions on Iran for Failure to Halt Uranium Enrichment, Unanimously Adopting Resolution 1737 (2006)," UN Doc. SC/8928, New York: Department of Public Information, 23 December 2006; available at ⟨http://www.un.org/News/Press/docs/2006/sc8928.doc.htm⟩ (accessed 14 November 2008).
United Nations Security Council, "Committee Monitoring Sanctions Against Iran Has Received 88 National Reports on Implementation of Those Measures, Chairman Tells Security Council," UN Doc. SC/9276, New York: Department of Public Information, 17 March 2008; available at ⟨http://www.un.org/News/Press/docs/2008/sc9276.doc.htm⟩ (accessed 14 November 2008).
United Nations Security Council, "Security Council Toughens Sanctions Against Iran, Adds Arms Embargo, With Unanimous Adoption of Resolution 1747 (2007)," UN Doc. SC/8980, New York: Department of Public Information, 24 March 2007; available at ⟨http://www.un.org/News/Press/docs/2007/sc8980.doc.htm⟩ (accessed 14 November 2008).
US Department of State, "North Korea and Iran: An Administration Perspective," Remarks at National Defense University Symposium by Patricia McNerney, Principal Deputy Assistant Secretary, International Security and Nonproliferation, Washington, DC, 8 May 2008; available at ⟨http://www.state.gov/t/isn/rls/rm/104548.htm⟩ (accessed 14 November 2008).

as a pawn in retaliating against the United States and Japan for what China might have perceived as their joint effort at containing it. Indeed, North Korea's neighbors did not see the situation as an arena to play out their geopolitical rivalry.

Unlike the North Korea case, key Arab players such as Egypt and regional organizations such as the GCC or the Arab League have had no role in the nuclear talks with Iran, thereby denying them regional legitimacy. There is no China-like actor in the case of the Iran negotiations: neither Egypt nor Russia can play that role. Perhaps the key to the Iranian case is China again, but Iran is less dependent on Beijing economically than is North Korea. Furthermore, China's own dependence on Iran for energy security undermines its ability to shape the course of negotiations with Iran in the manner of North Korea.

Sanctions

With regard to sanctions, although both North Korea and Iran have been subject to international sanctions, North Korea has received fewer sanctions and more incentives than Iran. China has consistently thwarted Security Council sanctions on North Korea, to a much greater extent than China and Russia have resisted Security Council sanctions on Iran. Iran has been subject to three rounds of Council sanctions. One was imposed days after the IAEA's mixed findings on Iran's nuclear weapons program in February 2008. Another followed the November 2007 US National Intelligence Estimate, which concluded that Iran had halted its nuclear weapons program in the fall of 2003. And the United States maintains its "comprehensive sanctions" on Iran that were imposed after the 1979–1980 hostage crisis. The greater sanctions burden of Iran compared with North Korea is ironic, since North Korea has the more advanced nuclear weapons program and has arguably committed a more serious violation of the Nuclear Non-Proliferation Treaty (NPT).[18] Moreover, the most biting UN sanctions against North Korea came only after it conducted nuclear tests in 2006, whereas Iran has been punished preemptively for not stopping its uranium enrichment activity, which by itself is not forbidden under the NPT (although it is banned under Council resolutions).[19]

Incentives

The incentives offered to North Korea are more regionally based, apart from US assistance for civil nuclear technology and Western economic assistance. Under the terms of a possible agreement, North Korea also received substantial aid from China and South Korea under the Kim Dae-jung and Roh Myun-hee governments respectively.[20] The regional nature of assistance to North Korea is a key missing element in the case of Iran, although Saudi Arabia and other oil-rich GCC members are quite capable of offering economic assistance. Aid from neighbors is important because it creates a regional comfort zone for North Korea conducive to mitigating its regime and national insecurity.

Direct negotiations with the United States

Finally, US willingness to negotiate directly with North Korea but not with Iran has been an important factor. Although the George W. Bush administration formally refused to negotiate directly with North Korea, preferring the Six-Party formula (and some analysts would even view the Six-Party Talks as a ploy to deflect the need for direct talks with Pyongyang), the United States has had meetings with North Korea on the margins of UN and Asian regional meetings. The United States has made no comparable effort to talk to Iran directly. It has offered to talk directly with Iran only if the latter gives up its uranium enrichment. Direct negotiations have a symbolic significance in the sense that they satisfy the status needs of the regimes, especially important in the case of Iran.

In sum, in both the North Korea and Iran cases, the "axis of evil" concept has turned out to be a self-fulfilling prophecy. However, it was possible to control the damage in the case of North Korea owing to differing political conditions, especially cooperation from China, a belated pragmatism on the part of the United States in de-linking its regime change strategy from nuclear negotiations, and the backdrop of cooperative security frameworks that had developed in East Asia since the end of the Cold War.

Conclusion

"Obviously, there is no 'one size fits all' solution in diplomacy." This statement by senior Bush administration non-proliferation official Patricia McNerney in May 2008 was meant to differentiate Iran from North Korea,[21] wisdom that was conspicuously lacking when both were lumped together seven years previously by the same administration as the "axis of evil." Equally revealing was a statement by President Bush himself in October 2003. He described the role of "neighborhood" actors, particularly China, in facilitating a solution to the North Korean crisis.[22] Together, these statements offer powerful evidence from the policy world that *differentiated subsidiarity* and regional cooperative security are critical principles and tools in the hands of the international community in addressing regional security challenges.

The conclusions of this chapter concern both the theory and the practice of regional security arrangements. In terms of theory, the subsidiarity principle (RST) must permit consideration of inter-regional differences in context and capacity. The RSCT helps to fill the gap, but it requires a theory of conflict management. Hence, the idea of cooperative security (RCST), pursued through regional organizations and processes, is crucial.

This has implications for the role of the United Nations and the international community more broadly in addressing the proliferation of nuclear and other weapons of mass destruction. Differences in regional institutional contexts must be clearly understood and borne in mind in designing policy frameworks to deal with the spread of nuclear weapons.[23] Even die-hard Bush apologists came to agree that the "axis of evil" and the Bush doctrine were crude formulations that bracketed very different regimes operating in dramatically opposite regional contexts under one sweeping policy framework. This might have created easier tools for fear-mongering that is the central element of the global war on terror, but it also made for bad diplomacy and arms control. Whatever success the United States has achieved in North Korea was mainly owing to the implicit realization that North Korea cannot be subjected to regime change strategy.

Next, although one might argue that the presence of a regional organization is not a precondition for addressing nuclear proliferation, regional ownership and regional legitimation do play an important role in mitigating, managing, and even reversing nuclear proliferation. In the case of North Korea, the negotiating process not only involved key regional actors but also was normatively embedded in nascent Asia-Pacific regional norms and institutions, especially the doctrine of cooperative security. Regional actors such as South Korea and China kept the political and humanitarian engagement of North Korea going even at the height of the Bush doctrine's rabidly unilateralist pre-emption rhetoric. In contrast, there has been no such regional ownership and legitimation of the world's efforts to contain Iran's nuclear ambition.

How can regional approaches to addressing nuclear proliferation be legitimized and made more effective? This chapter has offered some lessons. The most important of these is that regional approaches are unlikely to be very useful in conflict management if undertaken by outsiders or if they are non-inclusive. Comparing the Gulf with Southeast Asia (where nuclear proliferation is not an issue), one finds that the relative stability of ASEAN is owing to its decision to bring Vietnam (through ASEAN) and China (through the ARF) quickly into its framework of regional security. The GCC, by contrast, has made no serious effort to engage Iraq or Iran, the two regional superpowers.[24] This means the states most threatened by Iran's nuclear ambitions, such as Saudi Arabia, have no means of dialogue and communication with Iran at the regional multilateral level.[25] Inclusiveness is not an idealistic notion, as its critics often allege; the examples of OSCE, ASEAN, and the Korean peninsula suggest that inclusiveness is an indispensable element of any approach to conflict resolution.

Hence, the development by the GCC of a mechanism for dialogue with Iraq and Iran is long overdue. The GCC is otherwise of limited relevance. On its own, it is not a credible military alliance against Iran.[26] Unable to act as a deterrent, it would be better off developing a diplomatic role in reducing and managing conflicts in the Gulf region. At the very least, the GCC should develop a multilateral dialogue with Iran, much in the way ASEAN did with Vietnam and China before making them formal members of regional cooperative security arrangements.[27]

To the extent that a regional element in addressing proliferation is important, some types of regional arrangements may be more effective than others. Regional security arrangements geared specifically to controlling nuclear weapons, such as nuclear-weapon-free zones (NWFZs), are best undertaken as preventive action rather than reactively. For example, Southeast Asia and the South Pacific have reasonably credible NWFZs, which were announced well before any member state took a serious step towards nuclear proliferation. The Antarctica Treaty provides a useful model of preventive action that should be considered by regions where there may be a long-term danger of nuclearization. The proposed NWFZ in the Gulf to deal with Iran's nuclear program (and Israel's) comes too late. An NWFZ in the Middle East is an unrealistic goal unless Israel can be persuaded to declare and reverse its nuclear capabilities, something that is highly unlikely even in the most optimistic case of current negotiations leading to the creation of a Palestinian state.[28] The Israel factor also ensures that Iran will not agree to a sub-regional NWFZ covering Gulf states only, as has been proposed by the GCC.[29] For Iran, the GCC proposal does little to address the issue of Israel's nuclear arsenal and the danger of Israeli pre-emption, which is a realistic possibility for any regional power seeking nuclear capability. Iran has instead "pursued the realization of a nuclear-weapon-free zone in the Middle East."[30]

A comprehensive regional organization is also not always the answer. These groups have their own baggage and can be unwieldy owing to larger membership. Ad hoc or à la carte regional multilateralism may be a more effective response than standing bodies. Hence, the subsidiarity principle and the RST must be reframed to include both formal and informal, standing and ad hoc multilateral instruments.

Although the United States and the European Union are important players in seeking solutions to the nuclear situation in Iran, they should also involve and defer to Asian regional powers, especially China and India, as closely as possible. This would be consistent with Iran's own "look east" policy, which led it to move away from the agreement with the EU-3 (France, Germany, and the United Kingdom) in November 2004 that had provided for the suspension of all processing activities. Ray Takeyh of the Council on Foreign Relations points to a foreign policy reorientation in Iran: "the idea of more of an Eastern orientation ... The idea being that the future of Iran lies in cementing its commercial and diplomatic ties with the emerging industrial giants of the East, whether it's India, whether it's China, Japan, and so on, as opposed to privileging the relationship with the West."[31]

It is counterproductive to pursue regime change alongside nuclear nonproliferation. This is because regime survival has emerged as the most distinctive feature of the "second nuclear age." This is quite different from the first nuclear age, when ideology and geopolitics were the main motives behind the nuclear arms race. Regime survival is the key factor behind the quest for nuclear arms in North Korea, Iran, and even Pakistan, where ex-President Musharraf and the Pakistani military constantly played the "loose nukes card" to deflate international pressure for democratic reform. As some have argued, would the United States have invaded Iraq if Saddam really had nuclear capabilities? North Korea's "nuclear blackmail" is another clear instance of the use of nuclear weapons in the service of regime security. In 2007, Pakistani opposition figure Nawaz Sharif started his quest to recapture power by proclaiming himself the leader who made Pakistan a nuclear power. Hence, a policy of regime change is at odds with the objective of reversing nuclear proliferation, whatever may be the geopolitical and moral imperative behind the latter.

We tend to think of regional regimes in isolation from one another, but the security strategies of regional regimes do impact on one another. There is an irony in the fact that despite having labeled both North Korea and Iran as members of the "axis of evil" – as part of a global strategy to combat terrorism and proliferation – the United States has shown a greater willingness to negotiate with North Korea than with Iran. This fact is unlikely to have been missed by Tehran. Regimes targeted by the United States do learn from each other. Although there is as yet insufficient evidence to support this claim, some analysts have argued in defense of the Bush administration's approach that the successful effort to force Libya's hand in the Lockerbie affair and its nuclear proliferation might have had a bearing on North Korea's decision to accept a deal over its nuclear program.

The international community's approach to nuclear proliferation must also pay particular attention to the nature of the nexus between the global and regional security dynamics that underpin the quest for nuclear weapons. For example, whereas the nuclear ambitions of North Korea and Iran are viewed by Washington and other Western capitals as a threat to both global and regional security, both countries' primary motivations for acquiring nuclear weapons are largely embedded in their regional security concerns. Yet the United States has often highlighted Iran (and to a lesser extent North Korea) as a threat to its global security interests (hence placing a missile defense system in Poland to counter Iran) while pursuing a global approach to containing Iran that neglects the regional dimensions of the equation. Avoiding this mismatch between the regional roots of nuclear ambition and the global counterproliferation strategies of the United States (as well as the United Nations) is important in devising effective diplomatic approaches to containing nuclear proliferation.

Another critical factor in conflict management concerns incentives and status. As this chapter has shown, Iran suffered more sanctions and received fewer incentives compared with North Korea. Of course, oil-rich Iran does not need handouts of the kind that the Kim Jong Il regime in North Korea desperately requires to survive. But Iran's reward might have been in the form of increased recognition of its security concerns and interests. Some argue that Iran has been treated with less respect as a regional power, even when the country was ruled by the considerably more moderate Mohammad Khatami regime.[32] Direct negotiations between the United States and Iran at ambassadorial levels, as happened over Iraq, should have long since taken place covering nuclear issues. Shortly before this book went to press, the Bush administration sent Under Secretary of State William Burns to attend talks between the European Union and Iran on 19 July 2008 in Geneva. The move was welcomed by Iran, but US participation was described by the State Department as a one-time occasion only, and at the meeting Burns insisted that Iran must first suspend uranium enrichment before it could expect to have direct negotiations with the United States. Iran promptly turned down this proposal.[33] The election of Barack Obama raises hopes for a direct US approach to Iran, but his campaign-time "speaking with the enemy" policy has been qualified since, and it is unlikely that an Obama administration will resort to unconditional talks with Tehran.[34]

It is clear that, in both cases analyzed, one of the motives of the party in question has been recognition of its status as an equal participant at the table. In the case of North Korea, the regional forum of Six-Party Talks has made this possible. Iran's status concerns have not been similarly addressed. This is something for the international community to consider in its ongoing efforts to address the problem of nuclear weapons proliferation.

Notes

1. Glenn Kessler, "N. Korea Nuclear Accord Reached: Side Deal with U.S. Involves Terror List," *Washington Post*, 3 October 2007, A14. The United States had been satisfied with North Korea's move to supply it with a list of its nuclear facilities. But in August 2008 the Bush administration refused to remove North Korea from its list of states that support terrorism until Pyongyang signed a protocol to verify the dismantling and accounting of its nuclear program. Pyongyang wanted to be removed from the list first, and on 14 August 2008 announced that it was stopping the disabling of the Yongbyon nuclear complex. See also "US Accuses North Korea of Violating Nuclear Accord," AFP via *Yahoo! News*, 27 August 2008. In October, the United States did remove North Korea from the list, but in November Pyongyang had threatened not to comply with the verification aspects of the nuclear agreement by insisting that it would not allow inspectors to remove samples from its nuclear sites. This shows the continuing uncertainties about the nuclear accord.
2. In August 2008, after the European Union imposed new sanctions on Iran over Tehran's refusal to accept a fresh package of incentives offered by it on behalf of the P-5 and Germany (see Table 12.2), Iran and the European Union agreed to continue talks to reach common ground. Iran had refused the demand by the European Union and the United States to halt its uranium enrichment program in return for a freeze on sanctions and incentives such as civilian nuclear cooperation.
3. In conceptualizing regional security orders, I acknowledge that the term "region" can have contested meanings. In this chapter, I define a region as a group of geographically proximate states that have a high degree of economic or security interdependence (whether cooperative or conflictual) and whose interactions are recognized as distinctive by actors within and outside. Regions can have overlapping boundaries and large "macro regions" can contain distinctive sub-regions. Both the Gulf and Northeast Asia are essentially sub-regions within the wider Middle East and East Asian regions. For further discussion on regions, see Amitav Acharya, "The Emerging Regional Architecture of World Politics," *World Politics* 59, no. 4 (2007): 629–652. Regional security arrangements/organizations as used in this chapter refer to multilateral forums whose main goal is the reduction and management of intra-regional conflict, rather than to alliance-type organizations whose main goal is to deter and defend against external threats.
4. Norman J. Padelford, "Regional Organizations and the United Nations," *International Organization* 8, no. 2 (1954): 203–216; Ernst Haas, "Regionalism, Functionalism and Universal Organization," *World Politics* 8, no. 2 (1956): 238–263; Minerva Etzioni, *The Majority of One: Towards a Theory of Regional Compatibility* (Beverly Hills, CA: Sage Publications, 1970); Joseph S. Nye, *Peace in Parts: Integration and Conflict in Regional Organization* (Boston: Little, Brown, 1971).
5. David O'Brien, "The Search for Subsidiarity: The UN, African Regional Organizations and Humanitarian Action," *International Peacekeeping* 7, no. 3 (2000): 57–83; Sorpong Peou, "The Subsidiarity Model of Global Governance in the UN-ASEAN Context," *Global Governance* 4, no. 4 (1998): 439–460; Connie Peck, "The Role of Regional Organizations in Preventing and Resolving Conflict," in *Turbulent Peace: The Challenge of Managing International Conflict*, ed. C. Crocker, F. O. Hampson and P. Aall (Washington, DC: USIP Press, 2001).
6. Barry Buzan and Ole Wæver, *Regions and Powers: The Structure of International Security* (Cambridge: Cambridge University Press, 2003).
7. For further discussion, see Amitav Acharya, "The Emerging Regional Architecture of World Politics."

8. On the origins and spread of cooperative security theory, see Amitav Acharya, "How Ideas Spread: Whose Norms Matter? Norm Localization and Institutional Change in Asian Regionalism," *International Organization* 58, no. 2 (2004): 239–275.
9. When Buzan first proposed the idea of a regional security complex in 1983, it designated a relationship of intense rivalry (e.g. India–Pakistan; the Arab countries–Israel, North and South Korea) and excluded cooperative relationships. Barry Buzan, "A Framework for Regional Security Analysis," in *South Asian Insecurity and the Great Powers*, ed. Barry Buzan and Gowher Rizvi (London: Croom Helm, 1986), 8. In the new formulation, regional security complexes may vary from anarchy ("conflict formations") to "security communities," the latter being cases where war has been rendered unthinkable.
10. Despite the greater economic weakness of the Pyongyang regime, this is as true of Iran as of North Korea. As Vali Nasr of the Naval Postgraduate School has said: "what matters to the Iranians essentially is regime survival. More than the nuclear issue, they want to make sure that there would not be either a military or a political push to topple the regime in Tehran. And they're going to bargain very hard with the Europeans and the Americans to get guarantees about the regime survival, both with regard to military action against Iran as well as supporting a democratic movement within Iran before they're going to make any concessions about the nuclear weapons issue." See "U.S. Agrees to Iran Incentives," PBS NewsHour with Jim Lehrer Transcript, 11 March 2005; available at ⟨http://www.pbs.org/newshour/bb/middle_east/jan-june05/iran_3-11.html⟩ (accessed 14 November 2008).
11. "Can We Prevent Nuclear Iran?" *Ynet News.com*, 11 May 2006. As Hassan Zekrgoo puts it, "there is talk on a daily basis about how the country is a superpower." Hassan Zekrgoo, "North Korean Nuclear Crisis: A Model for Iran?" *Aljazeera Magazine*, 1 January 2008; available at ⟨http://www.aljazeera.com/news/newsfull.php?newid=74060⟩ (accessed 14 November 2008).
12. Samuel Huntington, "The Clash of Civilizations?" *Foreign Affairs* 72, no. 3 (1993): 22–49.
13. Amin Saikal, "Setting the World of Islam Alight," *The Age* (Melbourne), 14 October 2005; available at ⟨http://www.theage.com.au/news/opinion/setting-the-world-of-islam-alight/2005/10/13/1128796647831.html⟩ (accessed 14 November 2008).
14. On the Six-Party Talks, see Carin Zissis, "The Six-Party Talks on North Korea's Nuclear Program," Council on Foreign Relations Backgrounder, 21 June 2007, updated 21 October 2008, available at ⟨http://www.cfr.org/publication/13593/⟩ (accessed 14 November 2008). China's position is well summed up here: "Beijing serves as Pyongyang's most long-standing ally and main trade partner, and has used its influence with the Kim regime to bring North Korea to the Six-Party negotiating table. China's ability to play such a role in the talks boosts its relations with Washington. Like South Korea, China fears a rush of refugees across its border and has provided North Korea with energy and food assistance. Beijing has been resistant to implementing stringent UN resolutions imposing sanctions against Pyongyang. North Korea also serves as a buffer zone between China and U.S. troops in South Korea."
15. "US Willing to Stick to Six-Party Talks: China's FM Spokesman," *People's Daily Online*, 28 April 2005; available at ⟨http://english.peopledaily.com.cn/200504/28/eng20050428_183118.html⟩ (accessed 14 November 2008).
16. ASEAN, "Regional Security Forum to Focus on North Korea, Terrorism," 27 June 2004; available at ⟨http://www.aseansec.org/afp/55.htm⟩ (accessed 14 November 2008).
17. Joseph E. DeTrani, Special Envoy for Six-Party Talks, "Six-Party Talks and China's Role as an Intermediary in the Process," Remarks to U.S.-China Economic Security Review Commission, Washington, DC, 10 March 2005; available at ⟨http://www.state.gov/p/eap/rls/rm/2005/43247.htm⟩ (accessed 14 November 2008).

18. The actual extent of Iran's breach of the NPT had been a matter of some controversy in the past. "Experts say Iran violated the NPT by introducing nuclear material into its centrifuges before it had declared them to the IAEA, which later found samples of enriched uranium there. Iran tried to shift blame to Pakistan, the alleged source of the centrifuges. The IAEA is unable to prove or disprove this claim, because Pakistan – not a signatory of the NPT – does not allow international inspectors access to its nuclear facilities." Esther Pan, "Iran: Curtailing the Nuclear Program," Council on Foreign Relations Backgrounder, 13 May 2004; available at ⟨http://www.cfr.org/publication/7821/iran.html⟩ (accessed 14 November 2008).
19. Gary Sick, a senior Jimmy Carter administration official, contends that the United States has shifted its "redlines" for Iran, first trying to prevent it from acquiring nuclear technology, then trying to prevent it from nuclear reactors, and now trying to prevent it from developing uranium enrichment capacity. "Iran's Strategic Concerns and U.S. Interests," Transcript, Middle East Policy Council Forums, Washington, DC, 18 January 2008.
20. "On China's Aid to North Korea and Sanctions," 9 July 2003; available at ⟨http://www.parapundit.com/archives/001464.html⟩ (accessed 14 November 2008); "S. Korea Suspends North Food Aid," *BBC News*, 7 July 2006; available at ⟨http://news.bbc.co.uk/go/pr/fr/-/1/hi/world/asia-pacific/5156464.stm⟩ (accessed 14 November 2008); "South Korea's Aid to North Korea Reaches New Record," Korean Information Service, 4 December 2006; available at ⟨http://www.reliefweb.int/rw/RWB.NSF/db900SID/KHII-6W69MK?OpenDocument⟩ (accessed 14 November 2008).
21. US Department of State, "North Korea and Iran: An Administration Perspective," Remarks at National Defense University Symposium by Patricia McNerney, Principal Deputy Assistant Secretary, International Security and Nonproliferation, Washington, DC, 8 May 2008; available at ⟨http://www.state.gov/t/isn/rls/rm/104548.htm⟩ (accessed 14 November 2008).
22. Joseph Curl, "Bush Hails Joint Effort on N. Korea; Role of 'Neighborhood' Vital in Nuke Standoff," *Washington Times*, 23 October 2003; available at ⟨http://goliath.ecnext.com/coms2/gi_0199-3384163/Bush-hails-joint-effort-on.html⟩ (accessed 14 November 2008).
23. Amitav Acharya and Alastair Iain Johnston, eds, *Crafting Cooperation: Regional International Institutions in Comparative Perspective* (Cambridge: Cambridge University Press, 2007); Amitav Acharya, "Protecting Sovereignty in an Age of Regionalism," ECSSR 11th Annual Conference, "Current Transformations and Their Potential Role in Realizing Change in the Arab World," 12–14 March 2006, Abu Dhabi, United Arab Emirates, organized by the Emirates Center for Strategic Studies & Research (ECSSR), United Arab Emirates.
24. Ghanim Alnajjar, "The GCC and Iraq," *Middle East Policy*, 10 January 2000; David Priess, "The Gulf Cooperation Council: Prospects for Expansion," *Middle East Policy*, 1 January 1998.
25. Amitav Acharya, "So Similar, Yet So Different," *Straits Times* (Singapore), 4 January 2006.
26. Amitav Acharya, *The Gulf Cooperation Council and Security: Dilemmas of Dependence 1981–88* (London: Gulf Centre for Strategic Studies, 1989); Amitav Acharya, "Gulf States' Efforts to Ensure Collective Security," *Pacific Defence Reporter* 12, no. 10 (1986): 11–13.
27. Such proposals have already been made and discussed. See, for example, Joseph McMillan, Richard Sokolsky, and Andrew C. Winner, "Toward a New Regional Security Architecture," *Washington Quarterly* 26, no. 3 (2003): 161–175; Amitav Acharya, "Managing Challenges to Sovereignty in an Era of Regionalism: Asia and the Arab World," in *Current Transformations and Their Potential Role in Realizing Change in*

the Arab World (Abu Dhabi: Emirates Center for Strategic Studies and Research, 2007). See also the two reports issued by the Stanley Foundation: "The Future of Persian Gulf Security: Alternatives for the 21st Century," 3–5 September 2005, and "The United States, Iran, and Saudi Arabia: Necessary Steps Toward a New Gulf Security Order," *Policy Dialogue Brief*, 20–22 October 2005 (Warrenton, VA: The Stanley Foundation).

28. Savita Pande, "Nuclear Weapon-Free Zone in the Middle East," *Strategic Analysis* (New Delhi), 22, no. 9 (1998).

29. "Arab Gulf Mulls Nuclear Weapons-Free Zone, Asking Iran to Join," *China Daily*, 19 December 2005; available at ⟨http://www.chinadaily.com.cn/english/doc/2005-12/19/content_504602.htm⟩ (accessed 14 November 2008).

30. General Debate on All Disarmament and International Security Items, General Assembly, Fiftieth session, First Committee, 11th meeting, 26 October 1995, New York, UN document A/C.1/50/PV.11; available at ⟨http://daccessdds.un.org/doc/UNDOC/GEN/N95/864/50/PDF/N9586450.pdf?OpenElement⟩ (accessed 14 November 2008).

31. "Iran and Nuclear Proliferation," transcript of Council on Foreign Relations conference call discussion on Iran, 13 September 2005, Federal News Service; available at ⟨www.cfr.org/publication/8877/iran_and_nuclear_proliferation_rush_transcript_federal_news_service_inc.html⟩ (accessed 14 November 2008).

32. As Sharam Chubin, director of research at the Geneva Center for Security Policy, argues: "Iran considers itself not a rogue state. It doesn't consider itself Iraq, it's not like North Korea, it's not Libya, it's not been under U.N. sanction. The image depicted at home is that all this stuff about rogue states and axis of evil is an American political ploy because they dislike the independence of the Islamic Republic." Quoted in "Iran Threatens to Limit Co-operation with IAEA," Voice of America News Report by Marlene Smith, 6 September 2004; available at ⟨http://www.globalsecurity.org/wmd/library/news/iran/2004/iran-040919-34f1a038.htm⟩ (accessed 14 November 2008). Iran's sense of national identity as a civilization and its regional ambitions are recognized by India and China, but seldom by Western policy-makers. Insulting Iran's leaders, who have more domestic democratic legitimacy than the leaders of the Soviet Union had during the Cold War, may be good for domestic audiences in the United States but it does not help the cause of Iran's nuclear reversal. Recognizing Iran's legitimate security interests and its desire to be treated as a regional power that is to be consulted on major initiatives about regional security would be crucial to nuclear negotiations with Iran.

33. "U.S. Attends Iran-EU Talks," *International Herald Tribune*, 19 July 2008.

34. Jim Muir, "Obama Quashes Iran's Hopes for Change," *BBC News*, 9 November 2008; available at ⟨http://news.bbc.co.uk/1/hi/world/americas/us_elections_2008/7718603.stm⟩ (accessed 4 December 2008).

13
NPT regime change: Has the good become the enemy of the best?

Ramesh Thakur

Since the end of the Cold War, the risk of total nuclear war between the major powers has diminished. Yet the prospect of nuclear weapons being used is more plausible. There were two great pillars of the normative edifice for containing the nuclear horror: the doctrines of strategic deterrence, which prevented their use among those who had nuclear weapons; and the non-proliferation regime, centered on the Nuclear Non-Proliferation Treaty (NPT), which both outlawed their spread to others and imposed a legal obligation on the nuclear weapons states (NWS) to eliminate their own nuclear arsenals through negotiations – their only explicit multilateral disarmament commitment. The NPT was signed in 1968 and came into force in 1970 as the centerpiece of the global non-proliferation regime that codified the international political norm of non-nuclear-weapons status.[1] It tries to curb proliferation by a mix of incentives and disincentives. In return for intrusive end-use control over imported nuclear and nuclear-related technology and material, non-NWS were granted access to nuclear technology, components, and material on a most-favored-nation basis.

The NPT regime also includes a number of treaties restricting nuclear testing. The Partial Test Ban Treaty (1963) outlawed atmospheric, space, and underwater nuclear testing. The Threshold Test Ban Treaty (1974) outlawed underground tests of more than 150 kilotons yield. The elusive goal of a total ban on nuclear testing was seemingly realized in 1996 with the endorsement by the General Assembly of the Comprehensive Nuclear-Test-Ban Treaty (CTBT). But, in part owing to the rigid

The United Nations and nuclear orders, Boulden, Thakur and Weiss (eds), United Nations University Press, 2009, ISBN 978-92-808-1167-4

entry-into-force provisions of the CTBT,[2] and in part owing to changed administrations in Washington and the altered climate of arms control after the attacks of 11 September 2001, the CTBT is unlikely to enter into force in the foreseeable future.

Today both pillars are at risk of crumbling. Some commentators fear that arms control is at an impasse and disarmament could be reversed. Tellingly, there are no ongoing discussions between the nuclear powers for reducing their nuclear stockpiles still further, nor the intensity of concerns and demands from non-nuclear states from earlier decades. Treaties already negotiated and signed could unravel through non-ratification or breakouts. The testing of nuclear weapons could be resumed. Revelations of a previously unsuspected underground nuclear bazaar run by Abdul Qadeer Khan, the "father" of Pakistan's bomb, came as quite a shock. Kofi Annan noted in 2005 that the NPT "faces a crisis of confidence and compliance born of a growing strain on verification and enforcement."[3] Revelations that, on 29 August 2007, a B-52 bomber carrying six air-launched cruise missiles armed with nuclear warheads had made an unauthorized flight from North Dakota to Louisiana did nothing to diminish the sense of crisis afflicting the nuclear weapons agenda.[4] A quartet of American national security heavyweights caution: "The accelerating spread of nuclear weapons, nuclear know-how and nuclear material has brought us to a nuclear tipping point."[5]

The lengthening list of proliferation-sensitive concerns includes North Korea's weaponized nuclear capability and its nuclear test of 2006;[6] worries expressed by the International Atomic Energy Agency (IAEA) about Iran's nuclear program;[7] reports that Saudi Arabia might be contemplating an off-the-shelf purchase of nuclear weapons;[8] evidence of mild misdeeds by South Korea,[9] Taiwan,[10] and Egypt;[11] apprehensions about a new uranium enrichment plant that would give Brazil a nuclear breakout capability;[12] disappointment at the under-funding of the Nunn–Lugar Cooperative Threat Reduction program; dismay at Russia's retreat in the 1990s from its historical commitment to a no-first-use policy; anxieties about the 27,000 nuclear warheads (of which around 10,000 are operational and the rest are spares, in active and inactive storage, or slated for dismantlement) with a total yield of 5,000 megatons held by the five nuclear powers (with just Russia and the United States accounting for more than 26,000 warheads); fears that Washington is lowering the threshold of normative barriers to the use of a new generation of nuclear weapons; evidence of an extensive multinational nuclear black market, which demonstrated the inadequacy of the existing export controls system; and the prospect of terrorists acquiring nuclear weapons. Rounding out this list of concerns, Pakistan is often dubbed the most dangerous place on earth because of the lethal nexus of an unstable military dictatorship, Islamist groups bitterly hostile to the West, terrorists, and nuclear weapons.[13] These anxieties are hardly allayed by multilateral action. Washington announced its commitment to negotiate a legally binding fissile material cut-off treaty, but without verification provisions. Space talks remain blocked. The Six-Party Talks make but fitful progress in keeping North Korea from establishing a fully functioning nuclear weapons program. Iran sends conflicting messages on compliance with NPT commitments and its pursuit of a nuclear energy program for peaceful purposes. For four decades, the world has lived with five (the United Kingdom, China, France, Russia, and the United States), followed by eight (Israel, India, and Pakistan) and then nine (North Korea), nuclear powers. Can we live with a tenth, if that be Iran?

The disquieting trend of a widening circle of NPT-licit, NPT-illicit, and extra-NPT nuclear weapons powers in turn has a self-generating effect in drawing other countries into the game of nuclear brinkmanship. Concerns persist about the potential leakage of "loose nukes" from Russia to terrorists. Worst-case scenarios see terrorists using nuclear or radiological weapons to kill hundreds of thousands of people. As far as we know, however, no terrorist group has the competence to build nuclear weapons. Nor is there any evidence so far to suggest that nuclear weapons have been transferred to terrorist organizations. The only good news stories are that Libya walked away from that path in December 2003,[14] Iraq does not have nuclear weapons, and North Korea shut down its plutonium production in July 2007 under international inspection.[15]

Still, the global governance mechanisms for non-proliferation and disarmament are in a sorry state. The Conference on Disarmament (CD) has been immobilized, unable even to agree on an agenda for a decade. In a speech on 23 January 2008, Secretary-General Ban Ki-moon could only declare helplessly that he was "deeply troubled" by the CD's "impasse over priorities" and warned that it was "in danger of losing its way."[16] The UN reform summit in 2005 failed to agree on a single sentence on the hot subject. Reliance on the Security Council as the forum of choice for enforcing compliance is deeply problematical, since the five permanent members (P-5) are the five NPT-licit nuclear powers (N-5), the Council is severely unrepresentative and unaccountable, and the P-5/N-5 have been amongst the most arms-exporting and war-prone countries since 1945.

The United Nations' strengths and assets in arms control and disarmament are research, advocacy, norm-building, and networking. It has established procedures and forums for sustaining annual debates and discourses, provides a rare channel for non-nuclear countries to network with one another and exert pressure on nuclear holdouts, tries to coordinate global regimes and regional initiatives, and undertakes analytical, empirical, and problem-solving research. The organization's weaknesses are antiquated procedures that are easily captured by recalcitrant holdouts to block any initiative, meager resources devoted to what is said to be one of the gravest threats to international security, and the most powerful enforcers of peace and security being the worst offenders in terms of military arsenals and sales as well as engagements in armed conflicts. Although consciousness of the risks of nuclear weapons falling into the hands of terrorists, militant fanatics, and other non-state groups has grown enormously, the collective memories of the horrors of Hiroshima and Nagasaki have begun to fade in the world beyond Japan (where the memory remains intensely painful and powerful), lowering the normative barriers to the acquisition and use of nuclear weapons. In January 2007, the doomsday clock of the *Bulletin of the Atomic Scientists* was set at 11.55 p.m. – the closest to doomsday since the end of the Cold War – where it remains today.

The rising anxieties about nuclear weapons are rooted in two major and parallel developments: the so-called renaissance of nuclear power and a resurgence of old-fashioned national security threats that supposedly had ebbed with the end of the Cold War. Between them, the developments highlight how all three legs of the NPT's triangular linkage – nuclear power for civilian use, nuclear non-proliferation, and nuclear disarmament – are straining the regime. The widening circle of NPT-licit, extra-NPT, and NPT-noncompliant nuclear weapons powers indicates the extent to which the contradictions and tensions inherent to the NPT have ripened and the regime's weaknesses have become increasingly apparent. When we factor in also the regime's many weaknesses and anomalies, we begin to understand why it seems to be so close to breaking point. Can it be repaired and continue to form the centerpiece of global nuclear arms control policy? Or is it destined to go the way of Humpty Dumpty, in which case would it be better to abandon the NPT and look to a new nuclear weapons convention as the chief cure for the world's nuclear ailment?

This chapter begins by reviewing the two sets of concerns that form the roots of growing nuclear anxieties. It then highlights the weaknesses, deficiencies, and anomalies of the NPT before postulating the need to move beyond the sclerotic regime.[17]

A nuclear renaissance?

According to the International Energy Agency (IEA), the world's energy consumption will increase, based on current trends and policies, by more than 50 percent from 2005 to 2030, with just China and India accounting for 45 percent of the extra growth in demand.[18] Fluctuations in the price of oil in 2008 indicate that the IEA may have seriously underestimated the speed with which the world will experience a supply-side crunch and abrupt escalation in oil prices. Hence the interest of governments in increasing their exposure to nuclear energy in their total energy portfolio. After the well-publicized accidents at Three Mile Island (USA, 1979) and Chernobyl (Ukraine, but at the time the former Soviet Union, 1986), public and political opposition to nuclear power was so strong that many existing reactor plants were shut down, plans for new ones were cancelled, and virtually no new reactor was built over the last decade. Indeed, in the United States no new reactors have been built in three decades. With the escalating price of oil, caused by a spike in demand from booming major economies such as China and India and disruptions to supply because of conflicts in the Middle East, the economics of even risk-discounted nuclear power has changed. With the accelerating threat of global warming caused by greenhouse gas emissions, the balance of public anxiety between energy sourced in nuclear power and coal and fossil fuel has changed dramatically. Combined with technological developments, the changed financial and environmental equations have also altered the politics of constructing and operating nuclear power reactors.[19]

The net result is plans for building several new reactors in Asia, Australia, the Middle East, and even Europe to add to the 435 reactors in 30 countries that are providing 15 percent of the world's total electricity at present. According to the latest forecast of the International Atomic Energy Agency (IAEA), this particular renaissance is being led by Asia, with 18 of the 31 planned new reactors to be located there.[20] Nuclear power accounts for 2 and 3 percent, respectively, of China's and India's electricity at present, but it will jump by a factor of five and eight respectively by 2022. Whereas the spike in their demand is a function of booming economic growth and population, in Japan and South Korea interest in nuclear power arises from a lack of indigenous oil and gas resources and the desire for energy security and reducing greenhouse gas emissions. Other Asian countries planning or considering nuclear power reactors are Indonesia, Malaysia, Pakistan, Thailand, and Vietnam.

At the same time, the long lead times and high capital costs for nuclear construction mean that governments want to be assured that nuclear energy and plants are safe, secure, reliable, and cost-effective. All this throws up several clusters of concern:[21]
- How do we ensure that the plants are operated with complete safety, so that the chances of accidents are minimized, and mechanisms and procedures are put in place so that accidents are discovered immediately,

their effects are mitigated, and firewalls are constructed to prevent wider damage?
- How do we secure the plants against theft and leakage of weapons-sensitive material, skills, and knowledge? After all, the now notorious Abdul Qadeer Khan simply stole designs and material from places in the West he was working in, then returned to Pakistan and established a very effective global nuclear arms bazaar.[22]
- How do we protect civilian use of nuclear power from being employed for weapons-related purposes?
- How do we establish multinational regimes for the assurance of fuel supply, the management of spent fuel, the disposal of radioactive wastes, and the decommissioning of old reactors?

These concerns relate not just to the countries in which the reactors are located, but also to the international trade in nuclear material, skills, and equipment. As Mohamed ElBaradei – the IAEA director general and as such the person with the highest international authority on the subject – has noted: "Nuclear components designed in one country could be manufactured in another, shipped through a third, and assembled in a fourth for use in a fifth."[23]

Security threats

We would be foolish to believe that the renaissance of nuclear power is explained fully and solely by the interest in nuclear energy for civilian uses. Nuclear weapons can be sought for one or more of six reasons:[24] deterrence of enemy attack; defense against attack; compellence of the enemy to one's preferred course of action; leveraging adversary and great power behavior;[25] status; and emulation. Specific causes of proliferation are many, diverse, and usually rooted in a local security complex. On the supply side, a major challenge is the globalization of the arms industry, the flooding of the global arms market, and a resulting loosening of supplier constraints. Under modern conditions of globalized trade, instantaneous and voluminous electronic information exchanges, interlinked financial systems, and the sheer diversity of technology, the control of access to nuclear weapons technology and material has grown vastly more complex and challenging.

Proliferation refers to the dispersion of weapons, capabilities, and technologies. There are eight categories of proliferation-sensitive actors:
- Vertically proliferating NWS: those that increased their nuclear stockpiles and upgraded their nuclear lethality from inside the NPT regime, and by doing so undermined the non-proliferation regime and institutionalized international nuclear "apartheid."

- NPT-irresponsible NWS: those that export nuclear-missile materials, technology, and expertise in violation of international treaties, regimes, and commitments.
- Fragmenting NWS, or NPT splinters: when the old Soviet Union broke up, for instance, we faced the prospect of an additional three NWS (Belarus, Kazakhstan, Ukraine). Fortunately, they were persuaded to forgo the nuclear option.
- NPT cheats: those that have signed the NPT but are engaged in activities in violation of their obligations.
- Threshold NWS: those that do not claim possession of nuclear weapons, have not forsworn the nuclear weapons option, produce significant amounts of nuclear material or equipment, and refuse to accept international control over their material and equipment. With India and Pakistan coming out of the nuclear closet in 1998, and few left to deny Israel's nuclear weapons capability, the threshold status is in effect obsolete.
- Nuclear terrorists: it defies credulity that nuclear weapons and materials can be kept secure in government inventories and never be obtained by any terrorist group. Although a government's nuclear capability can be seized and destroyed, it is impossible to capture or kill every single terrorist and his/her last piece of dynamite, Semtex, or timing mechanism.
- "Virtual" NWS: the flow of enabling technologies, material, and expertise in the nuclear power industry can be used, through strategic prepositioning of materials and personnel, to build a "surge" capacity to upgrade to nuclear weapons within the time-frame of a crisis degenerating into conflict. Thus Ichiro Ozawa of Japan's Liberal Party warned China not to forget that Japan could easily make 3,000–4,000 nuclear weapons.[26]
- Missile proliferators: missiles are an acutely destabilizing form of weaponry because little defense is available against them. Armed with biological, chemical, or nuclear warheads, they can be lethal.

The challenge on the international security front is thus fourfold. First, the five NPT-licit nuclear powers have simply disregarded their NPT Article VI obligation to disarm. China continues to modernize its arsenal and in January 2007 demonstrated its space-war capabilities by shooting down a satellite in a controlled test. The United States has retreated from several arms control and disarmament agreements, including the Anti-Ballistic Missile, Nuclear Non-Proliferation (the 2005 Review Conference outcome documents), and Comprehensive Nuclear-Test-Ban treaties. It is asserting the right to develop new generations of earth-penetrating, bunker-busting nuclear weapons and battlefield "mini-nukes" and to refine the doctrines underpinning the deployment and possible use of nuclear weapons. With US plans to install a new missile shield along Russia's borders, Moscow has warned of a new Cuban-type missile crisis. The United Kingdom has decided to upgrade its Trident strategic nuclear force to give it nuclear-weapons capability beyond 2020. The new nuclear doctrines indicate that retention and expanded use of these weapons are being contemplated for decades to come. To would-be proliferators the lesson is clear: nuclear weapons are indispensable in today's world and becoming more useful, not less, for dealing with tomorrow's threats.

Second, three states lie outside the NPT and have gone down the weapons path: India, Israel, and Pakistan. Israel, even though it is not an NPT signatory, will not openly admit to its nuclear weapons stockpiles. India and Pakistan have been accepted, more or less, as de facto nuclear weapons powers. The stop-start India–US civil nuclear cooperation deal proved extremely contentious. Supporters argue that it serves the strategic goals of both countries while also advancing the global non-proliferation agenda more realistically than any conceivable alternative. Yet it caused despondency among the arms control community for its breach of the NPT regime even as it made some Indians uncomfortable for drawing India into the US strategic embrace and others for constricting India's future nuclear options.[27] The constitutional and political crisis in Pakistan in 2007–2008 spread alarm in many sectors about how safe and secure its nuclear arsenal was from Islamists within and jihadists outside the military.

Third, the NPT is an intergovernmental agreement and therefore does not cover non-state groups, including terrorists, who might be pursuing nuclear weapons. It is not at all clear how the international normative architecture can be extended to cover them on legislative, operational, and compliance dimensions.

And, fourth, some NPT members may be trying to cheat on their non-proliferation obligations and pursuing the weapons option through stealth. Because of the robust international norm against nuclear weapons and the legal obligations of the NPT, which has been signed by all countries other than India, Israel, and Pakistan, countries planning to cross the line from civilian to weapons programs do so clandestinely.

For example, few believe Iran's professions of peaceful intent in its uranium enrichment drive. Yet the consequences of using military force to try to stop the drive may be worse than learning to live with the new reality. For far too many, the drumbeats of warnings and threats being sounded in Washington on Iran – US President George W. Bush has even spoken of World War III – brought back memories of 2002–2003. During the US presidential primary campaign, Hillary Clinton threatened to "obliterate" Iran if it dared to attack Israel with nuclear weapons.[28] This is an all too familiar story. Most did not like the ending the first time around in Iraq and are unlikely to like it any better the next time. In the same vein, there is the familiar discrepancy between the assessments of the IAEA and of some Western countries regarding the gravity and urgency of the threat of a nuclearized Iran.

NPT weaknesses and deficiencies

Thus there are several major gaps in the arms control and disarmament regime:[29]
- Lack of NPT universality
- Continuing existence of stockpiles of nuclear weapons
- Lack of a nuclear weapons convention outlawing the possession and use of nuclear weapons by all actors
- Lack of verification machinery and compliance mechanisms for the disarmament obligations (Article VI) of the NPT
- Lack of a credible and binding inspections regime for non-proliferation
- Lack of agreed criteria to assess proliferation threats
- Lack of a basis in international law to enforce non-proliferation norms for states outside the treaty regimes
- Inapplicability of norms and regimes to non-state actors

Some NPT weaknesses are not just intrinsic but were intentional. For example, the wording of Articles I and II deliberately permits the NWS to transfer nuclear weapons to other countries (Cold War allies at the time) – that is, engage in geographical proliferation – as long as control of the weapons remains in NWS hands. The subsequent popularity of regional nuclear-weapon-free zones owed much to the desire to plug this loophole. Such zones cover virtually the entire southern hemisphere but are conspicuously scarce north of the equator.[30] The desire to marry two possibly incompatible goals – President Dwight Eisenhower's vision of "atoms for peace" and non-proliferation – produced the odd juxtaposition of Articles III and IV, and opened the door for developments in North Korea and Iran. For nuclear energy for peaceful purposes can be pursued legitimately to the point of being a screwdriver away from a weapons capability.

Other NPT weaknesses became apparent with the benefit of hindsight. By failing to include clearly timetabled, legally binding, verifiable, and enforceable disarmament commitments, it temporarily legitimized the nuclear arsenals of the N-5. The imbalance of reporting, verification, and compliance mechanisms between non-proliferation and disarmament in the NPT regime has also over time served seriously to erode the legitimacy of this centerpiece of the global arms control effort. By relying on the promise of signatories to use nuclear materials, facilities, and technology for peaceful purposes only, it empowered them to operate dangerously close to a nuclear weapons capability. It proscribed non-nuclear states from acquiring nuclear weapons, but failed to design a strategy for dealing with non-signatory states parties. It permits withdrawals much too easily: North Korea joined the NPT in 1985, but in January 2003 announced its intention to withdraw. Because there is no standing agency or secretariat, the NPT depends on five-year Review Conferences for resolving implementation problems. These operate by the consensus rule, which does not make for decisive resolution of contentious issues. Verification and enforcement are one step removed to the extent that the IAEA acts as a buffer between the NPT and the Security Council.

The Iraq experience shows the enormous difficulty of ensuring compliance with international norms and commitments, even with respect to one of the world's most odious regimes pursuing the world's most destructive weapons.[31] The failure to find WMD since the war cannot eradicate the known historical record of Saddam Hussein's past pursuit of them, or his will to use them against outsiders as well as Iraqis. Moreover, there is an inherent tension between the IAEA's mandate for promoting peaceful nuclear energy use and the overall strategic goal of non-proliferation. This is best illustrated by the fact that India and Pakistan, which are outside the NPT regime, are on the IAEA board of governors. It is also increasingly a problem because more and more of nuclear technology, materials, and equipment are dual use. When the chief distinction between peaceful and offensive use rests on intent, there is a problem.

Strengthening treaty regimes requires national legislation and measures on criminalization of proliferation activities, effective protection of proliferation-sensitive personnel, materials, and equipment, control and accounting systems for monitoring materials and stocks, and regulation and surveillance of dual-use transfers. The NPT could be strengthened by making the IAEA Additional Protocol mandatory for all states parties, toughening up or even eliminating the exit clause, and making clear that withdrawal from the NPT will be treated as a threat to peace and security.[32] But these measures cannot be undertaken without also addressing gaps on the disarmament side of the NPT and reform of the composition and procedures of the Security Council. A body that is itself seen as increasingly illegitimate by many members of the international community will have difficulty enforcing global norms in the name of that very same community.

The IAEA's reluctance to cite Iran for non-compliance with the NPT may indicate weaknesses in the treaty structure and procedures that reflect the world of 1968 rather than 2008. Moreover, Tehran joins Pyongyang in throwing down the gauntlet, yet again, to a basic inconsistency in our definition of the problem. Is it the very destructiveness of nuclear weapons that somehow makes them so evil that they should be proscribed for all, including the N-5? Or is the problem rogue states, whose behavior is so bad that they cannot be trusted with weapons that are tolerable, if not desirable, in more mature and responsible hands?

NPT anomalies

The many internal inconsistencies and tensions notwithstanding, the NPT has been the symbol of the dominant arms control, disarmament, and non-proliferation paradigm. Over the course of four decades, however, six significant anomalies have accumulated and now weigh it down close to the point of rupture.

First, the definition of a nuclear weapons state is chronological – a country that manufactured and exploded a nuclear device before 1 January 1967. India, Pakistan, Israel, North Korea – even Iran – could test, deploy, and even use nuclear weapons, but cannot be described as nuclear powers. Conversely, the United Kingdom and France could dismantle their nuclear edifice and destroy their nuclear arsenals, but would still count as nuclear powers. This is an Alice-in-Wonderland approach to affairs of deadly seriousness. But can the NPT definition be opened up for revision through a formal amendment of the treaty, with all the unpredictable consequences?[33]

Second, even as the threat from non-state actors has grown frighteningly real, multilateral treaties such as the NPT can regulate and monitor the activities only of states. A. Q. Khan's underground nuclear bazaar that merrily sold nuclear technology, components, and weapons designs to Iran, Libya, and North Korea showed how porous is the border between private and state rogue actors. Protestations of innocence by the Pakistan government are simply not credible. It was either actively complicit in, connived in and facilitated, or at the very least knew about and tolerated the existence and activities of the network. The "hero of the nation" was placed under a comfortable version of house arrest by his "friend" General Pervez Musharraf. Moreover, it is at the very least arguable that the Khan network still exists and is active, and that Pakistan's nuclear weapons are not safe.[34] A robust and credible normative architecture to control the actions of terrorist groups that can acquire and use nuclear weapons must be developed outside the NPT.

The problem of non-parties and non-state actors could be taken care of by accepting the suggestion that the fruitless search for universal membership should be replaced by "universal compliance" with the terms of arms control regimes. The Carnegie Endowment for International Peace lists a set of six obligations to make this a reality: making non-proliferation irreversible; devaluing the political and military currency of nuclear weapons, including the steady, verified dismantlement of nuclear arsenals; securing all nuclear materials through robust standards for monitoring and accounting for fissile materials in any form; enforceable prohibitions against efforts by individuals, corporations, and states to assist others in secretly acquiring the technology, material, and know-how for nuclear weapons; a commitment to conflict resolution; and persuading India, Israel, and Pakistan to accept the same non-proliferation obligations as the NWS signatories to the NPT.[35]

Third, North Korea's open defiance, spread over many years, shows that decades after a problem arises we still cannot agree on an appropriate response inside the NPT framework. It becomes increasingly difficult to de-fang tyrants of nuclear weapons the day after they acquire them. The United Nations seems incapable of doing so the day before. If international institutions cannot cope, states will try to do so themselves, either unilaterally or in company with like-minded allies. If prevention is strategically necessary and morally justified but legally not permitted, then the existing framework of laws and rules – not preventive military action – is defective. In other words, where for decades countries such as India argued that the NPT, although legal, was illegitimate because of the nuclear apartheid built into it, can the "good cops" now turn the legality–legitimacy argument on its head?

The fourth anomaly is lumping biological, chemical, and nuclear weapons in one conceptual and policy basket. They differ in their technical features, in the ease with they can be acquired and developed, and in their capacity to cause mass destruction. Treating them as one weapons category can distort analysis and produce flawed responses. There is also the danger of mission creep. Justifying nuclear weapons as a useful tool in countering biological and chemical weapons may be one step too far. If nuclear weapons are accepted as having a role to counter biochemical warfare, then how can we deny a nuclear weapons capability to Iran, which actually suffered chemical weapons attacks from Saddam Hussein?

Fifth, not a single country that had nuclear weapons when the NPT was signed in 1968 has given them up. Their behavior fuels the politics of grievance and resentment. Can the country with the world's most powerful nuclear weapons rightfully use military force to prevent their acquisition by others? From where do the leaders of nuclear-armed France and the United Kingdom derive the moral authority to declare that a nuclear Iran is unacceptable and must be stopped by force if necessary?

The final anomaly concerns the central doctrine underpinning the contemporary Westphalian system, which holds that sovereign states are equal in status and legitimacy. In reality, states are not of equal worth and significance, either militarily, economically, politically, or morally. It seems unlikely that, in the eyes of most people and countries, nuclear weapons in the hands of the United Kingdom and North Korea are equally dangerous.[36] This is why President George W. Bush warned of the threat of the world's most destructive weapons falling into the hands of the world's worst regimes: it is the conjunction of the two that is especially dangerous. Granted, the Iraq war has been a disaster richly foretold. But was there any moral equivalence between Saddam Hussein, on the one hand, and George W. Bush, Tony Blair, and John Howard – leaders of the three countries that waged the war – on the other hand?

Similarly, how reasonable or logical is it to lump India, Iran, Israel, North Korea, and Pakistan together without discriminating between their respective records, yet to continue to distinguish between non-proliferation and disarmament? Even with regard to the latter, it is already a decade since India and Pakistan gate-crashed into the nuclear club. Any effort to roll back their nuclear weapons capability amounts to nuclear disarmament, not non-proliferation. Analyzing the problem from within the conceptual lens of non-proliferation is simply inappropriate. The logical policy implication is either to condemn nuclear weapons for everyone, or to distinguish bad and rogue behavior from responsible behavior and to oppose regimes, not the weapons. But that threatens the core assumption of the NPT, that nuclear weapons are immoral for anyone. This has been the central bone of contention between the proponents and opponents of the India–US civil nuclear cooperation deal: that it acknowledges India's responsible nuclear stewardship or that it threatens the core integrity of the NPT.

Nuclear proliferation or nuclear abolition, the NPT is history

In practice, we face four nuclear choices: the status quo, proliferation, nuclear rearmament, or abolition.[37] The tests by India, Pakistan, and North Korea confirmed the folly of believing – in defiance of common sense, logic, and history – that a self-selecting group of five powers could indefinitely retain their monopoly on the world's most destructive weaponry.

It truly is remarkable how those who worship at the altar of nuclear weapons threaten to excommunicate for heresy others wishing to join their sect. The first country to engage in nuclear breakout in 1998 – India – deplored North Korea's test in 2006 as a threat to regional peace and stability and as highlighting the dangers of clandestine proliferation.

Thus did India, quickly followed by Pakistan, join the ranks of the nuclear powers preaching nuclear abstinence for others while engaged in consenting deterrence themselves. Other members of the nuclear club condemned North Korea's test as "brazen," "grave," "provocative," "intolerable," etc. That test and Iran's ongoing defiance are symptoms, not the cause, of the NPT being a broken reed. Maybe it is time to return with some seriousness and urgency to the dream of a nuclear-weapon-free world.

In a major foreign policy speech at DePaul University in Chicago on 2 October 2007, Democratic presidential hopeful Senator Barack Obama declared (and repeated in his Berlin speech on 24 July 2008 as the presumptive Democratic nominee): "America seeks a world in which there are no nuclear weapons." In this he followed in the footsteps of an eminent panel of former US secretaries of defense and state – George Shultz, William Perry, Henry Kissinger – and Senator Sam Nunn, former chairman of the Senate Armed Services Committee, who published an opinion article that electrified disarmament activists by calling on Washington to take the lead in the abolition of nuclear weapons.[38] They did not dispute that nuclear weapons confer many national security benefits. Rather, they argued that these were subordinate to the threats posed to US security by the uncontrolled proliferation of nuclear weapons. As startling as their conversion – on the road to Tehran rather than Damascus – was the newspaper in which it was published, the very bastion of US conservatism. They followed a year later by publishing a second article, also in the *Wall Street Journal*, noting the worldwide positive response that their call had evoked and the serious and substantive work that it had produced among a coalition of Americans aiming to marry the vision of a nuclear-weapon-free world to a series of progressive steps to pull the world back from the nuclear precipice, such as reducing warhead numbers and limiting the role of nuclear weapons in security policy.[39]

Ironically, therefore, sections of the admittedly retired national security elite are coming around to embracing and championing the nuclear-weapon-free cause in a decade in which the formerly energized popular movement has been largely dormant. But their views are not universally shared. A group of retired NATO generals argued recently for a NATO "policy of deterrence by proactive denial," which includes both preemption and prevention. They put forward the concept of "interactive escalation" based on "escalation dominance," which can use "all instruments of soft and hard power, ranging from the diplomatic protest to nuclear weapons." In their view, "nuclear weapons – and with them the option of first use – are indispensable ... and nuclear escalation continues to remain an element of any modern strategy."[40]

In this context, it is worth recalling three further pointers from post-

1945 history. First, the most spectacular Soviet territorial and political advances in Europe came during the period of US atomic monopoly. Second, the implosion, collapse, and disappearance of the Soviet Union occurred after its achievement of strategic parity with the United States. And, third, the dramatic reductions in nuclear arsenals in the first half of the 1990s resulted from unilateral initiatives (reinforced by the power of positive reciprocity) by Mikhail Gorbachev and George H. W. Bush, not from verifiable agreements signed after protracted negotiations. They reflected and in turn contributed to improved political trust and the dismantling of "the vast apparatus of ideological hostility that had been built up" over four decades.[41]

The NPT can fairly be judged to have been the most brilliant half-successful arms control agreement in history. The number of countries to sign it embraced virtually the entire family of nations. Yet, at the same time, the nuclear arsenals of the N-5 (of which France and China signed the NPT only much later) expanded enormously. The total number of nuclear warheads climbed steadily after 1945, peaked in the mid-1980s, fell dramatically for about a decade, and then stabilized to date in the new millennium (see Table 13.1).[42] With four decades having elapsed since 1968, the N-5 must be deemed to be in violation of their solemn obligation to disarm, reinforced by the Advisory Opinion of the International Court of Justice in 1996 that Article VI requires them to engage in *and bring to a conclusion* negotiations for nuclear abolition.

Despite this history and background, a surprising number of arms control experts focus solely on the non-proliferation side to demand denial of technology and materiel to all who refuse to sign and abide by the NPT, and punishment of any who cross the threshold. The term "non-proliferation ayatollahs" is applied pejoratively to them.

The symbiotic link between non-proliferation and disarmament is integral to the NPT. Most countries gave up the weapons option in return for a promise by the N-5 to engage in good-faith negotiations to eliminate nuclear weapons. It was expected that nuclear disarmament could take some time. Accordingly, unlike the non-proliferation obligations, the Article VI disarmament obligation was not brought under international monitoring and enforcement.

The logics of nuclear disarmament and non-proliferation are inseparable. The most powerful stimulus to nuclear proliferation by others is the continuing possession of nuclear weapons by some. After all, Iraq was attacked when it did not have nuclear weapons (having been disarmed not by US bombs but by UN inspectors) whereas North Korea, which had nuclear weapons but not oil, was spared.[43] The unintended but entirely predictable consequence for any regime that feared US attacks was: if you wish to avoid Saddam Hussein's fate, do not cooperate in efforts to

Table 13.1 Number of nuclear warheads in the inventory of the five NPT nuclear weapons states, 1945–2005

Year	USA	USSR/Russia	UK	France	China	Total
1945	6					6
1950	369	5				374
1955	3,057	200	10			3,267
1960	20,434	1,605	30			22,069
1965	31,982	6,129	310	32	5	38,458
1970	26,662	11,643	280	36	75	38,696
1975	27,826	19,055	350	188	185	47,604
1980	24,304	30,062	350	250	280	55,246
1986	24,401	45,000	300	355	425	70,481[a]
1990	21,004	37,000	300	505	430	59,239
1995	12,144	27,000	300	500	400	40,344
2000	10,577	21,000	185	470	400	32,632
2005	10,295[b]	17,000[b]	200	350	400	28,245

Source: Hans M. Kristensen and Robert S. Norris, "Nuclear Notebook," *Bulletin of the Atomic Scientists* 62, no. 4 (2006): 64–67, using data from the Natural Resources Defense Council.

Notes: Of the non-NPT nuclear weapons states, Israel is estimated to have 60–85 warheads, India and Pakistan about 110 between them, and North Korea could have around 10. Altogether, more than 128,000 nuclear warheads are estimated to have been built since 1945, with the United States and the former Soviet Union/Russia accounting for 55 and 43 percent of them respectively.
[a] Peak year.
[b] Slightly less than half the US and Russian stockpiles are considered operational, with the balance in reserve, retired, or awaiting dismantlement.

disarm but instead get the bomb as quickly as possible. By worsening regional and global insecurities, the Iraq war increased the attractiveness of the nuclear option and strengthened the motivation to get nuclear weapons by any means necessary.[44] And the threat to use nuclear weapons, not just to deter their use by others but to prevent others from acquiring them in the first place as part of a counter-proliferation strategy,[45] *legitimizes their possession and use.*

Hence the axiom of non-proliferation: as long as any one country has nuclear weapons, others, including terrorist groups, will try their best (or worst) to get them. There is a marked contradiction between rhetoric and example. Nuclear weapons were invented to cope with Germany, used to defeat Japan, and deployed most extensively against the Soviet Union. As their primary strategic rationale disappeared with the end of the Cold War, Washington's evolving nuclear policies acquired greater regional specificity. In East Asia, for example, continued US attachment to nuclear weapons and doctrines was seen as proof of a shift in stance – from deterrence to compellence and coercion – and provoked more assertive Chinese nuclear policies and nuclear brinkmanship by North Korea, which in turn produced self-vindication in Washington.[46] Conversely, even a cursory probing of the sources of instability that impel countries towards nuclear acquisition confirms the link between the denuclearization of individual states, the regions in which they are located, and universal disarmament. Iran, for example, has hostile and potentially hostile nuclear weapons and troops of nuclear-armed powers all around it. With India and Pakistan to the east, Russia to the north, and US forces patrolling its southern shores and occupying its immediate neighbors in Iraq and Afghanistan, the reasons why Iran's national security strategy cannot be de-linked from regional and global dynamics are obvious.

The Bush administration has justified new weapons and additional uses by shifting the US nuclear posture from deterrence to use, redefining its mission from a nuclear stalemate with a superpower peer to waging and winning wars against countries that cannot fight back in kind. (To paraphrase Donald Rumsfeld apropos of coalitions, the existence, numbers, and lethality of nuclear weapons will determine missions, not the other way round.) It is not possible to convince others of the futility of nuclear weapons when the facts of continued possession and of doctrines and threats of use prove their utility for some. Refining and miniaturizing nuclear weapons, developing new doctrines and justifications for their use, and lowering the threshold for their use weaken the taboo against them and erode the normative barriers to nuclear proliferation.

The problem is not nuclear proliferation but nuclear weapons. They could not proliferate if they did not exist. Because they do exist, they will proliferate. The policy implication of this logic is that the best guarantee of nuclear non-proliferation is nuclear disarmament through a universal, non-discriminatory, verifiable, and enforceable nuclear weapons convention that bans the possession, acquisition, deployment, testing, transfer, and use of nuclear weapons by everyone. This would solve the problems of non-proliferation as well as of disarmament. The focus on non-proliferation to the neglect of disarmament ensures that we get neither. If we want non-proliferation, we must prepare for disarmament.

How do we move from analysis and prescription to action and nuclear abolition? To begin with, some practical and concrete measures are long overdue: bringing the CTBT into force, negotiating a verifiable fissile materials treaty, retrenching from launch-on-warning postures, standing down nuclear forces, to name but a few[47] – that is, reviving, implementing, and building on existing agreements for reducing the role, readiness, and numbers of nuclear weapons and introducing further degrees of separation between the possession and launch of nuclear weapons by modifying the doctrines and practices of deployment.

But these amount to tinkering, not a bold and comprehensive vision of the final destination. What we need are rules-based regimes anchored in the principles of reciprocity of obligations, participatory decision-making, and independent verification procedures and compliance mechanisms. In the words of a former US Deputy Secretary of Defense, "America is sleepwalking through history, armed with nuclear weapons. The Cold War left us with a massive inventory of weapons we no longer need, an infrastructure we can no longer use or maintain, and no thought of where our future lies."[48] The three policy imperatives are to encourage the reduction of nuclear inventories among the NWS, strengthen controls over nuclear stocks and material among them, and minimize the attraction of the nuclear option to those who do not have these weapons.

Annan argued that the unique status of the NWS "also entails a unique responsibility," and they must do more, including further and irreversible reductions in non-strategic nuclear arsenals, reaffirmation of negative security assurances, swift negotiation of a fissile material cut-off treaty, and the maintenance of the moratorium on nuclear testing until the entry into force of the CTBT. He strongly urged states to agree on these measures at the 2005 NPT Review Conference. On the non-proliferation side, he urged a strengthening of the IAEA verification machinery through universal adoption of the Model Additional Protocol and the creation of incentives for states to forgo uranium enrichment and plutonium separation capacities, with the IAEA to act as a guarantor for the supply of fissile material to civilian nuclear users at market rates.[49]

In the end, the seventh NPT Review Conference in May 2005 ended in complete collapse. It failed to address the vital challenges or to offer practical ideas for preventing the use, acquisition, and spread of nuclear weapons. The first half of the conference was dogged by procedural wrangling, and the second half was equally rancorous. The exercise ended in acrimony and recriminations over where the primary blame lay for the lost opportunity to bolster the NPT. Washington, which has historically led international efforts to reinforce the NPT regime, faulted the international community, yet again, for failure to confront the reality of the threat of proliferation by countries such as Iran and North Korea. Arms control advocates countered that the US delegation had come intent on focusing on the proliferation side of the equation and was totally intransigent with regard to previously agreed-to commitments on arms control and disarmament measures by the existing nuclear powers. In an echo of communist systems, the information booklet produced by the US government during the conference blanked out milestones no longer popular with the current administration, including the 1996 CTBT and the 2000 NPT Review Conference. Joseph Cirincione commented that "official disdain for these agreements seems to have turned into denial that they existed."[50]

Most countries concluded that the nuclear powers had no intention of fulfilling their NPT-based disarmament obligations and agreed commitments from the 1995 and 2000 conferences. This had a triple negative effect: it eroded support for US proposals for strengthening the non-proliferation elements of the treaty, weakened support for strong action against possible Iranian and North Korean transgressions, and may soften adherence to NPT obligations over the long run.

The September 2005 World Summit similarly failed to come to any agreement on non-proliferation and disarmament, a failure described as "inexcusable" and "a disgrace" by Annan and blamed on "posturing" getting in the way of results.[51] Some senior diplomats blamed the 2005 summit's failure to tackle the nuclear threat in effect on Washington.[52] The US refusal to countenance any form of disarmament blocked attempts to adopt measures that would prevent regimes seeking to develop a nuclear capability. One diplomat remarked that Washington refused to accept the "logical premise" that it must engage in disarmament if it wants to discourage a "new nuclear arms race."

The NPT may be creaking beyond repair even with respect to its nuclear energy bargain because the nexus of security, economic, energy, and environmental imperatives can no longer be adequately nested within that one old regime. More countries are bumping against the nuclear weapons ceiling at the same time as the world energy crisis is encouraging a move to nuclear energy. The bulk of the international market is controlled by the P-5/N-5 and their allies such as Australia, Canada, Germany, and Japan. As West as well as East Europeans have discovered, Russia is an unreliable supplier of energy, not averse to using it as a political weapon. But so too is Washington prone to imposing sanctions on regimes it dislikes, which constitutes a threat to the security of nuclear supplies. There is therefore growing interest in creating a new international market under the auspices of multilateral nuclear arrangements in order to assure the continued supply of nuclear fuel and services even without ownership, which would raise suspicions about motives and complications about civilian–military firewalls.[53] Internationalizing the nuclear fuel cycle and entrusting supply to a body such as the IAEA would simultaneously ensure security of supply divorced from political hostilities and reduce-cum-eliminate the need for enrichment and reprocessing plants in countries interested in acquiring nuclear power for civilian use.[54]

Too many have paid lip-service to the slogan of a nuclear-weapon-free world but have not pursued a serious program of action to make it a reality. The elegant theorems, cogent logic, and fluent reasoning of many authoritative international commissions have made no discernible impression on the old, new, and aspiring nuclear powers. A coalition between

Table 13.2 Public opinion on nuclear weapons (percent)

	France	UK	USA
NPT has been effective	22.0	25.0	15.9
NPT has been ineffective	47.6	40.4	46.3
Strongly/moderately agree that non-nuclear states should be prevented from developing them	88.3	84.9	82.3
Eliminate NW worldwide	39.0	50.9	48.7
Reduce global numbers of NW	44.6	39.7	33.6
Maintain current number/develop new weapons	13.5	5.8	8.9
Eliminate nuclear testing worldwide	58.8	60.8	52.8
Nuclear weapons make world safer	11.6	18.2	10.2
Nuclear weapons make world more dangerous	76.9	73.4	79.3
Support eliminating NW through enforceable agreement	86.6	84.5	73.5
Oppose eliminating NW through enforceable agreement	6.5	8.5	16.7

Source: The Simons Foundation, *Global Public Opinion on Nuclear Weapons* (Vancouver, Canada, September 2007).
Notes: The other countries included in the survey, which asked a total of 15 questions, were Germany, Israel, and Italy.

nuclear-armed and non-nuclear countries – for example India, which has crossed the threshold from a disarmament leader to a hypocritical nuclear power, and Japan, the only country to have suffered an atomic attack – might break the stalemate and dispel the looming nuclear clouds. Critical introspection and self-reflection are required also on the part of civil society actors and arms control non-governmental organizations: does the focus on the NPT play into the hands of the non-proliferation hawks, divert attention and effort from nuclear disarmament, and in effect thereby undermine the pursuit of nuclear abolition? That is, has the good – non-proliferation via the NPT – become the enemy of the best – nuclear abolition?

A cross-national survey of public attitudes in the three Western nuclear-armed countries shows some interesting and surprising features (see Table 13.2). First, people are clearly convinced of the failure of the NPT regime. Second, they are just as firmly convinced that nuclear weapons make the world more dangerous rather than safer. And, third, they are willing to see this belief translated into policy by supporting with almost equal conviction the twin goals of preventing further proliferation and eliminating nuclear weapons entirely through an enforceable agreement.

The articles by Kissinger et al. gave "street credibility" to the goal of nuclear disarmament within the US political process and political legitimacy to it worldwide. There is a gathering sense around the world that nuclear threats are intensifying and multiplying. There is a matching growing conviction that existing policies have failed to mute the threats.[55] In the meantime, scientific and technological advancements since the NPT was signed in 1968 have greatly expanded our technical toolkit for monitoring and verifying weapons reduction and elimination. It is time to supplement and then supplant the sword-and-shield nuclear diplomacy of the United States with the pen diplomacy of a multilaterally negotiated, non-discriminatory, and universal nuclear weapons convention. The emergence of new leaders in a range of nuclear policy-relevant countries brings into power a post–Cold War generation less burdened by the rigid analytical and policy framework of the second half of the twentieth century. The mindset, world-view, and policies of the next US administration in particular will be critical to driving or blocking efforts at nuclear arms control and disarmament.

Time is running out for the contradictions, hypocrisy, and accumulated anomalies of global nuclear apartheid. Either we will achieve nuclear abolition or we will have to live with nuclear proliferation followed by nuclear war. If the non-proliferation end of the NPT bargain collapses, the regime will become obsolete. If the disarmament goal of the NPT is realized, the regime is completed but also becomes redundant. Either way, the NPT regime as we have known it has passed its use-by date. Better the soft glow of satisfaction from the noble goal realized of nuclear weapons banned, than the harsh glare of the morning after these weapons are used.

Notes

1. I use the term "regime" to refer to norms, rules, and behavior around which actor expectations converge in the issue area of non-proliferation even in the absence of formal international organization. The non-proliferation regime includes the norms of international nuclear behavior and the network of international treaties, institutions, export controls, and nuclear trade agreements.
2. All 44 countries with operational nuclear reactors, listed in Annex 2 of the treaty, are required to sign and ratify the CTBT before it can come into force. China joined the NPT regime in March 1992, followed by France in August, thereby bringing all five known NWS within the NPT fold. Thus, if analogous clauses had been written into the NPT, that treaty would never have entered into force.
3. Kofi A. Annan, *In Larger Freedom: Towards Development, Security and Human Rights for All. Report of the Secretary-General*, UN document A/59/2005, 21 March 2005, para. 97; available at ⟨http://www.un.org/largerfreedom/contents.htm⟩ (accessed 18 November 2008).
4. For the *New York Times* editorial on the chilling incident, see "The Wake-Up Flight of a Wayward B-52," *New York Times*, 15 February 2008.
5. George P. Shultz, William J. Perry, Henry A. Kissinger, and Sam Nunn, "Toward a Nuclear-Free World," *Wall Street Journal*, 15 January 2008.
6. See International Institute for Strategic Studies, *North Korea's Weapons Programmes:*

A Net Assessment (London: Palgrave Macmillan, 2004); Wade Huntley, "Ostrich Engagement: The Bush Administration and the North Korean Nuclear Crisis," *Nonproliferation Review* (Summer 2004): 1–35; and International Crisis Group (ICG), *North Korea: Where Next for the Nuclear Talks?* Asia Report No. 87 (Brussels: ICG, 15 November 2004).

7. ICG, *Iran: Where Next on the Nuclear Standoff?* Middle East Briefing No. 15 (Brussels: ICG, 24 November 2004).
8. Jonathan Power, "Turning a Blind Eye to Nukes: The U.S. and Saudi Arabia?" *International Herald Tribune*, 4 August 2004.
9. "South Korea Says It Enriched Uranium Four Years Ago," *Japan Times*, 3 September 2004; "Top Scientist Acknowledges Uranium Tests," *Japan Times*, 5 September 2004; "ROK Enrichment Tests Conducted '3 Times'," *Daily Yomiuri*, 5 September 2004; "Seoul Admits Scientists Extracted Plutonium in '82 Experiment," *Japan Times*, 10 September 2004; James Brooke, "Report Details South Korean Cover-up," *International Herald Tribune*, 25 November 2004; "S Korea Chided for Nuclear Tests," *BBC News*, 11 November 2004; available at ⟨http://news.bbc.co.uk/2/hi/asia-pacific/4004865.stm⟩ (accessed 18 November 2008).
10. "Taipei Held Nuke Experiments as Late as Mid-1980s," *Japan Times*, 14 October 2004, and "Concern over Taiwan Nuclear Ambitions," *Japan Times*, 17 October 2004.
11. "Egyptian Scientists Produced Nuclear Material: Diplomats," *Japan Times*, 6 January 2005.
12. Larry Rohter, "If Brazil Wants to Scare the World, It's Succeeding," *New York Times*, 31 October 2004.
13. For a hilarious, tongue-very-firmly-in-cheek parody of a press conference by a Pakistani military spokesman pointing to US command and control being lax relative to Pakistan, the history of nuclear accidents in the United States, the record of US proliferation to allies the United Kingdom and France, a commander-in-chief who confessed to having been an alcoholic, and the fundamentalism and religious fervor of the American people and administration, see Hugh Gusterson, "A Pakistani View of U.S. Nuclear Weapons," *Bulletin of the Atomic Scientists*, 4 February 2008; available at ⟨http://www.thebulletin.org/web-edition/columnists/hugh-gusterson/a-pakistani-view-us-nuclear-weapons⟩ (accessed 18 November 2008). The Pakistani general even offered technical advice and assistance to the United States to improve its nuclear weapons handling procedures, to which Pentagon officials responded stiffly that the US role was to give, not receive, advice on nuclear weapons safety and security issues.
14. The Bush administration was quick to claim the Libyan renunciation of the nuclear option as a tangible success of its Iraq war policy. It is just as plausible to link the Libyan decision to domestic political compulsions, the adverse impact of the international sanctions imposed on it in the 1980s, and the trend line for a negotiated end to the stalemate visible since the Clinton administration. See Thomas E. McNamara (a former ambassador and Assistant Secretary of State who developed and implemented the UN sanctions policy against Libya as a special assistant to President George H. W. Bush in 1991–92), "Why Qaddafi Turned His Back on Terror," *International Herald Tribune*, 5 May 2004; Flynt Leverett, "Why Libya Gave up the Bomb," *New York Times*, 23 January 2004; Geoff D. Porter, "The Faulty Premise of Pre-emption," *New York Times*, 31 July 2004; and Thomas E. McNamara, "Unilateral and Multilateral Strategies against State Sponsors of Terror: A Case Study of Libya 1979–2003," in *Uniting against Terror: Cooperative Nonmilitary Responses to the Global Terrorist Threat*, ed. David Cortright and George A. Lopez (Cambridge, MA: MIT Press, 2007). Many Arabs believe that, as a result of the difficult insurgency in Iraq after the war, it is Washington that became more receptive to long-standing Libyan overtures and signals for an end to the confron-

tation. Thus both versions agree on the war being the deal maker, but for opposite reasons. In truth, the Libyan case is a good example of an integrated strategy of diplomacy, economic engagement, and security assurances. The crisis with North Korea was exacerbated by the Bush administration's abandonment of just such a strategy that had been followed by the Clinton administration.

15. Having said that, on 19 September 2008 North Korea said it had stopped disabling the Yongbyon nuclear reactor and was making "thorough preparations" to restart it. Foreign ministry official Hyun Hak-bong said that Pyongyang had suspended work to put the plant out of action because the United States had not fulfilled its part of a disarmament-for-aid deal. "North Korea 'to restore reactor'," *BBC News*, 19 September 2008; available at ⟨http://news.bbc.co.uk/2/hi/asia-pacific/7624601.stm⟩ (accessed 18 November 2008).
16. Secretary-General Ban Ki-moon, "Statement to the Conference on Disarmament in Geneva," *UN News Centre*, 23 January 2008; available at ⟨http://www.un.org/apps/news/infocus/sgspeeches/statments_full.asp?statID=174⟩ (accessed 18 November 2008).
17. I am grateful to all the participants in the two workshops for this project, and in particular to M. J. Peterson, for their many helpful and constructive comments on earlier drafts of this chapter.
18. *World Energy Outlook 2007* (Paris: IEA, 2007).
19. Those who remain skeptical of any nuclear solution continue to advocate renewables such as wind and solar energy, as well as increased energy efficiency.
20. *Energy, Electricity and Nuclear Power Estimates for the Period up to 2030*, Reference Data Series No. 1 (Vienna: IAEA, 2007).
21. See *20/20 Vision for the Future: Background Report by the Director General for the Commission of Eminent Persons* (Vienna: IAEA, 2008). The panel's report was published in May: *Reinforcing the Global Nuclear Order for Peace and Prosperity: The Role of the IAEA to 2020 and Beyond. Report Prepared by an Independent Commission at the Request of the Director General of the International Atomic Energy Agency* (Vienna: IAEA, 2008); available at ⟨http://www.iaea.org/NewsCenter/News/PDF/2020report0508.pdf⟩ (accessed 18 November 2008).
22. See Christopher Clary, "Dr. Khan's Nuclear WalMart," *Disarmament Diplomacy* 76 (March/April 2004): 31–35; and Douglas Frantz and Catherine Collins, "Those Nuclear Flashpoints Are Made in Pakistan," *Washington Post*, 11 November 2007.
23. Mohamed ElBaradei, "Preserving the Non-Proliferation Treaty," *Disarmament Forum* 4 (2005): 5.
24. This is developed more fully in Ramesh Thakur, "Arms Control, Disarmament, and Non-Proliferation: A Political Perspective," in *Arms Control in the Asia–Pacific Region*, ed. Jeffrey A. Larsen and Thomas D. Miller (Colorado Springs: USAF Institute for National Security Studies, US Air Force Academy, 1999), 39–61.
25. Many of the newer proliferating materials and processes are "leveraging" technologies that allow poorer countries to offset high-technology advantages. By demonstrating the acquisition of just a few key capabilities, developing countries can affect the perceptions and alter the decision calculus of diplomacy and war of the advanced military powers.
26. As reported in the *Japan Times*, 6 April 2002.
27. See Ramesh Thakur, "U.S.-India Nuclear Accord a Win-Win Outcome for All," *Daily Yomiuri*, 27 November 2005, and "Don't Let the India-U.S. Nuclear Deal Unravel," *Globe and Mail*, 27 April 2007. For a view that highlights the non-proliferation costs and risks of the deal, see Jayantha Dhanapala and Daryl Kimball, "A Nonproliferation Disaster," *Proliferation Analysis* (Carnegie Endowment for International Peace), 10 July 2008; available at ⟨http://www.carnegieendowment.org/publications/index.cfm?fa=view&id=20292&prog=zgp&proj=znpp,zsa⟩ (accessed 18 November 2008).

28. Ewen MacAskill, "'Obliteration' Threat to Iran in Case of Nuclear Attack," *Guardian*, 23 April 2008. See also Norman Podhoretz, "The Case for Bombing Iran," *Commentary* 123, no. 6 (2007): 17–23.
29. See Natasha Bajema, rapporteur, *Weapons of Mass Destruction and the United Nations: Diverse Threats and Collective Responses* (New York: International Peace Academy, June 2004).
30. See Ramesh Thakur, ed., *Nuclear Weapons-Free Zones* (London/New York: Macmillan and St. Martin's Press, 1998).
31. See Waheguru Pal Singh Sidhu and Ramesh Thakur, eds, *Arms Control After Iraq: Normative and Operational Challenges* (Tokyo: United Nations University Press, 2006).
32. This will always be problematic, in that all countries insist on exit options in international treaties.
33. See Jenny Nielsen, "Engaging India, Israel and Pakistan in the Nuclear Non-Proliferation Regime," *Disarmament Diplomacy* 86 (Autumn 2007): 13–28.
34. See Adrian Levy and Catherine Scott-Clark, *Deception: Pakistan, the United States, and the Secret Trade in Nuclear Weapons* (New York: Walker, 2007); David Armstrong and Joseph J. Trento, *America and the Islamic Bomb: The Deadly Compromise* (Hanover, NH: Steerforth, 2007); International Institute for Strategic Studies (IISS), *Nuclear Black Markets: Pakistan, A.Q. Khan and the Rise of Proliferation Networks. A Net Assessment*, IISS Strategic Dossier (London: IISS, May 2007); and Selig S. Harrison, "What A. Q. Khan Knows," *Washington Post*, 31 January 2008.
35. George Perkovich, Jessica Tuchman Mathews, Joseph Cirincione, Rose Gottemoeller, and Jon Wolfsthal, *Universal Compliance: A Strategy for Universal Compliance* (Washington, DC: Carnegie Endowment for International Peace, March 2005).
36. Thus the conservative columnist Charles Krauthammer: "During the Cold War, we worried about Soviet nukes, but never French or British nukes. Weapons don't kill people; people kill people" ("Deterring the Undeterrable," *Washington Post*, 18 April 2008). The same point on differentiating by regimes rather than denouncing nuclear weapons per se was made in an editorial criticizing Obama's adoption of the nuclear-free goal ("Obama's A-Bomb," *New York Sun*, 4 October 2007).
37. See Ramesh Thakur, "The Desirability of a Nuclear Weapon Free World," in Canberra Commission on the Elimination of Nuclear Weapons, *Background Papers* (Canberra: Department of Foreign Affairs and Trade, 1996), 74–88.
38. George P. Shultz, William J. Perry, Henry A. Kissinger, and Sam Nunn, "A World Free of Nuclear Weapons," *Wall Street Journal*, 4 January 2007.
39. Shultz, Perry, Kissinger and Nunn, "Toward a Nuclear-Free World," *Wall Street Journal*, 15 January 2008. They were joined by Madeleine Albright, James Baker, Zbigniew Brzezinski, Frank Carlucci, Warren Christopher, Melvin Laird, and Colin Powell – all former secretaries of state and defense and national security advisers – as well as a number of scholars in a project housed at Stanford University's Hoover Institute. The two factors different from their time in office that might explain their conversion to the abolitionist cause is the fear of terrorists acquiring nuclear weapons and the far bigger gap between the conventional capabilities of the United States and any other single power or coalition of states.
40. Klaus Naumann, John Shalikashvili, Lord Inge, Jacques Lanxade, and Henk van den Breemen, *Towards a Grand Strategy for an Uncertain World: Renewing Transatlantic Partnership* (Lunteren, Germany: Noaber Foundation, 2007), 96, 97. For a contrary view of what NATO should be doing with nuclear weapons, see John Burroughs, "Visible Intent: NATO's Responsibility to Nuclear Disarmament," Middle Powers Initiative Briefing Paper, New York, January 2008; available at ⟨http://www.middlepowers.org/pubs/NATO_brief_2008.pdf⟩ (accessed 18 November 2008).

41. David Cortright, "Overcoming Nuclear Dangers," Policy Analysis Brief, The Stanley Foundation, Muscatine, IA, November 2007, 10; available at ⟨http://www.fourthfreedom.org/pdf/0711_stanley.pdf⟩ (accessed 18 November 2008).
42. The two parts of the story are told well in Richard Rhodes, *Arsenals of Folly: The Making of the Nuclear Arms Race* (New York: Knopf, 2007), and Jonathan Schell, *The Seventh Decade: The New Shape of Nuclear Danger* (New York: Metropolitan, 2007). See also Paul Lettow, *Ronald Reagan and His Quest to Abolish Nuclear Weapons* (New York: Random House, 2005).
43. The hindsight verdict on Israel's attack on the Iraqi nuclear reactor at Osirak in June 1981 is kinder than the contemporary condemnations. Yet, as a counterpoint, it is worth noting the judgment of a retired senior Egyptian ambassador that Egypt's ratification of the NPT in February 1981 would have been seriously imperiled if the attack on Iraq had preceded it. Mohamed I. Shaker, "An Egyptian Perspective," in Sidhu and Thakur, *Arms Control After Iraq*, 257.
44. See Ramesh Thakur, *War in Our Time: Reflections on Iraq, Terrorism and Weapons of Mass Destruction* (Tokyo: United Nations University Press, 2007).
45. *The National Security Strategy of the United States of America* (Washington DC: The White House, 2002); available at ⟨http://www.whitehouse.gov/nsc/nss.pdf⟩ (accessed 18 November 2008).
46. See Wade L. Huntley, "Nuclear Threat Reliance in East Asia," in Sidhu and Thakur, *Arms Control After Iraq*, 181–199.
47. See "LockDown, CleanOut, Fissban," Policy Dialogue Brief, The Stanley Foundation, Muscatine, IA, 2007; available at ⟨http://www.stanleyfdn.org/publications/pdb/SPC07PDB_Lockdown.pdf⟩ (accessed 18 November 2008).
48. John J. Hamre, "Toward a Nuclear Strategy," *Washington Post*, 2 May 2005.
49. Annan, *In Larger Freedom*, paras 97–100. See also Mohamed ElBaradei, "Seven Steps to Raise World Security," *Financial Times*, 2 February 2005.
50. "U.S. 'Rewrites History' of Arms-Control Deals in Conference Brochure," *Japan Times*, 26 May 2005.
51. David Usborne, "Annan Launches Tirade at World's Leaders for Abandoning Disarmament and Development," *The Independent*, 15 September 2005; available at ⟨http://www.independent.co.uk/news/world/politics/annan-launches-tirade-at-worlds-leaders-for-abandoning-disarmament-and-development-506895.html⟩ (accessed 4 December 2008).
52. Mark Townsend, "Summit Failure Blamed on US," *Observer* (London), 18 September 2005.
53. Downstream agenda would have to include also the conversion of existing national facilities to international control while ensuring that new facilities being constructed are multinational from the start.
54. See John Thomson and Geoffrey Forden, "Multilateralism as a Dual-Use Technique: Encouraging Nuclear Energy and Avoiding Proliferation," Policy Analysis Brief, The Stanley Foundation, Muscatine, IA, March 2008.
55. See Joseph Cirincione, "A Critical Mass for Disarmament," *Los Angeles Times*, 4 June 2008.

Index

"t" refers to table; "n" to notes.

ABACC. *See* Brazilian-Argentine Agency for Accounting and Control of Nuclear Materials [Agência Brasileiro-Argentina de Contabilidade e Controle de Materiais Nucleares] (ABACC)
ABM Treaty. *See* Treaty on the Limitation of Anti-Ballistic Missile Systems (ABM Treaty)
Acharya, Amitav, 12, 19, 248–72, 269n3, 269n7, 270n8, 270n23, 270n25–27, viii
al-Qaeda, 2, 127–28, 135, 198, 208n27, 222, 242, 247n24, 256, xiii
Algeria, 17, 174, 198, 219
Annan, Secretary-General Kofi, 3, 25n2, 84–86, 96–99, 104n62, 106n135–36, 107n141, 107n143, 225, 229n48, 233, 246n5, 274, 290–91, 293n3, 297n49, 297n51
ARF. *See* ASEAN Regional Forum (ARF)
Argentina, 192–95
arms race, 194
ASEAN (Association of Southeast Asian Nations), 250, 252, 265–66, 269n5, 270n16
ASEAN-Plus-Three framework, 257

ASEAN Regional Forum (ARF), 254, 257, 265–66
Aum Shinrikyo, 135, 208n27, 222
Australia, 22–23, 64, 67, 172, 184n14, 185n24, 194, 200, 216–17, 277, 291
Austria, 23, 88, 155
"axis of evil"
    Iran, 248, 264, 267, 272n32
    Iraq, 248
    North Korea, 175, 248, 264, 267, 272n32
    President Bush's, 137, 264–65
    talks with, 20
    weapon(s) of mass destruction (WMD), 248

Ban Ki-moon, 51n40, 87, 97, 104n80, 275, 295n16
Baruch, Bernard, 11, 25n14, 245, 247n28
BBC China (German freighter), 224, 229n46
Belarus, 193–94, 246n4, 279
Belgium, 23, 195
biological weapons, 37–38, 63–64, 143, 222
Blair, Prime Minister Tony, 134, 285
Blix, Hans, 9, 25n9, 114, 116–17, 130n11, 130n20, 131n25, 158, 168n9, 168n15, xv
Boulden, Jane, 1–27, viii, xiv, xvii n1, xvii n4

298

INDEX   299

Boutros-Ghali, Boutros, 82–83, 95–97, 99, 106n130–31, 253t12.1
Brazil, 22, 64, 90, 192–95, 274, 294n12
Brazilian-Argentine Agency for Accounting and Control of Nuclear Materials [Agência Brasileiro-Argentina de Contabilidade e Controle de Materiais Nucleares] (ABACC), 158–59, 168n21
Burma, 197
Burns, Under Secretary of State William, 268
Burns, Under Secretary R. Nicholas, 123, 186n38–39, 260t12.2
Bush, President George W., 35, 49n23, 62, 64, 121, 123–26, 132–34, 137, 147n1, 201, 218, 228n28, 248, 256–57, 260t12.2, 264–65, 267–68, 269n1, 271n22, 280, 285, 287, 289, 294–95n14, 294n6, xiv
Bush, President H. W., 113, 130n6

Campaign for Nuclear Disarmament, 72n35
Canada, 23, 134, 194–95, 200, 236, 242, 245, 246n19, 247n23, 291
Canada's Global Partnership Program, 247n23
CD. *See* Conference on Disarmament (CD)
Centre for Disarmament Affairs, 84, 99
CFE. *See* Treaty on Conventional Forces in Europe (CFE)
chemical weapons, 37–38, 42, 63–64, 115, 117, 143, 165, 198, 222
Cheney, Vice President Richard, 114, 121, 130n12, 134, 254
Chernobyl (Ukraine) nuclear accident, 240, 277
Chile, 64
China
  arms race, 194
  ASEAN-Plus-Three framework, 257
  ASEAN Regional Forum (ARF), 257, 265–66
  Conference on Disarmament, 60
  CTBT ratification, 73, 173, 212, 219
  East Asian RSC, 251
  energy consumption and nuclear energy, 276–77
  EU-Iran dialogue support, 259t12.2
  FMCT, 220
  geopolitical rivalries, 255

  illicit trading practices, 208n15
  India and, 56, 215–16
  Iran, 263, 266–67, 272n32
  Japan and nuclear weapons, 279
  National Defense white paper, 141, 149n36
  North Korea, 163, 257, 259t12.2, 263–65, 271n20
  NPT nuclear state, 58, 212, 293n2
  nuclear arsenal, 31, 60, 191–94, 287, 288t13.1
  nuclear power, 275
  nuclear weapon accumulation and mutual distrust, 56
  nuclear weapon modernization, 279
  nuclear weapon use, 42
  nuclear weapons free zone, 272n29
  nuclear weapons stalemate, 64
  nuclear weapons tests, 58, 211
  P-5/N-5, 45
  plutonium and HEU production, 48n7
  Proliferation Security Initiative (PSI), 142
  Resolution 36/100, 62
  Samuel Huntington's characterization, 255
  Security Council, 31–32, 41, 215, 263
  Six-Party Talks, 257, 259t12.2, 261t12.2, 270n14–15, 270n17
  UFP in Kosovo, 140
  US-led "war on terror," 256
  war on Korean peninsula, 257
  WMD proliferation, 141
Clinton, President Bill, 113, 124, 126, 173, 184n16, 216, 258t12.2, 294–95n14
Clinton, Senator Hillary, 280
codification and legal issues
  Article I, prohibitions on aiding the acquisition of nuclear explosive devices, 178
  Article IV, selectivity in cooperation, 178–79
  Article VI, obligations to negotiate disarmament, 179–80
  Article VIII, legal meaning of NPT Review Conferences, 180–81
  Article X, withdrawal, 181–82
  codification of constraints on weapons prior to the nuclear age, 171–72
  conclusion, 182–83
  ICJ advisory opinion on legality of use or threat of use of nuclear weapons, 173–76

codification and legal issues (cont.)
  introduction, 170–71
  NPT regime, specific issues relating to, 177–82
  nuclear testing, attempt to codify restraints on, 172–73
  Security Council as law-making forum, 176–77
Cold War, 1, 3, 5, 7, 12, 20, 22, 25n3, 25n16, 26n26, 34, 49n17, 57, 59–60, 62, 65, 75, 133, 142, 179, 193, 195, 251–52, 254, 264, 272n32, 281, 296n36
Commission on the Intelligence Capabilities of the United States, 245n3
Comprehensive Nuclear-Test-Ban Treaty (CTBT)
  about, 7, 12, 33, 35, 39, 63–64, 77, 87, 172, 184n13, 185n18, 216–17, 219–21, 227n1, 273–74, 279, 289–90, 293n2, xiv
  China, 73, 173, 212, 219
  General Assembly, 63
  India, 23, 67, 73, 173, 216, 219
  Iran, 73, 173, 214
  Israel, 73, 173, 214, 219
  Libya, 23
  North Korea, 73, 173, 219
  Pakistan, 73, 173, 217, 219
  United States, 73, 173, 212, 219
Conference on Disarmament (CD), 7, 23, 33, 36, 39, 44, 54, 60, 63, 65, 76, 86, 216, 219–20, 225, 228n37, 229n38, 275, 295n16
Convention on the Physical Protection of Nuclear Material (CPPNM), 237
Cortright, David, 111–31, viii–ix
Council on Foreign Relations, 267
CPPNM. *See* Convention on the Physical Protection of Nuclear Material (CPPNM)
CTBT. *See* Comprehensive Nuclear-Test-Ban Treaty (CTBT)
Cuba, 4, 57, 88, 92, 105n108, 170, 183n1–2, 280
Cuéllar, Javier Pérez de, 80, 94–95, 99, 106n129

Daalder, Ivo, 19, 26n23
Damrosch, Lori Fisler, 16–17, 34, 170–87, 184n17, 186n32, ix

DDA. *See* Department of Disarmament Affairs (DDA)
"Declaration on the Prevention of Nuclear Catastrophe", 61
Democratic People's Republic of Korea (DPRK). *See also* North Korea
  IAEA, 227n4
  non-proliferation regime, 212
  NPT, 187n52–53
  NPT withdrawal, 139, 149n24, 181–82
  nuclear program, xiv
  nuclear safeguards, 187n51, 207n13
  nuclear tests, 139, 211
  Six-Party Talks, 222
Denmark, 88, 200
Department of Disarmament Affairs (DDA), 80–82, 85–89, 94–95, 97–98, 102n25, 104–5n84, 169n32, 182, 187n53, 228n37
Department of Political Affairs (DPA), 82–83, 86–89, 95, 103n50
Department of Political and Security Council Affairs (DPSCA), 78, 93–94
Dhanapala, Jayantha, 85–86, 295n27, xiii–xv
DPA. *See* Department of Political Affairs (DPA)
DPRK. *See* Democratic People's Republic of Korea (DPRK)
DPSCA. *See* Department of Political and Security Council Affairs (DPSCA)
dual-use technology
  arms trade, 199
  commercial products, 194, 197
  hardware and weapons materials, 115, 198–99
  human talent, 196
  item list, 200
  nuclear technologies, 96, 196, 198, 244, 258t12.2, 297n54
  transfers, 282

East Asian RSC, 251
East Europeans, 291
Egypt, 22, 41, 46, 64, 73, 88, 104n56, 107n56, 173, 194, 198, 214, 219, 263, 274, 294n11, 297n43
Eight-Nation Initiative, 22
Eighteen-Nation Disarmament Conference (ENDC), 215, 217

INDEX 301

Eisenhower, President Dwight, 11, 191, 207n3, 221, 281
ElBaradei, Mohamed, 115, 117, 124, 130n16, 131n24, 158, 214, 243, 278, 295n23, 297n49
11 September 2001, 2, 85, 102n14, 103n52, 116, 132, 177, 202, 218, 248, 274, xiii. *See also* 9/11
ENDC. *See* Eighteen-Nation Disarmament Conference (ENDC)
EU. *See* European Union (EU)
EU-3. *See* France, Germany and the United Kingdom (EU-3)
Europe, 26n26, 57, 89, 122–23, 168n6, 192, 196, 252, 253t12.1, 277, 287
European neutral states, 59, 62, 277
European Union (EU)
 EURATOM, 159
 incentives, 128
 Iran, 259t12.2, 266–68, 269n2
 non-proliferation strategy, 141
 North Korea, 270n10
 regional organization, 158–59, 251
 regional security complex (RSC), 251
 Security Council (P-5), 257
 security dilemma, 152–53
 Six-Party talks, 257
 terrorism and proliferation, 141
Evans, Nicole, 19, 22, 230–47, ix
Expert Group on Multilateral Approaches to the Nuclear Fuel Cycle, 166, 169n34
extra-NPT actors and non-state actors
 extra-NPT actors, three approaches, 219–22
 historical overview, 212–19
 India, 215–17
 introduction, 210–11
 Israel, 212–15
 non-state actors, two approaches, 223–25
 non-state actors of concern, 222–23
 Pakistan, 217–19
 United Nations, implications for, 225–26

Financial Action Task Force (FATF), 202, 209n35–36
Finland, 185n24, 200
Finlay, Brian, 18, 191–209, 209n30, ix
First Committee of the General Assembly, 7–8, 76

Fissile Material Cut-off Treaty (FMCT), 49–50n24, 167, 219–20, 275, 290
five declared nuclear powers (N-5), 138, 143
five declared nuclear weapons states (N-5), 172–73
five NPT-licit nuclear states (N-5), 13, 21, 31–32, 39, 275, 279, 281, 283, 287
five permanent members of the Security Council (P-5), 21, 24, 31–32, 39, 43, 112, 129, 133, 138, 140–43, 145, 147, 157, 162–63, 165, 192–93, 195–96, 216, 220–21, 225, 257, 259t12.2, 260t12.1, 269n2, 275
FMCT. *See* Fissile Material Cut-off Treaty (FMCT)
force
 conclusion, 146–47
 events, accumulation of, 125–37
 General Assembly and peaceful resolution, 140
 interdiction, 143–44
 introduction, 132–33
 plea of necessity, 137–38
 pre-emption and anticipatory self-defense, doctrine of, 133–35
 security assurances, 143
 Security Council, collective action by, 142–43
 Security Council, legal authority of, 138–40
 Security Council, role of, 138
 Security Council action, 141–42
 Security Council's criteria, 144–46
 self-defense, 133–38
France
 arms race, 194
 dual-use nuclear technologies, 196–97
 EU-3 high-level negotiations, 122–23, 225–26, 257, 259t12.2, 260t12.2, 267, 269n2
 EU-Iran dialogue support, 259t12.2
 ICJ on atmospheric testing, 172
 Indian nuclear test, 215
 Iran, 123, 267, 284
 Iraq, 118, 141
 NPT, 41, 58, 212, 275, 283, 293n2
 nuclear arsenal, 31, 194, 287, 288t13.1
 nuclear power, 275
 nuclear proliferation, 222
 nuclear weapon accumulation and mutual distrust, 56

INDEX

France (cont.)
  nuclear weapons, public opinion, 292t13.2
  nuclear weapons tests, 58, 172, 184n14, 191, 211
  nuclear weapons use, 41–42
  OMV system in Iraq, 118
  plutonium and HEU production, 48n7
  security assurances, 143
  stove-piped policy structures, 200
  test-ban treaties, 172
  Treaty on the Non-Proliferation of Nuclear Weapons, 41
France, Germany and the United Kingdom (EU-3), 222, 225–26, 267

G-8. *See* Group of Eight (G-8)
G-8 Kananaskis Summit, 242
G-77. *See* Group of 77 (G-77)
GCC. *See* Gulf Cooperation Council (GCC)
General Assembly
  resolution 1/1, 4, 11, 32–33, 54, 56, 75
  resolution 14/1378, 58
  resolution 16/1653, 61, 71n15
  resolution 21/2153B, 70n10
  resolution 22/2346B, 70n10
  resolution 23/2456C, 70n9
  resolution 24/2605B, 70n9
  resolution 26/2828A, 59, 70n11
  resolution 26/2829, 70n9
  resolution 30/3472B, 59
  resolution 30/3478, 59
  resolution 30/3484, 70n9
  resolution 31/90, 79
  resolution 33/71, 227n9
  resolution 33/71B, 71n14
  resolution 34/87[E], 102n13
  resolution 36/27, 227n12
  resolution 36/100, 61–62
  resolution 37/ 99[K], 80
  resolution 37/85, 60
  resolution 38/73G, 60
  resolution 38/75, 61–62
  resolution 39/63[J], 81
  resolution 40/151[G], 81
  resolution 41/60[J], 102n23
  resolution 42/39[D], 102n24
  resolution 42/78, 227n11
  resolution 43/66, 228n22
  resolution 43/76[H], 102n23
  resolution 44/117[F], 102n24
  resolution 46/232, 103n37
  resolution 47/49, 228n22
  resolution 47/54 G, 103n47
  resolution 49/75[I], 71n21
  resolution 49/78, 227n11
  resolution 50/73, 227n11
  resolution 50/250, 67
  resolution 51/45[C], 71n22
  resolution 51/48, 227n11
  resolution 52/12, 85
  resolution 52/35, 228n22
  resolution 60/92, 227n11
  resolution 60/288, 97
  resolution 61/257, 90
  resolution 62/24, 71n31
  resolution 62/25, 71n31
  resolution 62/33, 71n30
  resolution 62/37, 65, 71n31
  resolution 62/39, 65, 71n31
  resolution 62/42, 65, 71n31
  resolution 62/51, 71n31
  resolution 502(VI), 75
  resolution 1378, 75
  resolution 2951 (XXVII), ifc
  resolution 3263 (XXIX), 227n7
  resolution 3265 (XXIX), 228n21
  resolution 3484[B], 102n8
  resolution A/RES/50/245, 221
  resolution S-10/2, 70n3, 70n12, 75
  resolution S/1995/263, 150n44
  resolutions (general), 10–12, 23, 53–57, 59–61, 68, 70n2, 76–77, 81, 162, 176, 179, 185n27
  resolutions on Centre for Disarmament Affairs, 99
  resolutions on CTBT, 63
  resolutions on India, 215
  resolutions on Iran, 212–13
  resolutions on nuclear issues, 59, 69–70
  resolutions on nuclear-weapon-free zones, 64, 215
  resolutions on nuclear weapons, 4, 60, 62–63, 65–66
  resolutions on Office for Disarmament Affairs, 84
  resolutions on Uniting for Peace, 140, 163
General Assembly majorities on preferred nuclear order. *See also* United Nations and nuclear orders
  conclusion, 69–70
  General Assembly, what it can/can't do, 65–69

General Assembly resolution on nuclear weapons, political context of, 55–57
General Assembly's approach and working methods, 53–55
General Assembly's resolution on nuclear weapons, 57–65
introduction, 52–53
Germany
  Advisory Opinion, 185n24
  dual-use nuclear technologies, 196–97
  EU-3 high-level negotiations, 122–23, 225–26, 257, 259t12.2, 260t12.2, 267, 269n2
  India, 217
  Iran, 123, 259t12.2, 267, 269n2
  non-nuclear weapons, 195
  NPT state, 194
  nuclear energy, 291
  nuclear proliferation, 222
  nuclear weapons, 288
  nuclear weapons proliferation network, 238
  stove-piped policy structures, 200
  United States, 130n6, 149n39
Global Initiative to Combat Nuclear Terrorism, 242
Global Partnership Against the Spread of Weapons and Materials of Mass Destruction, 242
Global Public Opinion on Nuclear Weapons (Simons Foundation), 292t13.2
Global South, 54, 192, 205
"A Global Strategy for Fighting Terrorism" (Annan), 246n5
Goldsmith, Attorney-General Lord, 134
Gorbachev, Mikhail, 287
Grossman-Vermaas, Rita, 18, 191–209, ix–x
Group of 77 (G-77), 88–89, 99, 163, 198
Group of Eight (G-8), 199, 224, 242
Gulf Cooperation Council (GCC), 254–55, 263–66, 271n24, 271n26

Hammarskjöld, Dag, 73, 77–78, 88, 91–92, 99, 101n3, 105n89–93, 105n95, 105n97
HEU. *See* highly enriched uranium (HEU)
High-level Panel on Threats, Challenges and Change (HLP), 3, 15, 25n1, 64–65, 71n25–26, 72n34, 134, 144–45, 169n32

highly enriched uranium (HEU), 48n7, 231, 233, 238, 242–44
Hiroshima, 7, 184n9, 276
HLP. *See* High-level Panel on Threats, Challenges and Change (HLP)
Howard, Prime Minister John, 285
human rights, 5, 111, 126, 150n48, 173, 176, 204, 207n1, 252, 293n3
Huntington, Samuel, 255
Hussein, Saddam, 4, 113, 116, 120

IAEA. *See* International Atomic Energy Agency (IAEA)
ICJ. *See* International Court of Justice (ICJ)
IHL. *See* international humanitarian law (IHL)
ILC. *See* International Law Commission (ILC)
India
  CD veto, 23
  cessation of nuclear testing, 22
  China, 56, 215–16
  Conference on Disarmament (CD), 216, 229n38
  CTBT ratification, 23, 67, 73, 173, 216, 219
  Eighteen-Nation Disarmament Conference (ENDC), 215, 217
  energy consumption and nuclear energy, 276–77
  export controls, 228n34
  extra-NPT actor, 211
  FMCT, 219–22
  General Assembly resolution, 215
  Germany, 217
  IAEA Safeguards Agreement, 178, 217
  international nuclear exports, 195
  Iran, 272n32, 289
  Japan, 217
  joint Vision Statement, 216
  N-5/P-5 roles and responsibilities, 21
  non-NPT nuclear state, 145, 228n33, 234, 280, 282
  non-proliferation obligations, 284
  North Korea, 285–86
  NPT norms, 221
  NSG Guidelines, 221
  nuclear ambitions of, 192
  nuclear power, 275, 277, 292
  Nuclear Suppliers Group (NSG), 39–40, 49–50n24, 215

304   INDEX

India (cont.)
  nuclear warheads, 288t13.1
  nuclear weapon accumulation and mutual distrust, 56
  nuclear weapons, 14, 32, 34, 56, 68, 195, 227n19, xiv
  nuclear weapons state (NWS), 2, 58, 127, 279, 283
  nuclear weapons tests, 22–23, 26n29, 27n33, 38–39, 59, 173, 186n33, 215–17, 228n20, 228n29, 234, 283, 285
  P-5/N-5 nuclear testing *vs.*, 39
  Pakistan, 56
  proliferation, abstain on resolutions, 64
  regional security complex, 270n9
  sanctions, punitive trade and technology, 112
  Security Council, 12–13, 34
  Security Council resolution 1172, 13, 39, 216–17, 220
  Security Council resolution 1540, 37
  Singh–Talbott dialogue, 216
  United States, 125–26, 228n31, 240, 280
Indian Ocean tsunami (2004), 204
Indo-US nuclear agreement, 13–14, 186n36, 217, 222, 226, 228n30, 259t12.2, 280, 285, 295n27. *See also* United States-India Civil Nuclear Cooperation Initiative
Indonesia, 64, 73, 103n47, 173, 185n31, 277
Intermediate-Range Nuclear Forces Treaty, 3, 184n5, 233
International Atomic Energy Agency (IAEA)
  about, 168n10–13, 227n16, 295n21
  Action Team, 115
  actor in international nuclear trade, 230
  Additional Protocol, 168n12, 235, 241, 282
  Annan, Kofi, 290
  board of governors, 157, 282
  Chernobyl accident, 246n4
  Commission of Eminent Persons, 67
  compliance promotion and enforcement, 54, 151, 155
  Consolidated Report of, 130n14
  Department of Safeguards, 241
  disarmament process, 128, 155
  dual role of, 160

ElBaradei, Director Mohamed, 124, 130n16, 181, 214, 243, 278
EURATOM and, 158–59
Expert Group on Multilateral Approaches to the Nuclear Fuel Cycle, 166, 169n34
extra-NPT states, 221
General Assembly, 59, 162
Hammarskjöld, Dag, 92
history of, 168n10, 169n24
ICJ and, 166
Illicit Trafficking Database, 236, 241
India, 125, 217
Indo-US Agreement, 226–27
inspections and monitoring, 22, 36, 114–15, 117, 127
inspections in Iraq, 22, 36, 57, 113–20, 125, 130n16, 131n32, 156, 159
inspectors, 115, 125, 153, 155
International Physical Protection Advisory Service (IPPAS) mission, 239
Iran, 34, 122, 161, 166, 248, 258–59t12.2, 263, 271n18, 272n32, 281–83
Iraq, 4, 82, 114–17, 125, 128, 141, 156, 158–62, 166, 282, xiii
Model Additional Protocol, 290–91
Multilateral Approaches to the Nuclear Fuel Cycle, 169n34
non-compliance reporting, 33, 47
non-proliferation enforcement mechanisms, horizontal, 47
non-proliferation management, 263t12.1
North Korea, 124–25, 161, 163, 166, 181, 187, 227n4, 260t12.2, 274
NPT, 112, 235, 241, 282
NSG and, 234
nuclear forum, 66
nuclear fuel *vs.* weapons material, 69
nuclear power plants, 277
nuclear proliferation, 138
nuclear reactor renaissance, 277
Nuclear Security – Measures to Protect Against Nuclear Terrorism (Annual Report), 246n11
Nuclear Security Plan, 245
nuclear trade analysis unit (NUTRAN), 235–36
Office of Nuclear Security, 236, 241
Pakistan, 125

Plan of Activities to Protect Against Nuclear Terrorism, 236
regional bodies and, 158–60
role of, 4, 8, 72n37, 149n30–31, 151, 235, 295n21
safeguards, 25n15, 39, 49n24, 182, 186n39, 213–14, 217, 220, 236, 241, 243
Safeguards Agreements, 33, 53, 178, 227, 233, 235, 241
Secretariat, 158, 169n31
Secretary General and, 162
Security Council, 33, 111, 138, 159, 164–65, 167, 182, 207n13, 209n33, 282
Security Council Chapter 7, 15
"special inspections", 152, 155, 235
as specialized agency, 165
state sovereignty and, 239
Statute, 16, 33, 138, 159
 Article III.B.4, 33
 Article VI, 16
 Article XII.C, 33, 149n30
support of major actors, 155
Syria's nuclear site, 214
technical assistance, 160
technical assistance to civilian programs, 57
Trade and Technology Analysis (TTA), 241
UN Charter, 160
UN diplomatic offensive and, 111
UN nuclear inspector, 234
United Nations and, 138, 149n30, 156
United States *vs.,* 158, 207n3, 214, 236
UNSCOM, 82, 115, 141, 156
Update Report, 131n23
US nuclear industry, 236
verification activities, 152–53, 155, 160–61, 164, 166–67
International Convention for the Suppression of Acts of Nuclear Terrorism, 221, 223, 237
International Convention for the Suppression of the Financing of Terrorism, 201
International Court of Justice (ICJ)
 about, 17, 36, 45, 51n38, 62, 149n25, 185n29, 185n31
 Advisory Opinion, 17, 36, 171, 173, 184n11, 185n24, 185n28, 186n44, 287

Advisory Opinion on nuclear weapons, 62–63
Advisory Opinion on Palestinian Territory, 148n17, 176
Bedjaoui, President, Judge Mohammad, 17
disarmament, obligations to negotiate, 179–81
French atmospheric testing, 172
General Assembly and peacekeeping, 140
IAEA and, 166
"Legality of the Threat or Use of Nuclear Weapons," 17, 49n16, 51n38, 65, 71n17, 150n45, 165, 169, 169n33, 171, 173–76, 179, 181, 184n8–11, 185n19–21, 185n23–25
military action against nuclear threats, 140
NPT's Article VI, 38
"nuclear disarmament in all its aspects", 45, 287
nuclear terrorism, threats of, 135
nuclear weapon prohibition, 143
nuclear weapons, 4, 38, 62–63, 150n45, 169n33, 171, 184n3, 185n22, 185n30, 186n33, 186n44
nuclear weapons states (NWS), 172
"on any legal question", 17
Palestinian Territory, 148n17, 185n28
role of, 165–66
self-defensive, 135
state party reports, 36
unilateral action, theory for, 137
United Nations, 151, 167, 171
verification/compliance interface role, 165
international humanitarian law (IHL), 171–72, 174, 176
International Law Commission (ILC), 137–38, 149n26, 177
international nuclear trade
 background, 231–33
 challenges and threats, 237–41
 conclusion, 244–45
 framework, 233–35
 introduction, 230
 solutions, 241–44
 United Nations, role of in, 235–37
 weapons-usable nuclear material from existing source, 232–33
International Physicians for the Prevention of Nuclear War, 72n35

Iran
  Arab–Israeli conflict, 255
  "axis of evil," 248, 264, 267, 272n32
  breakout state, potential, 192
  China, 263, 266–67, 272n32
  civilian nuclear energy, 254
  Conference on Disarmament, 219
  Council on Foreign Relations, 267
  CTBT ratification, 73, 173, 214
  DDA non-involvement, 87
  economic–security, 255
  EU-3 high-level negotiations, 122–23, 225–26, 257, 259t12.2, 260t12.2, 267, 269n2
  European Union, 128, 258t12.2, 268, 269n2
  Financial Action Task Force (FATF), 202
  fissile materials, 2, 219
  FMCT, 219, 259t12.2
  General Assembly resolution, 103, 212
  Gulf Cooperation Council (GCC), 254, 266
  IAEA, 4, 34, 122, 161, 166, 248, 259t12.2, 263, 274, 282–83
  Iraq, 256
  Israel, 175, 214, 227n14, 255
  Khan network, 218, 238, 283
  national security strategy, 289
  nonproliferation vs. disarmament, 285
  North Korea vs., 258–61t12.2
  NPT disarmament obligations, 128, 275, 291
  NPT member state, 220–21, 271n18
  nuclear ambitions, 129, 192, 233, 265–66
  nuclear energy needs, 281
  nuclear program, 192, 233, 248, 254, xiv
  nuclear technicians, Soviet, 196
  nuclear-weapon-free zone in the Middle East, 266, 272n29
  nuclear weapons program, 123, 195, 248, 263, 283–84
  nuclear weapons proliferation network, 238, 272n31
  nuclear weapons state (NWS), 283
  NWFZ, sub-regional, 266
  NWFZ in the Gulf, 266
  P-5/N-5 states, 44
  pre-emptive strikes against, 132, 136, 284
  regime survival, 270n10, 272n32
  regional and international ambitions, 254–55
  regional entity, absence of a strong, 19, 254, 263
  regional security complex (RSC), 251, 289
  rivalry between Shiite Islam and Sunni Islam, 252–53, 255
  Russia, 256, 259t12.2, 289
  sanctions, ineffectiveness of, 128, 142, 268
  sanctions and denuclearizing, 122–23, 270n11
  sanctions on trade in sensitive nuclear materials, 112, 122–23
  Security Council, 12, 34, 122, 161, 257
  Security Council resolutions, 13, 186n33, 207n13, 220
  Security Council sanctions, 87, 112, 122, 214, 258t12.2, 263
  UN and right to develop nuclear reactors, 128
  United States, 112, 122–23, 128, 148n19, 256, 259t12.2, 260t12.2, 264, 267–68, 269n2, 270n10, 271n19, 271n21, 272n27, 272n33–272n34, 280
  uranium enrichment, 128, 258t12.2, 269n2, 280
  US-led "war on terror", 256
  weapons expertise, attracted, 196
Iraq
  about, 25n6, 25n10, 26n18, 48n4, 129n2, 130n7–8, 147n8, 149n40, 168n22
  Additional Protocol, 159
  "axis of evil," 248
  Blix, Hans, 9, 25n9, 168n9
  chemical, biological, and nuclear weapons program, 12, 116
  ElBaradei, Mohamed, 115
  France, 118, 141
  Hussein, Saddam, 4, 113, 116, 120
  IAEA, 4, 82, 114–17, 125, 128, 141, 156, 158–62, 166
  IAEA inspections, 22, 36, 57, 113–20, 125, 130n16, 131n32, 156, 159
  invasion of Kuwait, 8, 82, 213
  Iraq Survey Group, 161, 169n26–27
  Israel, plan to obliterate, 136
  Israeli attack on Iraqi nuclear facility, 12, 46, 148n20, 213
  Libya, 121
  Niger uranium import, 115
  nonproliferation war doctrine, preventive, 224
  NPT disarmament obligations, 128

NPT member state, 25n15, 159, 194–95, 211–12, 220–21
NSG members export to, 215–16
nuclear ambitions of, 192
nuclear arsenal, elimination of, 114–16
OMV system, 117–18
P-5 and military action, 141–42, 186n32
pre-emptive military action, 134
Safeguards Agreement, 159
sanctions-based diplomacy and weapons inspections, 117–19
Scud missiles, 115–16
Secretary-General, 82, 161–62
Security Council, 4, 8, 12, 14, 43–44, 116, 159–61
Security Council resolutions, 8, 14, 34, 113, 117, 147n5, 186n33
Security Council sanctions, 113, 116–18, 129–30n3–5
Survey Team, post-invasion, 9
UN inspections, 4, 9, 114–20
UN policy of military containment, 120
UN Special Commission for disarming, 43
UN weapons inspectors and vacuum pumps, 200
United Nations' role, 5
United States, 113–14, 116
Uniting for Peace procedure (UFP), 162
UNMOVIC, 8–9, 15, 114–17, 156
UNSCOM, 9, 15, 82, 114–19, 128, 156
US hoax justifying invasion, 154, 161, 200
US invasion of, 8–9, 15, 114, 121, 147n7, 210
US Maritime Interception Force, 119
US violation of UN Charter, 15, 116, 146, 149n38
US vs. IAEA, 158
weapons-program dossier, 216
WMD, blocking imports, 119–20
WMD, non-existent, 4, 116
WMD program, 8–9, 117, 130n10, 130n13, 141
Ireland, 22, 49n11, 64
Israel
  about, 148n19, 227n6, 227n13, 227n15
  Arab–Israeli conflict, 255
  attack on Iraqi nuclear facility, 4, 12, 46, 148n20, 213
  bombing of nuclear site in Syria, 136, 214
  bombing of the Osirak reactor (Iraq), 4, 136, 210, 297n43

breakout state, potential, 192
Conference on Disarmament, 229n38
CTBT ratification, 73, 173, 214, 219
extra-NPT actors and non-state actors, 211–15
GCC proposal, 266
General Assembly resolution, 212–13
historical overview, 212–15
IAEA safeguards, 25n15, 212–13
Iran, 123, 175, 214, 227n14, 255, 266, 280
Iraq's plan to obliterate, 136
Middle East WMDFZ, 213
non-NPT nuclear state, 145, 212, 228n33, 280
non-proliferation, 284–85
NPT, 13, 58, 212, 221, 280, 283–84, 296n33
NSG Guidelines, 221
nuclear ambitions of, 192
nuclear power/energy, 275
nuclear programs, 62
nuclear proliferation, 64
Nuclear Suppliers Group (NSG), 214–15
nuclear test blasts, 283
nuclear warheads, 266, 288t13.1
nuclear weapons, 68, 71n20, 195, 211, 214, 279, xiv
nuclear weapons state (NWS), 212, 283
NWFZ in the Gulf, 266
NWFZ in the Middle East, 266
Palestinian territory, 176
proliferation, abstain on resolutions, 64
regional security complex, 270n9
Secretary General report, 95
Security Council resolutions, 34, 213, 220
South Africa, 213
Italy, 192, 194–95, 208n26

Japan
  DDA, 88
  geopolitical rivalries, 255
  India, 217
  International Commission on Nuclear Nonproliferation and Disarmament, 22
  North Korea, 123, 251, 255, 259t12.2, 263
  NPT, 194–95, 291
  nuclear energy, 277, 291
  nuclear weapons potential, 279
  ODA funding, 103n47
  RSCT and Korean peninsula, 257

308 INDEX

Japan (cont.)
  Samuel Huntington's characterization, 255
  Six-Part Talks on North Korea, 259t12.2
  US atomic bombs (1945), 194, 276, 288, 292
  war on Korean peninsula, 257
Johnstone, Ian, 15, 132–50, 148n17, 149n28–29, 149n38, 149n41, 150n54–55, 186n34, x

Kazakhstan, 104n63, 112, 193–94, 279
Khan, Abdul Qadeer, 2, 121, 218, 238, 274, 278, 283
Kissinger, Henry, 26n22, 38, 49n15, 65, 71n29, 229n50, 286, 292, 293n5, 296n38–39

landmines, 8, 23, 63
League of Arab States, 212
Libya
  CTBT, 23
  dual-use hardware and weapons materials, 198–99, 224, 238
  Khan network, 121, 218, 238, 283
  nuclear ambitions of, 192
  nuclear program, 121, xiv
  nuclear turnabout, 120–21, 131n38, 194, 275, 294–95n14
  nuclear weapons program, 2, 13
  Security Council sanctions, 13, 112, 120–21, 128, 186n33, 272n32
  South Africa, 239
  US diplomacy, 112, 120–21, 267, 294n14
  US Libya Sanctions Act, 122
Lie, Trygve, 73, 90, 101n2
Lieber Code, 171, 184n9
Limited Test Ban Treaty (LTBT), 58–59, 63, 70, 172, 184n4
Lodal, Jan, 19, 26n23
Lopez, George A., 14, 26n17, 111–31, 129n1, 129n3, 130n5, 130n8, 131n38, 131n40, 294n14, x
LTBT. *See* Limited Test Ban Treaty (LTBT)

Malaysia, 88, 185n31, 197, 224, 277
  dual-use nuclear technologies, 196–97
Manhattan project, 20
Mexico, 22, 64, 103n47, 185n31

Middle East, 19, 25n13, 63–64, 99, 212–13, 215, 221, 227n8, 239, 247n22, 251–52, 255, 262t12.2, 266, 269n3, 271n24, 272n28, 277
military force. *See* force
Müller, Harald, 15, 151–69, 168n3, 168n8, 168n17, 169n26, 169n28, x–xi

N-5. *See* five declared nuclear powers (N-5); five declared nuclear weapons states (N-5); five NPT-licit nuclear states (N-5)
NAC. *See* New Agenda Coalition (NAC)
Nagasaki, 7, 184n9, 276
NAM. *See* Non-aligned Movement (NAM)
National Defense white paper (China), 141, 149n36
National Security Strategy (NSS), 133–34, 147n2–3
The National Security Strategy of the United States of America, 147n2, 297n45
National Security Strategy to Combat Weapons of Mass Destruction, 134, 147n3
NATO. *See* North Atlantic Treaty Organization (NATO)
Netherlands, 185n24, 195
New Agenda Coalition (NAC), 22, 64, 96, 98, 107n137
New Dimensions of Arms Regulation and Disarmament in the Post-Cold War Era (Boutros-Ghali), 83, 95, 103n43, 106n131
New Zealand, 22, 49n14, 64, 88, 172, 184n14–184n15
NGO. *See* non-governmental organization (NGO)
NGO Committee on Disarmament, Peace, and Security, 83–85
Nigeria, 103n47, 192
9/11, 136, 229n42–229n43, 236. *See also* 11 September 2001
  before, 135
  post, 125, 127–28, 142, 147n4, 148n10, 206, 222, 245n1, 245n3, 256
NNWS. *See* non-nuclear-weapon state(s) (NNWS)
Non-aligned Movement (NAM), 54, 57, 59, 61–62, 87–89, 99, 234

non-governmental organization (NGO), 9, 16, 18, 26n21, 50n25, 51n42, 76, 83, 87–89, 98–99, 103n48, 103n53, 160, 204, 222, 292
non-nuclear-weapon state(s) (NNWS), 35, 37, 40–43, 47, 50n26, 58–60, 63–65, 143, 156–57, 159, 166, 178, 211, 215, 231, 233
non-nuclear-weapons status, 273
non-proliferation
  horizontal, 31, 36–38, 40, 43–44, 46–47, 129
  India, 125–26
  International Commission on Nuclear Nonproliferation and Disarmament, 22
  Iran, 285
  Iraq, 224
  Israel, 285
  Pakistan, 125–26
  Subcommittee on Terrorism, Nonproliferation and Trade, 247n22
  talks, 123
  vertical, 31, 33, 37–38, 40, 43–44, 129, 278
North Atlantic Treaty Organization (NATO), 7, 140, 153, 174, 250, 286, 296n40
North Korea. *See also* Democratic People's Republic of Korea (DPRK)
  about, 131n39, 149n32–33, 227n5, 270n11, 270n16, 294n6
  ASEAN Regional Forum (ARF), 257, 265
  "axis of evil," 175, 248, 264, 267, 272n32
  ballistic missile test, 136, 142
  breakout state, potential, 192
  China, 163, 257, 259t12.2, 263–65, 271n20
  CTBT ratification, 73, 173, 219
  denuclearization in, 123–25
  East Asian RSC, 251
  European Union, 270n10
  Financial Action Task Force (FATF), 202
  IAEA and, 128, 161, 163, 166, 181–82, 274
  illicit trading practices, 208n15
  incentives, 263–64, 268
  India's response to, 285–86
  inspection cycles, 155
  inspectors expelled, 124, 136
  Iran *vs.*, 258–61t12.2, 258–62 t12.1, 272n32

Khan network, 218, 238, 283
  military sanctions against, 163
  non-NPT nuclear state, 145
  non-NPT nuclear weapons, 288t13.1
  NPT member state, 220–21, 275, 281–82
  NPT withdrawal, 49n21, 124, 136, 139, 181–82, 195
  nuclear ambitions of, 129, 192, 268, 274
  nuclear testing, 124, 142, 173, 274, 283, 285
  nuclear weapons program, 13, 195, 257, 293–94n6
  nuclear weapons state (NWS), 283
  P-5/N-5 states and, 44
  Pakistan's response to, 286
  policy of nuclear brinkmanship, 2, 289
  political utility of nuclear weapons, 232
  politicized environment, 4
  pre-emptive strike against, 132
  Pyongyang's plutonium production program, 124, 275, 295n15
  Pyongyang's uranium enrichment program, 124
  regime survival, 267–68, 270n10
  regional accord, 248
  Russia and, 139
  Security Council, 12, 34, 112, 139, 161, 181–83, 186n33
  Security Council resolutions, 34
  Security Council sanctions, 87, 112, 124–25, 129, 263
  Six-Party Talks, 14, 19, 87, 124, 142, 254, 256–57, 264, 268, 270n14, 275
  subregional context, 252, 254–55
  Syria's nuclear site, 136, 214
  United Kingdom, 139
  United States, 123–25, 137, 139, 181, 248, 256–57, 264–65, 267–68, 269n1, 270n10, 271n21, 287–88, 291, 295n14
  US-led "war on terror,' 256
  weapons expertise, attracted, 196
Norway, 23, 64, 80, 88, 99, 194–95
Norway Group, 64
NPT. *See* Treaty on the Non-Proliferation of Nuclear Weapons (NPT)
NSG. *See* Nuclear Suppliers Group (NSG)
NSS. *See* National Security Strategy (NSS)
nuclear, biological or chemical weapons, 37–38, 50n29, 71n28, 75, 115, 117, 119, 121, 192, 207n11, 208n27, 209n34, 224, 279, 284, xv

nuclear arsenal
  China, 31, 60, 191–94, 287, 288t13.1
  France, 31, 194, 287, 288t13.1
  Iraq, 114–16
  Pakistan, 280
  Russia, 77, 194, 288t13.1
  Soviet Union, 31
  United Kingdom, 194, 288t13.1
  United States, 77, 194, 288t13.1
nuclear disarmament
  Annan, Kofi, 85–86
  Atomic Energy Agency (IAEA), 82, 155–56, 159, 167
  Ban Ki-moon, 87–88
  Bliss, Hans, 25n9
  Boutros-Ghali, Boutros, 96
  Conference on Disarmament, 65, 229n38
  Cuéllar, Javier Pérez de, 94–95
  EURATOM, 159
  FMCT, 219
  General Assembly, 69–70
  ICJ Advisory Opinion, 38, 45, 51n38, 174, 179–80, 287
  Kissinger, Schultz, Perry, Nunn, 65, 292
  Lie, Trygve, 90
  NATO, 296n40
  New Agenda Coalition, 98
  non-proliferation and, 287, 289
  NPT, 22, 34–36, 50n36, 179, 233, 276, 285, 287, 292
  NWS, 58
  P-5/N-5, 34, 37–38, 43, 45
  Secretary-General, 46
  Security Council, 31–32, 34–36, 44–45
  Security Council resolutions, 39, 49n14
  specialists, 18
  transnational environmental groups, 72n35
  U Thant, 92
  UN Charter, 32, 76
  UN Department of Disarmament (DDA), 85
  UN Disarmament Commission, 76
  UN Secretariat, 100–101
nuclear order(s). *See* General Assembly majorities on preferred nuclear order; United Nations and nuclear orders
nuclear proliferation and regional security orders
  conclusion, 264–68

  conflict management, approaches to, 256–57, 263–64
  framework, negotiating, 256–57
  incentives, 263–64
  introduction, 248–49
  North Korea and Iran, 258–62t12.2
  regional security orders, theories of, 253t12.1
  regional security orders, three perspectives, 249–52, 253t12.1
  sanctions, 263
  tale of two regions, 252–56
  United States, direct negotiations with, 264
Nuclear Security – Measures to Protect Against Nuclear Terrorism (UN Secretary General), 246n11
Nuclear Suppliers Group (NSG), 39–40, 49n24, 50n24, 68, 195, 214–18, 221, 227n1, 227n15, 228n23, 228n32, 234, 241, 245, 246n6
Nuclear Terrorism Convention. *See* International Convention for the Suppression of Acts of Nuclear Terrorism
nuclear testing
  codifying restraints on, 172–73
  Democratic People's Republic of Korea (DPRK), 139, 211
  India, cessation of, 22
  India's test, response to, 39, 215–16
  Israel, 283
  North Korea, 124, 142, 173, 274, 283, 285
  P-5/N-5 *vs.*, 39
  Pakistan, 22, 38–39, 173, 186n33, 216–17, 228n29, 283, 285
  restraints on, attempt to codify, 172–73
  South Africa, 211
nuclear weapon accumulation and mutual distrust, 56
nuclear-weapon-free zone (NWFZ)
  about, 27n31, 227n1, 281
  Africa, 150n43
  Caribbean, 104n63
  Central Asia, 86, 150n43
  China and, 42
  Cold War Assembly debates, 60, 62
  in Gulf, 266
  Latin America, 104n63, 150n43
  Middle East, 212, 215, 227n8, 266
  Security Council and, 33

South Asia, 64, 215, 217
South Pacific, 22, 150n43, 266
Southeast Asia, 150n43, 266
nuclear-weapons-based strategic deterrence, 3
nuclear weapons state(s) (NWS), 12, 16–17, 21, 24, 31, 40, 46, 58, 61, 71n26, 88, 99, 112, 128, 150n43, 156–57, 159, 165–67, 168n17, 172, 175, 183, 185n25, 186n44, 211–12, 216, 219–20, 233, 273, 283, 288t13.1
Nunn, Sam, 26n22, 38, 49n15, 65, 71n29, 229n50, 286, 292, 293n5, 296n38–39
Nunn–Lugar Cooperative Threat Reduction program, 274
NWFZ. *See* nuclear-weapon-free zone (NWFZ)
NWS. *See* nuclear weapons state(s) (NWS)

Obama, President Barack, 19, 64, 268, 272n34, 286, 296n36
ODA. *See* Office for Disarmament Affairs (ODA)
Office for Disarmament Affairs (ODA), 7, 84, 86, 89–90, 97, 99, 103n47
OMV. *See* Ongoing Monitoring and Verification (OMV)
Ongoing Monitoring and Verification (OMV), 117–18
OPCW. *See* Organisation for the Prohibition of Chemical Weapons (OPCW)
Organisation for the Prohibition of Chemical Weapons (OPCW), 8, 165
Organization for Security and Cooperation in Europe (OSCE), 251–52, 266
OSCE. *See* Organization for Security and Cooperation in Europe (OSCE)

P-5. *See* five permanent members of the Security Council (P-5)
P-5/N-5 states, 31–47, 50n33, 275, 291
Pakistan
  CTBT ratification, 73, 173, 217, 219
  Eighteen- Nation Disarmament Conference (ENDC), 217
  export controls, 228n34
  Export Policy and Procedures Order, 218
  extra-NPT actor, 211, 217
  FMCT, 219

illicit trading practices, 208n15
India, 56
international nuclear exports, 195
Iran, 289
Khan's network, 126, 218–19
non-NPT nuclear state, 145, 228n33, 234, 280, 282
non-proliferation obligations, 284
North Korea testing, 285–86
NSG Guidelines, 218
nuclear ambitions of, 192
nuclear arsenal, securing from Islamists and jihadists, 280
"nuclear blackmail", 267
nuclear power, 275
nuclear testing, 22, 38–39, 173, 186n33, 216–17, 228n29, 283, 285
nuclear warheads, 288t13.1
nuclear weapon accumulation and mutual distrust, 56
nuclear weapons, 32, 34, 68, 195, xiv
nuclear weapons state (NWS), 2, 127, 279, 283
P-5/N-5 nuclear testing *vs.*, 39
proliferation, abstain on resolutions, 64
regime survival, 267
sanctions, punitive trade and technology, 112
Security Council, 12–13
Security Council resolution 487, 220
Security Council resolution 1172, 13, 39, 218, 220
Security Council resolution 1540, 37
Security Council resolutions, 34
uranium-enrichment technology, 218
US aid program, 126–27
US nonproliferation policies, 125–26
US Nuclear Non- Proliferation Act, 218
US sanctions, 218
Perry, William, 26n22, 38, 49n15, 65, 71n29, 229n50, 286, 292, 293n5, 296n38–39
Peterson, M. J., 11, 52–72, 72n39, 72n42, 169n29–30, 185n26, 295n17, xi
Plan of Activities to Protect Against Nuclear Terrorism, 236
plutonium and HEU production
  China, 48n7
post-cold War, 32, 34, 36, 83, 85, 99, 195–99, 201, 203, 207n7, 210, 212, 216, 249, 251–52, 253t12.1, 254, 273, 276, 288, 290, 293

"Principles and Objectives for Nuclear Non-Proliferation and Disarmament", 35, 45, 48n6
Proliferation Security Initiative (PSI), 18, 68, 142, 144, 150n46–47, 150n50, 222, 224–25, 229n46, 242, 253t12.1
PSI. *See* Proliferation Security Initiative (PSI)

Qaddafi, Colonel Muammar, 121, 294n14

RCST. *See* regional cooperative security theory (RCST)
Regehr, Ernie, 12, 31–51, xi–xii
regional cooperative security theory (RCST), 249, 251–52, 265
regional security complex (RSC), 251
regional security complex theory (RSCT), 249–52, 254, 257, 265
regional subsidiarity theory (RST), 248–52, 253t12.1, 265–66
Richardson, Bill, 85
Romania, 64, 194
RSC. *See* regional security complex (RSC)
RSCT. *See* regional security complex theory (RSCT)
RST. *See* regional subsidiarity theory (RST)
Russia. *See also* Soviet Union
  al-Qaeda negotiating for nuclear arms, 135
  Beslan school tragedy, 141
  Chechen insurgency, 141
  Chernobyl nuclear accident, 246n4, 277
  Conference on Disarmament, 60
  dual-use nuclear technologies, 196–97
  energy supplier, unreliable, 291
  EU-Iran dialogue support, 259t12.2
  ex-warhead HEU recycling, 243–44
  Global Partnership Against the Spread of Weapons and Materials of Mass Destruction, 242
  High-level Panel discussion, 71n26
  Indian nuclear test, 215–16
  International Convention for the Suppression of Acts of Nuclear Terrorism, 237
  Iran, 256, 259t12.2, 289
  Iraq, 115, 118, 141, 143, 216
  "loose" nukes in, 128–29, 275
  no-first-use policy, retreat from, 274

North Korea, 263
NPT, 41, 139, 170
NSG member, 216
nuclear arms use, 42
nuclear arsenal, 77, 194, 288t13.1
nuclear power, 208n16, 275
nuclear warheads, 274, 288t13.1
nuclear weapon accumulation and mutual distrust, 56
nuclear weapons stalemate, 64
nuclear weapons use, 42
OMV system in Iraq, 118
P-5/N-5 reporting obligations, 45
plutonium and HEU production, 48n7
security assurances, 143
Security Council, 263
Six-Part Talks on North Korea, 259t12.2
terrorism and proliferation, 141
Treaty on the Non-Proliferation of Nuclear Weapons, 41
UFP, opposition to, 140
US missile shield along Russian's borders, 280
US–Russian Megatons to Megawatts Program, 243–44
US–Soviet/Russian arms control negotiations, 170, 184n6
weapons stockpiles and proliferation risks, 101
WMD and disarmament, 44
WMD proliferation, 141
Rydell, Randy, 10, 73–107, xi

SALT-I. *See* Strategic Arms Limitation Talks Treaty I (SALT-I)
Secretary-General and the Secretariat
  Annan, Kofi, 3, 25n2, 84–86, 96–99, 104n62, 106n135–36, 107n141, 107n143, 225, 229n48, 233, 246n5, 274, 290–91, 293n3, 297n49, 297n51
  Ban Ki-moon, 51n40, 87, 97, 104n80, 275, 295n16
  Boutros-Ghali, Boutros, 82–83, 95–97, 99, 106n130–31, 253t12.1
  Cuéllar, Javier Pérez de, 80, 94–95, 99, 106n129
  disarmament mandate, origin and evolution of, 74–75
  Hammarskjöld, Dag, 73, 77–78, 88, 91–92, 99, 101n3, 105n89–93, 105n95, 105n97

introduction, 73–74
Lie, Trygve, 73, 90, 101n2
organizational change within the Secretariat, 77–90
preliminary conclusions and look ahead, 98–101
specific approaches to disarmament by the Secretaries General, 90–98
Thant, U, 92–93, 99, 105n100, 105n108
UN disarmament machinery and its mandates, 75–77
Waldheim, Kurt, 93–94
Security Council. *See also* five permanent members of Security Council (P-5)
China, 31–32, 41, 215, 263
European Union, 257
force, action by, 141–42
force, collective action by, 142–43
force, criteria of, 144–46
force, legal authority of, 138–40
force, role of, 138
forensics, 164–65
India, 12–13, 34
Iran, 12, 34, 122, 161, 257
Iraq, 4, 8, 12, 14, 43–44, 116, 159–61
as law-making forum, 176–77
North Korea, 12, 34, 87, 112, 124–25, 129, 139, 161, 181–83, 186n33, 263
nuclear disarmament, 31–32, 34–36, 39, 44–45, 49n14
Pakistan, 12–13, 34, 37, 39, 218, 220
resolution 255, 16, 41, 50n26, 149n42
resolution 487, 12, 46, 148n21, 213–14, 220
resolution 687, 8, 12, 82, 102n29, 113, 116, 118, 130n5, 130n15, 130n17, 161, 186n33, 213, 220
resolution 715, 117–18
resolution 748, 186n33
resolution 825, 187n50
resolution 885, 186n33
resolution 984, 41–42, 50n27, 143, 186n33, 186n43
resolution 1051, 130n14
resolution 1115, 118
resolution 1172, 13, 37, 39–40, 42, 49n12, 186n33, 216–18, 220
resolution 1284, 8, 117
resolution 1373, 13, 142, 177, 223
resolution 1441, 8, 131n23, 141, 147n5, 149n39, 161

resolution 1540, 4, 13, 16, 18–19, 37–38, 44, 46–47, 49n10, 49n14, 51n45, 53, 87, 104n64, 142–43, 177, 182–83, 186n35, 201–2, 204, 206, 209n33, 220, 222–24, 229n41, 229n45, 245
resolution 1566, 149n37
resolution 1673, 223
resolution 1695, 186n33, 187n54
resolution 1696, 186n33
resolution 1718, 124, 149n33, 186n33, 187n54–55, 207n13, 258t12.2
resolution 1735, 223
resolution 1737, 186n33, 207n13, 262t12.2
resolution 1747, 207n13, 262t12.2
resolution 1803, 186n33, 207n13
resolution 1810, 223
resolution 2373, 221
resolutions (general), 10, 47, 144
resolutions on India, 34, 37, 39
resolutions on Iraq, 14–15, 34, 82, 113, 116–18, 142, 161
resolutions on Israel, 34
resolutions on Myanmar and Zimbabwe, 141
resolutions on non-state actors, 223
resolutions on non-state actors in nuclear proliferation, 201–2
resolutions on North Korea, 34, 139, 181
resolutions on nuclear disarmament, 39
resolutions on nuclear proliferation, 47–48
resolutions on Pakistan, 34, 37, 39, 218
resolutions on peaceful settlement of disputes., 83
resolutions on pre-emptive military action, 134
Russia, 263
WMD, 141, 220
Security Council and nuclear disarmament
introduction, 31–32
nuclear disarmament agenda, 34–36
outliers, challenge of the, 38–40
security assurances, negative, 40–42
Security Council as a disarmament body, 42–48
UN Charter framework, 32–34
vertical-horizontal connection, 36–38
Security Council Summit (1992), 139
Shultz, George, 26n22, 38, 49n15, 65, 71n29, 229n50, 286, 292, 293n5, 296n38–39

314 INDEX

Sidhu, Waheguru Pal Singh, 18, 25n6, 26n18, 48n4, 129n2, 130n9, 168n22, 210–29, 227n5, 228n20, 229n38, 229n44, 296n31, 297n43, 297n46, xii, xvii n3
Singh–Talbott dialogue, 216
Six-Party Talks
  China, 257, 259t12.2, 261t12.2, 270n14–15, 270n17
  Democratic People's Republic of Korea, 222
  European Union (EU), 257
  North Korea, 14, 19, 87, 124, 142, 254, 256–57, 264, 268, 270n14, 275
Slovenia, 22
South Africa
  Eight-Nation Initiative, 22
  Israel, 213
  Libya, 239
  NAM, 89
  New Agenda Coalition, 64
  NPT, 195, 211
  nuclear ambitions of, 192–93
  nuclear facility housing weapons-grade HEU, 242
  nuclear program, 62, 71n20
  nuclear reduction decision, 112
  nuclear tests, 211
  nuclear weapons proliferation network, 199, 238
  nuclear weapons renunciation, 2, 193–94
  Secretary General report, 95
  terrorist movements, 198
South Korea, 123, 136–37, 194–95, 252, 255, 259t12.2, 263, 265, 270n9, 270n14, 271n20, 274, 277, 294n9
Soviet republics, 1–2, 199
Soviet Union. *See also* Russia
  arms race, 192, 194
  atomic weapons, testing and deploying, 191
  Chernobyl nuclear accident, 246n4, 277
  Cold War and UN Assembly, 60
  Department for Disarmament Affairs, 80
  Group of Eight Global Partnership, 224, 242
  Indian nuclear test, 215
  Intermediate Range Nuclear Forces agreement, 3, 184n5, 233
  joint statement on general and complete disarmament, 92

NPT, 143, 187n52
nuclear arsenal, 31
nuclear fuel cycle goods and services, exports of, 196–97, 199–200, 208n27, 208n29, 224, 242
nuclear fuel cycle under control of United Nations, 11
nuclear parity with US, 287
nuclear warheads, 288t13.1
nuclear weapons tests, 191
NWS after breakup, prospect of, 279
proliferation, second-tier, 199
Secretary General report, 95
Security Council member, 31
Special Session on Disarmament, 63
World War II target for nuclear weapons, 288
Spain, 194, 246n5
Special Session on Disarmament (SSOD), 12, 76
  First (SSOD-I), 7–8, 60, 70n12, 75, 79–80, 94
  Fourth (SSOD-IV), 63
  Second (SSOD-II), 61, 80, 94, 106n121
  Third (SSOD-III), 94, 106n121–06n122
SSOD. *See* Special Session on Disarmament (SSOD)
START. *See* Strategic Arms Reduction Treaty (START)
Stockholm International Peace Research Institute, 32
Strategic Arms Limitation Talks Treaty I (SALT-I), 60
Strategic Arms Reduction Treaty (START), 37, 184n5
Sudan, 197–98
Sweden, 22, 64, 78–79, 88, 99, 102n12, 102n19, 192, 194–95, 200, 212
Switzerland, 194–95
Syria, 136, 192, 210, 214, 227n13

Taiwan, 41, 192, 194, 274, 294n10
technology proliferation, globalization and the role of United Nations
  "back to the future?", 192–94
  conclusion, 205–6
  non-proliferation toolkit, gaps in international, 199–203
  post-Cold War world and globalization, 195–99

post-World War II non-proliferation regime, 194–95
United Nations' role in a new nuclear age, 203–5
terrorism
  about, 2–3, 5, 8, 12–13, 229n43, 297n44
  acts of, 141
  Africa and, 198
  Annan, Kofi, 246n5
  anti-, 87
  armed attack concept, 148n17
  ASEAN and, 270n16
  China and, 141
  conventional, 201
  counter, 19, 51n45, 77, 107n139, 120, 123, 125, 141, 202
  funding, 202, 208n25
  G-7 finance ministers and, 209n34
  global, 120, 267
  Global Initiative to Combat Nuclear Terrorism, 242
  international, 121, 248
  International Convention for the Suppression of Acts of Nuclear Terrorism, 221, 223, 237
  International Convention for the Suppression of the Financing of Terrorism, 201
  Iraq and, 142
  Libya's support of, 112, 120–21
  mass, 223
  North Korea, 259t12.2, 269n1, 270n16
  nuclear, 97, 132, 135–36, 144–46, 148n16, 195, 201, 208n27, 222–23, 227n2, 234, 237, 244–45, 245n1, 247n27
  nuclear proliferation and, 142, 177
  P-5 and, 141
  Plan of Activities to Protect Against Nuclear Terrorism, 236
  proliferation-related financial networks, 202
  Secretary General report, 246n11
  self defense and, 145, 148n9, 148n13
  spread of, 111
  states sponsoring, lists of, 122, 125, 131n34, 131n36
  Subcommittee on Terrorism, Nonproliferation and Trade, 247n22
  UN Global Counter-Terrorism Strategy, 97, 208n26
  WMD, 16, 97, 142, 148n14, 229n44

Thakur, Ramesh, 1–27, 25n4, 25n6–8, 25n16, 25n18, 26n27, 26n30, 27n33, 39, 48n3–4, 49n19, 129n2, 130n9, 168n22, 186n44, 227n5, 229n38, 229n44, 273–97, 295n24, 295n27, 296n30–31, 296n37, 297n43–44, 297n46, xii, xiv, xvii n2–4
Thant, U, 92–93, 99, 105n100, 105n108
Three Mile Island (USA) nuclear accident, 240, 277
toxin weapons, 63
Treaty on Conventional Forces in Europe (CFE), 37, 152
Treaty on the Further Reduction and Limitation of Strategic Offensive Arms (START II), 184n5
Treaty on the Limitation of Anti-Ballistic Missile Systems (ABM Treaty), 2, 60, 184n5, 233
Treaty on the Non-Proliferation of Nuclear Weapons (NPT), 31, 37, 41, 48n6, 48n8, 50n26, 50n35, 50n37, 51n38, 58, 70n8, 77, 149n30, 151, 168n11, 170, 182, 192, 226–27n1
  anomalies, 283–85
  Article I, 43, 178, 281
  Article II, 37, 281
  Article III, 37, 43, 281
  Article IV, 178–79, 186n40, 215, 221, 281
  Article V, 221
  Article VI, 35–38, 43–45, 47–48, 50n36, 51n38, 58, 165, 179–81, 186n44, 220, 239, 244, 279, 281, 287
  Article VIII, 180–81
  Article IX(2), 187n52
  Article IX(3), 70n8
  Article X, 33, 149n33, 181–82, 220
  Article X(1), 181
  Article X(2), 180
  Article XIV, 219
  China, 58, 212, 293n2
  France, 41, 58, 212, 275, 283, 293n2
  IAEA, 112, 235, 241, 282
  introduction, 273–76
  Iran, 128, 220–21, 271n18, 275, 291
  Iraq, 25n15, 128, 159, 194–95, 211–12, 220–21
  Israel, 13, 58, 212, 221, 280, 283–84, 296n33
  North Korea, 49n21, 124, 136, 139, 181–82, 195

Treaty on the Non-Proliferation of Nuclear Weapons (NPT) (cont.)
  nuclear disarmament, 22, 34–36, 50n36, 179, 233, 276, 285, 287, 292
  nuclear proliferation or nuclear abolition, 285–93, 288t13.1, 292t13.2
  nuclear renaissance, 276–78
  nuclear warheads in inventory of five NPT states, 288t13.1
  public opinion on nuclear weapons, 292t13.2
  regime, specific issues relating to, 177–82
  Review and Extension Conference, 85, 219, 234
  Review Conference, 17, 46, 66, 90, 107n140, 153, 166, 175, 180–81, 187n47, 226, 290
  Russia, 41, 139, 170
  security threats, 278–81
  South Africa, 195, 211
  Soviet Union, 143, 187n52
  United Kingdom, 139, 143, 187n52, 283
  United States, 139, 143, 170, 187n52, 212
  weakness and deficiencies, 281–83
Treaty on the Reduction and Limitation of Strategic Offensive Arms (START I), 184n5
Truman, President, 26n24

UFP. *See* Uniting for Peace (UFP)
UK. *See* United Kingdom (UK)
Ukraine, 112, 128, 193–94, 246n4, 277, 279
UN. *See* United Nations (UN)
United Kingdom (UK)
  arms race, 192, 194
  atomic weapons, testing and deploying, 191
  counter-terrorism policy *vs.* sanctions over nuclear development, 125
  EU-3 high-level negotiations, 122–23, 225–26, 257, 259t12.2, 260t12.2, 267, 269n2
  Indian nuclear test, 215
  Iran, 123, 267, 284
  Iraq, 118, 141–42
  Iraq and UN Charter violations, 14–15, 146
  Iraqi nuclear weapons program, 158
  North Korea, 139
  Norway Group, 64
  NPT, 139, 143, 187n52, 283

nuclear arsenal, 194, 288t13.1
nuclear proliferation, 222
nuclear weapon accumulation and mutual distrust, 56
nuclear weapons, public opinion on, 292t13.2
nuclear weapons tests, 58, 191
nuclear weapons use, 41
OMV system in Iraq, 118
plutonium and HEU production, 48n7
proliferation, self-interest *vs.* judicial review, 165
security assurances, 143
Security Council member, 31
stove-pipes across government departments, 200
Treaty on the Non-Proliferation of Nuclear Weapons, 41
Trident strategic nuclear force up-grade, 280
UFP resolution, 140
United Nations (UN).
  about, 1, 3–7, 9, 11, 14–15, 17–24, 25n11–12, 25n14, 26n25, 26n27–28, xiv
  Commission for Conventional Armaments, 75
  Disarmament Commission, 8, 22, 33, 53, 66, 75–76, 81
  Disarmament Committee, 22, 54, 58–59
  General Assembly (Article 11), 139
  Global Counter-Terrorism Strategy, 97, 208n26
  inspections, 4, 9, 114–20, 235
  International Court of Justice (ICJ), 151, 167, 171
  international nuclear trade, 235–37
  Regional Centre for Peace, Disarmament and Development in Latin America, 81
  Regional Centre for Peace and Disarmament in Africa, 81
  Regional Centre for Peace and Disarmament in Asia, 81
  Secretary-General (Article 99), 139, 161
United Nations and nuclear orders. *See also* General Assembly majorities on preferred nuclear order
  the actors, 9–14
  changing environment, 17–20
  concluding thoughts, 20–25

context, 1–5
General Assembly, 11–12
introduction, 1
Secretariat and Secretary General, 10–11
Security Council, 12–14
UN arms control and disarmament
   machinery, 7–9
UN Charter, 6–7
UN tools, 14–17
United Nations Charter
   Article 1(1), 139
   Article 2(4), 136, 174
   Article 6, 13
   Article 11, 32, 101n4, 139
   Article 11(1), 6, 46
   Article 11(2), 140
   Article 12(1), 162
   Article 13(1)(a), 184n7
   Article 24, 6, 32
   Article 26, 6, 32, 46, 101n4
   Article 35, 139
   Article 39, 134
   Article 47, 6, 101n4
   Article 47(1), 33
   Article 51, 132–34, 148n17, 174
   Article 96, 17
   Article 96(1), 173, 185n20
   Article 96(2), 185n20
   Article 97, 74
   Article 98, 74
   Article 99, 10, 74, 139, 161–63
   Article 100, 74
   Article 101, 74
   Chapter VII, 20, 47, 139, 160, 177, 182, 214, 220
   Charter, about, 1, 3, 5–7, 9–10, 14–16, 20, 24–25, 26n25, 31, 41, 52, 61, 74, 77, 93, 132, 143
   Charter and General Assembly, 180
   Charter and IAEA, 138
   Charter and Security Council, 136
   Charter and self-defense, 135
   Charter framework, 32–34
   Charter mandate, 67
United Nations Monitoring, Verification
   and Inspection Commission
   (UNMOVIC), 8–9, 15, 82, 102n32, 114, 116–17, 130n19–20, 131n32, 156, 158, 168n22
United Nations sanctions and nuclear
   weapons

current and future issues, 127–29
India and Pakistan, 125–27
introduction, 111–12
Iran, sanctions and denuclearizing,
   122–23
Iraq, blocking WMD imports into, 119–20
Iraq and critical role of inspections and
   monitoring, 117
Iraq and sanctions-based diplomacy and
   weapons inspections, 117–19
Iraq the bitter irony of, 113–14
Iraq's nuclear arsenal and UN
   inspections, 114–16
Libya, nuclear turnabout in, 120–21
North Korea, denuclearization in, 123–25
United Nations Special Commission on Iraq
   (UNSCOM), 9, 15, 82, 114–19, 128, 141, 156, 168n14, xiv
United States (US)
   aid program, 126–27
   arms race, 192, 194
   Burns, Under Secretary of State William, 268
   Burns, Under Secretary R. Nicholas, 123, 186n38–39, 260t12.2
   Bush, President George W., 35, 49n23, 62, 64, 121, 123–26, 132–34, 137, 147n1, 201, 218, 228n28, 248, 256–57, 260t12.2, 264–65, 267–68, 269n1, 271n22, 280, 285, 287, 289, 294–95n14, 294n6, xiv
   Bush, President H. W., 113, 130n6
   Clinton, President Bill, 113, 124, 126, 173, 184n16, 216, 258t12.2, 294–95n14
   Clinton, Senator Hillary, 280
   command and control, lax, 294n13
   counter-terrorism policy vs. sanctions
      over nuclear development, 125
   CTBT ratification, 73, 173, 212, 219
   Cuban missile crisis, 92, 105n108, 170, 183n1–2, 280
   dual-use nuclear technologies, 196–97
   EU-Iran dialogue support, 259t12.2
   Germany, 130n6, 149n39
   Global Nuclear Energy Partnership, 240
   High-level Panel discussion, 71n26
   IAEA, 158, 207n3, 214, 236
   India, 228n31, 240, 280
   India Civil Nuclear Cooperation
      Initiative, 178, 186n36–39, 217 (*See
      also* Indo-US nuclear agreement)

United States (US) (cont.)
  Indian nuclear test, 215
  Indian Peaceful Atomic Energy Cooperation Act, 186n36, 295n27
  Intermediate Range Nuclear Forces agreement, 3, 184n5, 233
  International Atomic Energy Agency (IAEA), 158, 207n3, 214
  Iran, 112, 122–23, 128, 148n19, 256, 259t12.2, 260t12.2, 264, 267–68, 269n2, 270n10, 271n19, 271n21, 272n27, 272n33–272n34, 280
  Iraq, 113–14, 116, 118, 141–42, 158
  Iraq and UN Charter violations, 14–15, 146
  joint statement on general and complete disarmament, 92
  Libya, 112, 120–21, 267, 294n14
  Libya Sanctions Act, 122
  Manhattan project, 20
  missile shield along Russian's borders, 280
  nonproliferation policies, 125–26
  North Korea, 123–25, 137, 139, 181, 248, 256–57, 264–65, 267–68, 269n1, 270n10, 271n21, 287–88, 291, 295n14
  NPT, 139, 143, 170, 187n52, 212
  nuclear arms use, 41–42
  nuclear arsenal, 77, 194, 288t13.1
  Nuclear Non-Proliferation Act, 218
  nuclear power, 275
  nuclear proliferation and regional security orders, 264
  nuclear warheads, 274
  nuclear weapon accumulation and mutual distrust, 56
  nuclear weapons, public opinion on, 292t13.2
  nuclear weapons stalemate, 64
  nuclear weapons use, 42
  OMV system in Iraq, 118
  plutonium and HEU production, 48n7
  proliferation, self-interest vs. judicial review, 165
  Russian Megatons to Megawatts Program, 243–44
  security assurances, 143
  Security Council member, 31
  Six-Part Talks on North Korea, 259t12.2
  Soviet/Russian arms control negotiations, 170, 184n6
  stove-piped policy structures, 200
  stove-pipes across government departments, 200
  Three Mile Island nuclear accident, 240, 277
  Treaty on the Non-Proliferation of Nuclear Weapons, 41
  Truman, President, 26n24
  UFP resolution, 140
  violation of UN Charter, 15
  "war on terror", 256
  WMD and disarmament, 44
  WMD proliferation, 141
Uniting for Peace (UFP), 67, 72n38, 140, 162–63
UNMOVIC. *See* United Nations Monitoring, Verification and Inspection Commission (UNMOVIC)
UNSCOM. *See* United Nations Special Commission on Iraq (UNSCOM)
US. *See* United States (US)

verification and compliance
  compliance, defined, 152–53
  conclusion, 166–67
  ICJ, role for, 165–66
  introduction, 157
  Security Council forensics, 164–65
  United Nations, role of, 160–63
  verification, defined, 151–52
  verification, meaning under the security dilemma, 153–55
  verification and compliance in crisis (short of enforcement), 157–58
  verification and compliance in routine operations, 155–57
  verification apparatus: IAEA and regional bodies, 158–60
Vietnam, 265–66, 277

weapons
  biological, 37–38, 63–64, 143, 222
  chemical, 37–38, 42, 63–64, 115, 117, 143, 165, 198, 222
  landmines, 8, 23, 63
  nuclear, biological or chemical, 37–38, 50n29, 71n28, 75, 115, 117, 119, 121, 192, 207n11, 208n27, 209n34, 224, 279, 284, xv
  toxin, 63

INDEX 319

Weapons of Mass Destruction Commission, 45, 50n29, 50n34
weapon(s) of mass destruction (WMD). *See also* zone free of weapons of mass destruction in the Middle East (WMDFZ)
about, 207n12, 296n29
Annan, Kofi, 85
"axis of evil," 248
Ban Ki-moon, 97
Boutros-Ghali, Boutros, 96
Cold War norms, 193
Commission on the Intelligence Capabilities of the United States, 245n3
Dhanapala, Jayantha, 86
Disarmament Department, 165
Global Partnership, 242
Hammarskjöld, Dag, 88
in hands of "mad" or "rogue" governments, 62
Hussein, Saddam, 113
international legal architecture for controlling, 183
in Iraq, 4, 116, 119–20, 130n13, 186n32, 297n44
Libya, 121
Michael Doyle's standards for preventive action, 145
Millennium Summit, 63
OMV system, 117–18
proliferation of, 127, 182, 265
PSI Agreement, 143, 150n46
resolution 1540, 38, 53, 87, 128, 143, 177
Secretary-General and Secretariat, 73
Security Council, 141, 220
Security Council Summit (1992), 139
terrorist use of, 98, 133, 148n14
as threat to international peace and security, 37, 47
UN provisions to eliminate, 15

UN Special Commission, 43
UNMOVIC and Iraq, 9
UNSCOM chairman Ekéus, 119
verifying disarmament, in Iraq, 8
weapon(s) of mass destruction (WMD)
China, 141
Iraq, 4, 8–9, 116–17, 119–20, 130n10, 130n13, 141
Russia, 44, 141
terrorism, 16, 97, 142, 148n14, 229n44
United States, 44, 141
Weapons of Terror: Freeing the World of Nuclear, Biological and Chemical Arms (Hans Blix et al.), 50n29, xv
Weiss, Thomas G., 1–27, 25n12, 26n17, 26n27, xii, xiv, xvii n1–2, xvii n4
West Germany, 194
Western Europe, 196, 198
WHO. *See* World Health Organization (WHO)
WMD. *See* weapon(s) of mass destruction (WMD)
WMDFZ. *See* zone free of weapons of mass destruction in the Middle East (WMDFZ)
Women's International League for Peace and Freedom, 72n35
World Disarmament Campaign, 80–81, 95
"A World Free of Nuclear Weapons" (Kissinger et al.), 26n22, 38, 49n15, 65, 71n29, 229n50, 286, 292, 293n5, 296n38–39
World Health Organization (WHO), 17, 173

Yugoslavia, 194

zone free of weapons of mass destruction in the Middle East (WMDFZ), 213, *See also* weapon(s) of mass destruction (WMD)